THE BURDEN OF THE FLESH

Volume Editor
L. Michael White

THE BURDEN
OF THE FLESH

*Fasting and Sexuality
in Early Christianity*

Teresa M. Shaw

Fortress Press
Minneapolis

THE BURDEN OF THE FLESH
Fasting and Sexuality in Early Christianity

Scripture translations from the Revised Standard Version of the Bible, copyright © 1946, 1952, and 1971 by the Division of Christian Education of the National Council of Churches of Christ in the United States of America, are used by permission.

Cover design: Joe Bonyata
Cover graphic: Edward Burne-Jones, "The Days of Creation (The Sixth Day)," watercolor, c.1875–76. Courtesy of The Fogg Art Museum, Harvard University Art Museums. Bequest of Grenville L. Winthrop.
Interior book design: The HK Scriptorium, Inc.

Library of Congress Cataloging in Publication Data

Shaw, Teresa M., 1958–
    The burden of the flesh : fasting and sexuality in early
  Christianity / Teresa M. Shaw.
      p.   cm.
  Includes bibliographical references and index.
  ISBN 0-8006-2765-2 (alk. paper)
    1. Fasting—History of doctrines—Early church, ca. 30–600.
  2. Chastity—History of doctrines—Early church, ca. 30–600.
  3. Woman (Christian theology)—History of doctrines—Early church,
  ca. 30–600. I. Title.
  BV5055.S43   1998
  248.4'7'09015—dc21   98-5098

Manufactured in the U.S.A.   AF 1-2765

02   01   00   99   98   1   2   3   4   5   6   7   8   9   10

for Jeff

Contents

Acknowledgments

It is a pleasure to acknowledge the many people who contributed to the completion of this project. First, I must express my gratitude to the members of my dissertation committee at Duke University: Elizabeth Clark, Kent Rigsby, Dale Martin, Bruce Lawrence, and Susan Keefe. Their suggestions pointed me in the right direction for turning the dissertation into the book. My advisor, Elizabeth Clark, was, and continues to be, extremely generous with her time and serves as an unsurpassed role model and mentor not only for me, and other Duke graduates, but for many young scholars throughout the country. Several scholars have generously read all or parts of the study at varying stages and offered expert suggestions and corrections. These include Elizabeth Clark, Cynthia Eller, Susanna Elm, James Francis, James Goehring, Jeffrey Groves, Dale Martin, and Kent Rigsby.

I am especially grateful to L. Michael White of the University of Texas at Austin. Working at first in conjunction with a projected Fortress Press series, he provided helpful responses and suggestions throughout the later stages of writing, helping to make the eventual book more interdisciplinary.

For several years, my work has been greatly enriched by my participation in the research group on Ascetic Behavior in Greco-Roman Antiquity. That community proved to be the primary ground for my early scholarly formation and continues to inspire me; thanks are due in particular to Richard Valantasis, James

Goehring, and Vincent Wimbush. For sharing with me his mastery of the Greek language and helping me to make sense of a particularly difficult passage, I thank Howard M. Jackson. Richard Smith and Jonathan Reed offered advice on Coptic, and Eloisa Rivera checked my Spanish translation.

My mother, Audrey Shaw, and sisters, Cynthia Colbert and Janice Shaw-Morgan, have honored me with their respect and pride in my work and sustained me with their love. My dear friend and colleague, Cynthia Eller, has helped me in so many ways it's downright embarrassing. I thank her for her keen editorial advice and bibliographic help, but most of all for her delightful presence and good humor. Finally, this book is dedicated to my husband, Jeffrey Groves. To thank Jeff properly would change the nature of this work from scholarly monograph to epic saga. He has read every chapter and shared wise comments, and helped me to conquer an eccentric word processing program. His unwavering faith in me and my work has encouraged me, his own scholarship and teaching have inspired me, and his love has nourished me. Most of all, he has created with me a happy and adventurous life.

Abbreviations

AP	*Apophthegmata Patrum*
CSCO	Corpus Scriptorum Christianorum Orientalium
CSEL	Corpus Scriptorum Ecclesiasticorum Latinorum
HL	Palladius, *Historia Lausiaca*
HM	*Historia monachorum in Aegypto*
PG	J. Migne, *Patrologia Graeca*
PL	J. Migne, *Patrologia Latina*
PO	Patrologia Orientalis
Pr.	Evagrius of Pontus, *Praktikos*
SC	Sources Chrétiennes
SVF	Hans von Arnim, ed., *Stoicorum Veterum Fragmenta*
TU	Texte und Untersuchungen

CHAPTER ONE

Introduction

THE RELIGIOUS PRACTICE of fasting, or abstinence from certain foods for certain periods of time, was nothing new when Christianity became a strong cultural and social force in the ancient Mediterranean world. Yet fasting took on a central role in Christian piety, both as a practice that marked the rhythms of the week and the year for the entire community and as a feat of endurance and discipline that distinguished the elite and heroic few. Why was fasting so important? The author of a Greek treatise on virginity (probably dating to the fourth century) offers a clue in this assessment of fasting:

> Observe what fasting does: it heals diseases, dries up the bodily humors, casts out demons, chases away wicked thoughts, makes the mind clearer and the heart pure, sanctifies the body and places the person before the throne of God. . . . For fasting is the life of the angels, and the one who makes use of it has angelic rank.[1]

What is the modern reader to make of this catalog of benefits? These lofty claims for the usefulness of fasting concern not only

---

1. Pseudo-Athanasius, *De virginitate* 7 (Eduard F. von der Goltz, ed., Λόγος σωτηρίας πρὸς τὴν παρθένον *(De virginitate): Eine echte Schrift des Athanasius,* TU 29, 2a [Leipzig: J. C. Hinrichs, 1905], 41). Athanasius, bishop of Alexandria, died in 373 C.E. See chap. 6, n.10, for sources on the question of authenticity. All translations from ancient and modern languages are mine unless otherwise noted.

physiological effects and health advantages, but also protection from demons, improvements in mental facility and moral excellence, and preparation for paradise itself. The author is as concerned with specific instructions on what, when, where, how, and with whom to eat as with assurances of the eschatological value attached to dietary renunciation. Further, this treatise, like many others of its type in the fourth and fifth centuries, focuses on female virginity and the particular interpretation and concerns of female bodily renunciation. Thus, according to the author, the virgin's fasting acts like a kind of cosmetic which makes her more attractive to her bridegroom, Christ: "Adorn your body with this virtue, O virgin, and you will please the heavenly bridegroom;" for Christ does not require worldly cosmetics, but only "a pure heart and an undefiled body which has been mortified by fasting."[2]

These brief passages from the pseudo-Athanasian treatise highlight what will become standard features in the Christian discussion of fasting in late antiquity: arguments concerning the effects of diet on the condition of the body and the soul interweave with eschatological images (placing the one who fasts regularly among the angels and in paradise), with instructions for the daily practice of female chastity and with the theological interpretation of creation, embodiment, and gender. In this volume I will discuss the ways in which these types of arguments reinforce and inform each other in Christian ascetic literature of the fourth and early fifth centuries, in the context of late ancient medicine and ethics. Overall, I hope to demonstrate how fasting is connected to the ascetic ideal of virginity while considering the relationship between behavior and theory, the body and belief, and physical asceticism and theological speculation. Like the ancient authors, modern readers and scholars struggle to understand the place of "the body" and behavior in the early Christian world. One is struck by what seems to be a profound ambivalence. The stuff of the body, the flesh itself, weighs heavily. Jerome, writing in the late fourth century, describes the flesh as a "burden" (*sarcina*) borne along by the spirit through its pilgrimage in this world, like

2. Ibid., 6 (von der Goltz, 40).

bulky baggage that will be cast off only after death.[3] For Basil of Ancyra, the flesh tugs at the "wings of the soul" like a leaden weight (ἡ μολιβδὶς τῶν σαρκῶν)[4] that pulls fishing nets down into the waters. At the same time, it is the flesh itself that is the subject of so much speculation, interpretation, scrutiny, management, and even—in the case of the ascetic body—praise.

To explore these issues, I will examine a variety of ancient texts dating from the seventh century B.C.E. to the seventh century C.E. The sources include medical treatises from late antiquity, especially the works of Galen; philosophical writings, Christian homilies, and theological treatises not directly addressing ascetic issues or audiences; and more specifically ascetic sources, including letters, treatises, homilies, instructions, rules, hagiographies, and sayings collections. It must be noted that virtually every one of these sources was—as far as we know—written by a male. Many of the Christian texts addressed to or concerning female ascetics are of a prescriptive nature. Therefore it is not possible for the modern scholar to have a strong sense of or to make claims about what ancient Christian ascetic women—much less married women—were themselves thinking. We cannot know how a virgin of the fourth century interpreted her own sexual renunciation, nor how she would want herself to be represented by others. This fundamental limitation in early Christian studies must be kept in mind throughout this investigation.

My main focus is the written Christian discourse concerning ascetic fasting and sexual abstinence from the late fourth and early fifth centuries in the Eastern Mediterranean and Egypt. Most of the primary texts are in Greek, but some are in Latin, Coptic, and Syriac. Of these, several are translations of lost Greek originals. As I have limited my subject, in general, to the East, I have used few Latin sources, with two important exceptions. Jerome (c.342–420) and John Cassian (c.365–c.433) were both directly influenced by the Eastern ascetic tradition and spent significant amounts of time in the East. Jerome's is a crucial voice in the debate over ascetic theology and practice for our period.

3. Jerome, *Epistula* 39.1 (Isidorus Hilberg, ed., *Eusebii Hieronymi Epistulae*, CSEL 54 [Vienna: Tempsky, 1910], 295).
4. Basil of Ancyra, *De vera virginitatis integritate* 10 (*PG* 30.688D–689A).

Cassian saw as his task the transplanting of the wisdom and lifestyle of the Egyptian desert fathers—in a somewhat milder form—into Western soil. His writings preserve the views of his teacher, Evagrius of Pontus (c.345–399), who is one of the most influential thinkers in the history of Eastern ascetic spirituality.

This book is in no way intended to be a history of the development of fasting in Greco-Roman antiquity or early Christianity. Modern sources are available that survey the most important texts, developments, and types of fasts in ancient Judaism, pagan philosophy and religions, and Christianity.[5] And although I examine fasting in relation to female asceticism and theological understandings of gender and sexuality, I am not attempting to survey the history and ideology of female asceticism or monasticism in early Christianity.[6] Finally, I give little attention to regular eccle-

---

5. The works of P. Rudolph Arbesmann are especially informative on pagan and Christian food abstinence; see *Das Fasten bei den Griechen und Römern,* Religionsgeschichtliche Versuche und Vorarbeiten 21/1 (Giessen: Alfred Töpelmann, 1929; reprint, Berlin: Alfred Töpelmann, 1966); idem, "Fasten, Fastenspeisen, Fasttage," in *Reallexikon für Antike und Christentum,* ed. Theodor Klauser (Stuttgart: Anton Hiersemann, 1969), 7:447–524; idem, "Fasting and Prophecy in Pagan and Christian Antiquity," *Traditio* 7 (1949–1951): 1–71. See also Fernand Cabrol, "Jeûnes," *Dictionnaire d'archéologie chrétienne et de liturgie* 7 (1927): 2481–2501; Placide Deseille, "Jeûne," *Dictionnaire de spiritualité* 8 (1974): 1164–1175; Alexandre Guillaume, *Jeûne et charité dans l'église latine des origines au XIIe siècle en particulier chez saint Léon le Grand* (Paris: n.p., 1954); Johannes Haussleiter, *Der Vegetarismus in der Antike,* Religionsgeschichtliche Versuche und Vorarbeiten 24 (Berlin: Alfred Töpelmann, 1935); J. A. MacCulloch, "Fasting (Introductory and non-Christian)," and A. J. Maclean, "Fasting (Christian)," in *Encyclopaedia of Religion and Ethics,* ed. James Hastings (Edinburgh: T. & T. Clark, 1937), 5:759–771; Herbert Musurillo, "The Problem of Ascetical Fasting in the Greek Patristic Writers," *Traditio* 12 (1956): 1–64; Theodorich Pichler, *Das Fasten bei Basileios dem Grossen und im antiken Heidentum,* Commentationes Aenipontanae 11 (Innsbruck: Universitätsverlag Wagner, 1955); Rosemary Rader, "Fasting," in *Encyclopedia of Religion,* ed. Mircea Eliade et al. (New York: Macmillan, 1987), 5:286–290; Johannes Schümmer, *Die altchristliche Fastenpraxis mit besonderer Berücksichtigung der Schriften Tertullians,* Liturgiegeschichtliche Quellen und Forschungen 27 (Munich: Aschendorff, 1933); Ludwig Ziehen, "Νηστεία," in *Realencyclopaedie der classischen Altertumswissenschaft,* ed. A. Pauly and G. Wissowa, revised ed. (Stuttgart: J. B. Metzler, 1936), 17/1:88–107.

6. Useful secondary sources on these developments include Susanna Elm, *'Virgins of God': The Making of Asceticism in Late Antiquity,* Oxford Classi-

siastical fasts—such as the normal Wednesday and Friday fasts or the Lenten fast—observed generally and locally by the wider Christian populace. Rather, I focus on the practice and theory of fasting among *ascetic* Christians as a central aspect of their worldviews and lifestyles.

What Is Asceticism?

Asceticism, from the Greek ἄσκησις (*askesis*), indicates athletic training, exercise, practice, or discipline. In antiquity, *askesis* could apply to any regimen of exercise with a goal of improvement—in performance, in manner of life, or in health and effectiveness of body and mind. The athletic terminology became a metaphor implying rigorous dedication, hard work, and discipline, to the point of self-denial, in a particular philosophical or religious mode of life. Ascetic disciplines may involve bodily renunciations (for example, sexual chastity, food abstinence, or poverty) or contemplative disciplines (for example, meditation or study). Some scholars interpret asceticism in a fairly narrow sense, as religiously motivated acts of physical discipline with the

cal Monographs (Oxford: Clarendon Press, 1994); David Amand de Mendieta, "La virginité chez Eusèbe d'Émèse et l'ascétisme familial dans la première moité du IVe siècle," *Revue d'histoire ecclésiastique* 50 (1955): 777–820; Peter Brown, *The Body and Society: Men, Women and Sexual Renunciation in Early Christianity*, Lectures on the History of Religions 13 (New York: Columbia University Press, 1988); P. Thomas Camelot, "Les traités 'de virginitate' au IVe siècle," in *Mystique et Continence: Travaux scientifiques du VIIe Congrès international d'Avon*, Études Carmélitaines (Brugge: Desclée de Brouwer, 1952), 273–292; Elizabeth A. Clark, "Ascetic Renunciation and Feminine Advancement: A Paradox of Late Ancient Christianity," *Anglican Theological Review* 63 (1981): 240–257; idem, *Jerome, Chrysostom, and Friends: Essays and Translations*, Studies in Women and Religion 2 (Lewiston, New York: Edwin Mellen Press, 1979); idem, "Theory and Practice in Late Ancient Asceticism: Jerome, Chrysostom, and Augustine," *Journal of Feminist Studies in Religion* 5 (Fall 1989): 25–46; Kate Cooper, *The Virgin and the Bride: Idealized Womanhood in Late Antiquity* (Cambridge: Harvard University Press, 1996); Ross Kraemer, "The Conversion of Women to Ascetic Forms of Christianity," *Signs* 6 (1980–1981): 298–307; Rosemary Radford Ruether, "Misogynism and Virginal Feminism in the Fathers of the Church," in *Religion and Sexism: Images of Women in the Jewish and Christian Traditions*, ed. Rosemary Radford Ruether (New York: Simon and Schuster, 1974), 150–183; Anne Yarbrough, "Christianization in the Fourth Century: The Example of Roman Women," *Church History* 45 (1976): 149–165.

purpose of "subordinating the lower appetites to the dictates of right reason and the law of God."[7] Here the emphasis is on asceticism as a means of self-conquest, ruling the impulses of the flesh by the power of the mind or spirit.[8] But this more narrow definition, with its stress on physical self-denial and the primacy of the spiritual over the physical, is rooted in the later Christian ascetic ideal that developed out of the ancient setting. It would be dangerous to apply later definitions and models in the context of a study like this one that attempts to trace the construction of the Christian ascetic ideal. A useful definition would see asceticism more broadly and with general cultural connotations, for example, as "any act of self-denial undertaken as a strategy of empowerment or gratification."[9]

In this study I have understood asceticism as a way of life that requires daily discipline and intentionality in bodily behaviors. I have tried to approach early Christian *askesis* in its proper ancient contexts; chapter two is devoted to a discussion of some of the key aspects of late ancient understandings of body, soul, ethics, regimen, and physiology—understandings that shape Christian ascetic behaviors and argumentation. I have also focused more specifically on asceticism as a factor in determining group status. That is, by "ascetic Christians" I indicate those who, by their physical renunciations, distinguish themselves from the wider Christian populace. In antiquity all Christians were encouraged to fast on certain days and to maintain a level of fidelity and chastity in marriage, and these may be considered as ascetic constraints; but certain individuals and groups devoted themselves to perpetual food abstinence and complete sexual chastity. Ascetic behaviors are thus not exclusive to any one group, but rigorous observance of such behaviors can define a particular type of Christian.

The Greek terms for the fast or fasting are νηστεία or νῆστις and the Latin *ieiunium* or *ieiunus*. In the strict sense the terms refer to absolute avoidance of eating and drinking for a fixed amount of

7. Arbesmann, "Fasting and Prophecy," 37.
8. See also Musurillo, "The Problem of Ascetical Fasting," 3.
9. Geoffrey Galt Harpham, *The Ascetic Imperative in Culture and Criticism* (Chicago: University of Chicago Press, 1987), xiii.

time, but they can also refer to abstinence from particular kinds of food or drink, such as meat and wine, or to reduced food intake.[10] We shall see that in early Christian ascetic sources *fasting* is most often used in this broader sense to indicate the regular, daily observance of a restricted diet as well as regular rejection of certain types of nourishment. Thus there is significant overlap in meaning and usage between νηστεία and ἐγκράτεια (*enkrateia*: self-control, temperance, or abstinence).[11] I will use the term *fasting* broadly, to indicate a range of intentional food abstinence.

Although modern studies of early Christian asceticism have tended to emphasize self-denial of bodily pleasures and the battle between flesh and spirit, it should become clear that such a view does not do justice to the complex meanings of such terms as *askesis* and *enkrateia*. Rather, ancient insights concerning the control of desires that lead to pleasure (and pain) and concerning the careful management and training of the body with the soul, as well as ancient anthropological and physiological models, give much of the shape and contours to early Christian understandings of the body, creation, and, indeed, salvation.

The various texts examined in the following chapters, though from a range of genres, share some common, sometimes standardized, themes in the discourse concerning fasting, as will become obvious. But we will nevertheless see an incredibly rich fabric of distinctive detail and nuance of personality, obsessions, prescriptions, praise, and condemnation. The individuals who are the heroes or villains of ascetic texts exhibit a range of lifestyles and backgrounds, from genteel urban settings to harsh and solitary subsistence in the deserts of Egypt, Syria, and Palestine. Thus Jerome devotes more than one epistle to the upbringing and regimen of very young girls whose elite Roman families have dedicated them to virginity. In contrast, the *Life of Pelagia* praises the

---

10. Arbesmann, "Fasting and Prophecy," 1–2; idem, "Fasten, Fastenspeisen, Fasttage," 447–449; idem, *Das Fasten*, 3–7; Ziehen, "Νηστεία," 88–89.

11. While *enkrateia* is associated with *askesis* as the endurance of hardship or exercise of self-mastery as part of training or discipline, the connotation of abstinence (for example, *enkrateia* in diet) is common in Christian texts. Other Greek terms include ἀσιτία (fasting) and ἀποχή (abstinence).

former prostitute who, upon her dramatic conversion, fled to the desert disguised as a monk. She died alone in a secluded cell, her body wasted and emaciated from years of fasting, and unrecognizable as female save for her breasts, which hung from her body like withered leaves.

The type and intensity of ascetic fasting attested in our sources is likewise varied. While, on the one hand, John Chrysostom urges his lay congregations to show more discipline in observing the regular Wednesday and Friday fasts as well as the Lenten and pre-eucharistic fasts, on the other hand, records from church councils condemn those enthusiastic ascetics who refuse to ease their rule of fasting, even on Sundays. While Bishops Basil of Ancyra and Gregory of Nyssa, who both authored lengthy treatises on the topic of virginity, call for the careful moderation and control of eating so that the body's elements and fluids are maintained in harmony and its desires held in check, others' texts glorify the pallor, weakness, suffering, and emaciation of the mortified body. So Jerome describes with some pride young Blesilla's weak neck and staggering steps and twelve-year-old Asella's habit of eating only bread, salt, and water every two or three days—a regimen that kept her always hungry.

The level of physiological detail and dietary specificity in ascetic texts, including those that offer advice as well as those that extol the virtues of the exemplary individual, is often striking. Recommendations to eat a light meal once a day and avoid foods such as meat, wine, and delicacies are quite common. But individual texts and authors provide insight into specific—sometimes even seemingly quirky—habits and avoidances. Basil of Ancyra warns against the indiscriminate use of fruit, salt, and other condiments that lead to passion. The author of the treatise on virginity attributed to Athanasius instructs virgins to eat bread, vegetables, and oil once a day, and notes that all non-animal food is pure. John Cassian describes the regimens of Egyptian monks (the champions of ascetic discipline) in admiring detail, noting carefully how many dried biscuits were eaten, how many drops of oil were consumed, and which types of vegetables were prepared in which manner. And Paula so despised food that although she allowed other women in her monastery to eat meat and drink wine when they became ill, she herself refused such remedies in her own grave sickness.

Evagrius's advice to monks and virgins illuminates the daily fears and obsessions of those who fast rigorously. He encourages them to resist thoughts for their own health, desires for the comfort of vegetables, and the temptation to relax their fast on feast days. Though he warns against the pride that may infect the one who fasts with great austerity, he also urges the virgin not to let self-pity over her wasting flesh and bloodshot eyes distract her from her goal of a pure soul. In the same way, the author of the pseudo-Athanasian treatise exhorts the virgin to stop up her ears when others discourage her from fasting so rigorously. And Syncletica, we are told, had such a love of fasting and was so repulsed by eating that, when she did eat, her body's health did not improve or thrive. Rather, she became more pale and emaciated.

These examples illustrate the variety and intensity of fasting practices found in the sources for this study; the sources also claim numerous benefits and effects for fasting that, as in the quotation at the beginning of this chapter, interweave physiological concerns with models of piety, gender, human creation, and salvation. Authors credit fasting with reducing passions and establishing the foundation for virtues, inhibiting sexual desire, and limiting nocturnal emissions of semen. Fasting makes the body more obedient and controllable while it makes the soul lighter, quiets the restless mind, and aids in prayer and penitence. It is a potent weapon against demons and evil thoughts. Just as Adam and Eve sinned by eating, so fasting offers redress for their gluttony and leads Christians back to paradise. And while some arguments highlight the value of dietary restrictions for the body's health, others recognize the physical toll of long-term fasting; both arguments give these physical changes theological significance. Finally, the rigorous fasts of female ascetics are credited with destroying the distinctively female features of the body while at the same time making the body more attractive to Christ, the virgin's bridegroom. In the following chapters I will draw out some of the implications and interdependencies of the

physical behavior described, advocated, or criticized and the theoretical or theological frameworks in which the behavior is presented in our sources.

Fasting in Sources on Early Desert Monasticism

It is instructive at this point to consider the fasting practices
among the earliest participants in the monastic movement as it
developed in the early fourth century—especially among monks
in the Egyptian desert. The desert monastic tradition provides
essential background for later ascetic theory and practice. Many
of the authors central to this study—including Jerome, John Cassian, Evagrius of Pontus, John Chrysostom, and Basil of Caesarea—
spent significant amounts of time in the Egyptian, Palestinian, or
Syrian deserts, visiting the monks there or living the ascetic life
(with varying degrees of success).[12] Further, the heroic figures of
the desert remained models for inspiration and imitation as
monasticism developed in the East and West.[13]

---

12. Detailed discussions of fasting regimens as presented by Jerome, John
Cassian, Evagrius, and others appear in the following chapters.

13. Useful secondary texts on the development and sources for early
monasticism include Derwas J. Chitty, *The Desert a City: An Introduction to
the Study of Egyptian and Palestinian Monasticism under the Christian
Empire* (Crestwood, N.Y.: St. Vladimir's Seminary Press, 1966); Jean
Gribomont, "Monasticism and Asceticism: 1. Eastern Christianity," in *Chris-
tian Spirituality: Origins to the Twelfth Century*, ed. Bernard McGinn, John
Meyendorff, and Jean Leclercq, trans. Marie Miklashevsky, World Spirituality
16 (New York: Crossroad, 1985), 89–112; Elm, *Virgins of God*; Philip
Rousseau, *Ascetics, Authority, and the Church in the Age of Jerome and
Cassian* (Oxford: Oxford University Press, 1978); idem, *Pachomius: The Mak-
ing of a Community in Fourth-Century Egypt*, The Transformation of the
Classical Heritage 6 (Berkeley: University of California Press, 1985); Arthur
Vööbus, *History of Asceticism in the Syrian Orient*, 2 vols., CSCO 184 (Subsidia 14) and 197 (Subsidia 17) (Louvain: Secrétariat du CorpusSCO),
1958–1960; Armand Veilleux, "The Origins of Egyptian Monasticism," in
*The Continuing Quest for God: Monastic Spirituality in Tradition and Tran-
sition*, ed. William Skudlarek (Collegeville, Minn.: Liturgical Press, 1982),
44–50; Gabriele Winkler, "The Origins and Idiosyncrasies of the Earliest
Form of Asceticism," in *The Continuing Quest For God*, ed. William Skudlarek, 9–43; and now Samuel Rubenson, *The Letters of St. Antony: Monasticism and the Making of a Saint*, Studies in Antiquity and Christianity
(Minneapolis: Fortress Press, 1995).

Important sources for the early stages of cenobitic (communal) and eremitic (solitary) monasticism include the *Apophthegmata* or "Sayings" collections,[14] the *Life of Antony* by Athanasius of Alexandria,[15] the *History of the Monks in Egypt* (an anonymous record of the pilgrimage of seven Palestinian monks to the Egyptian desert in the last decade of the fourth century),[16] the *Lives* and *Rules* of Pachomius,[17] and Palladius's *Lausiac History* (a record of personal experiences and stories told of the female and male ascetics of Egypt, Palestine, Syria, and Asia Minor).[18] Each of these texts reveals the importance of diet and fasting in community and individual asceticism. Although we find some significant variations in observances, we can also describe typical monastic regimens.[19]

14. *Apophthegmata Patrum* (*PG* 65.71–440). There are several different collections of sayings; I am using the alphabetical collection, organized according to the name of person whose sayings are recorded. The sayings were compiled and written down in Greek, probably in the fifth and sixth centuries.

15. Athanasius, *Vita Antonii* (*PG* 26.837–976). Antony died in 356 C.E. and Athanasius wrote the *Vita* soon after.

16. Greek text edited by André-Jean Festugière, *Historia monachorum in Aegypto*, Subsidia hagiographica 53 (Brussels: Société des Bollandistes, 1971); Latin translation of Rufinus, *PL* 21.387–462. See also Benedicta Ward, "Introduction" to *The Lives of the Desert Fathers: The Historia Monachorum in Aegypto*, trans. Norman Russell (London: Mowbray; Kalamazoo, Mich.: Cistercian Publications, 1981).

17. Translated by Armand Veilleux, *Pachomian Koinonia: The Lives, Rules, and Other Writings of Pachomius and his Disciples* 1, *The Life of Saint Pachomius and his Disciples* 2, *Pachomian Chronicles and Rules*, Cistercian Studies Series 45–46 (Kalamazoo, Mich.: Cistercian Publications, 1980–1981).

18. Palladius, *HL* (Cuthbert Butler, ed., *The Lausiac History of Palladius*, 2 vols., Texts and Studies 6/1–2 [Cambridge: Cambridge University Press, 1898, 1904]). Palladius spent twelve years in the Egyptian desert, where he was a disciple of Evagrius of Pontus, and wrote the *HL* around 419.

19. Of course, in the Egyptian villages and deserts, one would not expect to find great variety in diet among the wider population. For a discussion of peasant and monastic diet as described in Byzantine hagiography, see Evelyne Patlagean, *Pauvreté économique et pauvreté sociale à Byzance: 4e–7e siècles*, Civilisations et sociétés 48 (Paris: Mouton, 1977), 36–53. On monastic diet see also Aline Rousselle, *Porneia: De la maîtrise du corps à la privation sensorielle IIe–IVe siècles de l'ère chrétienne*, Les chemins de l'Histoire (Paris: Presses Universitaires de France, 1983), 205–215; idem, "Abstinence et continence dans les monastères de Gaule méridionale à la fin de l'Antiquité et au

The recommendation to eat a small amount of food once a day is common. Antony, perhaps the most famous of the early monks, is reported to have eaten bread, salt, and water once a day in his early renunciations,[20] and Poemen taught that it was better to eat a little every day. The recorder of this saying notes that this was the consensus of the fathers after their experiments with different regimens.[21] And both Cassian[22] and Evagrius of Pontus[23] report that eating once a day without satiety was the custom in the Egyptian desert. Some individuals, however, ate less often. Elias, for example, ate only once a week when he was young, but later ate a small amount of bread daily.[24] Palladius relates separate stories of a virgin[25] and a monk[26] who ate only on Saturdays and Sundays, traditional non-fasting days in Egypt.[27] And the record of the seven monks' pilgrimage to Egypt notes that the hermit John, who stood in prayer for three years, ate only the eucharist brought to him on Sundays during that time.[28] The Pachomian *Precepts* suggest that in the Pachomian communities of upper Egypt the monks ate two meals per day, one at noon and one in the evening.[29]

début de Moyen Age: Etude d'un régime alimentaire et sa fonction," in *Hommages à André Dupont: Etudes médiévales langue-dociennes* (Montpellier: Fédération historique du Languedoc méditerranéen et du Roussillon, 1974), passim; Maria Dembińska, "Diet: A Comparison of Food Consumption Between Some Eastern and Western Monasteries in the 4th–12th Centuries," *Byzantion* 55 (1985): 431–462; Violet McDermot, *The Cult of the Seer in the Ancient Middle East* (Berkeley: University of California Press, 1971), 39–43, 322–338; Alison Goddard Elliott, *Roads to Paradise: Reading the Lives of the Early Saints* (Hanover, N.H.: University Press of New England for Brown University Press, 1987), 137–140; A.-J. Festugière, *Les moines d'orient: Culture ou sainteté* (Paris: Éditions du Cerf, 1961–1964), 1:59–74; and Arbesmann, "Fasten, Fastenspeisen, Fasttage," 476–478, 495–500.

20. *Vita Antonii* 7 (*PG* 26.852C–853A).

21. *AP* Poemen 31; Megethius 2 (*PG* 65.329C; 301A).

22. John Cassian, *Conlationes* 2.19; 2.26 (E. Pichery, ed., *Jean Cassien: Conférences*, SC 42 [Paris: Éditions du Cerf, 1955], 133; 137).

23. *De diversis malignis cogitationibus* 25 (*PG* 79.1229C).

24. *HM* 7.3 (Festugière, 46).

25. *HL* 20 (Butler, 2:63).

26. Ibid., 48 (Butler, 2:142).

27. Butler, 2:198–199.

28. *HM* 13.4 (Festugière, 99).

29. *Precept* 103 (Veilleux [English translation], 162); and see Rousseau, *Pachomius*, 84–85.

The avoidance of meat and wine, except by those monks who fell ill, seems in my sources to be the general rule.[30] A fasting diet of bread, salt, and water is often recorded and recommended in my sources as the most basic and simple observance. This was Antony's diet, as noted above, and the practice of eating bread with salt seems to have been very common among Egyptian monks.[31] Typically bread was baked and dried in small loaves or biscuits, παξαμάτια, which could be easily stored for long periods of time[32] and soaked in water for easier consumption.[33] Bread could be eaten alone[34] or with oil,[35] or as part of a regimen that included vegetables.[36] Sources also mention fruits,[37] fish,[38] and gruels made from soaked or cooked legumes, grains, and cereals.[39] There tends to be a general distinction between "cooked" regimens (which would include cereals or soups made from boiled grains and legumes such as lentils or chickpeas) and "dry" or

30. *Vita Antonii* 7 (*PG* 26.853A); *AP* Theophilus the Archbishop 3; Macarius the Great 10; Xoius 1; Poemen 170; Peter the Pionite 1 (*PG* 65.200A; 268A–B; 312C; 364A; 376B–C); Palladius, *HL* 1 (Butler, 2:15). See also Patlagean, *Pauvreté,* 41–53, 137; idem, "Ancient Byzantine Hagiography and Social History," in *Saints and Their Cults: Studies in Religious Sociology, Folklore and History,* ed. Stephen Wilson, trans. Jane Hodgkin (Cambridge: Cambridge University Press, 1983), 106; and Schümmer, *Die altchristliche Fastenpraxis,* 45–47.
31. See, for example, Palladius, *HL* 47 (Butler, 2:141); *AP* Ares 1 [bread and salt prescribed]; John the Dwarf 29 ["the fathers of Scetis eat bread and salt"] (*PG* 65.132C; 213B–C). In the Pachomian communities, "Those who dedicate themselves to greater abstinence and do not want to eat in common with the others" are supplied with small loaves of bread which they keep in their cells and eat with salt (*Precept* 79 [Veilleux (English translation), 159]). On salt see also Patlagean, *Pauvreté,* 39.
32. *AP* Agathon 20; Macarius the Great 33 (*PG* 65.113C; 276C); Palladius, *HL* 22 (Butler, 2:72).
33. *AP* Achilles 3 (*PG* 65.124C–D).
34. Palladius, *HL* 19 (Butler, 2:60); *HM* 7.3 (Festugière, 46).
35. Palladius, *HL* 38 (Butler, 2:120).
36. Ibid., 2 (Butler, 2:17); *AP* Poemen 186 (*PG* 65.368B). The Pachomian *Precepts* mention a vegetable garden for the monastic community (71 [Veilleux (English translation), 158]).
37. *Precepts* of Pachomius, 75–77 (Veilleux [English translation], 158–159); *AP* Arsenius 19 (*PG* 65.92C); *HM* 1.17; 21.13–14 (Festugière, 15; 126–127).
38. Candida generally abstained from meat but ate fish, vegetables, and oil on feast days (Palladius, *HL* 57 [Butler, 2:150–151]).
39. *AP* Paul the Great 3 (*PG* 65.381C); *HM* 14.20; 15.4 (Festugière, 108–109; 111–112); Palladius, *HL* 18; 38 (Butler 2:48; 122).

"raw" regimens (based on dried bread or raw vegetables and soaked legumes).[40] But these regimens are not entirely exclusive. The place of bread is particularly illustrative: often it is excluded, along with cooked foods, from diets based on raw vegetables. For example, John of Lycopolis never ate bread or foods that required cooking.[41] Yet some ascetics apparently included bread in a raw diet. From a young age Ammonius, for example, "ate nothing that was prepared with fire except bread."[42] This ambiguity may be explained in part by the fact that dried breads such as παξαμάτια would not require preparation on a daily basis and so would fall into the same category as uncooked foods.[43]

Although, according to these sources, rigorous fasting is admired and clearly central to the way of life of the early desert ascetics (and there seems to have been rivalry and competition in ascetic prowess[44]) we also find a strong emphasis on humility, not fasting beyond one's strength, and placing the requirements of hospitality before fasting.[45] Further, the sources on early monasticism are distinguished by images of paradise on earth and miracles that often center around food issues.[46] This is especially true

40. Rousselle, *Porneia*, 211–213; cf. Elliott, *Roads to Paradise*, 138–140.
41. *HM* 1.17 (Festugière, 15).
42. *HL* 11 (Butler, 2:34). For other examples of abstinence from bread, vegetables, or cooked foods, see *AP* Dioscorus 1; Isaiah 6 (*PG* 65.160C; 181C); Palladius, *HL* 2; 11; 18; 19; 36; 38; 45; 52 (Butler, 2:17; 34; 48; 60; 107; 120–122; 133; 145); *HM* 2.4–5; 6.4; 8.9; 20.17 (Festugière, 36–37; 45; 49–50; 123.
43. Patlagean's structuralist analysis of different foods mentioned in fourth- to seventh-century sources distinguishes four classifications based on the type of preparation required, ranging from gathered foods eaten without preparation of any kind to cooked foods. Παξαμάτια, eaten dry, fall into the second level (cultivated and eaten without preparation), but dried bread eaten after soaking falls into the third level (cultivated foods requiring preparation but without cooking). Fresh and warm bread, however, belongs to the fourth level of prepared and cooked foods. It is thus clear that "bread" does not always indicate the same thing in our sources (*Pauvreté*, 38–44).
44. See especially *HM* prolog, 11; 20.5 (Festugière, 8; 120); Palladius, *HL* 18 (Butler, 2:48).
45. For example, see *AP* Anthony 13; Silvanus 1; Syncletica 15 (*PG* 65.77D–87A; 408C; 425C–D).
46. P. Suso Frank, *Angelikos Bios: Begriffsanalytische und begriffs-geschichtliche Untersuchung zum 'engelgleichen Leben' im frühen Mönchtum*, Beiträge zur Geschichte des alten Mönchtums und des Benediktinerordens, 26 (Munich: Aschendorff, 1964), 108–119; Brown, *The Body and Society*, 218–224; Ward, "Introduction," 36–37.

of the *History of the Monks in Egypt,* but also evident in Palladius and the *Apophthegmata.* The monk Apollo, for example, lived in a cave where he prayed continuously and was miraculously provided with food by an angel.[47] In a particularly striking story, Apollo and his disciples pray for food and are visited by strangers bearing amazing things: "fruits of paradise of every kind, grapes and pomegranates and figs and walnuts, all acquired out of season, and some honeycombs and a jar of fresh milk, and loaves of bread, still warm, although they were brought from a strange land."[48] This sensuous description of foods miraculously received gives readers a sense of the very human desires and vulnerability of the desert ascetics. Here the focus of the text is on the bounty, abundance, and delight of paradise rather than on frugality and abstinence. This same sense of abundance and blessing is found in the reports of agricultural miracles associated with monks. John of Lycopolis is said to have been able to predict the behavior of the Nile River (the flooding of which was critical in Egyptian farming) and periods of agricultural productivity.[49]

Finally, we are left with the difficult question of the motives for fasting. Because the sources were written at significant chronological distance from the first generation of monks and hermits, we can expect that the monks' deeds and words are filtered through the interpretations and worldviews of the later authors.[50] Thus we cannot be certain to what extent the stated motives for and effects of fasting reflect the understandings of the early monks themselves or the concerns of later advocates.[51] It will nevertheless be

47. *HM* 8.5–6 (Festugière, 48–49). For other examples of feeding miracles see also ibid., 1.45–58; 2.9; 10.8; 11.5; 12.2–4, 14–15 (Festugière, 26–32; 37–38; 78–79; 91; 92–93; 96–97); *AP* Zeno 5 (*PG* 65.177A); Palladius, *HL* 18; 36; 51; 71 (Butler, 2:50–51; 107; 144; 167–168).

48. *HM* 8.38–41 (Festugière, 62–63). Similarly, when Patermuthius was taken to paradise, he brought back a wonderful fig as proof of his journey (ibid., 10.21–22 [Festugière, 84]; and see also ibid., 21.5–12 [Festugière, 125–126]).

49. Ibid., 1.11; 10.28–29; 12.16 (Festugière, 12; 86–87; 97).

50. For example, Philip Rousseau has cautioned that the *Lausiac History* of Palladius as well as the writings of John Cassian "represent . . . a more reflective stage in the development of ascetic literature, a more conscious attempt to capture allegiance and to influence the organization of the ascetic life" (*Ascetics, Authority, and the Church,* 17).

51. In particular, Rousselle has raised the issue of the interpretation of the Egyptian ascetic diet by later Greek and Western theorists in terms of the

useful for this study to review some of the motives for fasting in the early monastic sources. In the *Apophthegmata*, fasting is said to help fight against evil thoughts,[52] sin,[53] and the enemy.[54] It consumes the body,[55] expresses the fear of God,[56] and distinguishes the ascetic from "the world" based on his or her paltry diet.[57] Palladius and the *History of the Monks in Egypt* likewise report that the monks and virgins looked on fasting as an aid in resisting desires,[58] passion,[59] and wicked images and dreams.[60] Some passages indicate that fasting was practiced in order to fight against sexual desire, but—in contrast to many of the texts examined in the following pages—generally no explicitly physiological model is used for the connection between food and sexual desire.[61]

Two apparent exceptions, both on the topic of noctural emissions, or wet dreams, invite comment. In the *Apophthegmata* and the *Letters* of Antony, we encounter Antony's teaching that there are three kinds of bodily "movements" or urges: one is natural and without passion, the second is caused by eating too much food (which warms the blood and "spurs the body to work"), and the third is caused by jealous demons.[62] And the *History of the*

Greco-Roman medical understanding of diet and sexual desire. She argues that compilers of the Coptic oral tradition and editors of monastic sources embellished the teachings of the early heroes to reflect their own obsession with achieving perfect sexual chastity as well as their own physiological models and nutritional techniques for maintaining chastity (Rousselle, *Porneia*, 215–222; see also Brown, *The Body and Society*, 217–218, 230; and see n.64, p. 17).

52. *AP* Syncletica 3 (*PG* 65.421B).

53. Ibid., Hyperechius 2 (*PG* 65.429C).

54. Ibid., Doulas 1; John the Dwarf 3 (*PG* 65.161B; 205A).

55. Ibid., Theodore of Eleutheropolis 2 (*PG* 65.197C).

56. Ibid., Poemen 181 (*PG* 65.365C).

57. Ibid., Syncletica 4 (*PG* 65.421C).

58. *HM* 1.29 (Festugière, 19).

59. Ibid.; Palladius, *HL* 45 (Butler, 2:133).

60. Palladius, *HL* 19 (Butler, 2:60–61).

61. For example, Philodormus fought against the passions of gluttony and lust by shutting himself in with irons and avoiding wheat bread and cooked food for eighteen years (Palladius, *HL* 45 [Butler, 2:133]); Poemen instructs the one fighting sexual desire to control the belly and the tongue and to live apart (*AP* Poemen 62 [*PG* 65.337A]). See also Rousselle, *Porneia*, 216.

62. *AP* Anthony 22 (*PG* 65.84A–B); *Epistle* 1.35–41 (English translation in Rubenson, *The Letters of St. Antony*, 199).

Monks in Egypt preserves an even more explicit teaching of Dioscorus in which he reminds monks that nocturnal emissions of semen can be reduced by means of fasting: by controlling the intake of food one reduces the buildup of "matter," or seminal fluid, in the body.[63] These two passages, connecting gluttony to the physical movements of desire, and fasting to their suppression, point to the types of concerns that will distinguish the developing discourse on fasting and sexual chastity.[64]

Bodily Practice and Ascetic Theory

In modern scholarly works dealing with early Christian asceticism, one detects a general mistrust or discomfort with the physical realities of fasting, especially as graphically depicted in some of the ancient sources on desert asceticism we have just examined. Until recently, much scholarship on fasting has tended to concern itself with the development of ecclesiastical fasts associated with the church calendar and rituals, and with making distinctions between types of fasting based on definitions of orthodoxy, moderation, and "true" Christian tradition. Johannes Behm, for example, in his article on fasting in the New Testament, seeks to separate the teaching and model of Jesus from Jewish fasting (which he characterizes as legalistic works-righteousness), as

---

63. *HM* 20.1–4 (Festugière, 118–119).

64. Rousselle has discussed both of these texts as examples from sources concerning early monasticism in which models from Greco-Roman medical physiology are applied to the desert tradition. She argues that while Coptic or Egyptian monks understood there to be a connection between food and sexual desire, later authors and compilers of sayings added models from Greco-Roman medicine that explicitly connect the buildup of heat and moisture with increase in seminal fluid and therefore increase in sexual desire (*Porneia*, 216–218). But this argument may require some modification in light of Samuel Rubenson's recent study of the letters of Antony. Rubenson's argument for the authenticity of the letters draws a much more direct line between the earliest Egyptian monks and the Alexandrian Origenist and Platonic traditions, thus challenging the typical scholarly distinction between the Greek and Coptic worlds (*The Letters of St. Antony*). David Brakke discusses the two passages on movements and seminal emissions in the context of Egyptian monasticism and the shifts in early Christian understanding of wet dreams in "The Problematization of Nocturnal Emissions in Early Christian Syria, Egypt, and Gaul," *Journal of Early Christian Studies* 3 (1995): 436–441.

well as the practice of the Christian church after the first century (which he labels "dualistic" and "a continuation of . . . Jewish piety"). He thus manages to separate Jesus from any ascetic taint, claiming that in the early church "there is no longer any clear awareness of the way in which Jesus viewed fasting." For Jesus, we are told, fasting was "no mere ascetic exercise" or "pious work," but a "sign and symbol of the inner attitude which perhaps hardly needs such a sign and symbol."[65]

Some modern writers have attempted to define a mainstream or norm of early Christian practice and interpretation and to bracket rigorous forms of dietary abstinence as fanciful, quaint, pagan-influenced, Judaizing, abnormal, or even heretical. The result is an emphasis on the "spiritual fast" as the primary, correct fast of the early church so that, strangely, fasting becomes a disembodied, nonthreatening spiritual exercise in abstaining from sin. For example, one historian argues that in spite of the continuities, influences, and similarities with Greek and Roman philosophical and religious food abstinence, Christian fasting is nonetheless *unique* because Christianity is founded not on certain acts and observances but on love.[66]

Herbert Musurillo, emphasizing the diversity in fasting practices, rightly criticizes others for dismissing ascetic behavior as dualistic or masochistic. Nevertheless he characterizes the food abstinence of the Egyptian, Palestinian, and Syrian desert ascetics as "abnormal" and writes of one ancient source: "The minute recording of the bizarre austerities, the number of ounces of greens a man ate per day, the abnormal (one is almost tempted to say morbid) interest in the body—this strikes us at the very least as childish and ridiculous."[67] His discomfort with the evidence that physical asceticism was an important mode of religious

---

65. Johannes Behm, "νῆστις, νηστεύω, νηστεία," in *Theological Dictionary of the New Testament*, ed. Gerhard Kittel, trans. and ed. Geoffrey W. Bromiley (Grand Rapids: Eerdmans, 1967; reprint, 1973), 4:924–935; see also Musurillo's criticism of Behm's "entirely over-simplified" approach ("The Problem of Ascetical Fasting," 43–45).

66. Festugière, *Les moines d'orient*, 1:65–67.

67. Musurillo, "The Problem of Ascetical Fasting," 28, on Palladius's *Historia Lausiaca*. Musurillo includes the sources on the desert tradition under the heading "Abnormality in the Practice of Fasting" (24–35).

expression is clear when he notes that "from the viewpoint of modern thought, perhaps, this practice of fasting and austerity may reflect a primitive conception of matter, and a misunderstanding of the role of the body and its impulses in the redemption of man."[68] It is not surprising, therefore, that Musurillo lays great stress on the motif of the spiritual fast (the allegorical or symbolic interpretation of fasting as avoidance of evil or sin), a motif found in texts throughout the patristic period.[69]

Other authors have, in their examination of the ancient sources, likewise sought to discover an "interior," spiritual fast and to elevate it over an "exterior," physical fast.[70] The problem with such an approach is not that there is no concept of a spiritual fast in the early sources or that there are no distinctions to be made between degrees of austerity or moderation in fasting. Rather, this approach tends not only to subordinate or dismiss the physical expressions of early Christian piety but also to ignore the role of bodily behaviors in religious expression and self-definition. This problem reflects, I think, what is a wider issue in historical studies as well as sociology and anthropology. It seems difficult for historians or external observers to approach practice first as practice, or bodily behaviors first as bodily. Thus scholars have tended to prioritize or privilege theory and belief over practice and action.

Several more recent studies, however, have both challenged this common scheme and raised new questions that are particularly important for the study of ascetic piety. Catherine Bell, for example, has analyzed and criticized a common approach to ritual studies that sees habitual action as something that encodes or expresses meaning and therefore something that requires interpretation and theory.[71] In particular, she has shown that

---

68. Ibid., 63.

69. For a discussion and texts see ibid., 35–42.

70. See for example Arbesmann, "Fasting and Prophecy," 38, 50; Guillaume, *Jeûne et charité*, passim; Pichler, *Das Fasten bei Basileios dem Grossen*, 71–74, 98, 101; Schümmer, *Die altchristliche Fastenpraxis*, 224–226, 234.

71. Catherine Bell, *Ritual Theory, Ritual Practice* (New York: Oxford University Press, 1992), esp. 13–66.

differentiations between ritual, activity, and practice on the one hand and myth, thought, and theory on the other not only distort both sides, but always lead to "the subordination of act to thought, or actors to thinkers."[72] Similarly, sociologist Pierre Bourdieu has dramatically described the ways in which the academic analysis of bodily behavior has been limited by its traditional privileging of observer over observed, knowing over doing, and theory over practice.[73] He notes that in much scholarly thought one can detect a "secret conviction that action is fully performed only when it is understood, interpreted, expressed," or that "a gesture or ritual act" must express something.[74] Bourdieu argues instead that there is a logic in practice, that it "makes sense" without the totalizing discourse and theoretical models that are usually applied to it. Thus practices "express" the socially constructed body as part of a particular context and are sensible within that context.

The study of early Christian asceticism presents a particularly acute example of these tensions. In recent years, historians have been interested in reconstructing bodily practices and expectations, especially in relation to gender and sexuality, in medicine, religion, culture, and society. In particular, recent studies on asceticism have rejected the view of bodily renunciation as dualistic, masochistic, or "mad"[75] and sought instead to interpret it as

72. Ibid., 48–49: "Indeed, no matter how provisional or heuristic, a distinction between thought and action is not a differentiation between two equally weighted terms. When used, it is rarely intended to be. Despite the seeming equality of abstract distinction—male-female, black-white, true-false, one-many—such dichotomies are implicitly employed to afford one term some purchase over another. To perceive this is to grasp differentiation itself *as an activity* and, therefore, to begin to appreciate the strategic activity of theory-making in general."

73. Pierre Bourdieu, *The Logic of Practice*, trans. Richard Nice (Stanford: Stanford University Press, 1990).

74. Ibid., 36–37.

75. See E. R. Dodds's now famous query regarding what he saw as the "repulsive" ascetic renunciations of the desert fathers: "Where did all this madness come from?" (*Pagan and Christian in an Age of Anxiety* [Cambridge: Cambridge University Press, 1965; reprint, New York: W. W. Norton, 1970], 33–34).

an integral aspect of piety and religious expression. The work of Peter Brown has been quite influential in this area.[76] Other new research on Christian and non-Christian asceticism has emphasized the interrelationship between physical representations and manipulations of the body and theology, meaning, interpretation, and social relations.[77] Steady interest and momentum have accompanied the collection and translation of ancient ascetic

76. Brown examines the variety of attitudes toward the body and sexuality in light of theology, culture, and the relationship between individual and society. Explicitly rejecting earlier characterizations of asceticism as body-hating and dualistic, he instead argues that early Christian asceticism by its nature includes matter and the body in spiritual progress (Brown, *The Body and Society*, 222–223, 235–237). Brown's study of early Christianity was in turn influenced by the work of such scholars as Aline Rousselle and Michel Foucault on topics of sexuality, desire, and gender in Greco-Roman antiquity (Aline Rousselle, *Porneia*; Michel Foucault, *The History of Sexuality:* vol. 2, *The Use of Pleasure*; vol. 3, *The Care of the Self*; trans. Robert Hurley [New York: Pantheon Books, 1985–1986]; see also Elizabeth A. Clark, "Foucault, the Fathers, and Sex," *Journal of the American Academy of Religion* 56 [1988]: 619–641). Both Rousselle and Foucault raise the issue of diet as a primary arena for analysis.

77. Representative texts among the secondary sources for this study include Rudolph M. Bell, *Holy Anorexia*, Epilogue by William N. Davis (Chicago: University of Chicago Press, 1985); Caroline Walker Bynum, *Holy Feast and Holy Fast: The Religious Significance of Food to Medieval Women*, The New Historicism: Studies in Cultural Poetics (Berkeley: University of California Press, 1987); Averil Cameron, "Virginity as Metaphor: Women and the Rhetoric of Early Christianity," in *History as Text: The Writing of Ancient History*, ed. Averil Cameron (Chapel Hill: University of North Carolina Press, 1989), 184–205; Cooper, *The Virgin and the Bride*; James A. Francis, *Subversive Virtue: Asceticism and Authority in the Second-Century Pagan World* (University Park: Pennsylvania State University Press, 1995); John G. Gager, "Body-Symbols and Social Reality: Resurrection, Incarnation and Asceticism in Early Christianity," *Religion* 12 (1982): 345–363; Harpham, *The Ascetic Imperative*; Margaret R. Miles, *Carnal Knowing: Female Nakedness and Religious Meaning in the Christian West* (Boston: Beacon Press, 1989); Patricia Cox Miller, "Desert Asceticism and 'The Body from Nowhere,'" *Journal of Early Christian Studies* 2 (1994): 137–153; Judith Perkins, *The Suffering Self: Pain and Narrative Representation on the Early Christian Era* (New York: Routledge, 1995); and see the sources on female asceticism in n.6, p. 4.

78. See for example Vincent L. Wimbush, ed., *Ascetic Behavior in Greco-Roman Antiquity: A Sourcebook*, Studies in Antiquity and Christianity (Minneapolis: Fortress Press, 1990); Sebastian P. Brock and Susan Ashbrook Harvey, eds. and trans., *Holy Women of the Syrian Orient*, The

texts,[78] and attention has turned as well to cross-cultural and theoretical approaches to the study of asceticism.[79] In general, then, recent scholarship has tended to recognize the centrality of perceptions of body, as both a physical reality and as a metaphor or construction, in religious experience and expression. Christian myth, scripture, and ritual are grounded in bodily acts and bodily symbols, including birth, crucifixion, resurrection, Eucharist, baptism, and martyrdom as well as the "mortification" of the flesh in asceticism.[80] And for all of the rhetorical condemnations of the flesh in ascetic literature, the steady, intent focus on the appearance of the body as a sign of holiness and sanctification refutes any easy dismissal of asceticism as bizarre or dualistic.

Nevertheless, we continue to face the difficulties, outlined by Bell and Bourdieu, inherent in the interpretation of ascetic practice. Patricia Cox Miller, for example, has expressed reservations about recent scholarship that emphasizes the body as the arena for religious or spiritual formation, an emphasis that, according to Miller, threatens to over-theologize bodily acts. Miller warns of the "danger of bypassing the body in the very act of trying to bring it forward for consideration." Her analysis stresses the performative aspects of ascetic behavior, an approach which, she argues, "enables the interpreter to focus on the doing and acting which

---

Transformation of the Classical Heritage 13 (Berkeley: University of California Press, 1987).

79. See, for example, the essays collected in Vincent L. Wimbush and Richard Valantasis, eds., *Asceticism* (New York: Oxford University Press, 1995) and the collection of articles on religion and food in *Journal of the American Academy of Religion* 63 (1995).

80. See especially Gager, "Body-Symbols," and Miles, *Carnal Knowing*.

81. Miller, "Desert Asceticism," 144–148. Miller's point may be related to the broader tension, in the history of the body as well social or cultural analysis, between approaches to "the body" that emphasize the flesh-and-bones, biological, or "lived" body and approaches that emphasize the cultural or social "construction" of the body in representation or discourse. For three discussions of this tension from the perspective of different fields, see Bryan S. Turner, "The Body Question: Recent Developments in Social Theory," in *Regulating Bodies: Essays in Medical Sociology* (London and New York: Routledge, 1992), 33–66; Roy Porter, "History of the Body," in *New Perspectives on Historical Writing*, ed. Peter Burke (University Park: Pennsylvania State University Press, 1991), 206–232; and Susan Bordo, *Unbearable Weight: Feminism, Western Culture, and the Body* (Berkeley: University of California Press, 1993), e.g., 38–42, 165–184.

are creative of meaning in the ascetic context."[81] Miller identifies what I think is a critical need in studies of asceticism, that is, the need to resist the temptation (to borrow ascetic language) simply to take over the theological or theoretical categories of our sources—ancient or modern. The difficulty is that because bodily behavior is presented to us through ancient texts, the body is already theorized, theologized, idealized, or—in many cases—made deviant. What is more, the very language of "theory" vs. "practice" (or "contemplation" vs. "*askesis*," or "spiritual" vs. "physical") is interwoven throughout both the ancient sources and modern interpretations of those sources. As historians, we should be suspicious of such categories and the values attached to them. It is to presume upon the ancients to suggest that ascetic practice was distinct from the nurturing of the soul. Such is not the case, as we shall see.

In this study I have tried, then, to make sense of ascetic fasting by integrating attention to both the practical experience of asceticism (that is, what the ancients might actually have been doing and what they expected from their bodies) and the theological and textual framework in which that behavior is presented and in which the ideal body is constructed. I have considered the context of late ancient assumptions, theories, and practices as well as Christian appropriations and applications. Thus my study reflects interweaving interests in the history of the body, social history, and the history of ideas. Early Christian fasting offers a particularly rich field for exploration. I make no attempt to locate or isolate a single, "correct" theory of ascetic fasting, but have assumed diversity in practice and interpretation.

To explore the issues of fasting, virginity, and ascetic theology I shall begin, in chapter two, with what I understand to be the essential context—that is, first- and second-century ethical and medical ideas about diet, *askesis,* and physiology—in order to illustrate the interdependence of practical bodily behaviors with ethics and the condition of the soul. I first discuss these themes in the ethical theory of the Stoics Musonius Rufus and Epictetus; the pseudonymous Cynic epistles; Plutarch; the Christian Clement of Alexandria; and the medical writer Galen. Next I will describe Greco-Roman medical material from late antiquity, especially the works of Galen, concerning the relationship between diet, digestion, the humors, and sexual desire in male and female bodies. Clement and Galen will be significant for the articulation of these ideas among later thinkers.

Chapter three presents close readings of four Christian ascetic theorists—Basil of Ancyra, Gregory of Nyssa, Jerome, and John Cassian—who use explicit medical or physiological models to argue for the usefulness of fasting in maintaining sexual chastity.[82] These authors, writing in the fourth and early fifth centuries, saw a direct causal connection between the amount and type of food consumed and the level of sexual humors and desire generated in the body. Thus fasting is a practical and necessary tool for the avoidance of passion.

The physiological connection of eating and sexual desire extends further to the link between gluttony and lust as passions of the soul. In chapter four I discuss the representation of the vice of gluttony, common in ancient literature, in two Christian writers: John Chrysostom (bishop of Constantinople) and Evagrius of Pontus. Chrysostom's homilies, addressed to a lay audience, emphasize the gross physical effects of gluttony and the damage it causes not only to one's body but to one's public honor as well. Evagrius's writings are addressed to a smaller ascetic audience and concentrate on the more subtle yet dynamic relationship between gluttony and sexual lust as vices of the soul. Still, both Chrysostom and Evagrius understand the intimate link between gluttony and lust and both expect visible and concrete physical changes as evidence of the successful repression of vice.

On the one hand, then, historians of antiquity cannot understand dietary asceticism without understanding late ancient medical notions of diet, physiology, and the relationship of body and soul. On the other hand, we cannot appreciate the social and ideological implications of physical behaviors and techniques without

82. Aline Rousselle has previously demonstrated clearly that Jerome and John Cassian use medical theory to argue that fasting reduces sexual heat and moisture in the body ("Abstinence et continence," 239–254). My study expands the analysis of these ancient authors and places them in the wider context of Christian discourse.

returning to the theological underpinnings of the ancient discussion. Chapter five deals with the protological and eschatological arguments for asceticism, that is, arguments based on ideals of first things and last things. Fasting and virginity are, according to several texts examined in this chapter, ways of imitating the original blessed human condition in paradise before the fall and life in the paradise to come. By fasting and sexual abstinence one also imitates the ways of the angels.

To present the ways in which eating (especially meat eating), sexuality, procreation, and gender differentiation were understood as being somehow tainted by the fall or degradation of humanity, I first discuss the ancient myths of the golden age and Prometheus, as presented and interpreted especially in Hesiod and Porphyry. Next I examine the interpretation of these issues by fourth-century Christian theorists, in relation to the myth of creation and the fall in Genesis and the promise of the coming kingdom. I will show that in Christian ascetic theory both eating and sexual activity take on the weight of the fall and its consequences of mortality, hierarchy, labor, and pain in human life. Thus the one who takes up a life of chastity and dietary renunciation becomes identified with original purity and immortality, and the ascetic body anticipates—or even returns to—the condition of original creation.

Chapter six focuses specifically on the female ascetic body as represented and portrayed in Christian texts. I draw together the ideas and reconstructions of the previous chapters to argue that ascetic authors interpreted the physical effects of fasting—including dryness, thinness, withered breasts, and the cessation of menstruation—as an obliteration of "female" nature, a concrete realization of the return to paradise, and a reversal of the power of procreation and death. At the same time, the female body remains essentially female, both by its continuing sexual danger to men and in its eroticized relationship with Christ the bridegroom. In this chapter we will also consider the place of fasting and virginity in the rhetorical construction of "heretical" *askesis.*

Overall, I will argue that ascetic dietary renunciation in general, and the fasting of female virgins in particular, lies at the intersection of ancient medical theory, psychological models, and eschatological hopes; it reflects theological ideas concerning the origins of the vulnerable and unruly human body, sexual differentiation, and hierarchy. The understanding of ascetic fasting demonstrates that many of its advocates saw release from the "burden of the flesh," paradoxically, as to a great extent accomplished through and inscribed in the human body itself.

CHAPTER TWO

Philosophy of the Body and Medicine of the Soul: Ethics, Diet, and Sexuality in Late Antiquity

MANY OF THE CONCEPTS and assumptions we will encounter in Christian ascetic discourse and theory are grounded in the wider context of Greco-Roman medical theory, moral philosophy, and contemporary understandings of the relationship between body and soul in the human being. This chapter will introduce two dynamically interrelated and interdependent fields of late ancient inquiry and concern: moral philosophy and dietetic and sexual physiology. In both arenas, the mutual dependence and influence of body and soul inform arguments concerning human health, character, and behavior. After reviewing these themes briefly in the works of several writers representing moralist philosophy or ethics in the early centuries of the common era, we will examine theories of diet, sexuality, and male and female physiology in the medical theory of the same period, represented primarily by Galen. This chapter will articulate much of the essential context for the fourth-century surge in Christian ascetic theory and practice, especially relating to sexual and dietary abstinence.

The Moralist Tradition

Scholars have recently called attention to a flowering of concern with the "care of the self" or "cultivation of the self"[1] in the first

---

1. The terms are from Michel Foucault, *The History of Sexuality:* vol. 3, *The Care of the Self,* trans. Robert Hurley (New York: Pantheon Books, 1986).

centuries of the common era, which featured a greater emphasis on ethical or moral formation; bodily needs, movements, and vulnerabilities; and the interior life and "health" of the soul— especially as these relate to regimen, public behavior, and self-presentation.[2] First- and second-century moral philosophers recognize not only that medicine and philosophy are analogous, but that their fields of interest are in fact overlapping. For example, Musonius Rufus (c.30–c.101 C.E.) often compares physicians and philosophers, and notes that both groups are skilled in the arts of observation, diagnosis and prescription, and that both require practical training.[3] Plutarch (c.47–c.120), goes beyond simple comparison and metaphor to argue that medicine and philosophy should be considered as one field, as they are both concerned with happiness, health, and daily lifestyle;[4] and the physician Galen (c.129–200) notes that the ideal doctor is also a philosopher (trained in logic as well as ethics), and that a healthy lifestyle is a sign of virtue. Further, Galen argues that the physician must not only be trained in *theoretical* knowledge, but also demonstrate virtue through *practical* application of the lessons of philosophy,[5]

---

2. In addition to Foucault, see also James A. Francis, *Subversive Virtue: Asceticism and Authority in the Second-Century Pagan World* (University Park: Pennsylvania State University Press, 1995); Maud W. Gleason, *Making Men: Sophists and Self-Presentation in Ancient Rome* (Princeton: Princeton University Press, 1995); Judith Perkins, "The 'Self' as Sufferer," *Harvard Theological Review* 85 (1992): 245–272; idem, *The Suffering Self: Pain and Narrative Representation in the Early Christian Era* (London: Routledge, 1995); Martha C. Nussbaum, *The Therapy of Desire: Theory and Practice in Hellenistic Ethics*, Martin Classical Lectures, n.s. 2 (Princeton: Princeton University Press, 1994); Peter Brown, *The Body and Society: Men, Women, and Sexual Renunciation in Early Christianity*, Lectures on the History of Religions 13 (New York: Columbia University Press, 1988), 5–32; and Owsei Temkin, *Hippocrates in a World of Pagans and Christians* (Baltimore: The Johns Hopkins University Press, 1991), 3–17.

3. For example, see Musonius Rufus *Discourses* 1; 5 in Cora B. Lutz, ed., "Musonius Rufus: The Roman Socrates," *Yale Classical Studies* 10 (1947): 32; 50.

4. Plutarch, *De tuenda sanitate praecepta* 1, 122c–e (Frank Cole Babbitt, ed., *Plutarch's Moralia*, Loeb Classical Library [Cambridge: Harvard University Press, 1971], 2:216–218).

5. See esp. *Quod optimus medicus sit quoque philosophus* (C. G. Kühn, ed., *Galeni Opera Omnia* [Leipzig: K. Knobloch, 1823–1833; reprint,

and assumes throughout his writings that the body's condition is linked to the soul's character.[6] In the late ancient Mediterranean context of early Christianity, then, we find a general convergence of concern in the areas of ethical formation, lifestyle, practical morality, and bodily regimen and behaviors. One indicator of this convergence is the overlapping of medical, philosophical, and athletic language ("disease," "training," "exercise," "health," etc.) in relation to what we might call an "ascetic" attitude, that is, a positive valuation of training and self-management for a particular goal or way of life.

These issues are especially critical for understanding concepts of the soul (ψυχή) and body (σῶμα) during this period. Although a comprehensive survey of philosophical and medical ideas of soul and body in antiquity is beyond the scope of this study, some general remarks on the topic will be helpful to situate our material.[7] The modern tendency to see body and soul as two distinct and unrelated or even conflicting spheres of activity and attention does not translate well to Greco-Roman antiquity, when medical and philosophical practitioners and theorists paint a more complicated and dynamic picture of their relationship.[8] Indeed, modern

---

Hildesheim: Georg Olms, 1965], 1:53–63) and the discussion in Temkin, *Hippocrates*, 47–50; and Tamsyn S. Barton, *Power and Knowledge: Astrology, Physiognomics, and Medicine under the Roman Empire*, The Body, in Theory: Histories of Cultural Materialism (Ann Arbor: The University of Michigan Press, 1994), 139, 171–172.

6. See the discussion of Galen on pp. 46–48.

7. The secondary literature on this topic is extensive, and should be consulted for more detailed analyses. Useful secondary sources include B. L. Hijmans, *Askesis: Notes on Epictetus' Educational System*, Wijsgerie Teksten en Studies (Assen: Van Gorcum, 1959); A. A. Long, *Hellenistic Philosophy: Stoics, Epicureans, Sceptics* (New York: Charles Scribner's Sons, 1974); idem, "Soul and Body in Stoicism," *The Center for Hermeneutical Studies in Hellenistic and Modern Culture: Colloquy 36* (Berkeley: Center for Hermeneutical Studies, 1980); John M. Rist, *Stoic Philosophy* (Cambridge: Cambridge University Press, 1969); and Wayne A. Meeks, *The Moral World of the First Christians*, Library of Early Christianity (Philadelphia: Westminster Press, 1986), 40–64.

8. In his recent study of conflicting views of the body in 1 Corinthians, Dale B. Martin addresses several of the issues in this chapter, especially concerning the ancient concepts of body and soul, with similar conclusions (*The Corinthian Body* [New Haven: Yale University Press, 1995], 3–37).

terminology, and modern interpretations of ancient terminology, prove inadequate to characterize ancient formulations.[9]

For much of the Greco-Roman philosophical tradition in the first and second centuries, the human soul remained a "vague kind of 'stuff.'"[10] Although Plato had characterized the soul as incorporeal (ἀσώματος), others—the Stoics and Epicureans in particular—continued to maintain bodily or materialist views.[11] For the Stoics, as A. A. Long writes, the human person—like all animals—is a unity of a body as we normally conceive it, a "flesh and bones body," and the soul which is itself a "body," a "substance in its own right which permeates the flesh and bones body." Its corporeal substance is warm or heated *pneuma* (breath, air, or spirit).[12] The Stoics distinguished eight "parts" or "faculties" of

9. As we will see, this is certainly the case with the concepts of body and soul, but also with the related areas of "physiology" and "psychology." The modern view of psychology as the "science of the mind" distinct from the body distorts the ancient picture. For this reason it may be better to avoid the term altogether, or substitute another. "Psychagogy" (from ψυχαγωγία leading the soul or persuasion), for example, captures the ancient medical and philosophical effort to care for souls and direct their progress. But this term also carries with it the negative connotation of deception or flattery. On psychagogy see Clarence Edvin Glad, "Adaptability in Epicurean and Early Christian Psychagogy: Paul and Philodemus" (Ph.D. diss., Brown University, 1992), 20–52. At minimum, it should be clear that "psychology" in the ancient world is not, finally, distinct from "physiology."

10. R. Renehan, "On the Greek Origins of the Concepts Incorporeality and Immateriality," *Greek, Roman, and Byzantine Studies* 21 (1980): 109. Renehan's remark concerns the "immediately post-Homeric period," but applies as well to certain schools of thought in the late ancient period.

11. Ibid., passim. On the archaic Greek understanding of the human body and the body of the gods see also Jean-Pierre Vernant,"Dim Body, Dazzling Body," in *Fragments for a History of the Human Body*, ed. Michel Feher, trans. Anne M. Wilson (New York: Zone, 1989), 1:19–47.

12. Long, "Soul and Body," 7–10. See also idem, *Hellenistic Philosophy*, 171; and Michel Spanneut, *Le Stoïcisme des pères de l'église de Clément de Rome à Clément d'Alexandrie*, new ed., Patristica Sorbonensia (Paris: Éditions du Seuil, 1957), 133–135. Long notes that the Stoic concept of soul as body must be interpreted in the larger context of the Stoic belief that anything that exists must be body ("Soul and Body," 3; and *Hellenistic Philosophy*, 152–153.) For examples of testimonies to the early Stoic position see Hans von Arnim, ed., *SVF* (Leipzig: B. G. Teubner, 1903–1924; reprint, 1964), 2:219–221 (soul as body) and 2:217–219 (pneuma as substance of the soul). Tertullian, who held a corporeal view of the soul, provides a brief and clear

the soul: the five senses, the voice, the procreative faculty (τὸ σπερματικόν), and the authoritative principle or *hegemonikon* (τὸ ἡγεμονικόν).[13] All animals have the same eight parts, but in an adult human, the authoritative principle develops rationality, which is the factor distinguishing humans from irrational animals.[14] The *hegemonikon* functions in most ways like what we might think of as the mind or consciousness. It governs the other parts of the soul and therefore also the activities of the body.[15]

Scholars have noted that these eight "parts" of the Stoic soul do not represent actual divisions or separate parts, but rather distinctive aspects or functions of a unified soul extending through the whole body.[16] Thus the Stoic distinction is not really analogous to what characterizes the Platonic view of the soul, namely a tripartite division. Briefly stated, in the Platonic theory there are three parts or aspects of the soul seated in three different parts of the body. The rational soul (τὸ λογιστικόν) is seated in the brain and is the incorporeal essence of reason, controlling the other two parts of the soul as a charioteer guides horses. Together the other parts constitute the "irrational soul": the irascible soul (τὸ θυμικόν, τὸ θυμοειδές) is seated in the heart and governs anger, passion, and courage while the concupiscible soul (τὸ ἐπιθυμητικόν) is seated in the liver and controls desire (useful and wicked), nutrition, and generation.[17]

---

summary of the Stoic position in his treatise *De anima* 5 (A. Reifferscheid and G. Wissowa, eds., *Tertulliani Opera*, CSEL 20 [Vienna: Tempsky, 1890], 304–305).

13. For texts see von Arnim, *SVF* 2:225–227.

14. Long, "Soul and Body," 12.

15. Long, *Hellenistic Philosophy*, 124, 171–172. Long elsewhere argues that the Stoics made a basic distinction between the soul in a general sense and soul in the specific sense, that is, soul as *hegemonikon* ("Soul and Body," passim). Later Stoic philosophers including Epictetus tended also to link the *hegemonikon* with God and with guardian angels (*daimona*). See Hijmans, *Askesis*, 13 and Rist, *Stoic Philosophy*, 261–272.

16. The authoritative principle, however, is seated in the heart or brain. Long, "Soul and Body," 12; Spanneut, *Le Stoïcisme*, 133–135.

17. See Plato, *Timaeus* 69b–72d (R. G. Bury, ed., *Plato: Timaeus, Critias, Cleitophon, Menexenus, Epistles*, Loeb Classical Library [Cambridge: Harvard University Press, 1966], 178–188); *Republic* 4.435–442 (Paul Shorey, ed., *Plato: The Republic*, 2 vols., Loeb Classical Library [Cambridge: Harvard

This image of the tripartite soul, which we will encounter often in the course of this study, finally proved to be more influential than the Stoic view in early Christian circles. On the other hand, the implications of the Stoic view for ethical theory and practice, if not the Stoic picture of the soul itself, continued to inform pagan and Christian moral philosophy. Indeed, the Platonic and the Stoic concepts of the soul and its relation to the body in many ways established the terms and issues for Christian discourse on the topic and—especially important for this study—for the theory and practice of asceticism.

In this arena, three overall themes emerge from both philosophical schools, themes that are critical for understanding asceticism. First, moral virtues and vices are linked to the soul's condition or health. Second, whatever the precise nature, substance, and constitution of the soul, it is somehow linked with the bodily senses and the procreative impulse. As noted above, the five senses and the power of generation are fully integrated as "parts" of the Stoic soul. But in the Platonic theory as well, the rational soul interacts with and struggles to control the irascible soul and the desiring soul, including the generative impulse, and is affected through the bodily senses. But third, at the same time both theories evince an elevation of either the *hegemonikon* or the rational soul and a theoretical tendency to *separate* it, to a greater or lesser extent, from the flesh and bones body, its functions, and its drives. This is clear even in the corporealist understanding of the Stoics, particularly in later articulations.[18] This

---

University Press, 1963], 1:374–410); and *Phaedrus* 253c–254e (Harold North Fowler, ed., *Plato: Euthyphro, Apology, Crito, Phaedo, Phaedrus*, Loeb Classical Library [Cambridge: Harvard University Press, 1966], 494–498). Long observes that "What Plato distinguishes as reason, spirit, and appetite are, in the Stoic soul, all activities of the dominant part, the *hegemonikon*" ("Soul and Body," 12).

18. This is one reason that the term "dualism" is not always a useful one, and is especially slippery in regard to the ancient material. R. Renehan points out in his discussion of concepts of the soul in the archaic period, for example, that scholars sometimes make the false assumption that "a soul which is independent of, indeed opposed to, the body is therefore free from matter and incorporeal." He also notes that a corporealist understanding of soul does not exclude the development of a "dichotomy" between body and soul ("On the Greek Origins," 107, 109). It is not enough simply to note that

contradiction or tension—between rhetorical hierarchy, or even opposition, of body and soul on the one hand and a practical recognition that the soul's condition and character are subject to bodily influence, and therefore also to bodily management, on the other—runs throughout pagan and Christian ascetic literature of late antiquity and most of the sources we will examine here.

Ethics and Askesis

In the following overview of ethical theory and ascetic ideals, we will focus on the practical philosophical tradition that became most prominent in the first and second centuries. Our principal sources are the Stoic philosophers Musonius Rufus and Epictetus, the unknown authors of the so-called Cynic Epistles, the middle-Platonic essayist Plutarch, the physician-philosopher Galen, and the Christian writer and teacher Clement of Alexandria. The remainder of the chapter will introduce dominant physiological and dietary theories of the same period, especially as they relate to the female body. Together, these form the theoretical and practical context of Christian ascetic fasting.

In the first and second centuries of the common era, Stoic influence was dominant in what has been called the philosophical, intellectual, and ethical "koine" or "common sense" of the larger culture.[19] Musonius Rufus and his student, Epictetus (c.55–c.135),

---

the Stoics held a corporealist view of the soul and assume that we know what that means about the soul's relationship to the body. As A. A. Long and others have shown, Stoic materialism does not necessarily avoid tension or even "dualism" between body and soul or *hegemonikon*. See Long, "Soul and Body," 2–3, 13, 16; Hijmans, *Askesis,* 15–16; Rist, *Stoic Philosophy,* 256–259; and Arthur Hilary Armstrong, "Gnosis and Greek Philosophy," in *Gnosis: Festschrift für Hans Jonas,* ed. B. Aland (Göttingen: Vandenhoeck & Ruprecht, 1978), 94.

19. See Spanneut, *Le Stoïcisme,* 50–53, 203; Francis, *Subversive Virtue,* 1–19. Although, in general, one can argue that Stoicism is prominent in the first and second centuries and that Platonic concepts and assumptions eventually eclipse the Stoic, it is nevertheless often difficult (and sometimes useless) to classify individual figures according to these categories. Marcus Aurelius and Clement of Alexandria are two important examples of thinkers who seem to some extent simply to have used what arguments seemed helpful or accurate. See John M. Rist, "Are You a Stoic? The Case of Marcus Aurelius," in *Jewish and Christian Self-Definition,* vol. 3, *Self-Definition in the*

together provide a rich sampling of late Stoic philosophy, in particular concerning the issues central to this study: the relationship between body and soul, and how that influences lifestyle, regimen, and behavior. Musonius and Epictetus represent the characteristic shift in late Stoicism toward ethics as an arena of philosophical discussion and witness to the growing emphasis in some Stoic circles on "practical" lifestyle issues.[20] In general, Musonius gives more specific attention to physical training and topics concerning bodily regimen than does Epictetus. Reflecting a common debate, he argues that, in the philosophical life, practice or habit (ἔθος) is more effective than theory (λόγος). Just as in medicine, music, or sailing it is more important to practice well than simply to understand the theory behind the art, so also in the pursuit of virtue it is better to be self-controlled and abstinent than to teach the same. Therefore, when one learns about a particular virtue, one should follow the lesson with training (askesis).[21] In his discourse "On Askesis," Musonius notes that "Since the human does not happen to be soul alone or body alone, but some synthesis of these two, it is necessary for the one in training (τὸν ἀσκοῦντα) to care for both." Although one may be more concerned with the soul, as the "better" part, one should care for and train the body, which is, after all, often the instrument of virtue.[22]

Musonius distinguishes two types of askesis: one that is proper to the soul alone and one that is common to both soul and body. The latter askesis involves becoming accustomed to bodily discomforts, including "cold, heat, thirst, hunger, plain food, hard

---

Greco-Roman World, ed. Ben F. Meyers and E. P. Sanders (Philadelphia: Fortress Press, 1982), 23–45; on Clement of Alexandria's Stoicism see Spanneut, Le Stoïcisme; and on Platonic elements in Clement's thought see Salvatore R. C. Lilla, Clement of Alexandria: A Study in Christian Platonism and Gnosticism, Oxford Theological Monographs (Oxford: Oxford University Press, 1971).

20. See Francis, Subversive Virtue, 2–6, and on the "Cynicizing" element in late Stoicism see Abraham J. Malherbe, "Self-Definition Among Epicureans and Cynics," in Jewish and Christian Self-Definition, vol. 3, Self-Definition in the Greco-Roman World, ed. Ben F. Meyers and E. P. Sanders (Philadelphia: Fortress Press, 1982), 46–59.

21. Musonius Rufus, Discourses 5–6 (Lutz, 48–52).

22. Discourse 7 (Lutz, 52–54).

beds, avoidance of pleasures, and endurance of suffering."[23] By such habituation to hardship the body becomes sturdy and ready for work, but the soul also is trained for certain virtues, "for courage (πρὸς ἀνδρείαν) through endurance and for self-control (πρὸς σωφροσύνην) through avoidance of pleasures."[24] Thus some virtues of the soul in particular are developed by bodily training and style of life (that is, δίαιτα or "diet"). In late ancient and early Christian moral theory (as in Musonius), the cardinal virtue of self-control (*sophrosyne*) becomes closely associated with practical issues of bodily management and control of appetites. *Enkrateia* appears with other lesser virtues as an aspect of *sophrosyne*, with its emphasis on the importance of struggle (ἀγών), labor (πόνος), training (ἄσκησις), and the endurance (καρτερία) of hardship in the virtuous life. This association is particularly significant in the Cynic-Stoic tradition. So Musonius observes that temperance (*enkrateia*) in eating and drinking lays the groundwork for self-control.[25] Later Christian authors focus especially on the relation of the virtues associated with *sophrosyne* to the ascetic life, sexual chastity, and the ideal of virginity. Thus the more restrictive meaning of *sophrosyne* in Christian discourse parallels that for *askesis* and *enkrateia*, while focus on the bodily appetites is not itself new or exclusive to Christian discourse.[26]

23. Ibid. (Lutz, 54).
24. Ibid.
25. *Discourse* 18A (Lutz, 112); see also *Discourses* 3; 4; 12 (Lutz, 38–48; 84–88).
26. On these developments, see Helen North, *Sophrosyne: Self-Knowledge and Self-Restraint in Greek Literature*, Cornell Studies in Classical Philology 35 (Ithaca, N.Y.: Cornell University Press, 1966), 227–231, 313–379. On the concept of *agôn* (struggle or hardship) see John T. Fitzgerald, *Cracks in an Earthen Vessel: An Examination of the Catalogues of Hardships in the Corinthian Correspondence*, SBL Dissertation Series 99 (Atlanta: Scholars Press, 1988); the interweaving of themes and terminology relating to *sophrosyne* and *enkrateia* is well-illustrated by the *Tabula of Cebes*, an eclectic work of moral philosophy dating to the early Roman empire. The *Tabula* describes a dialogue on the ethical life, complete with female personifications of virtues and vices, in which the goals are *paideia* and happiness. See e.g. *Cebetis tabula* 16.2; 20.3; 22;1 (John T. Fitzgerald and L. Michael White, eds., *The Tabula of Cebes*, Texts and Translations 24, Greco-Roman Religions Series 7 [Chico: Scholars Press, 1983], 86; 94; 96; n.53; n.74).

Askesis proper to the soul is concerned with developing the ability to discern that which is truly good and truly evil from that which only appears to be good or evil. By so doing, the philosopher learns to orient herself[27] or himself toward truly good pursuits, to turn away from attachments to false goods (such as wealth, pleasure, and even long life), and not to fear that which only seems evil (such as suffering and death).[28] These ascetic themes—the value of mental discernment, danger of false appearances, and acceptance of hardship—are common among pagan moral philosophers as well as many of the Christian ascetic theorists who will be discussed below.

Finally, Musonius is at times rather specific about the type of daily regimen or mode of life that best serves philosophical goals. He in no way argues that the philosopher should withdraw from the regular activities, relationships, and institutions of culture, but assumes, for example, that marriage is no impediment to philosophy.[29] Musonius nevertheless advocates an attitude of detachment and simplicity. In regard to clothing, housing, and furnishings, one should choose only that which meets the basic needs of the body and avoid that which leads to excess, physical weakness and vulnerability, and luxury (τρυφή). Luxury is a particular danger, as it injures both the body (through weakness) and the soul (through loss of self-control and courage).[30] When he discusses food and eating, Musonius connects bodily regimen even more directly to the soul's health, as one might expect. Not only does he argue that cheap, natural, and easily prepared foods are best for the simple lifestyle of the philosopher, he also notes that certain foods are better for the soul and more suitable for humans, who are like the gods and should therefore eat like the gods. Of course the gods are satisfied with "vapors rising up from the earth

27. Musonius argues that women should be trained in philosophy. He notes, however, that the value of such training for women is that it will make them more virtuous wives and daughters, better housekeepers, and more loving mothers (*Discourses* 3–4 [Lutz, 39–49]).

28. Ibid. (Lutz, 54–56).

29. Ibid., 15 (Lutz, 90–96).

30. Ibid., 19–20 (Lutz, 120–126).

and water"—not quite sufficient for most humans—so the human diet should be thin, light, and dry, in imitation of divine nourishment.[31] Meat fits none of these criteria and so should be avoided, not only because it is more suited to wild beasts than to civilized humans, but also because meat is a "heavy" food and therefore dulls the intellect and the reasoning process, and in general "darkens" the soul.[32] Musonius demonstrates, then, a widespread tendency in late ancient moral discourse; that is, to connect regimen in general and diet in particular to ethical formation.[33]

Epictetus's treatment of ascetic themes has much in common with Musonius Rufus's. In the philosophical life it is necessary to train oneself, through methods of self-examination and exercise, toward virtue.[34] From what Epictetus calls the beginning point of philosophy, namely, the "perception of how one's own *hegemonikon* is doing,"[35] one engages in continual scrutiny and correction of thoughts and habits. Specifically, Epictetus's method involves an almost medical treatment of weaknesses by the

---

31. Ibid., 18A–18B (Lutz, 112–120). Specific qualities and categorization of foods in medical and philosophical literature (light, heavy, dry, moist, etc.) will be discussed in greater detail below.

32. Ibid., 18A (Lutz, 112).

33. One of the favorite figures in moralist literature as well as satire is thus the glutton, whose revolting and shameful body displays his or her uncontrolled passions. Food avoidance and fasting in Greco-Roman religions and cultic practices, including Pythagorean and Orphic traditions, will not be addressed here. Useful discussions with reference to relevant texts include P. Rudolph Arbesmann, *Das Fasten bei den Griechen und Römern*, Religionsgeschichtliche Versuche und Vorarbeiten 21/1 (Giessen: Alfred Töpelmann, 1929; reprint, Berlin: Alfred Töpelmann, 1966); idem, "Fasten, Fastenspeisen, Fasttage," in *Reallexikon für Antike und Christentum*, ed. Theodor Klauser (Stuttgart: Anton Hiersemann, 1969), 7:456–471, 494–495, 503–506; idem, "Fasting and Prophecy in Pagan and Christian Antiquity," *Traditio* 7 (1949–1951): 1–32; and Johannes Haussleiter, *Der Vegetarismus in der Antike*, Religionsgeschichtliche Versuche und Vorarbeiten 24 (Berlin: Alfred Töpelmann, 1935). On Musonius's view of food and his influence on early Christian writers, see esp. 263–269.

34. See Hijmans, *Askesis*, 64. On Epictetus's ascetic method, in general, see also Francis, *Subversive Virtue*, chap. 1.

35. *Dissertationes* 1.26.15 (W. A. Oldfather, ed., *Epictetus: The Discourses as Reported by Arrian, The Manual, and Fragments*, Loeb Classical Library [Cambridge: Harvard University Press, 1966–1967], 1:168).

application of opposites. As bad bodily and mental conditions and vices are developed and maintained by bad habit (ἕξις) and repeated practice, so also good routines, attitudes, and virtues are cultivated by the opposite habit and practice. The method is refreshing in its straightforward clarity: goodness and wickedness both take time and practice to develop. If you want to be habituated to anger, for example, continue to react with anger to life's irritations. If you want to rid yourself of anger, do the opposite, that is, cultivate self-control. This is accomplished by learning philosophical principles and theories; observing your own reactions, emotions, and tendencies; and modifying your behavior and habits of lifestyle.[36] In regard to anger, Epictetus writes, "if you wish then not to be irascible, do not nourish your habit, set nothing promoting growth before it. At first, keep calm and count the days on which you have not been angry." In time, the bad habit of anger will become weaker and then be totally irradicated.[37]

Epictetus does not repeat Musonius's theory of the two types of asceticism related to body and soul, but instead posits three areas (τόποι) of training for the person who intends to be "good and excellent." These are concerned with mental attitudes, perceptions, and choices; namely, desire and aversion, choice and refusal, and discretion in judgments. By training oneself in these areas one can (respectively) develop control of passions or emotions; fulfill duties of appropriate social relationships; and cultivate the ideals of discretion, proper judgment, and freedom of choice.[38] Overall, Epictetus's *Discourses* reveal a keen and often touching awareness of basic human desires, needs, and fears, and the ways in which these can limit human potential and obscure freedom of choice by bad habit and compulsion. He describes vividly the real suffering and shame that result from common fears of illness and poverty.[39] The goal of philosophical training is thus to be free from attachment to externals or things over which

36. See, e.g., *Dissertationes* 1.27.3–5; 2.9.10–15; 2.18.1–32; 3.12.1–17 (Oldfather, 1:170–172; 268–270; 348–358; 2:80–86).
37. Ibid., 2.18.12–13 (Oldfather, 1:352).
38. Ibid., 3.2.1–18 (Oldfather, 2:20–28). See the discussions in Hijmans, *Askesis,* 64–91 and Francis, *Subversive Virtue.*
39. For example, *Dissertationes* 3.26 (Oldfather, 2:226–240).

one can have no real control—such as material wealth, health, possessions, status, and even family—and to cultivate freedom from desire, fear, and passion, thus cultivating self-sufficiency (αὐτάρκεια) and health in the *hegemonikon*.[40]

While Epictetus's three *topoi* of asceticism seem primarily concerned with mental exercises and self-reflection—he does not discuss bodily behavior at the level of detail that we find in Musonius Rufus—he acknowledges that some methods of bodily training may be useful to the philosopher so long as they relate to desire and aversion. He is very critical, however, of those who practice physical asceticism for the purpose of public display: for example, one who drinks only water but makes sure that everyone else knows about it, those who dress like philosophers in their rough cloaks and long hair but have none of the skills or behaviors of philosophy, or those who refuse to bathe.[41] Yet at the same time, Epictetus will call attention to external appearance and behavior as proofs of superior character. In this, he follows the conventions of ancient rhetorical, literary, and philosophical traditions, which interpreted character by physical appearance.[42] Thus he describes Socrates' body as "radiant," "attractive," and "sweet;" so sweet, apparently, that he needed only infrequent baths.[43] Socrates' superior character and the beauty of his soul are here translated to the surface of a body that is special—a body, Epictetus implies, that is not subject to the same level of daily cares and shameful excretions as most other bodies.

Likewise Epictetus notes that Diogenes the Cynic, whom he portrays as an ideal philosopher, attracted public attention by his radiant complexion and the appearance of his body. Indeed, the

40. See, for example, ibid., 4.1. (Oldfather, 2:244–304), esp. 62–85; 128–131 (Oldfather, 2:264–272; 288).

41. Ibid., 3.12.16–17; 3.14.4–6; 4.8; 4.11 (Oldfather, 2:86; 96; 374–390; 408–422).

42. Physiognomy, or the "art of interpreting character from the physique," was popular in late ancient philosophy as well as theater, art, rhetoric, and medicine. See Elizabeth C. Evans, *Physiognomics in the Ancient World*, Transactions of the American Philosophical Society 59/5 (Philadelphia: The American Philosophical Society, 1969); Barton, *Power and Knowledge*, 95–131; and Gleason, *Making Men*.

43. *Dissertationes* 4.11.19 (Oldfather, 2:414–416).

beauty and good condition of Diogenes' body reveal his soul's character and testify to his philosophical claim that it is possible to be a "good and excellent" person and to maintain health while following a simple lifestyle.[44] Epictetus holds Diogenes in such high regard because the Cynic seems to have fulfilled Stoic ideals of freedom, detachment, and lack of passion. The Cynic makes his or her way in the world relying not on status, wealth, or social networks, but on character, a pure *hegemonikon*, endurance, and self-respect.[45] If his noble, idealizing depiction of Diogenes and Cynicism should not be taken as an accurate representation by itself,[46] more evidence of later Cynic thought and behavior is found in the collection of pseudonymous "epistles" written under the names of prominent ancient figures, including Socrates, Heraclitus, Diogenes, and his disciple, Crates.[47]

The Cynics have the reputation (then and now) as either the "bad boys" of the ancient city or wandering teachers whose often provocative behavior and biting social criticism reveal profound, even prophetic, insight into the human condition. Whatever the case, scholars have recently observed that Cynicism in late antiquity does not represent a particular school of thought comparable to Stoicism or Epicureanism, but rather indicates a recognizable style of behavior, a mode of life, that may be adapted to any number of philosophical "systems" (hence the interweaving with

44. Ibid., 3.22.86–89; 4.11.21–23 (Oldfather, 2:160–162; 416). Epictetus clearly wants to separate himself, his students, and the reputation of Diogenes from ascetic practices that valued bodily neglect to the point of repulsive appearance and poor health. Instead, he emphasizes the good health and pleasant demeanor resulting from his brand of ascetic renunciation. We will see in the following chapters that in much of the Christian hagiographical tradition it is precisely the haggard, weak, and repulsive body of the heroic ascetic that not only testifies to her or his higher spiritual achievement, but also attracts the attention and devotion of others.

45. Ibid., 3.22 (Oldfather, 2:130–168). On Epictetus's own social network see Ronald F. Hock, "'By the Gods, It's My One Desire to See an Actual Stoic': Epictetus' Relations with Students and Visitors in his Personal Network," *Semeia* 56 (1992): 121–142.

46. Malherbe, "Self-Definition Among Epicureans and Cynics," 50.

47. See Abraham J. Malherbe, ed., *The Cynic Epistles: A Study Edition*, Society of Biblical Literature Sources for Biblical Study 12 (Missoula, Mont.: Scholars Press, 1977).

Stoicism in late antiquity).[48] Malherbe writes, "What made a Cynic was his dress and conduct, self-sufficiency, harsh behaviour towards what appeared as excesses, and a practical ethical idealism."[49] Key to that way of life and to Cynic ethics was physical asceticism displayed in the public arena. Indeed, Marie-Odile Goulet-Cazé locates the key distinction between late Stoicism and Cynicism in the centrality of corporeal *askesis* for the latter.[50] Thus the Cynic was known by his (or her)[51] behavior, demeanor, and appearance, which witnessed to a fundamental detachment (ἀταραξία) and self-sufficiency (αὐτάρκεια).

In the collected Cynic letters we find an interweaving of themes concerning the proper attitude to body and soul and recommendations for bodily regimen. On the one hand, several writers advocate indifference to and separation from the body and its needs and desires (a standard ascetic theme). By freeing herself or himself from the slavery to bodily concerns, the philosopher practices for death (which is the separation of soul from body), even while living.[52] The body is dangerous because in satisfying its needs one can easily lose control to passions and desires. (Here we find the same insight into the shortcomings of human embodiment and the value of freedom that we saw in Musonius and Epictetus.[53]) On the other hand, this harsh attitude is matched by

48. See especially Malherbe, "Self-Definition;" Francis, *Subversive Virtue*, 53–81; and Marie-Odile Goulet-Cazé, "Le Cynisme à l'époque impériale," *Aufstieg und Niedergang der Römischen Welt* 2.36.4:2720–2833. On Cynicism and Stoicism see also Rist, *Stoic Philosophy*, 54–80.

49. Malherbe, "Self-Definition," 49.

50. "Le Cynisme," 2817. Goulet-Cazé notes, however, regarding the relationship between the two in late antiquity that "between a rigorist Stoic and a Cynic, one would not see much difference on the exterior" (2810). See also Francis, *Subversive Virtue*, 64–66; and Meeks, *The Moral World of the First Christians*, 52–56.

51. The Cynic epistles, like the evidence from Musonius Rufus, make it clear that women practiced the Cynic lifestyle. On Hipparchia, e.g., see Ps.-Crates, *Epp.* 28–33 (Malherbe, 78–82).

52. Ps.-Diogenes, *Epistle* 39; Ps.-Aeschines, *Ep.* 14 (Malherbe, *The Cynic Epistles*, 164; 256–258).

53. E.g., Ps.-Crates, *Ep.* 35, where Crates observes that because we live with the body and with other people, there will necessarily be hardship in this life. But those who expect to live without hardship bring suffering on

the view that the body must be tolerated and cared for as a "fellow citizen" to the soul and not despised.[54] The philosopher should therefore follow a very simple lifestyle, eating plain foods, requiring only a few things to preserve health, and avoiding the excess and extravagance that feed passion.[55]

The distinctively Cynic style of satisfying bodily needs immediately (exemplified in the notorious tales of Diogenes urinating or masturbating in public) should thus be understood not as the overindulgence of every bodily whim, but rather as a strategy for enhancing freedom. As James Francis observes, "By gratifying instinct immediately, simply, and naturally, the Cynic ceased to be in thrall to desire and its ever-escalating demands."[56] In this way the ascetic logic particular to Cynic behavior and stance toward culture and society becomes clear.[57]

In the Stoic and Cynic sources reviewed thus far, several themes relating to soul and body have emerged. First, the soul is not unaffected by the body's condition. Rather, bodily behaviors, regimen, and lifestyle can lead toward either virtue or vice and passion in the soul. Second, while issues of bodily behavior and appearance permeate each text, at the same time priority of rhetorical concern is given to the *hegemonikon* or authoritative principle of the soul, as well as to the mental activities associated

---

themselves while the one who understands this reality is wise and happy (Malherbe, 88).

54. E.g., Ps.-Heraclitus, *Ep.* 9.7 (Malherbe, 214).

55. Ps.-Crates, *Epp.* 3; 11; 14; 18 (Malherbe, 54; 62; 64; 68). On food abstinence among the Cynics see also Haussleiter, *Der Vegetarismus,* 167–184.

56. Francis, *Subversive Virtue,* 65. On the Cynic ideal of freedom see also Rist, *Stoic Philosophy,* 58–63.

57. Malherbe has discussed two distinct models or types of Cynicism that appear in the ancient sources: the harsh, wandering, anti-social Cynic represented by Diogenes, Crates, and the hero Heracles; and the mild, settled, and persuasive Cynic teacher represented by Cynic figures such as Demonax, the ideal Cynic of Epictetus, and the hero Odysseus ("Self-Definition," 51–59). It is difficult to know, however, the extent to which these models were a literary convention and where they reflect actual factions. Clarence Glad has cautioned that the contrast of "harsh" and "gentle" is traditional in "religious, socio-political, and philosophic-ethical" contexts, and that while the ancient sources use this classification, scholars cannot take it at face value. Glad's remarks are related particularly to forms of moral exhortation ("Adaptability in Epicurean and Early Christian Psychagogy," 217–228).

with it. Third, in order to achieve a life in accord with nature and to maintain a healthy condition in the soul, one must not only apply techniques of mental self-examination and evaluation, but also make practical, daily steps toward virtue. Training or *askesis* toward virtue and autonomy involves the whole person. Finally, my sources exhibit both a healthy suspicion of false appearances as well as a tendency to demonstrate or depict superior character by attractive and even extraordinary appearance. Thus soul and body are in a dynamic, mutually dependent relationship.

This seems reasonable in the context of Stoic thought and the corporealist understanding of the soul. If the soul is some combination of God and "stuff," it is no wonder that it is affected by the body's condition.[58] But even when we turn to Plutarch and the Platonic traditions that view the soul as incorporeal, we find the same assumptions about this dynamic relationship. Plutarch (c.47–c.120) is an apt representative of middle Platonism in the first and second centuries and useful for this study in particular because several of his essays revolve around the topics of our inquiry. As noted earlier, Plutarch held that philosophy and medicine dealt with essentially the same issues of health, happiness, and virtue. The philosopher, according to Plutarch, should quite naturally be interested in health and a healthy lifestyle. At least in several of his own essays, Plutarch certainly lives up to this expectation, as his writing is filled with tidbits of information on regimen, diet, bathing, sleeping, relations between men and women, remedies, and more. But Plutarch reveals more than a fashionable obsession with bodily care. At base, Plutarch's concern for the quotidian is interwoven with his belief that it is precisely these details that influence character, that is, the health of the soul.

In his treatise "Advice on Keeping Well," Plutarch weaves an intricate relationship of influence and dependence between soul and body. A dominant metaphor is the body as a ship which must be kept clean, trim, and seaworthy by means of a healthy lifestyle. Just as a ship cannot sail smoothly when it is overloaded with cargo, so also the body, when it is overloaded with food or drink,

58. See Long, "Soul and Body," 15.

is unable to perform and becomes subject to disease.[59] Thus much of the essay is given to strategies for avoiding overindulgence in food and drink on a daily basis as well as at feasts and social gatherings. In general, Plutarch recommends not only that one should get used to eating less food and having fewer baths,[60] but also that the foods one does eat should be of the "light" and "thin" type, such as vegetables and some fish and birds.[61] Like Musonius Rufus, Plutarch singles out meat as not only unnatural but also the least healthy for the body and for the soul. Meat is a "heavy" food that makes the rational faculty of the soul likewise heavy and dull, unable to operate with clarity and brilliance.[62]

While one's physical behavior can have negative or positive effects on the soul, the reverse is also true. When the soul is bothered by its own passions and desires (such as lust, greed, and jealousy), it becomes neglectful of the body's needs and the body suffers. The body also reacts physically to the soul's passions, for example, when the face reddens from anger.[63] Likewise, unusual dreams may be signs of illness or some disturbance in spirit. The careful one should therefore monitor both the body and the soul for indications and symptoms of disease.[64]

But what exactly are the diseases of the soul? Here we encounter the concept of the soul's passions (πάθη), a concept which is common in various pagan and Christian formulations but with key distinctions. The Greek pathos (plural: pathe) is

---

59. On the body as a ship see De tuenda sanitate praecepta 4, 123e; 10, 127c–d; 11, 128b; 13, 128f; 22, 134c (Babbitt, 224; 242; 246; 250; 276).

60. Ibid., 3, 123b–c; 4, 123d–124a; 6–12, 124d–128e (Babbitt, 220–222; 222–224; 228–248).

61. Ibid., 18, 131e (Babbitt, 262). See the discussion of different types of food in the following section.

62. Ibid., 18, 131f–132a (Babbitt, 264); see also De usu carnium 6, 995d–996a (Harold Cherniss and William C. Hembold, eds., Plutarch's Moralia, Loeb Classical Library [Cambridge: Harvard University Press, 1957], 12:554–556). In general, on Plutarch's dietary views see also Haussleiter, Der Vegetarismus, 212–228.

63. De tuenda sanitate praecepta 24, 135e–f (Babbitt, 282); Quaestiones convivales 5.7, 681d–f (Paul A. Clement and Herbert B. Hoffleit, eds., Plutarch's Moralia, Loeb Classical Library [Cambridge: Harvard University Press, 1969], 8:424–426).

64. De tuenda sanitate praecepta 14, 129a–c (Babbitt, 250–252).

translated into English as "passion," "emotion," or "disease." A list of the soul's passions might include greed, lustful desire, sadness, anger, love of glory, envy, and pride. In late antiquity two points in particular distinguish views of the passions: how the passions are related to the soul, and what the goal of their treatment should be. Stated simply, those articulating or influenced by the Platonic tradition, which held a tripartite view of the soul (described above), located the passions in the irrational part of the soul and emphasized their irrational nature. The passions are thus the product of the concupiscible or irascible parts of the soul, while the rational part is untainted by their presence.

Although there is significant variation in the Stoic tradition, perhaps the classic theory, or at least the theory that both ancient and modern sources inevitably dispute or justify, is Chryssipus's assertion that the passions are "judgments" of the *hegemonikon*, or the soul's rational, authoritative principle. That is, the passions are not set in opposition to "rationality" understood in an abstract and absolute sense, but are somehow related to our faculty for perception, judgment, and mental assent. Nevertheless, passions may be described as false judgments or "not rational" because, though involving human rational faculties and processes, passions are excessive impulses assented to by wrong reason.[65]

Another important distinction, and one that influences ascetic discourse, relates to the therapeutic goal in dealing with the passions. Here the Stoic ideal is the state of *apatheia* (ἀπάθεια), or "passionlessness," while the Platonic tradition points toward the goal of controlling the passions and putting them to good use. John Rist has argued that the Stoic notion should not be understood as the wiping out of all "emotion," but as the eradication of the *pathe* as "diseases" of the soul, as "pathological disturbances of the personality."[66] Hence the state of *apatheia* may be

---

65. For detailed discussions of the Stoics on passions and rationality, see Rist, *Stoic Philosophy*, 22–36; Long, *Hellenistic Philosophy*, 175–178; and Nussbaum, *The Therapy of Desire*, 366–386. On certain ambiguities in the Stoic concept see Robert J. Rabel, "Diseases of the Soul in Stoic Psychology," *Greek, Roman, and Byzantine Studies* 22 (1981): 385–393.

66. Rist, *Stoic Philosophy*, 26–27. Rist further argues that the Stoic and

described as a state of health or balance in the soul, one in which judgments and acts of assent are made by right reason free of excessive impulse. Plutarch and others in the Platonic line of thought envision moderation of passions, and turning them to good use, rather than their suppression. Specifically, desire and anger may be useful in, say, sustaining the desire for the good or for God as well as the courage and drive toward virtue.

While the Stoic and Platonic concepts of the passions and their treatment can be thus distinguished, and while these distinctions are certainly key to the development of Greco-Roman ethical theory, many writers incorporate aspects of both strains of thought. This brings us to the last two figures to be discussed in this section: the medical theorist Galen and the Christian writer Clement of Alexandria. Both writers brilliantly embody what has been termed the "eclecticism" of the second century as well as the convergence of philosophy and medicine around issues of "the care of the self" and ethical formation.

Galen (c.129–200) was a Greek from Pergamon who became physician to the emperor Marcus Aurelius. He demonstrates as well as any figure in antiquity that the modern disciplinary boundaries between science and religion or philosophy and medicine are artificial. Galen's interest in questions concerning the nature of the soul, the passions, and how to treat the passions is integral to his understanding of human life and the human body. In the next section Galen's physiological and dietetic theories will be discussed in some detail. At this point it is important to note that his concepts are grounded in contemporary Stoic and Platonic moral philosophy and notions of body and soul. He accepts the Platonic tripartite division of the soul into rational, concupiscible, and irascible parts which are "seated" in three parts of the body,[67] but not the Platonic argument that the soul is incorporeal. Here Galen seems to agree with the Stoics that the soul must be of corporeal nature, though he stops short of endors-

---

Platonic concepts are not really that far apart if one considers their different definitions of "passion."

67. See for example *Quod animi mores corporis temperamenta sequantur* ("That the faculties of the soul follow the bodily constitution") 2–3 (Kühn 4:770–772).

ing the view. Instead he simply states his inability to understand how the soul could possibly be incorporeal, as even Plato acknowledged the effect of bodily temperament and condition on the soul.[68] He feels free now to use Stoic language of the passions as diseases of the soul and the ideal of *apatheia,* and to follow the Platonists of his day in allowing for the moderation and good use of passions and the application of opposites as a tool for controlling desire and anger.[69]

Galen's trust in the value of a healthy regimen is as strong as one would expect from a professional physician. But his concern is always for the relationship between the mundane details of bodily care and the condition of the whole person, body and soul. Galen's underlying model recognizes that the body's state or "temperament" influences the soul's character, including intelligence, virtue, and passions. Thus one's diet, body type, ethnicity, location, and daily habits all have an effect on character (ἦθος).[70]

68. Ibid., 3; 5–6; 9–10 (Kühn 4:772–776; 785–790; 804–813). See Temkin, *Hippocrates,* 204–205; idem, *Galenism: Rise and Decline of a Medical Philosophy* (Ithaca: Cornell University Press, 1973), 44–45. G. E. R. Lloyd has analyzed Galen's use of Plato, Aristotle, and Hippocrates in *quod animi* and concludes that Galen is willing to take liberties with his sources in order to support his general claim that character is influenced by bodily condition. Further, he argues that Galen's unstated agenda has to do with "medical apologetics" and the authority of the doctor: "his contributions to the debates on the relations between the soul and the body, and to moral philosophical issues, are in places subordinated to a strategic concern with the prestige and power of the doctor" ("Scholarship, Authority and Argument in Galen's *Quod animi mores,*" In *Le opere psicologiche di Galeno,* ed. Paola Manuli and Mario Vegetti [Naples: Bibliopolis, 1988], 40–42).

69. Galen, *De cognoscendis curandisque animi morbis* 3; 6; 7 (Kühn 5:7–14; 26–30; 35). On the structure and substance of the soul in Galen see also James Hankinson, "Galen's Anatomy of the Soul," *Phronesis* 36 (1991): 197–233, and on Galen's "therapy" of the soul's passions see idem, "Actions and Passions: Affection, Emotion, and Moral Self-management in Galen's Philosophical Psychology," in *Passions and Perceptions: Studies in Hellenistic Philosophy of Mind,* ed. Jacques Brunschwig and Martha C. Nussbaum (Cambridge: Cambridge University Press, 1993), 184–222.

70. This is the main argument of Galen's *Quod animi* (Kühn 4:767–822). See also Richard Waltzer, "New Light on Galen's Moral Philosophy," *Classical Quarterly* 43 (1949): 82–96 concerning another treatise, "On Character," in which Galen argues much the same point and discusses what things are inborn and to what extent the personality may be shaped through training. Galen compares moral training to raising young plants, which are more yielding and open to shaping than old plants.

While some factors in this mix, such as ethnicity, are beyond one's control, in general one can make active choices in regard to the body through lifestyle and mental regimen in order to influence health.[71] Training or *askesis* for virtue, like training for physical health, is effective. Here is the essential tie between medicine and philosophy and the shared responsibility of the philosopher and the doctor.[72] Galen writes:

> The character of the soul (τὸ τῆς ψυχῆς ἦθος) is corrupted by poor habits (μοχθηρῶν ἐθισμῶν) in food, drink, exercise, sights, sounds, and all the arts. Therefore the one pursuing health (τὴν ὑγιεινὴν) should be practiced in (ἔμπειρον) all these things, and should not think that it is proper only for the philosopher to shape the character of the soul.[73]

In Galen, then, regimen and lifestyle are directly and causally linked to morality and to an ideal of individual perfection through *askesis*.[74] If we turn to a Christian writer roughly contemporary with Galen, Clement of Alexandria (c.160–c.215), we find a similarly striking union of ethics, asceticism, and bodily behavior. Clement was, according to the fourth-century historian Eusebius, a teacher of Origen and head of the catechetical school in Alexandria.[75] His work represents vividly his sense of "continu-

71. *Quod animi* 1 (Kühn 4:767–768): "when we achieve a good temperament in the body by means of food and drink and further through our daily management, we also contribute to some virtue in the soul." See also *De cog. cur. animi morbis* where Galen presents a full-blown program for treating diseases of the soul. He advocates mental excercises including self-observation and scrutiny of one's own daily emotional state, continued practice, the guidance and criticism of one who is older and wiser, and a simple diet and lifestyle (Kühn 5:1–57).

72. In general, see Nussbaum, *The Therapy of Desire* and Jackie Pigeaud, *La maladie de l'âme: Étude sur la relation de l'âme et du corps dans la tradition médico-philosophique antique* (Paris: Les Belles Lettres, 1981).

73. *De sanitate tuenda* 1.8 (Kühn 6:40). Using the Platonic tripartite division of the soul, Galen argues that both the rational principle of the soul as well as the "mortal part" (the irascible and concupiscible souls) are affected by the body. For example, intelligence is fostered by dryness in bodily constitution while too much moisture leads the rational soul toward foolishness (*Quod animi* 4 [Kühn 4:781–782]).

74. *De cog. cur. animi morbis* 4 (Kühn 5:14): "Each of us needs almost a whole life of training to become a perfect man (τέλειος ἀνήρ)."

75. Eusebius of Caesarea, *Historia ecclesiastica* 6.6; 6.11.6; 6.13–14 (J. E. L. Oulton and H. J. Lawlor, eds., *Eusebius: The Ecclesiastical History*, Loeb

ity"[76] between classical culture, arts, and learning and the Christian life and Christian formation. Nowhere is this more apparent than in the *Paedagogue*, Clement's book of moral instructions and advice for newer Christians.[77] The second and third books of the *Paedagogue* address a myriad of topics related to daily life and activities, such as dress and ornamentation; sexual relations; hair style; behavior at banquets; styles of laughter; talking to children; animal lore; sneezing and hiccups; physiology and digestion; and proper voice, walk, and deportment. Clement's intention is to describe "what the one who is called a Christian must be," and "how each one of us should behave in regard to the body, or rather how we should regulate (the body)." In short, Clement proposes an "art of life (τέχνη . . . περὶ βίου)"—informed by classical elite sensibilities—for the Christian community.[78] Behavior and lifestyle are thus for Clement vehicles or visible markers by which the individual and the group define themselves.[79]

Throughout his writings, Clement demonstrates the same "vague eclecticism"[80] as we saw in Galen's. That is, Clement's ethical constructions show the influence of not one but several identifiable and prominent philosophical schools, including Stoicism and Platonism, as well as contemporary medical theory.[81]

Classical Library [Cambridge: Harvard University Press, 1980], 2:26–28; 38; 42–48).

76. See R. A. Markus, *Christianity in the Roman World,* Currents in the History of Culture and Ideas (London: Thames and Hudson, 1974), 48–69. Markus distinguishes two ways of thinking about Christianity's relationship to "the world": one of discontinuity (represented by Tertullian of Carthage) and one of continuity (represented by Clement of Alexandria).

77. *Paedagogus.* (Henri-Irénée Marrou, Marguerite Harl, Claude Mondésert, and Chantal Mantray, eds. and trans., *Clément d'Alexandrie: Le Pédagogue,* SC 70, 108, 158 [Paris: Les Éditions de Cerf, 1960–1970]). See Marrou's introduction, SC 70:7–22, and Peter Brown's lively discussion of Clement's relationship to Stoic and Platonic thought (*The Body and Society,* 122–139).

78. *Paed.* 2.1.1; 2.2.25; 3.11.59 (SC 108:10; 58; 158:122).

79. See now Blake Leyerle, "Clement of Alexandria on the Importance of Table Etiquette," *Journal of Early Christian Studies* 3 (1995): 123–141.

80. Marrou, "Introduction générale," SC 70:50.

81. Marrou identifies Stoicism as the most pervasive influence on Clement's thought, as does Michel Spanneut (*Le Stoïcisme*). But Salvatore Lilla argues that in spite of the clearly Stoic touches in Clement, nevertheless

This is certainly the case in regard to the issues discussed thus far, including the nature of the soul and its passions.[82] In particular, Clement's instructions reveal an understanding of the effect of body on soul and soul on body that is now quite familiar. For the pursuit of virtue and progress in the Christian life, the body is, according to Clement, the kin and fellow worker to the soul. In this way the fate and condition of both are intertwined.[83] Thus the centrality of bodily behavior in the *Paedagogue*, where the intention is to give Christians the tools necessary for the art of the Christian life.

In his desire to regulate Christian lifestyle, appearance, and deportment in Alexandrian society, Clement shows three primary areas of concern: first, the establishment and preservation of group and individual honor; second, the effects of physical activities on the health of the soul; and third, preparation for higher learning and the attainment of higher knowledge through practical training.[84] These three concerns run throughout the various topics addressed in the *Paedagogue*, but it may be most useful for this study on fasting to trace them specifically in relation to food and diet. Significantly, Clement's treatment of these themes is dependent on Plato and especially Musonius, whom he actually

---

such elements are more often than not filtered through the middle Platonism or "school-Platonism" of the second century. Thus Lilla would emphasize much more the Platonic Clement (*Clement of Alexandria*, 227 and passim). See also H. Chadwick, "Origen, Celsus, and the Stoa," *Journal of Theological Studies* 48 (1947): 34–49. Chadwick argues that Stoic influence on Clement, Origen, and middle Platonism is seen primarily in the emphasis on ethics (46–49).

82. For detailed discussions of Clement's view of the soul (its nature and "parts," the passions, the goal of *apatheia*, and virtues of the soul), comparison to earlier philosophical ethics, and relevant texts see Marrou's introduction to the *Paedagogue* (SC 70), Lilla, *Clement of Alexandria*, and Spannuet, *Le Stoïcisme*.

83. *Paed.* 1.13.102 (SC 70:292). Clement also links the body and the soul in sanctification (*Paed.* 2.2.20; 3.12.98 [SC 108:48; 158:184]). See Peter Brown's discussion in *The Body and Society*, 127.

84. In relation to this third area of concern, the *Paedagogus* represents the level of practical training. The distinction between practice and theory (or *gnosis*, or higher teaching), which we have already seen briefly with the Stoics, and which will be discussed below in relation to Evagrius of Pontus, is common in ancient moral philosophy.

quotes.[85] Much of Clement's discussion aims at the desire for honor and respect among one's peers and in society. Thus he paints an amusing (if often disgusting) picture of the glutton or the drunkard as a laughingstock, one whose obsession with food, drink, and exotic dishes is translated to a body which appears shameful and worthy of ridicule. The refined Christian, in contrast, eats and drinks with the moderation and decorum worthy of honor.[86]

But proper dietary regimen is essential not only for a healthy body and a healthy self-respect, but also for a healthy, finely tuned soul and a keener intellect. In this, Clement reflects what seems to be the consensus of ancient medicine and moral philosophy: a light and dry diet is good for the soul. Heavy and moist foods and drinks, especially meat and wine, obscure and "corporify" the soul, make it heavy and dull, and lead to evil thoughts.[87] But by avoiding excess in wine, Clement writes, the soul "will be pure and dry and luminous; 'a ray of light, the dry soul is wisest and finest,'"[88] Thus the soul is at least in part readied for contemplation and for higher knowledge by dietary management and self-conscious lifestyle.[89]

---

85. See L. Michael White, "Scholars and Patrons: Christianity and High Society in Alexandria," in *Christian Teaching: Studies in Honor of LeMoine G. Lewis*, ed. Everett Ferguson (Abilene: ACU Press, 1981), 328–342; and Marrou's comments (SC 70:74; 108:38–39).

86. See especially *Paed.* 2.1.1–18; 2.2.19–34 (SC 108:10–44; 46–74). For a discussion of gluttony as vice of the soul and destroyer of the body in John Chrysostom and Evagrius of Pontus see below, chap. 4.

87. *Paed.* 2.1.11; 2.2.20–21; 2.2.29. 2.10.90 (SC 108:30; 50; 64; 174). On meat and sexual desire see also *Stromata* 2.20.105 (Claude Mondésert, ed., *Clément d'Alexandrie: Les Stromates. Stromate II*, SC 38 [Paris: Éditions du Cerf, 1954], 114).

88. *Paed.* 2.2.29 (SC 108:64 and 65, n.8). Clement here quotes Musonius Rufus, who in turn refers to Heraclitus for this idea (*Discourses* 18A [Lutz, 112]). It should be noted that Clement very intentionally separates himself from "encratite" Christians who would *require* certain types of abstinence (most notably, of course, from meat and wine). See for example *Paed.* 2.2.32–33 (SC 108:68–70). This proviso becomes standard in early Christian discourse on food abstinence, as the chapters below will show.

89. For discussions of the relationship between Clement's views on the usefulness of physical asceticism for the soul and his understanding of the irrational parts of the soul as being related to the body and constituting a

Finally, Clement's treatise frames much of the impact of these issues in terms of the appearance of the body and the interpretation of that appearance by the public eye. Thus Clement reminds his readers that physical behaviors and habits signify elements of character: a weak voice is a sign of effeminacy; loud sneezing and hiccuping are signs of arrogance and lack of discipline; outlandish clothes and hairstyles are signs of lust; and shifting around in one's place at banquet is a sign of lightmindedness.[90] In contrast, the ideal body testifies to self-control, decorum, and honor. Christian formation and self-definition are, for Clement, displayed in the body and its activities. In his emphasis on the public scrutiny of the body managed by *askesis*, Clement is firmly in the moralist tradition, seen here especially in Epictetus.

Clement, Epictetus, Musonius, the pseudonymous Cynic letters, Plutarch, and Galen have established for us much of the territory or context for early Christian ascetic practice and argumentation. In particular, they demonstrate the extent to which medicine and philosophy converge in the arena of ethics.[91] Their practical advice and reflections demonstrate moreover that it is simply artificial and somewhat dangerous to apply modern distinctions of physiology and psychology to the ancient formulations—at least without careful definition. If this caution is important to bear in mind when approaching late ancient philosophy, it is no less so when we examine Greco-Roman medical theory, physiology, and dietetics. Thus the soul's passions or diseases, as well as the soul's proper balance, are directly related to sexuality and procreation, just as sexual activity and generation are functions of the soul (at least part of the soul) in both Stoic and Platonic physiology.

"corporeal soul" or a "fleshly spirit," see Spanneut, *Le Stoïcisme,* 170–175 and Lilla, *Clement of Alexandria,* 84–92.

90. *Paed.* 2.7.55; 2.7.59; 2.7.60; 2.10.105 (SC 108:114; 118; 122; 200). Here Clement makes use of the long tradition of physiognomy, the "art of interpreting character from the physique," which was popular in late ancient philosophy as well as theater, art, rhetoric, and medicine. See Evans, *Physiognomics in the Ancient World,* Gleason, *Making Men,* and Barton, *Power and Knowledge.*

91. Pigeaud writes, "Medicine and ethics are not developed as two independent techniques, they are deeply connected by a certain understanding of the human" (*La maladie de l'âme,* 27).

Diet and the Physiology of Sexual Desire

Patristic views of ascetic fasting cannot be understood apart from Greco-Roman medical theories of physiology, sexuality, and diet. Fourth-century medicine was dominated by the influence of Galen, although Galen himself was a contemporary of several important medical writers, including Rufus of Ephesus (c.110–c.180) and Soranus (fl. c.98–138), and was strongly influenced by earlier thinkers, particularly Hippocrates and Aristotle.[92] Fundamental to Galen's system is his use and development of the ancient theory of the four elements (fire, earth, air, and water), the four qualities (warm, cold, dry, and moist), and the four main bodily humors or fluids (blood, black bile, yellow bile, and phlegm). These elements, qualities, and humors are variously combined in individual bodies, and good health arises from and is maintained by their proper proportion or mixing (κρᾶσις).[93] Conversely, their imbalance can lead to behavioral disorders and diseases such as epilepsy, melancholy, and hysteria.[94]

Galen emphasizes that individual bodily constitutions—which can be variously categorized as dry, moist, bilious, phlegmatic, et cetera—differ and are affected by diet, environment, and lifestyle. In turn, as we have seen, the bodily κρᾶσις and habits produce an effect on the state of the soul.[95] Nutrition and diet are central to Galen's system in that the four principal humors are products of

92. See Vivian Nutton, "From Galen to Alexander, Aspects of Medicine and Medical Practice in Late Antiquity," *Dumbarton Oaks Papers* 38 (1984): 2–5; Temkin, *Galenism*, 28–34, 51–94; and idem, *Hippocrates*. General secondary material on medicine and medical schools in late antiquity includes Howard Clark Kee, *Medicine, Miracle and Magic in New Testament Times*, Society for New Testament Studies Monograph Series 55 (Cambridge: Cambridge University Press, 1986), 27–66; John Scarborough, *Roman Medicine* (Ithaca: Cornell University Press, 1969); Owsei Temkin, *Soranus' Gynecology* (Baltimore: Johns Hopkins Press, 1956), xxi–xliv; and Heinrich von Staden, "Hairesis and Heresy: The Case of the *haireseis iatrikai*," in *Jewish and Christian Self-Definition*, vol. 3, *Self-Definition in the Greco-Roman World*, ed. Ben F. Meyer and E. P. Sanders (Philadelphia: Fortress Press, 1982), 76–100.

93. Galen, *De san. tuenda* 1.1; 5 (Kühn 6:2; 15); *De naturalibus facultatibus* 3.7 (Kühn 2:167–168).

94. Galen, *De locis affectis* 3.9–10 (Kühn 8:173–193), 6.5 (Kühn 8:413–437).

95. *Quod animi* 1 (Kühn 4:767–768) and passim (Kühn 4:767–822); *De loc. aff.* 3.10 (Kühn 8:191); *De san. tuenda* 1.8 (Kühn 6:39–40).

the process of digestion.[96] For example, if too much food is taken into the body some of it will go undigested, which leads to an excess of excretions and an unhealthy state of these and other humors.[97]

According to Galen's theory of sexual physiology, blood and semen are the "elements of our generation":

> Each one is a mixture of the same type of elements, (that is) of moist, dry, warm, and cold, or—if one prefers to name these not by their qualities but according to their substances (κατὰ τὰς οὐσίας)—of earth and water, of air and fire. . . . But they differ in the quantity of the mixture. For in semen there is more fiery and airy substance, while in blood there is more earthy and watery substance.[98]

Both male and female bodies produce semen when blood and *pneuma* are "concocted" or "cooked" (πέττεται) in the coiled spermatic and ovarian vessels until the humor becomes white and is delivered to the male and female testicles (ὄρχεις) for further concoction.[99] Male and female genitals are basically the same but with one crucial difference: the greater natural heat of the male body causes the male genitals to develop more completely and protrude outside the body. The female, being colder, lacks the heat necessary for the full development of these parts.[100]

Galen shares the ancient understanding of semen as a kind of "vital life fluid" which contains *pneuma* and transmits the

96. See especially *De nat. fac.* (Kühn 2:1–214) and *De usu partium corporis humani* 4 and 5 (Kühn 3:266–408).

97. *De san. tuenda* 4.11 (Kühn 6:301–302); *De cog. cur. animi morbis* 9 (Kühn 5:45–46).

98. *De san. tuenda* 1.2 (Kühn 6:3).

99. Ibid., 14.10 (Kühn 4:183–184). What Galen considered to be the female testicles we would call the ovaries.

100. Ibid., 14.6 (Kühn 4:158–163). These issues will be discussed in more detail. The idea that the female body is colder than the male is common, but not universal, in ancient medical texts. See Erna Lesky, *Die Zeugungs- und Vererbungslehren der Antike und ihr Nachwirken* (Wiesbaden: Akademie der Wissenschaften und der Literatur, 1950), 1255–1262; G. E. R. Lloyd, "The Hot and the Cold, the Dry and the Wet in Greek Philosophy," *Journal of Hellenic Studies* 84 (1964): 102–106; and Margaret Tallmadge May, trans., *Galen: On the Usefulness of the Parts of the Body* (Ithaca: Cornell University Press, 1968), 1:382, n.78. See also Plutarch, *Quaestiones convivales* 3.4, 650f–651e for a debate on whether females are hotter or colder than males (Clement and Hoffleit, 230–234).

soul.[101] The production of this airy and vital humor is dependent on factors of diet and nutrition. Certain foods tend to generate semen while others tend to suppress it. The knowledge of the

---

There are several recent studies on the female body in Greco-Roman medicine. See esp. Danielle Gourevitch, *Le mal d'être femme: La femme et la médecine dans la Rome antique*, Realia (Paris: "Les Belles Lettres," 1984); Aline Rousselle, "Observation féminine et idéologie masculine: Le corps de la femme d'après les médecins grecs," *Annales: Économies, Sociétés, Civilisations* 35 (1980): 1089–1115; idem, *Porneia: De la maîtrise du corps à la privation sensorielle IIe–IVe siècles de l'ère chrétienne*, Les chemins de l'Histoire (Paris: Presses Universitaires de France, 1983), 37–63; Lesley Dean-Jones, "The Cultural Construct of the Female Body in Classical Greek Science," in *Women's History and Ancient History*, ed. Sarah B. Pomeroy (Chapel Hill: University of North Carolina Press, 1991), 111–137; Ann Ellis Hanson, "Continuity and Change: Three Case Studies in Hippocratic Gynecological Therapy and Theory," in *Women's History and Ancient History*, ed. Sarah B. Pomeroy (Chapel Hill: University of North Carolina Press, 1991), 73–110; idem, "The Medical Writers' Woman," in *Before Sexuality: The Construction of Erotic Experience in the Ancient Greek World*, ed. David M. Halperin, John J. Winkler, and Froma I. Zeitlin (Princeton: Princeton University Press, 1990), 309–337; and Giulia Sissa, *Greek Virginity*, trans. Arthur Goldhammer, Revealing Antiquity 3 (Cambridge: Harvard University Press, 1990). See also Thomas Laqueur, "Orgasm, Generation, and the Politics of Reproductive Biology," *Representations* 14 (1986): 1–41; and idem, *Making Sex: Body and Gender from the Greeks to Freud* (Cambridge: Harvard University Press, 1990) for interesting discussions of the interpretation and representation of female and male bodies in late antiquity and the eighteenth-century enlightenment.

101. Richard Broxton Onians, *The Origins of European Thought About the Body, the Mind, the Soul, the World, Time, and Fate*, Philosophy of Plato and Aristotle Series (Cambridge: Cambridge University Press, 1951; reprint, New York: Arno Press, 1973), 109–119. Galen, in his treatise *De semine* (Kühn 4:512–651), disagrees with Aristotle's theory of generation on several points, including Aristotle's assumption that only the male produces seed (Aristotle, *De generatione animalium* 1.20, 727b–729a [A. L. Peck, ed., *Aristotle: Generation of Animals*, Loeb Classical Library (Cambridge: Harvard University Press, 1979), 100–110]) and his argument that the male contributes form, but no matter, to the fetus (ibid., 2.4, 738b [Peck, 184]). See Anthony Preus, "Galen's Criticism of Aristotle's Conception Theory," *Journal of the History of Biology* 10 (1977): 65–85 (esp. 78–85); Michael Boylan, "The Galenic and Hippocratic Challenges to Aristotle's Conception Theory," *Journal of the History of Biology* 17 (1984): 83–112 (esp. 99–110); Jan Blayney, "Theories of Conception in the Ancient Roman World," in *The Family in Ancient Rome: New Perspectives*, ed. Beryl Rawson (Ithaca: Cornell University Press, 1986), 233–236; Rousselle, *Porneia*, 40–47; and Giulia Sissa, "Subtle Bodies," in *Fragments for a History of the Human Body*, ed. Michel Feher, trans. Janet Lloyd (New York: Zone, 1989), 3:135–141.

faculties of various foods is thus crucial for the treatment of diseases, the control of sexual desire, and the maintaining of balance in the bodily κρᾶσις. Again, since individual constitutions vary, proper dietary regimens will also vary.

Galen's treatise *On the Faculties of Foods* is in the tradition of Hippocratic and other ancient lists of foods and their powers.[102] It also represents one of the implications of Galen's theory of the humors and qualities, namely, that by careful control of diet and daily regimen one can maintain bodily health, including sexual health, and fertility. Further, since Galen argues—along with "all the best physicians and philosophers"—that the condition of the body and its humors changes the activity of the soul,[103] it follows that dietary practice influences behavior. As medical historian Owsei Temkin writes, "dietetic medicine, itself a product of rational study, thus becomes a powerful ally of moral philosophy."[104]

Throughout Galen's writings, then, he refers to the "faculties" or "powers" (δυνάμεις) of various foods. In general, foods can be classified as heating, cooling, drying, moistening, or a combination of these. To cite just a few examples, the parsnip (ἐλαφόβοσκον) is classified as heating, thinning, and drying;[105] wheat (πυρός) is heating, while barley (κριθή, πτισάνη) is cooling;[106] and wine (οἶνος) is heating and moistening.[107] Further, certain foods tend toward the production of certain humors. Thus "warmer" foods tend to produce bile, while "cooler" foods produce phlegm. Likewise, there are environments, phases in life, occupations, and seasons that correspond to the four qualities and four humors. Diseases are also classified accordingly and often treated by the

102. *De alimentorum facultatibus* (Kühn 6:453–748). On the Hippocratic *De victu* and its influence, see Wesley D. Smith, "The Development of Classical Dietetic Theory," in *Hippocratica: actes du Colloque hippocratique de Paris, 4–9 septembre 1978*, ed. M. D. Grmek, Colloques internationaux du Centre national de la recherche scientifique 583 (Paris: Éditions du Centre national de la recherche scientifique, 1980), 439–448.

103. *De loc. aff.* 3.10 (Kühn 8:191).

104. Temkin, *Galenism*, 85.

105. *De simplicium medicamentorum temperamentis ac facultatibus* 6.5.6 (Kühn 11:873).

106. *De alim. fac.* 1.9 (Kühn 6:501).

107. *De san. tuenda* 1.11; 5.5 (Kühn 6:54–55; 334).

careful intake of those foods that counteract the troublesome humors.[108]

Galen's ideas about the effect of diet on the development of semen in both men and women are particularly informative for an understanding of ascetic fasting. This issue appears in three main contexts: in general explanations of the effects or faculties of foods; in descriptions of various diseases for which an excess or lack of semen and moisture is a symptom; and in advice on reducing sexual desire. Thus Galen writes that foods that are very nourishing (τρόφιμα) and at the same time flatulent (φυσώδη) are generative of semen, the substance of which has its origin in excess nutrition (τὸ περίττωμα). On the other hand, those foods that are drying (ξηραίνοντα) and cooling (ψύχοντα) repress semen.[109] As examples of foods generative of semen, Galen lists bulbs (βολβοί), the chickpea (ἐρεβίνθος), beans (κύαμοι), octopus (πολύποδες), and the pinecone (κῶνος). Linseed (λίνου σπέρμα) and rocket (εὔζωμον) are plants that may be taken as foods or as medicines to

---

108. *De nat. fac.* 2.8–9 (Kühn 2:107–140). The humors are not contained in the foods themselves, but are produced in the individual body and in relation to the individual constitution. It is therefore possible for the same food item to produce different humors in different bodies. Honey, for example, becomes yellow bile in those who are young or naturally warm, but it produces blood in older persons or those with colder temperaments (ibid., 2.8 [Kühn 2:107–124]).

In contrast to the humoral theory of Galen and the Dogmatist school, physicians of the so-called "Methodist" school (including Soranus and Caelius Aurelianus [fl. c. 410]) emphasized "general states" of the body that correspond to three basic types of disease: (1) dry, tense, and constricted; (2) fluid, relaxed, and loose; and (3) a mixture of both. Treatment of diseases focuses on counteracting these states with relaxing or astringent measures and often includes fasting periods of one to three days followed by successive periods of specified dietary regimens. Foods likewise are characterized as "binding," "astringent," "loosening," "warm," "cold," etc. See, e.g., Caelius Aurelianus, *De morbis acutis* 3.18 (I. E. Drabkin, ed., *Caelius Aurelianus on Acute Diseases and on Chronic Diseases* [Chicago: University of Chicago Press, 1950], 412–416); *De morbis chronicis* 1.1; 1.3; 5.7 (Drabkin, 452–456; 474–476; 958–962). See also Owsei Temkin's compiled list of foods and their uses in Soranus's *Gynecology* (215–243).

109. *De simp. med. temp. ac fac.* 5.23 (Kühn 11:776–777). Galen also notes that those foods which are warming but at the same time drying (e.g., rue) reduce semen.

produce semen.[110] Foods inhibiting the production of semen
include lettuce (θριδακίνη, θρίδαξ),[111] the vegetable blite (βλίτον),
orach (ἀτράφαξυς), gourd (κολοκύνθη), black mulberry (μόρον),
melon (μηλοπέπων), cucumber (σίκυος), and rue (πήγανον).[112]

These foods and others are mentioned often in connection with
the treatment of diseases and physical problems. In *On the Preservation of Health*, Galen discusses the "most miserable" condition
of the body—the production of excessive and warm semen. If not
treated, the abundance of fluid presses the individual to frequent
sexual intercourse. The patient then becomes weak, dry, thin, and
hollow-eyed. But if the semen is not expelled through intercourse,
the patient develops headaches and stomach trouble. Galen therefore recommends abstinence from foods that produce semen; the
application of lead plasters and cooling ointments to the loins;
and the eating of foods that prevent the production of semen and
are easily digested.[113] Galen's treatment for "plethoric" conditions in general includes the reduction—in quantity and quality—
of dietary intake. He recommends eating foods such as vegetables
(λάχανα) and those legumes (χέδροπα), fish (ἰχθῦς), and birds
(ὄρνιθας) that are "not very nutritious" and would, therefore, not
contribute even more to the excess in bodily humors and excrements.[114] Similarly, Galen's discussion of gonorrhea (the involuntary discharge of semen and not the modern sexually transmitted

110. Ibid.

111. Aline Rousselle notes that that lettuce is not universally regarded as
an antiaphrodisiac in antiquity. While Greek writers such as Galen understood lettuce to be cooling and repressive of sexual desire, in the Egyptian tradition lettuce is an aphrodisiac (Rousselle, *Porneia*, 221). On the former view
see also the texts cited from Rufus of Ephesus in n.115, pp. 59–60; Pliny, *Historia naturalis* 20.26,64 (W. H. S. Jones, ed., *Pliny: Natural History*, Loeb
Classical Library [Cambridge: Harvard University Press, 1951], 6:38); Marcel
Detienne, *Dionysos Slain*, trans. Mireille Muellner and Leonard Muellner
(Baltimore: The Johns Hopkins University Press, 1979), 105–106, n.168. For
the latter view in Egypt see William J. Darby, Paul Ghalioungui, and Louis
Grivetti, *Food: The Gift of Osiris* (London: Harcourt Brace Jovanovich, Academic Press, 1977), 2:675–680. On Evagrius of Pontus's abstention from lettuce
see chap. 4, p. 142.

112. Ibid. In general on rue see Alfred C. Andrews, "The Use of Rue as a
Spice by the Greeks and Romans," *Classical Journal* 43 (1948): 371–373.

113. *De san. tuenda* 6.14 (Kühn 6:443–448).

114. Ibid., 6.6 (Kühn 6:407–410).

disease) and priapism (the increase in the size of the male genitals without sexual desire or increased heat) emphasizes the need for dietary therapy.[115]

115. *De loc. aff.* 6.6 (Kühn 8:437–451). Rufus of Ephesus describes similar treatments for gonorrhea and satyriasis (insatiable desire for sexual activity along with abundant semen). In his treatise *On Satyriasis and Gonorrhea,* and in fragments attributed to Rufus in other medical writers, Rufus recommends a regimen which includes bloodletting, mild evacuants, cooling ointments, the avoidance of erotic thoughts and images, and a carefully-considered "light and thin diet," all intended to reduce semen. The patient must avoid food that is heavy, phlegmatic, difficult to digest, laxative, diuretic, or flatulent. Such foods include meat, sweets, milk, cheese, beans, chickpeas, pease, sage, hedge mustard, acorns, dates, bulbs, octopus, fish without scales, rocket, radishes, turnips, asparagus or "stalks" (ὄρμενοι), and the leek (πρά-σον). Many of these are known to stimulate sexual desire. Recommended foods that reduce the production of semen and sexual desire include rue, thin porridge, mallow, patience, beets, gourd, lettuce, blite, and orach (C. Daremberg and C. E. Ruelle, eds. *Oeuvres de Rufus d'Ephèse* [Paris: 1897; reprint, Amsterdam: Adolf M. Hakkert, 1963], 64–84; 318–323; 429–431; 508–509). Rufus considers rue (πήγανον) to be the best substance—whether taken as food or applied as an ointment—for dulling "the impulses to sexual intercourse" (Daremberg and Ruelle, 73). He also recommends the fruit of the *agnus castus* (or chaste tree, ἄγνος) for drying sperm (Fragment #109 from Alexander of Tralles [Daremberg and Ruelle, 429]). Galen writes that the *agnus castus* has warming and drying faculties and restrains the impulses to sexual pleasures. He refers to its use as an antiaphrodisiac by Athenian women in the rituals of the *Thesmophoria,* and its power to help the menstrual flow (*De simp. med. temp. ac fac.* 6.1.2 [Kühn 11:807–810]). See also Detienne, *Dionysos Slain,* 105–106, n.168, on the anemone, lettuce, and the *agnus castus* as at the same time inhibiting of sexual desire and effective in stimulating the processes of menstruation and lactation: "As for the chaste tree, its effects concern the woman alone: the plant that clamps shut her body's desire is also the one that, by bringing on the menses and causing milk to mount, favors reproductive activity in her." But Heinrich von Staden has argued that, in Dioscorides, Galen, and other post-Hippocratic medical writers, "both the capacity of the chaste tree to promote reproductive normalcy and its power to blunt sexual desire cross gender lines." Galen, for example, writes that the chaste tree is effective in stopping wet dreams and curing priapism. Von Staden argues that the apparent paradox between the effects of the chaste tree (promotion of reproductive capabilities and repression of sexual desire) points to a general concern with preserving the reproductive and social orders ("Spiderwoman and the Chaste Tree: The Semantics of Matter," *Configurations* 1 [1992]: 28–32). On the chaste tree and the willow as symbols for chastity in early Christian interpretation see John T. Noonan Jr., *Contraception: A History of Its Treatment by the Catholic Theologians and Canonists,* enlarged edition (Cambridge: Harvard University Press, Belknap Press, 1986), 102–104. John M. Riddle has discussed the uses of *agnus castus* as an

On the other hand, Galen's recommendation for those suffering from extreme dryness is, predictably, a regimen of moistening, nutritious, and abundant food. Thus, for example, in the case of a patient whose urinary passages are thin and dried out from poor nutrition, Galen prescribes extra nourishment and oily ointments.[116]

There is a certain tension in Galen's writings on these matters between the danger of retention or excess of semen in the body and the desire not to weaken the body by the loss of vital *pneuma* in semen.[117] For example, Galen identifies the cause of hysteria in females as the retention of semen or menses and claims that more harm is done by the retention of the former than of the latter.[118]

---

abortifacient (due to its ability to bring on menstruation) in ancient and medieval traditions in *Contraception and Abortion from the Ancient World to the Renaissance* (Cambridge: Harvard University Press, 1992). Finally, Soranus recommends a potion made from seed of *agnus castus*, hemp, or rue in the treatment of "gonorrhea" in women. He describes gonorrhea as a chronic condition of the relaxed and fluid kind. Thus his treatment focuses on cooling and astringent measures (*Gyn.* 3.12,45–46 [Temkin (English translation), 168–170]). Cf. Caelius Aurelianus on satyriasis in *De morbis acutis* 3.18 (Drabkin, 412–416) and on priapism in *De morbis chronicis* 5.9 (Drabkin, 964); and Celsus, *De medicina* 4.28 (W. G. Spencer, ed., *Celsus: De Medicina*, Loeb Classical Library [Cambridge: Harvard University Press, 1948], 1:450–452).

116. *De usu partium* 14.11 (Kühn 4:191–192). On the use of "fasting cures" in Greco-Roman medicine see also Arbesmann, "Fasten," 467–468; and idem, *Das Fasten*, 118–126.

117. Galen writes that semen is "full of vital *pneuma*" (*De usu partium*, 14.9 [Kühn 4:183]). Vital *pneuma* passes with blood from the heart into the arteries leading to the base of the brain, where animal or "psychic" *pneuma* is produced from the vital *pneuma* (ibid., 9.4 [Kühn 3:696–703]). On weakness and the loss of vital *pneuma* in ejaculation see Rousselle, *Porneia*, 23–27, and Foucault, *The Care of the Self*, 112–123. The connection of vital *pneuma* with semen and also with the arteries at the base of the brain relates Galen to ancient Greek and Egyptian traditions connecting semen to cerebro-spinal fluid and the spinal column. See Françoise Héritier-Augé, "Semen and Blood: Some Ancient Theories Concerning Their Genesis and Relationship," in *Fragments for a History of the Human Body*, ed. Michel Feher, trans. Tina Jolas (New York: Zone, 1989), 3:159–175; Sissa, "Subtle Bodies," 141; Onians, *The Origins of European Thought*, 109–119; Lesky, *Die Zeugungs- und Vererbungslehren*, 1233–1254; Preus, "Galen's Criticism," 70–71.

118. *De loc. aff.* 6.5 (Kühn 8:413–436). See Ilza Veith, *Hysteria: The History of a Disease* (Chicago: University of Chicago Press, Phoenix Books, 1970), 31–38; Rousselle, *Porneia*, 89–102; and Gourevitch, *Le mal d'être femme*, 113–128.

The disease is most often found in widows and others who have been deprived of sexual activity. Since their semen is not expelled regularly, as is natural, it becomes burdensome.[119] Galen therefore recognizes the need to rid oneself of excess (nevertheless he argues that those who are temperate and self-controlled will participate in sexual activity not for pleasure, but for health, as the example of Diogenes the Cynic demonstrates).[120] Galen also argues, however, that sexual activity makes the body cold, dry, and weak. It is therefore dangerous for those with cold and dry constitutions. Indeed, sex is harmless (or beneficial) only for those with warm, moist constitutions who are in the prime of life.[121] Thus while some people become ill from lack of sexual activity, others are made weak from indulgence in the *aphrodisia*.[122] In these matters, as throughout his writings, Galen argues for moderation, discrimination, and control in every aspect of the daily regimen.

Finally, in *On the Usefulness of the Parts of the Body*, Galen offers an explanation of the physiological processes of sexual desire, pleasure, and ejaculation, and the relationship between nature, immortality, and procreation. Since the material of the

---

119. *De loc. aff.* 6.5 (Kühn 8:417). Cf. Soranus's description of hysteria and hysterical suffocation in *Gyn.* 3.5,26–30 (Temkin [English translation], 149–154). Soranus describes hysteria as a disease of constriction which is usually "preceded by recurrent miscarriages, premature birth, long widowhood, retention of menses and the end of ordinary childbearing or inflation of the uterus" (3.5,26 [Temkin (English translation), 149]). His treatment focuses on relieving the constriction and congestion and includes bloodletting.

120. *De loc. aff.* 6.5 (Kühn 8:419). Galen reports that Diogenes had sexual relations only in order to rid himself of excess semen.

121. *De san. tuenda* 2.2; 3.11; 6.4 (Kühn 6:84; 224; 401–402). Cf. Rufus of Ephesus, who acknowledges that the sexual act, as natural, is not harmful in itself. Immoderate use of sexual activity, however, can lead to illness, especially for those of weak, dry, and cold constitutions. The healthful effects of the sex act are many, according to Rufus. For example, it rids the body of excess, makes one more virile, and helps to cure melancholy and epilepsy. For those who indulge frequently Rufus recommends a warm and moist regimen that includes meat, vegetables such as rocket, beans, chickpeas, and flatulent and filling pods (λοβοί) (Fragment 60, Περὶ ἀφροδισίων, from Aetius [Daremberg and Ruelle, 318–323]).

122. *De loc. aff.* 6.5 (Kühn 8:417–418). See also Foucault, *The Care of the Self*, 112–123.

human body is not immortal or incorruptible, nature (ἡ φύσις) devised a clever method (τὸ σόφισμα) to guarantee the continuation of human and animal life through procreation. To the "organs of conception" nature added the power to produce pleasure and to the soul added the ineffable desire to exercise these instruments. Thus even the most ignorant creatures will be incited to the work of procreation.[123]

Pleasure and desire, then, are instrumental and essential to the purpose of generation. But there are also physiological reasons for their association with sexual activity. Here Galen describes the physiological process of desire in the female body. The collection of sharp and bitter serous moisture as well as warm *pneuma* in the uterus stimulates the sexual organs to action (expulsion) and makes that action pleasurable—much like scratching an itch.[124] A moistening humor in the male likewise incites to intercourse and makes it pleasurable. When the semen is expelled—in the female, from the ovaries ("testicles") into the fallopian tubes and the uterus; in the male, through the urethra—these moistening humors are also expelled. The tightening and tensing of the sexual organs during intercourse are, according to Galen, similar to the violent spasms of epilepsy, during which semen is often expelled due to the convulsions which overtake the entire body.[125]

In Galen's scheme, desire (ἐπιθυμία) and pleasure (ἡδονή) are physical aspects of the cause and effect of sexual activity. They are, indeed, as ordinary as itching and scratching, yet as overwhelming in impact as epileptic convulsions. The production of semen and the need for ejaculation are the normal physiological effects of nutrition and the process of digestion. Yet orgasm and ejaculation can be dangerous and harmful to all but the most hearty in physical constitution.[126] Because the type and quantity

123. *De usu partium* 14.1–2 (Kühn 4:142–144). Note that Galen's association of sexual desire and physical pleasure with the human problems of mortality and corruptibility anticipates some of the themes we will find in Christian ascetic discourse.

124. Ibid., 14.9 (Kühn 4:179–182).

125. Ibid., 14.10–11 (Kühn 4:185–191).

126. For fuller discussions and influential treatments of these issues see Foucault, *The Care of the Self*, 104–144; Rousselle, *Porneia*, 13–63; and Laqueur, *Making Sex*, 43–52.

of food eaten has a direct effect on the production of semen and other humors, those with constitutions not suited to frequent sexual activity, or those who suffer from gonorrhea, priapism, or the retention of semen, are able to reduce and indefinitely limit the production of semen—and therefore sexual desire—by careful moderation and control of diet. In addition, Galen emphasizes the power of erotic thoughts, images, and memories to stimulate desire. Thus those who avoid such erotic indulgences have more control over their bodies.[127]

In the mass of Galen's medical and philosophical writings, the image emerges of the human body perfectly designed by nature but delicately balanced and vulnerable to any change in regimen. This is especially striking in Galen's arguments on the effects of diet on the production or reduction of bodily humors, including semen, and in his descriptions of the physiology of desire, pleasure, orgasm, exhaustion, and depletion. Indeed, modern scholars have characterized the sexually active body in Galen as a "great steam generator"[128] or a "human Espresso machine":

> To make love was to bring one's blood to the boil, as the fiery vital spirit swept through the veins, turning the blood into the whitened foam of semen. It was a process in which the body as a whole—the

---

127. *De loc. aff.* 6.6 (Kühn 8:450–451). Galen is discussing priapism, which he claims is not a problem for the athlete who completely refrains from eroticism. The idea that mental or visual images can stimulate desire and thus complicate the treatment of certain diseases is common in medical writers. See e.g. Soranus (*Gyn.* 3.12,45–46 [Temkin (English translation), 168–170]) who suggests that the woman suffering from a flow of semen ("gonorrhea") not be exposed to erotic paintings or stories, and Caelius Aurelianus (*De morbis chronicis* 5.7 [Drabkin, 960]) who writes that the one experiencing nocturnal emissions must avoid erotic thoughts that lead to erotic dreams and the movement of semen. Self-control and freedom from the passions of the soul, including immoderate sexual desire, are the central themes of Galen's treatise *De cog. cur. animi morbis* (Kühn 5:1–57). Here Galen advocates a lifetime of training (ἄσκησις) and the guidance of an older, virtuous man in order to achieve such freedom (3–4 [Kühn 5:8–14]). Of course Galen assumes that the individual pursuing such training is a free, slave-owning male with leisure time, much as he recognizes that optimum health is usually attainable only for one who is free and wealthy (*De san. tuenda* 2.1 [Kühn 6:81–83]).

128. Laqueur, "Orgasm," 7.

brain cavity, the marrow of the backbone, the kidneys, and the lower bowel region—was brought into play.[129]

Since every activity, habit, and condition of the human body is thus interrelated, great care is required to maintain its health.

But Galen is optimistic. If the human body, which is his subject, is not perfectible, it is at least knowable,[130] controllable, and responsive to the manipulations of its wise owner. In closing his book *On the Preservation of Health,* Galen offers general advice to his readers, both laypersons and physicians: "Do not eat and behave as do most people, like irrational animals, but discriminate based on experience which foods and drinks are harmful, and which and how many actions." Likewise with "the use of sexual pleasures," one should determine whether they are harmful or not, and at what frequency they are harmless or become dangerous. Finally, to those who are educated or cultured (τοῖς πεπαιδευμένοις), Galen recommends simply that they note which things are beneficial and which are harmful—in this way they will have little use of physicians, as long as they are healthy.[131]

Ancient Medical Representations of the Female Body

Scholars have, in recent years, given increasing attention to the topic of the female body in ancient medical and philosophical

129. Brown, *The Body and Society,* 17.
130. Perkins, *The Suffering Self,* 142–172. Perkins's discussion emphasizes that with Galen the human body becomes knowable, "a subject to be understood, a text to be read" (152). She writes, "Galen's body, when known inside and out, was discovered to be essentially a body at risk; it was always verging toward dysfunction, needing careful, constant monitoring and outside control. It was a body that mattered, that signified and was significant, very unlike the body offered in Epictetus's narratives that was to be bracketed off from the 'real' self" (145). She thus contrasts Galen's attention to the risks of the body and focus on the body as object with the Stoic emphasis on detachment from bodily concerns in favor of an *askesis* of the mind. Perkins's point is important; I would nevertheless keep Galen and Epictetus in the same conversation. That is, if Epictetus's ideal subject is one "that passed through suffering unaffected and unchanged by the experience" (83), such an ideal is conceived in response to the reality of suffering and pain. The "real" self is precisely the one who is unmoved by pain, but pain is still very much the issue. In short, both Galen and Epictetus can be understood as responding to embodiment and theodicy.
131. *De san. tuenda* 6.14 (Kühn 6:449–450).

writings, especially those of the Hippocratic authors Aristotle, Galen, and Soranus.[132] Many of these scholars note that while we tend to assume that medicine, biology, and other sciences concerned with the human body have as their subjects concrete, identifiable "realities" and "facts," these sciences—and consequently the "facts" they pronounce—are culturally and historically influenced. Helen King, for example, writes:

> New approaches to medical history . . . explore discourse about the body as a means both of reflecting and confirming dominant social values. For example, the way in which differences between male and female bodies are expressed derives from particular social structures and the places of the sexes within these, but also reinforces such structures by locating their origin in unquestionable, 'natural' facts. The power of medicine lies in its ability to make the social appear natural.[133]

Thus the reader must recognize that the ancient medical text, like any historical text, can and does reflect ideology.[134] Nowhere is this better illustrated than in the descriptions of biological gender. As Bryan Turner writes, biological differences between male and female are "culturally mediated and historical. . . . What stands behind 'gender' is not an unmediated reality but another level of social constructs and classifications; the anatomy of the body is precisely such a classification."[135] A useful example of this interrelatedness of ideology and scientific theory is the common (though debated) ancient principle that the male body is

---

132. See the sources cited in n.100, pp. 54–55.

133. Helen King, "The Daughter of Leonides: Reading the Hippocratic Corpus," in *History as Text: The Writing of Ancient History*, ed. Averil Cameron (Chapel Hill: University of North Carolina Press, 1989), 13.

134. G. E. R. Lloyd explores the relationship between ancient sciences and ideology in *Science, Folklore and Ideology: Studies in the Life Sciences in Ancient Greece* (Cambridge: Cambridge University Press, 1983). See also Françoise Héritier-Augé, "Older Women, Stout-Hearted Women, Women of Substance," in *Fragments for a History of the Human Body*, ed. Michel Feher, trans. Leigh Hafrey (New York: Zone, 1989), 3:288–289; Dean-Jones, "The Cultural Construct," 111–137; Hanson, "Continuity and Change," 73–110; and idem, "The Medical Writers' Woman," 309–337. See also Martin, *The Corinthian Body*, 198–228.

135. Bryan S. Turner, *The Body and Society: Explorations in Social Theory* (Oxford: Basil Blackwell, 1984), 28.

hotter than the female, with heat being a more positive quality than cold.[136] Aristotle is one of the strongest representatives of the use of hot and cold as positive and negative categories.[137] He argues that male and female are distinguished by an ability and inability: the male is able to concoct or cook (πέττειν) and form semen from the blood, while the female receives the semen but is incapable, through her own digestive process, of concocting it fully or discharging it. Because all concoction takes place by means of heat, Aristotle concludes, the male is therefore hotter than the female, and, because of its coldness and inability to concoct fully, the female body retains more blood than the male.[138]

Galen rejects Aristotle's notion that only the male produces semen and argues (with the benefit of Herophilus's identification of the female testicles in the third century B.C.E.[139]) that the female also produces seed. He nevertheless agrees with Aristotle and others that the female is colder and less perfect than the male, and that her semen is likewise more scanty and less perfectly concocted.[140] Further, the degree of innate heat in the body is not a value-neutral feature. Rather, as heat is the principal instrument of nature, the excess of heat in the male is that which makes him a more perfect creation.[141] Differences in heat determine not only the production and quality of humors, but also the apparent anatomical features of gender. Galen explains that all of the parts of the body are common to men and women. The generative parts differ in appearance and function because for men the parts are outside of the body, while for women they remain within the body. Indeed, Galen suggests that his reader imagine the male parts turned inside out and inward. The penis would then become the vagina, the foreskin would become the labia, and the scrotum and testicles would become the uterus and ovaries. In the same

136. See the texts cited in n.100, pp. 54–55.

137. G. E. R. Lloyd, "The Hot and the Cold," 103.

138. Aristotle, *De gen. an.* 4.1, 765b; 1.19, 726b (Peck, 384–386; 92–94).

139. On the debate between Aristotle, Galen, and others on female anatomy and the female role in generation see the sources cited in n.101, above. Michael Boylan is especially careful to point out that Aristotle's theory of the seed is not completely clear or consistent in *On the Generation of Animals* ("The Galenic and Hippocratic Challenges," 83–112).

140. Galen, *De usu partium* 14.6 (Kühn 4:158–164).

141. Ibid. (Kühn 4:161).

way, the female parts imagined inside out and projecting outside of the body seem like the male genitalia. It is, again, the abundance of heat in the male which causes his parts to develop completely and protrude outside of the body, and the "defect" in heat that causes the female parts to remain inside, imperfect.[142] And that makes all the difference.

In this model, the female sex is defined in large part as a cold, defective, incompletely developed version of the male. Thomas Laqueur has explored the implications of this model for the ancient and modern understandings of "sex" and "gender." He writes concerning Galen's theory: "Instead of being divided by their reproductive anatomies, the sexes are linked by a common one. Women, in other words, are inverted, and hence less perfect, men. They have exactly the same organs but in exactly the wrong places."[143] Galen's theory is perhaps the best example for what Laqueur calls the "one-sex body," a theory which, he argues, dominated philosophy, anatomy, and medicine from antiquity to the eighteenth century. The understanding of biological "sex" as a scientifically verifiable fact upon which gender roles are based is, according to Laqueur, a modern one. The older model, exemplified by Galen's description of the male and female genitals, saw biological sexual differences as "matters of degree rather than kind."[144] The differences that really mattered to Galen and others were differences in what we now call "gender," that is, gender as socially, politically, economically, and culturally constituted.[145]

Laqueur reminds modern readers that what we think of as biological sex is not necessarily what earlier physicians and philosophers had in mind when they delineated male and female bodies:

> At the very least, what we call sex and gender were in the "one-sex model" explicitly bound up in a circle of meanings from which escape

142. Ibid. (Kühn 4:158–162).

143. Laqueur, *Making Sex*, 26.

144. Ibid., 125. I have found Laqueur's description of the "one-sex model" to be very useful, and his analysis has influenced my own in this section.

145. While it may be a useful theoretical tool for social and historical analysis, the distinction between "sex" as a biological category and "gender" as a cultural category also poses certain dangers, as Laqueur notes (*Making Sex*, 12–14). Laqueur's work demonstrates clearly the extent to which physical "description" and cultural "interpretation" are consistently intertwined.

to a supposed biological substrate—the strategy of the Enlighten-ment—was impossible. In the world of one sex, it was precisely when talk seemed to be most directly about the biology of two sexes that it was most imbedded in the politics of gender, in culture.[146]

Laqueur, King, and other scholars who have dealt with Greco-Roman discourse on the female body provide a useful corrective to the view that "sex" is somehow a timeless biological fact that ancient writers either correctly or incorrectly described and articulated.[147] Rather, ancient gynecological and anatomical theories—and ethical models of the moralists as well—in many ways reflect and express gender hierarchy and social realities.[148] The structure and physiological processes of the female body are thus represented and defined in relation to the male standard. The female body is a lesser version of the "canonical body" of the male.[149]

The Products of Nutrition: Semen, Menses, and Milk

In the major medical or biological writings of antiquity, including Hippocrates, Aristotle, and Galen, the reproductive fluids of the body are products of nutrition and digestion. In particular, semen, menstrual blood, and milk are produced out of the concocting of blood, itself one of the four main humors produced from food. Thus, as Anthony Preus writes concerning Aristotle, "the fluids of the body are generative of each other."[150] In Aristotle's description, menses (τὰ καταμήνια) and semen are both residues from nourishment and the concoction (πέψις) of blood. They are alike materially until the residue undergoes a further concoction in the

146. Ibid., 8.
147. See also esp. Lloyd, *Science*, 58–111; Gourevitch, *Le mal d'être femme*; Rousselle, *Porneia*; Sissa, *Greek Virginity*; Dean-Jones, "The Cultural Construct;" and Hanson, "The Medical Writers' Woman."
148. Lloyd argues as well that ancient zoological theory reflects the ideo-logical hierarchy of human over animal (*Science*, 7–57).
149. Laqueur, *Making Sex*, 34–35. Kirsten Hastrup, "The Semantics of Biology: Virginity," in *Defining Females: The Nature of Women in Society*, ed. Shirley Ardener (New York: John Wiley and Sons, Halsted Press, 1978), 53–55.
150. Preus, "Galen's Criticism," 78.

male and becomes semen. As the female body lacks the heat with which to achieve this final change, Aristotle refers to the menses as "impure" semen.[151] Indeed, Aristotle writes, it is this inability to concoct nutriment completely into semen that defines a female as female—she is, finally, an "infertile male" (ἄρρεν ἄγονον).[152] Blood, then, is, according to Aristotle, the source of semen in males and menstrual blood and milk in women. This assumption that the substance of menses and milk is the same explains why a woman does not menstruate during lactation; the nutritional byproduct is completely used up in either one process or the other.[153]

Galen also understands menses and milk to be of the same substance or material.[154] Milk, like semen, is produced from blood that is more perfectly concocted than the menses. This is because the blood spends more time in the vessels that conduct it to the breasts or to the male testicles; the longer the time spent in these vessels, the more thorough the concoction.[155] Further, the breasts and the uterus are interrelated. If the blood is carried to either the uterus or the breasts, Galen writes, the other part becomes dry.

151. *De gen. an.* 1.18–19, 726a–727b; 1.20, 728a; 2.3, 737a; 4.1, 765b (Peck, 88–100; 102–104; 172–174; 384–386). See also Boylan, "The Galenic and Hippocratic Challenges," 95, 98, 105–106. Boylan notes that Aristotle seems in certain places to suggest that the menses may in fact undergo some type of further *pepsis* in the uterus (98).

152. *De gen. an.* 1.20, 728a (Peck, 102). It is important to emphasize that although Aristotle argues that only the male produces semen, nevertheless semen and menses are residues from nourishment which are "analogous to each other" (Lloyd, *Science*, 97). Further, his language is often ambiguous enough (menses as "impure semen," for example), that one should not overstate Aristotle's distinction between male and female fluids. Laqueur writes, "Even in Aristotle's one-seed theory, *sperma* and *catemenia* [sic] refer to greater or lesser refinements of an ungendered blood" (*Making Sex*, 38; see also Boylan, "The Galenic and Hippocratic Challenges," 106). On the other hand, Aristotle's theory allows him to attribute efficient causality in generation to the male and insist that the female menses supply only material to the process. The implications of this gender hierarchy of causality should not be understated.

153. *De gen. an.* 2.4, 739b; 4.8, 776a–777a (Peck, 190–192; 466–474).

154. *De venae sectione adversus Erasistratum* 5 (Kühn 11:164); *De simp. med. temp. ac fac.* 5.22 (Kühn 11:773).

155. *De usu partium* 16.10 (Kühn 4:183–186).

Thus if blood is concocted into milk and collects in the breasts, the monthly flow does not occur, and if blood travels to the menses, the breasts are dry.[156] It follows, then, that the methods for provoking or retaining menstrual flow and lactation are inter-related. This applies to both foods and medicines. Menstrual fluid and milk are, like semen, products of nutrition and are affected by dietary regimens. The chickpea, for example, is generative of milk and provokes menses; we saw earlier that the chickpea is also recommended for the production of semen.[157]

According to Galen, semen is produced and the excess must be expelled in both males and females. Further, the buildup of semen is one of the causes of sexual desire, and the retention of semen is dangerous to male and female health.[158] He describes one case, in which a woman with a large amount of retained semen experienced relief from the symptoms of hysteria after the heat of the applied medicine caused sensations of pleasure and contractions like those experienced during sexual intercourse, and she expelled the semen.[159] It is significant that Galen relates this case immediately after the story of Diogenes the Cynic, who is said to have masturbated rather than wait for the services of a tardy prostitute, thus demonstrating that ejaculation is necessary for health, not pleasure.[160] By using parallel examples of the dangers of retained semen, Galen asserts that the production and release of this fluid are the same in females and males. Indeed, women can experience

---

156. Ibid., 14.8 (Kühn 4.176); *De simp. med. temp. ac fac.* 5.22 (Kühn 11:773–774).

157. *De simp. med. temp. ac fac.* 5.22; 6.5.16 (Kühn 11:774–775; 876). Compare this to the fruit of the chaste tree, which provokes menstruation and lactation but also represses sexual desire (n.115, above).

158. On female sexual desire in ancient medicine and philosophy see Rousselle, "Observation féminine," 1092–1113; idem, *Porneia*, 7–64; Laqueur, "Orgasm," 4–12; idem, *Making Sex*, 43–51.

159. Galen, *De loc. aff.* 6.5 (Kühn 8:420). On simulation of intercourse as therapy see Hanson, "The Medical Writers' Woman," 318–320. In ancient medicine, "hysterical" diseases were those thought to result from various forms of uterine suffering, including constriction and "suffocation" of the uterus as well as the so-called wandering womb (see sources cited in n.192, below).

160. Galen, *De loc. aff.* 6.5 (Kühn 8:419–420).

nocturnal emissions or wet dreams.[161] Likewise, the regimens for reducing and building semen are not gender-specific.

Aetios of Amida, court physician to Justinian in the sixth century C.E., discusses female fertility, diet, and sexual humors in the sixteenth book of his compilation of ancient medical learning, *The Tetrabiblion.*[162] Aetios's sources include the Hippocratic writers Galen, Soranus, Rufus of Ephesus, and other physicians of late antiquity. His work is significant for this study because he elaborates on much of Galen's teaching concerning the effects of diet on the production of humors and the stimulation of sexual desire and applies it specifically to questions concerning menstruation and female semen. His dietary advice is quite similar to that found in the writings of Galen and Rufus of Ephesus: heating foods generate semen, while cooling or drying foods, such as drinks made from rue or *agnus castus,* inhibit semen.[163] If a woman wishes to maintain fertility, she will follow a diet that helps to incite libido and increase semen, and she will add to her diet those foods that keep menstrual flow regular, as good menstrual flow is necessary for conception.[164] Menstrual regularity is here directly correlative with both fertility and sexual desire; and thus food and medicine are linked to both as well.

In Galen, discussions of menstrual fluid often focus on problems or abnormalities in the flow. The suppression or retention of the menses without pregnancy can cause melancholy[165] and hysteria.[166] Galen notes that the uterus will waste away if the necessary blood is hindered from entering, and that this congestion of blood in the vessels will cause tension in the surrounding

161. Galen, *De semine* 2.1 (Kühn 4:598–601).

162. James V. Ricci, trans., *Aetios of Amida: The Gynaecology and Obstetrics of the VIth Century, A.D.* (Philadelphia: Blakiston, 1950).

163. *Tetrabiblion* 16.26; 72 (Ricci [English translation], 37; 76–77). Aetios also relates a story similar to Galen's about a woman suffering from hysterical symptoms because of an accumulation of semen in the uterus. The woman was cured when a midwife rubbed and massaged the genital area, arousing the patient's lust and causing the semen to be ejaculated (16.68 [Ricci (English translation), 71]).

164. Ibid., 16.26 (Ricci [English translation], 36–37).

165. *De loc. aff.* 3.10 (Kühn 8:183).

166. Ibid., 6.5 (Kühn 8:413–436).

ligaments which pull on the womb. The symptoms of such retention include a feeling of heaviness, nausea, loss of appetite, chills,
and pains in the back, neck, and head.[167] Even a small amount of
retained or abnormal menstrual fluid or semen can cause serious
symptoms, just as even a small amount of poison affects the
entire body.[168]

Soranus, on the other hand, recognizes that some women experience amenorrhea because of lifestyles or activities which cause
excess nutriment to be diverted from the menses and used up
elsewhere in the body. Women who lead active lives, such as
singers and athletes, or women whose bodies are "masculine" (in
appearance and habits), normally do not menstruate, according to
Soranus. Amenorrhea in these women is a sign not of the retention of the menses, but of their absence—there is no menstrual
fluid to be expelled. This is not a cause for alarm and does not
require treatment, unless a particular woman wants to conceive,
in which case she should restrict her activity so that her body
becomes more "feminine" and her monthly flow resumes.[169]

The *retention* of menstrual fluid is, however, a serious condition and signals a disease of the uterus or of the rest of the body:
thus some injury, growth, or inflammation of the uterus might
block the normal flow. Conditions of the body that might cause
the excess nutriment to be used elsewhere include undernourish-
ment and the resulting wasting of the flesh, illness, fever, vomiting, or nosebleeds. Soranus's treatments for retention range from
the mild and practical (feeding one who is undernourished; reducing fever; prescribing rest, massage, and compresses) to the severe
(bloodletting, applying leeches).[170] Galen also suggests blood-

---

167. Ibid. (Kühn 8:428–435).
168. Ibid. (Kühn 8:421–423).
169. Soranus, *Gyn.* 1.4, 23; 3.1, 6–9 (Temkin [English translation], 19–20;
132–135). Aline Rousselle notes that Soranus's view of amenorrhea as a rather
frequent occurrence reflects his knowledge of Roman women who did not
tend to breast feed and so had their periods through much of their adult lives
(*Porneia*, 54). See also Ann Ellis Hanson's discussion of the shift from the
Hippocratic view of menstruation, intercourse, and childbirth as necessary
for female health and the later view, found here in Soranus (and again in
Aetios), that menstruation is not an essential component of health ("The
Medical Writers' Woman," 330–334).
170. Soranus, *Gyn.* 3.1, 7–16 (Temkin [English translation], 133–143).

letting as a treatment for some cases of retention,[171] and names several plants that may be used in preparations to provoke retained or obstructed menses, including lupine,[172] wild leek,[173] sabina, iris, and calamintha.[174]

Aetios of Amida prescribes various dietary regimens for maintaining regular menses according to whether the individual constitution is hot, cold, dry, or moist. These regimens correspond with Galen's classification of the faculties of foods. For example, if a woman's constitution is warmer and she exercises frequently, she should eat plenty of moistening foods such as lettuce, gourds, melons, and cucumbers.[175] If she is of a colder temperature, however, her diet should emphasize foods and blended juices with the opposite faculties. One recommended drink is made from cumin seeds, fennel, and chickpeas.[176]

Aetios echoes Soranus's assertion that amenorrhea is not always an abnormal condition. That is, in women who exercise vigorously or work hard, in women with masculine body types (broad shoulders, more hair, many veins), or in women who are quite thin or overweight, excess nutrition is directed to other parts of the body and little or no menstrual fluid is produced.[177] In fact, Aetios argues that it might be better for female health if menstruation were not necessary:

> It would be preferable indeed to prescribe a way of living (leading) to a complete preservation of health by which (means) the body of a woman may become so dry that it is not necessary (for her) to have menstrual periods. This of course would be harmful to conception; for those who do not have their menses do not conceive. Therefore for the sake of conception, and because almost all women live with that purpose, monthly periods are necessary.[178]

171. Galen, *De curandi ratione per venae sectionem* 19 (Kühn 11:307–308).

172. *De simp. med. temp. ac fac.* 6.8 (Kühn 11:886).

173. Ibid., 6.1 (Kühn 11:825).

174. Ibid., 5.22 (Kühn 11:774–775).

175. *Tetrabiblion* 16.53 (Ricci [English translation], 56–57).

176. Ibid., 16.54 (Ricci [English translation], 57).

177. This is also the case, writes Aetios, among women who perspire excessively or suffer from vomiting, diarrhea, loss of blood, or "pustular eruptions involving the skin" (ibid., 16.51; 57–58 [Ricci (English translation), 54–56; 60–61]).

178. Ibid., 16.53 (Ricci [English translation], 56).

Here Aetios follows the argument found also in Soranus, that menstruation is not healthy in itself, but useful only for conception.[179]

Smooth and regular menstruation is, of course, one of the most important signs and symbols of fertility, a sign that the woman is healthy and physically capable of bearing children, and a symbol of the social expectation that she will do so. Irregular menstruation and amenorrhea, then, are illnesses not of the physical body alone, but of the female social body as well. Danielle Gourevitch notes that in Greco-Roman medicine the link between menstruation, fertility, and femininity is so strong that "a woman who does not yet have or who no longer has periods is not truly a woman."[180] This interweaving of the physical body and its symbolic potential, especially in relation to female reproductive capacity, will be seen again in the Christian ascetic discourse on the female body.

It is important to remember that in the ancient medical discourse the physiological model for production of the fluids associated with generation—menses, semen, and milk—is much the same for the female and the male. All of these humors are useful residues from nutrition, produced out of blood. The primary, gendered, qualitative difference is the amount of innate heat in the body. This is so in both Aristotle and Galen, though they disagree on the question of female semen.

Mouth, Womb, and Belly

The ancient Greek poet Hesiod (who will be discussed again in chapter five) compares women to drones whose never-ending hunger drives worker bees (representing men) to continue their labors. If the metaphorical or symbolic connection between

---

179. Soranus, *Gyn.* 1.6, 27–29 (Temkin [English translation], 23–27).

180. Gourevitch, *Le mal d'être femme*, 96. Similarly, Aline Rousselle notes that in the Hippocratic writings as well as the writings of later physicians, especially Soranus and Rufus of Ephesus, the discussions of women's sexuality and the illnesses of women are focused on reproduction and maintaining fertility ("Observation féminine," 1092; *Porneia*, 37–57); see also Hastrup, "The Semantics of Biology," 60.

women and "bellies" informs Hesiod's poetic creations, the physiological connection between mouth, womb, stomach, and
appetite also informs medical imagery in our period. First, the
Greek terms overlap in meanings. The word γαστήρ, for example,
can refer to the abdominal cavity as "belly," but also as
"womb."[181] Likewise, στόμαχος is used in ancient and late ancient
medicine for the esophagus, mouth of the stomach, neck of the
bladder, womb, and vagina.[182] Galen relates the womb or uterus
to the stomach (γαστήρ) in his discussion of the retentive power of
certain organs. The uterus demonstrates this faculty of retention
best, as the uterus contracts upon and retains the fetus for a full
nine months, and the cervix closes completely so as not to allow
any material into or out of the uterus during that time.[183] The
stomach contracts on the food in the same way that the uterus
contracts on the fetus, while the food is retained for a much
shorter length of time for the process of digestion.[184]

Thus womb and stomach are linked by their locations in the
"belly," their shared names, and their similar retentive
functions.[185] Further, language and description link the mouth to
the womb and vagina in medical as well as philosophical and
mythological discourse.[186] Galen, for example, follows standard
usage when he refers to the cervix as the "mouth" (στόμα) and the
vagina as the "neck" or "throat" (αὐχήν) of the uterus.[187] But
the connection between *stomata* is not simply linguistic. Rather,
the tests for fertility, obstructions, and pregnancy described in the
Hippocratic treatises of the fifth and fourth centuries B.C.E. as well
as Aetios of Amida's *Tetrabiblion* of the sixth century C.E. reveal

181. See *Greek Virginity*, 53–70 (and references cited).
182. See the discussion and references in Lloyd, *Science*, 162.
183. *De nat. fac.* 3.3 (Kühn 2:147–152); *De usu partium* 14.3 (Kühn 4:146).
184. *De nat. fac.* 3.4 (Kühn 2:152–157). The gallbladder and urinary bladder are hollow organs that also demonstrate the retentive and expulsive faculties (3.5 [Kühn 2:157]).
185. Giulia Sissa discusses the image of the womb as jar or *pithos* in
Greek culture and mythology in *Greek Virginity*, 147–156; see also Hanson,
"The Medical Writers' Woman," 325–330.
186. See Sissa, *Greek Virginity*, passim; King, "The Daughter of
Leonides," 22–24; and Lloyd, *Science*, 83–84 for discussions of the Hippocratic material.
187. *De usu partium* 14.3 (Kühn 4:148–149); *De loc. aff.* 6.5 (Kühn 8:425).

the prevalent notion of a direct path between the mouth (or nostrils) and the entrance to the uterus.[188] Aetios recommends, for example, the following tests for female fertility:

> Burn resin under the lower garments so that the vapor enters the genital passage. If the odor passes through the body and reaches the mouth and the nostrils, she will conceive; otherwise, she will not conceive. Also, insert some peeled garlic wrapped in wool as a vaginal tampon at the time of retiring. If the odor reaches the mouth, she will conceive; otherwise, she is sterile.[189]

Here the free passage of the odor from one orifice to the other indicates that the passages of the body are free from obstructions, and that therefore the fluids necessary for conception and gestation will travel freely.

This suggests an ancient model of the female body which is generally permeable, even "spongy,"[190] seen further in the notion that menstrual blood might be diverted from the uterus to other openings of the body, resulting in nosebleeds or rectal bleeding.[191] It is also related to the use of "fumigations" or odor therapy in the treatment of the so-called wandering womb, and its theory that the womb is animal-like and moves around inside the body, searching for moisture, sometimes pushing against other organs and affecting respiration.[192] Galen and Soranus both reject the

188. On the Hippocratic treatises see King, "The Daughter of Leonides," 22–23, and sources cited.

189. *Tetrabiblion* 16.7 (Ricci [English translation], 19).

190. Hanson, "The Medical Writers' Woman," 317; idem, "Continuity and Change," 86; Dean-Jones, "The Cultural Construct," 114–115.

191. On the problem of nosebleeds in Hippocratic texts and on the passages and openings of the female body in general see both Helen King, "The Daughter of Leonides," 22 (and passim), and Ann Ellis Hanson "Continuity and Change," 85–6, 105 nn. 73 and 79. I am grateful to Dale Martin for the latter reference.

192. The theory of the wandering womb is found in ancient Egyptian medical papyri, Plato (*Timaeus* 91c), Hippocratic texts, and Aretaeus the Cappadocian. For a survey of this and other ancient material see Veith, *Hysteria: The History of a Disease;* Gourevitch, *Le mal d'être femme,* 113–128. See also Galen, *De loc. aff.* 6.5 (Kühn 8:425–430); Soranus, *Gyn.* 1.3, 8; 3.4, 26–29 (Temkin [English translation], 9; 149–154); Dean-Jones, "The Cultural Construct," 121–125; Hanson, "The Medical Writers' Woman," 319; and idem, "Continuity and Change," 81–87. Jean-Jacques Aubert has collected evidence

notion of the wandering womb and are aware that the uterus is held in its proper place. Soranus is especially opposed to the common treatment of the condition, which involves the introduction of foul-smelling materials such as burnt hair, burnt skin, or bitumen at the nostrils, in the belief that the uterus will "flee" the stench and return to its lower, proper position. Likewise, the afflicted woman underwent fumigations from below with pleasant-smelling materials, in the belief that the fumes would travel up the vagina and attract the womb downwards.[193]

Finally, the symbolic and physiological connections between the female belly, mouth, and womb come together in the notion of the appetite of the womb. Plato, for example, describes the animal-like womb as so desiring to be filled with fruit that, if unfilled, it wanders around the inside of the body causing obstructions and illness.[194] Centuries later, Soranus, who rejects this theory, nevertheless writes of the appetite necessary for conception to take place:

> Just as without appetite it is impossible for the seed to be discharged by the male, in the same manner, without appetite it cannot be conceived by the female. And as food swallowed without appetite and with some aversion is not well received and fails in its subsequent digestion, neither can the seed be taken up or, if grasped, be carried through pregnancy, unless urge and appetite for intercourse have been present.[195]

Laqueur observes of this passage, "a woman ingesting and a woman conceiving are engaged in analogous functions."[196] As the mouth opens to receive the food which will be retained for a time

---

concerning ancient magical spells and formulae pertaining to the reproductive functions of the womb, including menstruation, abortion, conception, and childbirth. Much of this material suggests the notion of the womb as an animal-like, independent entity which can be controlled by means of magic (Jean-Jacques Aubert, "Threatened Wombs: Aspects of Ancient Uterine Magic," *Greek, Roman, and Byzantine Studies* 30 [1989]: 421–449). I thank Kent J. Rigsby for this reference.

193. Soranus, *Gyn.* 3.4, 29 (Temkin [English translation], 152–153); Aetios of Amida, *Tetrabiblion* 16.68 (Ricci [English translation], 72).

194. Plato, *Timaeus* 91c (Bury, 248–250).

195. Soranus, *Gyn.* 1.10, 37 (Temkin [English translation], 36).

196. Laqueur, *Making Sex*, 51.

in the closed space of the stomach, so the "mouth" of the womb opens to receive the male semen and closes again to protect the fetus inside the retentive area of the womb.

In the anatomical descriptions of the openings and interior spaces of the female body—including those from late antiquity represented here by Galen, Soranus, and Aetios—eating and sexuality, lust and hunger, digestion and procreation, and food and sexual humors are woven into a web of symbolic and physiological meaning. Thus these medical texts will help us to understand the symbolic and physiological framework of the patristic argumentation concerning fasting and female virginity, eating and sexuality. Fasting and virginity can both be interpreted as the closing of *stomata*,[197] the withholding of the interior of the body. The medical representation of the orifices of the female body further illuminates the early Christian representation of the virginal body as closed to worldly pleasures. Moreover, if the various fluids of male and female sexual health are produced in the same manner and from the same products of digestion, nevertheless the anatomical connections between mouth, appetite, and womb give greater symbolic weight to female ascetic fasting. As we will see, fasting and sexual renunciation become inextricably bound in the ideal of virginity. To that end, we must now examine these themes of diet and sexual function as they are integrated into Christian ascetic arguments for chastity and virginity.

197. On this see Sissa, *Greek Virginity*, 121–122: "Defloration is the end of a kind of silence or fast."

The Physiology of Ascetic Fasting

THE PREVIOUS CHAPTER introduced essential concepts and contexts for the development of Christian ascetic theory and practice in late antiquity, including common understandings of the relationship between body, soul, and ethical formation as well as medical theories of nutrition and sexual function. In this chapter we will turn our focus to Christian ascetic literature of the fourth and early fifth centuries, specifically to four authors who exemplify the ways in which ascetic writers used Greco-Roman medical and dietetic theory to argue for the efficacy of fasting and food avoidance in maintaining sexual abstinence.

The fourth century brought a dramatic rise in the literature, theory, and institutionalization of Christian asceticism, a rise which may be related to the post-Constantinian status of Christianity and the resulting shifts in definitions of Christian holiness, the nature of the church, and ideas about proper stance toward "the world." Although—as is clear from chapter two—ascetic behavior and reflection are not unique to Christianity in late antiquity, nevertheless in their Christian context both developed distinct features. For example, during the fourth century various forms of ascetic lifestyle (including some, such as "home monasticism," that had developed earlier) were articulated and regulated. At the same time, a vast body of literature was produced: it included various "lives" of male and female ascetic heroes, "rules" for directing the daily life and activities of communities of monks and virgins, epistolary advice to individuals and groups in pursuit of the "perfect" life, and treatises and homilies intended to argue points of interpretation and behavior.

These sources testify to a range of behaviors, from rather mild forms of abstinence to extreme types of self-denial and bodily mortification. They also present themes that in general may be said to characterize Christian ascetic reflection during this period, such as attempts to justify ascetic behavior and theology by elaborate exegetical strategies, an increasing problematizing of desire—sexual desire in particular—and increasing attention to female virginity as the height of Christian renunciation and perfection. While male celibacy also remained an ideal, the ideology of the virginal life tended, during the fourth century, to become more and more directed toward *female* intactness and the interpretation of *female* renunciation of sexuality and procreation. Indeed, the fascination with female virginity led to the production of an increasing number of treatises and homilies devoted to the theme of virginity.[1]

In these and other texts of the period, practical aspects of the ascetic life—such as daily regimen and diet, clothing, relationships with family members and married or lay Christians, public activities, and scriptural study—are intertwined with the articulation and argumentation of ascetic ideology and theology. As we shall see, reflection on the value and meaning of abstinence, in particular sexual abstinence, necessarily involved questions of the origin, nature, and future of the world, the goodness of material creation, the nature of humanity and embodiment, and the role of marriage, procreation, and death. Thus cosmology, eschatology, and anthropology are always linked to ethics. In the emerging ascetic theories, to abstain from sexual relations and procreation, or to avoid food that is part of a typical diet, or to live in isolation and separation from the everyday activities and involvements of social existence, is to choose to align oneself in the sweep of cosmic and human history. Interpretation of the Genesis accounts of creation, embodiment, the fall, and the role of procreation, as well

---

1. While most sources in this genre assume a female subject, Gregory of Nyssa's *On Virginity* (discussed on pp. 92–96) is a notable exception.

as the possibilities for human progress and the condition of humanity in the future kingdom is therefore essential to the development of ascetic theory.

The following chapters will trace many of these themes through the particular expressions of fasting and celibacy, at least as they are textually represented. After considering diet and physiology in this chapter and theories of gluttony and desire in the next, we will examine more closely the theological and ideological elements, many of which will be introduced here, that link ascetic lifestyle—in particular fasting and female virginity—to understandings of creation, human fault, human perfection, and eschatology.

Basil of Ancyra

Although many of the ascetic theorists of the fourth and early fifth century were directly influenced by the practice and teachings of the masters of the Egyptian desert, when they presented the desert tradition to audiences in Mediterranean villages and cities, they filtered it through their own sets of concerns. The argumentation concerning fasting by these authors is by no means uniform. Nevertheless it is characterized by an interweaving of common elements—including physiological models, anthropological and eschatological formulations, and ecclesiastical concerns. In particular, the discussion focuses more and more on the struggle against sexual desire and the use of dietary renunciation as a practical method for maintaining chastity.

Many Christian ascetic theorists made free use of traditional and contemporary ethics and medical theory (now dominated in the East by Galen and Galenism).[2] In fourth-century treatises on the ascetic life and ascetic fasting, as well as in homilies dedicated to ecclesiastical or lay fasts, references to medical dietetic theory are most often incidentally used to strengthen arguments on fasting. For example, Basil of Caesarea exhorts his congregation to "ask the doctors" who will tell them that excessive nutrition is really a burden to the body and must be relieved through

2. Owsei Temkin, *Galenism: Rise and Decline of a Medical Philosophy* (Ithaca: Cornell University Press, 1973), 61; on Galen's prominence, see 51–94.

fasting. Thus fasting is "the preserver of good health" for every person in every walk of life.[3]

In some cases, however, medical or physiological notions are more central to the development of the argument for ascetic fasting. The most striking example of the explicit use of medical knowledge in ascetic argumentation is Basil of Ancyra's mid-fourth-century treatise *On the True Purity of Virginity*.[4] Basil became the bishop of Ancyra in Galatia in 336, and has been known in historical scholarship primarily as a leader of the so-called semi-Arian (or homoiousion) party during the mid-fourth-century period of the Arian controversy. He died shortly after his second exile in 360.[5] Jerome reports that Basil was trained as a physician, which may explain Basil's frank discussions of the physical and practical aspects of the virginal life in his treatise on virginity.[6] The work is addressed to one Letoios, bishop of

3. *De ieiunio homiliae* 2.7 (*PG* 31.193C–D).

4. *De vera virginitatis integritate* (*PG* 30.669–810). The text appears in this series (*Patrologia Graeca*) among the spurious works of Basil of Caesarea. Ferdinand Cavallera has argued persuasively, based on style, historical indications of the text, and the author's use of medical science, that the treatise was not written by Basil of Caesarea, but by Basil of Ancyra. He dates the treatise to sometime in the second third of the fourth century ("Le 'De Virginitate' de Basile d'Ancyre," *Revue d'histoire ecclésiastique* 6 [1905]: 5–14). See also F. J. Leroy, "La tradition manuscrite du 'de virginitate' de Basile d'Ancyre," *Orientalia Christiania Periodica* 38 (1972): 195–208. An Old Slavonic version of the treatise, which dates to the tenth century and is marked by significant lacunae, was published with a French translation by A. Vaillant (*De Virginitate de Saint Basile: Text vieux-Slave et traduction française*, Textes publiés par l'Institut d'Études slaves 3 [Paris: Institut d'Études Slaves, 1943]). For an important discussion of the treatise in the context of the development of female monasticism as well as the ascetic ideals of the homoiousion party, see Susanna Elm, '*Virgins of God': The Making of Asceticism in Late Antiquity*, Oxford Classical Monographs (Oxford: Clarendon Press, 1994), 113–136; and see also my "Creation, Virginity and Diet in Fourth-Century Christianity: Basil of Ancyra's *On the True Purity of Virginity*, " *Gender & History* 9 (1997): 579–596.

5. For general overviews of Basil of Ancyra's writings and career see Ferdinand Cavallera, "Basile d'Ancyre," *Dictionnaire de spiritualité* 1.2 (1932): 1283; R. Janin, "Basile d'Ancyre," *Dictionnaire d'histoire et géographie ecclésiastiques* 6 (1932): 1104–1107; X. Le Bachelet, "Basile d'Ancyre," *Dictionnaire de théologie catholique* 2 (1903): 461–463.

6. Jerome, *De viris illustribus* 89 (*PL* 23.731C). Jerome also reports that Basil of Ancyra wrote a treatise on virginity. Basil's focus on physical issues

Melitene, and is intended, Basil states, not as a hymn to virginity or an encomium glorifying those who live in poverty or mortify their bodies with excessive fasting, but as a careful instruction on true virginity—that is, the virginity of the soul—and how to pursue and protect it.[7] Basil compares his role as author of the treatise to that of a medical instructor, recalling the common connection made between philosophy and medicine in moral discourse. His subject is the female virgin, her daily regimen, proper conduct and decorum, and the many dangers and defilements threatening her body and soul with corruption and death. Throughout, Basil argues for increased seclusion of virgins from public activities, familial obligations, and contacts with ascetic men, as well as increased vigilance, control, and moderation in ascetic practices, especially fasting. Thus the body of the virgin— the central focus of Basil's work—is problematized and analyzed as the active agent of sin and especially sexual pleasures; it is guarded, moderated, and circumscribed as the necessary yet unruly servant of the soul on the ascetic course; and it is held up as the visible testimony and demonstration of the virgin's transformation into the intact and incorruptible bride of Christ. Indeed, Basil compares the virgin to a precisely painted image of God—from the top of her head to the bottom of her feet. She shows herself to be the "bride of the Lord" in her appearance and in her word (καὶ σχήματι, καὶ λόγῳ).[8]

---

has in the past caused no small amount of discomfort among patristics scholars. Cavallera notes the sometimes "disconcerting crudity" of the author's style ("Le 'de virginitate' de Basile d'Ancyre," 5). José Janini Cuesta seems scandalized that much of the text presents "scenes" of the physiology or pathology of physical pleasure and remarks, "It seems incredible to us that a physician worthy of such a title stoops to these accounts in a book that was intended for virgins" (José Janini Cuesta, "Dieta y virginidad: Basilio de Ancira y San Gregorio de Nisa," *Miscelánea Comillas* 14 [1950]: 190, n.6).

    7. *De virg.* 1 (*PG* 30.672A).

    8. Ibid., 36 (*PG* 30.740C–741A). Basil's appeal to the importance of both *word* and *appearance* in the virgin's self-presentation suggests a link with traditions of moral philosophy that emphasized consistency in word and appearance or behavior as a test of the philosopher's or psychagogue's authenticity. On this see Clarence Edvin Glad, "Adaptability in Epicurean and Early Christian Psychagogy: Paul and Philodemus," Ph.D. diss., Brown University, 1992, 2–3, 27–28, 39–42, 64.

Regular, daily dietary abstinence is a crucial element of the virgin's ascetic training. It is directly related to the success of her vow of sexual purity. But the place of fasting in Basil's program cannot be understood apart from his explanation of the creation and nature of male and female. At the time of creation, writes Basil, the Creator or Demiurge (ὁ Δημιουργός) divided the "root" of corporeal being for each species into male and female.[9] In order to populate the earth, the Creator placed in the nature of each "fragment" of original being an ineffable desire for union with the other through intercourse. To this the Creator also added the physical pleasure of sexual intercourse and the strong affection felt for offspring.[10] Subordinating the female to the power of the male and "taming" the male by the "pleasure" of the female, the Creator made the male active by nature and the female passive, since she was taken from the male. Thus, Basil writes, the female fragment, which was taken from the side of the (male) whole, will properly be obedient to the male. And the male, constantly yearning for that which was taken from him, will "by constraint of nature" regain "in his very self, through intercourse, his own member. Thus two out of one and back again to one from two."[11]

In order that the female not be entirely helpless in her subordination, the Creator placed in the female body the power of sexual attraction over the male. The shape, sight, and feel of her body were made more delicate to add to her allure. Just as iron is violently drawn toward a magnet, Basil writes, so the male body is pulled toward the female for the purpose of procreation. The male

9. Ibid., 3 (*PG* 30.673B). See also Plato, *Symposium* 189d–193b [Aristophanes' myth of the separated androgyne] (W. R. M. Lamb, ed., *Plato: Lysis, Symposium, Gorgias,* Loeb Classical Library [Cambridge: Harvard University Press, 1967], 134–146).

10. See also Galen, *De usu partium corporis humani* 14.2 (C. G. Kühn, ed., *Galeni Opera Omnia* [Leipzig: K. Knobloch, 1821–1833; reprint, Hildesheim: Georg Olms, 1964–1965], 4:144).

11. *De virg.* 3 (*PG* 30.673C–676A). Basil's idea that sexual desire was implanted by the creator in order to populate the world and therefore exists "naturally" in the human body must be considered along with his view (explored in chapter 5) that marriage and procreation are necessary because of the loss of immortality with the fall. If procreation previously made sexual activity a necessity, however, virginity is introduced with the time of Christ.

becomes a "prisoner of her pleasure." Basil is very clear that it is the *male* body which is drawn to the *female* and not the other way around. The female creature experiences sexual desire for the male, and female desire is one of Basil's concerns throughout the treatise, to be sure; but Basil explains that this power of drawing and holding the male was placed *in the female body itself* and is an inescapable and created feature of female nature.[12] In this sense the virgin's efforts to achieve sexual purity force her to battle her own female nature.

The virgin's goal, then, is to separate her soul from the passionate attraction of bodies, constraining her own nature in order to subdue the lust for intercourse as well as all other types of lust.[13] For lustful pleasure (ἡδονή) is like a single fountain "gushing forth from the flesh and dividing into the five senses, as into five streams, through which it flows violently toward objects of sensation," dragging the "slime" from the flesh along in the current and threatening to drown the soul in the tossing waves of passion.[14] Therefore the virgin must be extremely cautious in the necessary operation of the bodily senses. For sights, sounds, smells, and especially touches and tastes can easily agitate and trouble her with fantasies, memories, and images that propel her toward sexual intercourse. Particularly dangerous is the sense of touch: because it is coextensive with the entire surface of the body, it threatens in an instant to send shock waves of lustful pleasure through every inch of flesh.[15]

Here Basil explicitly links the sense of touch (ἁφή) existing in *taste* to the sense of touch located in the *genitals* and in sexual activity. The experiences of eating and intercourse are both incited and accomplished through sensual contact. Specifically, taste leads and sexual union follows: "through the sense of touch in tasting—which is always seducing toward gluttony by

---

12. Ibid. (*PG* 30.676B–C).

13. See n.11 above. For Basil, the need for procreation ceased with the time of Christ; thus the virgin resists the powers of sexual attraction and desire, even though they were implanted in bodies by a good God for a useful purpose.

14. Ibid., 4 (*PG* 30.677B–C).

15. Ibid., 5 (*PG* 30.680B–C).

swallowing—the body, fattened up and titillated by the soft
humors bubbling uncontrollably inside, is carried in a frenzy
towards the touch of sexual intercourse."[16] Thus indulgence in
the pleasures of eating leads directly and physiologically to the
buildup of bodily humors and the need for the pleasures of sex. In
addition, taste and sexual activity are those pleasures primarily
responsible for making the soul corporeal (σωματοῖ . . . τὴν ψυχήν).
Here Basil makes use of the Neoplatonic notion, found in Porphyry's De abstinentia, of the defiling or "corporifying" of the
soul by certain foods.[17]

The one who wishes to live in chastity must therefore first control her sense of taste—that which supplies the body with the
material (food and the humors produced from it) necessary for sexual function. Basil writes, "As the stomach grows heavy with
food, it becomes necessary for the organs underneath it, which are
overflowing with humors bubbling inside, to move toward their
natural function."[18] Thus the wise virgin uses all of the discretion
of the Platonic charioteer, placing the bit of rationality in the
mouth of her sense of taste, carefully moderating and guiding her
eating in order to protect her chaste body and soul.[19] The purpose

16. Ibid., 6 (PG 30.681C). Basil returns several times in his treatise to the
dangers of touching (see for example 43–45; 52; 62; 66 [PG 30.753B–760B;
773A–B; 797A–C; 804B]). When a man and a woman touch, he writes, their
natural tendency to unite in sexual intercourse is so strong that the touch
alone lights the flame of desire between them; they are like oakum that can
ignite spontaneously (45 [PG 30.757C–760A]).

17. Ibid., 6 (PG 30.681B–681C). See Porphyry, De abstinentia 4.20 (August
Nauck, ed., Porphyrii Philosophi Platonici: Opuscula Selecta [Leipzig:
Teubner, 1886; reprint, Hildesheim: Georg Olms, 1963], 262–266; and
Thomas Taylor, trans., Porphyry: On Abstinence from Animal Food [London:
Centaur Press, 1965], 175–179). Porphyry argues that the soul is defiled by
contact with dead matter such as meat or semen (when it is emitted without
conception). It is also defiled by the passions. Further, he argues that the soul
operates freely in a body that is dry and not clogged by humors.

18. Basil of Ancyra, De virg. 7 (PG 30.681C–684B).

19. Ibid., 5 (PG 30.680A–B). The metaphor of the body as a horse that must
be controlled with abstinence and guided by rationality as a charioteer is a
Platonic image popular with ascetic writers. Plato uses it to refer to rationality controlling the irascible and concupiscible souls (Phaedrus 246a–b;
253c–254e [Harold North Fowler, ed., Plato: Euthyphro, Apology, Crito,
Phaedo, Phaedrus, Loeb Classical Library (Cambridge: Harvard University
Press, 1966), 470; 494–498]). Among Christian writers see e.g. Evagrius, De
octo spiritibus malitiae 3 (PG 79.1148B–C); Gregory of Nyssa, De virginitate

of Basil's regimen is "to take into account both the condition of
the body and the qualities of foods (καὶ τὴν κατάστασιν . . . τοῦ σώ-
ματος, καὶ τὰς ποιότητας τῶν τροφῶν) and to keep in check the
thriving body and the increasing of natural heat besides, and by
means of diet to drive out heat."[20] The similarities in tone and
language between Basil's treatise and Aetios of Amida's medical
advice (discussed in chapter 2) is quite striking. Aetios writes for
the woman who desires to maintain fertility in order to conceive:
her diet should increase sexual desire as it promotes regular menstruation and the production of semen. Basil, on the other hand,
prescribes a regimen for the woman whose goal is lifelong virginity rather than fertility and reproduction. In both, the link
between diet and the procreative role of the female body is
explicit, and both authors encourage women to consider both
their own bodily constitutions and the effects of particular foods.
Basil compares the balance of the four elements and the four
qualities in the body to the harmony of a four-note scale. The
ascetic will maintain that harmony by preserving those qualities
of heat, cold, dryness and moisture necessary for the natural function of her body while reducing abundance. In this way, Basil
writes, she frees the body from discord, "as if preparing in the soul
the tetrachord of our bodies, for the melody of virtue."[21]

The virgin must wisely discern not only the quantity of food
necessary for preserving bodily strength, but above all the qualities and faculties of foods. For

> there are not only quite a few seeds (σπερμάτων) and legumes (ὀσπρίων)
> but even vegetables (λαχάνων) which, in spite of their common reputa-
> tion, are not absolutely useful as nourishment to the ascetic for the
> purpose of smooth [digestive] management, but tearing at the depths of
> the internal organs [lit. the flesh] and producing irritating gurgles—no
> less than is the case with those foods that are unquestionably
> avoided—they unexpectedly upset and stir up bodies.[22]

22.2 (Michel Aubineau, ed., *Gregoire de Nysse: Traité de la virginité*, SC
119 [Paris: Éditions du Cerf, 1966], 516–518); Basil of Caesarea, *Regulae fusius
tractatae* 16 (*PG* 31.957B); John Chrysostom, *Homilia XXVII in Acta* 3 (*PG*
60.209–210); idem, *Homilia I de statuis* 4 (*PG* 49.21); and Jerome, *Adversus
Jovinianum* 2.10 (*PL* 23.312C–313A).

20. Basil of Ancyra, *De virg.* 8 (*PG* 30.685B).

21. Ibid., 9 (*PG* 30.688B–C).

22. Ibid., 8 (*PG* 30.685C–D).

Unfortunately, Basil does not specify which seeds, legumes, and vegetables he includes in this dangerous group. He is more specific about condiments or seasonings that "entice toward sexual pleasure." Salt in particular should not be used indifferently. Certain well-meaning ascetics, because of extreme abstinence, have rejected all seasoning, but continue to use salt freely with bread. Basil suggests that they are unaware that salt is naturally fertile, produces itching in the body, and incites towards intercourse more than the other seasonings. Indeed, it is better for the virgin to avoid using salt with bread at all, because, not knowing what amount may be used safely, she may be fooled by her own sense of taste and find herself pursuing sexual pleasures in spite of her intentions.[23]

Throughout Basil's discussion of fasting and the effects of diet and the sense of taste on sexual desire he insists on the importance of moderation. Although he repeats the maxim that a fat body cannot produce a light or refined mind, he completes the sentence with the observation that excessive thinness and weakness of the body destroys whatever refinement of mind there is.[24]

23. Ibid., 9 (*PG* 30.685D–688B). Basil's warning on the dangers of salt is unusual because, as he himself notes and as was discussed in chap. 1, Egyptian ascetics are reported to have eaten salt with bread regularly. There is some indication, however, that even in Egypt salt was thought to have aphrodisiac powers (see William J. Darby, Paul Ghalioungui, and Louis Grivetti, *Food: The Gift of Osiris* [London: Academic Press, 1977], 1:447–449). Plutarch reports that Egyptian priests avoided salt with their food in their ritual purifications because it stimulates the appetite (see *De Iside et Osiride* 5, 352f [Frank Cole Babbitt, ed., *Plutarch's Moralia*, Loeb Classical Library (Cambridge: Harvard University Press, 1962), 5:14]). Elsewhere Plutarch suggests that the Egyptian priests abstained from salt because it was thought to lead to sexual activity due to its heat. Salt reportedly increases fertility in animals because it produces "itches" in the members (*Quaestiones convivales* 5.10, 684e–685f [Paul A. Clement and Herbert B. Hoffleit, eds., *Plutarch's Moralia*, Loeb Classical Library (Cambridge: Harvard University Press, 1969), 8:440–448]). Pliny discusses the types and properties of salt, and notes that it stimulates the appetite (*Historia naturalis* 31.39,73–31.45,105 [W. H. S. Jones, ed., *Pliny: Natural History*, Loeb Classical Library (Cambridge: Harvard University Press, 1963), 8:422–442]. On varieties of salt and salt production in antiquity see Robert J. Forbes, *Studies in Ancient Technology*, 2nd ed. (Leiden: E. J. Brill, 1965), 3:164–196.

24. Basil of Ancyra, *De virg.* 10 (*PG* 30.689A).

The "wings of the soul" are burdened as much by the weakness of the body as by the "lead weight of the flesh."[25] A horse is, after all, no good to the rider if it collapses on the road in exhaustion from weakness and physical neglect. So also a slave is useless to the master if he or she is so neglected and tortured that the master becomes a slave to the slave, due to the latter's infirmity and need for treatment. Thus the body is a necessary vehicle and servant to the soul on the road of virtue; it must be cared for properly, neither starved nor overfed. Virtue exists in the mean and in the harmony of body and soul.[26]

Basil's emphasis on moderation should not suggest, however, that he views fasting as an indifferent matter. Daily dietary restriction is a central, physical ascetic exercise in Basil's program. His physiological understanding of desire requires an equally physiological, essentially medical treatment of reducing the heat and moisture necessary for the production of those humors which increase itching sexual desire and the physical need for ejaculation. He speaks of abstinence (ἐγκράτεια)[27] as the red-hot sword with which the virgin cuts off and cauterizes the heads of the monster of lust, just as Heracles slew the multi-headed Hydra of Greek myth.[28] Abstinence is therefore expected to aid the physical requirements of sexual abstinence and thus to protect the virginity of the soul.[29]

---

25. Ibid. (PG 30.688C–689A).

26. Ibid., 8–11 (PG 30.684C–692D). Michel Aubineau has correctly observed that Basil's essentially moderate stance on ascetic fasting has been "misjudged" by scholars eager to portray Basil as excessively rigorous or narrow, especially in comparison to Gregory of Nyssa's De virginitate (SC 119:140). For examples of the harsh judgment of Basil's treatise see Janini Cuesta, "Dieta y virginidad," 193–197; Jean Daniélou, "Grégoire de Nysse et le Messalianisme," Recherches de science religieuse 48 (1960): 120; and idem, L'être et le temps chez Grégoire de Nysse (Leiden: E. J. Brill, 1970), 52.

27. Basil freely uses terminology and images from earlier non-Christian ethical theory, but emphasizes their more narrow application to the control of bodily desire and pleasure in the ascetic life.

28. Basil of Ancyra, De virg. 67 (PG 30.805B–808A).

29. Basil's choice of terms for food abstinence may reflect the debate over rigorous asceticism represented especially at this time and place by the more radical followers of Eustathius of Sebaste (discussed in more detail in chapter

In the final chapter of his treatise Basil uses the metaphor of sacrifice to discuss the best "manner of asceticism." This is indicated, he claims, by the manner in which Moses slaughtered a calf during the ritual for consecration to the priesthood (Exodus 29:1-13). Moses is instructed to burn "the lobe of the liver (τοῦ μὲν ἥπατος τὸν λοβὸν) but not the whole liver, and the fat covering the stomach but not the stomach itself, and not only the fat of the kidneys but the kidneys themselves with their fat."[30] The liver is the organ of desire or concupiscence (ἐπιθυμία).[31] But the lobe of the liver is the specific location for sinful desires as opposed to useful desire for the good. Thus the virgin will, like Moses, cut away the lobe of her liver—that is, sinful desire—while preserving her desire to serve God.

Likewise, because one cannot live in the body without eating, the virgin's stomach is stripped of its "fat"—that is, gluttony—but remains useful for the preservation of life and health. Here again Basil argues for the need for dietary abstinence while recognizing the requirements of nutrition. Finally, Basil writes that the kidneys are necessary neither to life, as is the stomach, nor to useful desire, as is the liver, but they harbor only the desire for sexual intercourse.[32] Therefore the virgin will "burn" the entire kidneys

---

6). Overall, Basil uses the more general terms for abstinence, ἐγκράτεια or ἀποχή, when giving advice on diet and avoidance of pleasures associated with food (e.g., De virg. 2; 8–12 [PG 30.672C; 684C–693A]). He seems on the other hand to choose the more specific word, νηστεία, in descriptions of excessive mortification, which he has no interest in praising (ibid., 1 [PG 30.669A–672A]), or physical fasting that may "make the body dead in regard to its own passions," but is useless when it is not linked with mortification of the passions of the soul (ibid., 47 [PG 30.761A–D]). Here, I think, Basil's language, while supporting his insistence on the need for both rigorous physical discipline as well as moderation and balance, may be further evidence for what Elm has identified as Basil's intention to defend Eustathian asceticism while criticizing its more extreme interpreters (Virgins of God, 124–131).

30. Basil of Ancyra, De virg. 68 (PG 30.808A–B).

31. On the association of the liver and the belly (γαστήρ) with desire see also Richard Broxton Onians, The Origins of European Thought About the Body, the Mind, the Soul, the World, Time, and Fate, Philosophy of Plato and Aristotle (Cambridge: Cambridge University Press, 1951; reprint, New York: Arno Press, 1973), 84–89.

32. See also De virg. 61 (PG 30.796A), where Basil writes that sexual desire "boils in the kidneys." On the link between the kidneys and sexual drive see

along with their fat, "for it is possible to live without the kidneys, that is without marriage, and from hence already in life to practice the angelic life of virginity."[33] Like the calf slaughtered by Moses, the virgin offers her own body as a sacrifice to God, "to consume in the divine flame of continence evil desire, like the lobe [of the liver], and the excess of food, like the fat covering the stomach, and all of the desire for marital sexual relations, like the kidneys."[34] In this vivid image of asceticism as bodily sacrifice Basil has incorporated aspects of the Platonic theory of the tripartite soul, specifically the link between the concupiscible soul—which concerns both good and illicit desire as well as sexual and nutritional drives—and the liver.[35]

In this passage we see again that the metaphorical, "physiological," and "psychological" connections between diet and sexual function are layered together to such an extent that distinctions are difficult and not, finally, as important as the whole. Gluttony and sexual desire are bound together in the soul as they are linked in the bodily processes of eating, digestion, and the production of sexual humors. Fasting takes on a necessary role as the method by which the sexually continent person physically protects herself or himself against the buildup in the body of the "materials" leading to desire for intercourse. The proper ascetic method, for Basil, takes into account the needs of the body and the usefulness of the body as the servant of the soul. The ascetic diet, therefore, will not be too harsh, but it will cut out gluttony like the fat of the stomach. While the desire for food and the act of eating cannot be entirely eliminated from any human life, the desire for and indulgence in sexual relations are cut away and sacrificed completely.

---

also Peter Brown, *The Body and Society: Men, Women, and Sexual Renunciation in Early Christianity*, Lectures on the History of Religions 13 (New York: Columbia University Press, 1988), 232.

33. Basil of Ancyra, *De virg.* 68 (*PG* 30.808B–D).

34. Ibid. (*PG* 30.808D–809A).

35. See Galen *De cognoscendis curandisque animi morbis* 6 (Kühn 5:26–31); *De locis affectis* 3.5 (Kühn 8:157–160); and *De usu partium* 4.13 (Kühn 3:308–310) where Galen agrees with Plato (*Timaeus* 70e) that the liver is like a "wild beast" which must be nourished in order to further the human species. The irascible soul assists the rational soul in controlling and guarding against this beast.

Basil has taken ideas about diet, digestion, and sexual function from his medical training and applied them to the daily life and training of one who chooses to live in perpetual chastity. Galen, Rufus, and others debated the benefits and dangers of sexual activity and recommended dietary regimens to increase or reduce the production of semen according to the needs and afflictions of their patients. Basil uses explicit, graphic physiological arguments to respond to the needs of virgins who have opted out of the human process of generation, yet must complete their earthly lives in bodies in which the desire for sexual union has been implanted.

In his treatise on virginity, then, Basil of Ancyra reveals himself to be very much the physician. This is so not simply in his focus on the body of the virgin or his use of notions of diet, the humors, and sexual desire found in Galen's and other Greco-Roman medical writings. Rather, Basil displays a physician's sense of confidence that the body can be controlled, indeed transformed, by means of the correctly prescribed ascetic regimen. Further, Basil displays the same confidence, seen earlier in the Stoics, Plutarch, and Clement of Alexandria, that bodily *askesis* helps perfect and protect the soul. His intention is to assist the one who is in training for the course of virginity and virtue by describing the physical realities of chastity as well as the potential defilements in food, activities, and associations.[36] Only by understanding these realities and dangers can the virgin hope to pursue her goal safely and to become the incorruptible bride of Christ.

Gregory of Nyssa

Basil's treatise raises many of the issues central to the general patristic discussion of fasting, gluttony, and desire. While the claims that overeating inflames lust or that fasting reduces evil desire are fairly common in Christian ascetic literature,[37] some

---

36. Basil of Ancyra, *De virg.* 9 (*PG* 30.688C).

37. E.g., Basil of Caesarea, *Regulae fusius tractatae* 19.2 (*PG* 31.964A–B); John Chrysostom, *Homilia III de statuis* 4 (*PG* 49.51); Jerome, *Epistola* 22.11 (Isidorus Hilberg, ed., *Eusebii Hieronymi Epistulae*, CSEL 54:158); Evagrius, *Sententiae ad virginem* 40 (Hugo Gressman, ed., *Nonnenspiegel und Mönchsspiegel des Euagrios Pontikos*, TU 39,4b [Leipzig: Hinrichs, 1913], 149); and idem, *De diversis malignis cogitationibus* 2 (*PG* 79.1201D).

authors, like Basil, are more specific about the medical theories that support these claims.[38] This is the case with the Cappadocian writer Gregory of Nyssa (c.335–394), the younger brother of Basil of Caesarea and Macrina, whose theological work has had profound influence on the development of Christian asceticism and mysticism. Gregory's treatise *On Virginity* (370–371 C.E.), thought to be his earliest known work, shows the influence of Basil of Ancyra's arguments on diet, taste, and pleasure.[39] Yet although Gregory's subject is Christian virginity, his approach in this particular text is more "philosophical" and abstract than Basil's. For while Basil's treatise on virginity is steeped in many of the same Neoplatonic images as Gregory's, Basil's treatment is much more practical and specific. His intention is to describe in detail the realities and dangers of the life of female chastity in order to assist the virgin in becoming the incorruptible bride of Christ. Gregory's stated purpose is rather "to create in the readers a desire for the life of virtue."[40] Further, while Gregory's "virgin" is not identified as being either male or female, Basil focuses specifically on the female dedicated to the life of perpetual chastity.

Keeping these differences in approach and subject in mind, one can nevertheless trace the influence of Basil's text and ideas. Scholars have identified several parallel passages in the two treatises. For example, in chapter twenty-one, Gregory compares pleasure to a stream from one source which divides into the streams of the senses, using language similar to Basil's.[41] Gregory also

38. Basil of Ancyra's work nevertheless remains distinct among early Christian writings on virginity for its very frank use of physiological details and images (P. Thomas Camelot, "Les traités 'de virginitate' au IVe siècle," in *Mystique et Continence: Travaux scientifiques du VIIe Congrès international d'Avon,* Études Carmélitaines [Brugge: Desclée de Brouwer, 1952], 290–291).

39. Michel Aubineau writes that, of the sources for Gregory's treatise, "no text exerted a more profound and clear influence on this work" than Basil of Ancyra's *De virginitate* (*Grégoire de Nysse,* SC 119:137). On Gregory's treatise in general see Aubineau's introduction (SC 119:29–243) and Jean Gribomont, "Le panégyrique de la virginité, oeuvre de jeunesse de Grégoire de Nysse," *Revue d'ascétique et mystique* 43 (1967): 249–266.

40. Prologue 1 (SC 119:246).

41. This parallel is noted by José Janini Cuesta, "Dieta y virginidad," 194–195. The Greek in Basil's text reads: Μία γὰρ οὖσα τῷ γένει ἡ ἡδονή, ὥσπερ πηγή τις ἀπὸ σαρκῶν ἀναβλύζει, καὶ καθάπερ εἰς πέντε ὀχετούς, τὰς

argues that the sense of taste must be guarded especially, since it "seems somehow to be the most direct [of the senses], as if the mother of that which is forbidden." He explains that the pleasures of immoderate eating and drinking necessarily produce an abundance of "evils that are independent of one's own will" in the body.[42] Gregory does not identify these "evils" nor does he equate them with the abundance of sexual humors produced by overeating, as does Basil. Thus one does not find an explicit physiological argument connecting the pleasures of eating to the physical need for sexual activity. Nevertheless the connection is implied in Gregory's well-tempered language.

Using the medical imagery familiar from Basil's treatise, Gregory writes that in order to separate the soul from temptations to pleasure and to keep the body calm and free from the "troubles of satiety," the "practitioner of temperance" will carefully measure and fulfill bodily need, distinguishing it from pleasure.[43] Gregory recommends that one maintain the body's health through a balance of the four qualities of hot, cold, moist, and dry, not allowing any one quality to dominate by a deviation in diet. Like the wise charioteer, the mind holds the reins of the body and will meet its needs in moderation and self-control. If the body is already in a state of excessive heat due to youthfulness, the mind

---

πέντε αἰσθήσεις διαιρεθεῖσα, διὰ τούτων ἐπὶ τὰ αἰσθητὰ ἔνδοθεν ῥεῖ (PG 30.677B). The Greek in Gregory's text reads: Μία γὰρ οὖσα τῷ γένει ἡ ἡδονή, καθὼς ἀκούειν ἔστι τῶν σοφῶν, ὥσπερ τὸ ὕδωρ ἐκ μιᾶς πηγῆς εἰς διαφόρους ὀχετοὺς μεριζόμενον, δι' ἑκάστου τῶν αἰσθητηρίων τοῖς φιληδόνοις ἐγκαταμίγνυται (SC 119:504). Although the language is very close, Michel Aubineau hesitates to call Basil of Ancyra's treatise a *direct* influence on this passage, recognizing the possibility of a common source, particularly in view of Gregory's reference to "the philosophers." Nevertheless there are several other parallel passages in the two treatises on virginity. In addition, Aubineau identifies what he considers an example of direct influence in the authors' common use of the very rare word συναποσχίζεσθαι (to be torn in two) in connection with the woes of marriage and child rearing, and with similar accompanying metaphors and use of scripture (PG 30.716C [chapter 23] and SC 119:288 [chapter 3.6]). See Aubineau, *Grégoire de Nysse*, SC 119:138–139.

42. Gregory of Nyssa, *De virginitate* 21.2 (SC 119:506); see Basil of Ancyra, *De virg.* 6 (PG 30.681B–C).

43. Gregory of Nyssa, *De virg.* 21.2–3 (SC 119:506–510). In general on Gregory and medicine see Mary Emily Keenan, "St. Gregory of Nyssa and the Medical Profession," *Bulletin of the History of Medicine* 15 (1944): 150–161.

will certainly not add to the fire, nor will the mind allow the body that has been chilled by disease or the passage of time to be filled with that which is excessively cooling or weak.[44] Gregory argues that the mind is hindered as much from weakness of the body caused by excessive mortification as from indulgence in sensual pleasure.[45] "This is the most perfect goal of abstinence, not to focus on the sufferings of the body, but on the facility of the instruments of the soul."[46] In these arguments for moderation in asceticism and diet, then, one detects what one scholar calls "an undeniable exploitation of Basil of Ancyra's text by Gregory of Nyssa."[47]

Gregory does not discuss the ascetic diet in any detail, nor does he classify any foods as dangerous or useful to the ascetic regimen of moderation. He criticizes unnamed ascetics who through lack of discipline trust their own judgment rather than the teachings of the Gospels, commandments, or an ascetic rule. They rely on dreams for revelation and guidance, and prefer "idleness" to honest work for their food. Further, Gregory condemns the errors of those he knows who "persist in hunger to the point of death, as if 'such sacrifices are pleasing to God' [Hebrews 13:16]," as well as those who not only indulge the pleasures of the stomach but cohabit openly with women.[48] Gregory thus points to broader

44. Gregory of Nyssa, *De virg.* 22.2 (SC 119:516–518). On heating and cooling the body according to its condition and age, see Basil of Ancyra, *De virg.* 8 (*PG* 30.685B–C) and 12 (693B). In the latter passage Basil writes: "Just as in the case of those who are boiling with heat because of (their) youthfulness and (are) vigorous in body, one must not add fire to the fire, . . . so also one must not even more harmfully pour cold (substances) over one who has grown cold due to infirmity. But just as in the former case we exhaust the natural heat by taking away external materials (τὰς ἔξωθεν ὕλας), so also in the latter case we will revive the one who is consumed by labors and already dried up because of age and sickness by assisting with external stimulus."

45. Gregory of Nyssa, *De virg.* 22.1–2 (SC 119:510–520); Basil of Ancyra, *De virg.* 8; 10 (*PG* 30.684C–685C; 688C–689A).

46. Gregory of Nyssa, *De virg.* 22.2 (SC 119:520); Basil of Ancyra, *De virg.* 12 (*PG* 30.692D–693B).

47. Aubineau, *Grégoire de Nysse*, SC 119:40–41.

48. *De virg.* 23.3–4 (SC 119:530–540). Many of these criticisms may be aimed at Messalianism (SC 119:534–540), an elusive movement with possible Syrian origins, which emphasized continual prayer and seems to have downplayed the ascetic value of labor. Recent scholarship points to Gregory's own

discussion and controversy over issues of authority, inspiration, and moderation in ascetic lifestyle and discipline—issues that will continue to shape ascetic discourse through the late fourth century and into the fifth. This will become more clear as we encounter other sources and personalities, including Jerome.

Jerome

Jerome (c. 342–420) is known for his Latin translations of the Bible and numerous ancient texts, his scholarship and commentaries on scripture, his extensive network of correspondence, his entanglement in more than one bitter dispute, and his ascetic theory and lifestyle. Educated in Rome, Jerome also traveled widely in the East, where he perfected his Greek and Hebrew and spent two disappointing years as a solitary monk in the Syrian desert of

sympathies for and connections with Messalian teachings and teachers. And Susanna Elm's recent study of female monasticism argues that common threads connecting Gregory of Nyssa, the Messalians, Eustathius, Basil of Caesarea, and Basil of Ancyra are the issues of communal ascetic life of men and women, and the role and prominence of female ascetics within the group or community (*Virgins of God,* 190–196). On Messalianism see also Daniélou, "Grégoire de Nysse et le Messalianisme, 119–134; Jean Gribomont, "Le dossier des origenes du Messalianisme," in *Epektasis: Mélanges Patristiques offerts au Cardinal Jean Daniélou,* ed. Jacques Fontaine and Charles Kannengiesser (Paris: Beauchesne, 1972), 621–625; idem, "Le monachisme au IVe s. en Asie Mineure: de Gangres au Messalianisme," *Studia Patristica* 2, TU 64,9 (Berlin: Akademie-Verlag, 1957), 400–415; Reinhart Staats, "Basilius als lebende Mönchsregel in Gregors von Nyssa De virginitate, " *Vigiliae christianae* 39 (1985): 228–255; idem, "Messalianism and Anti-Messalianism in Gregory of Nyssa's *De virginitate,* " *Patristic and Byzantine Review* 2 (1983): 27–44; and Columba Stewart, 'Working the Earth of the Heart': The *Messalian Controversy in History, Texts, and Language to AD 431,* Oxford Theological Monographs (Oxford: Clarendon Press, 1991). For the important ancient sources on Messalianism, also see Michael Kmosko, ed., *Liber Graduum, Patrologia Syriaca* 1,3 (Paris: Firmin-Didot, 1926), clxx–ccxciii (Kmosko does not include Gregory of Nyssa's treatise in his survey). On the issue of spiritual marriage or cohabitation see especially Hans Achelis, *Virgines Subintroductae: Ein Beitrag zum VII Kapitel des I Korintherbriefs* (Leipzig: J. C. Hinrichs, 1902); Elizabeth A. Clark, "John Chrysostom and the *Subintroductae,* " *Church History* 46 (1977): 171–185; and idem, *Jerome, Chrysostom, and Friends: Essays and Translations,* Studies in Women and Religion 2 (Lewiston, N.Y.: Edwin Mellen Press, 1979). Gregory's condemnation of cohabitation shows parallels in language and argumentation with Basil of Ancyra, *De virg.* 43 (*PG* 30.756A–B); see Aubineau (SC 119:539).

Chalcis (375–377). After alienating many in Roman social and ecclesiastical circles with his rigid and elitist views, he left Rome (in 385) and founded men's and women's monasteries in Bethlehem with his dear friend Paula.[49]

Jerome's writings are key to our understanding of fourth- and fifth-century ascetic theory, especially as it relates to the developing ideology of virginity. If virginity for Gregory of Nyssa can be described as "close to being a metaphor for an inner attitude of detachment and spiritual uplifting of the mind,"[50] in the writings of Jerome virginity and chastity are drawn in starkly physical lines. Like Basil of Ancyra, Jerome reminds his readers that sexual desire was implanted in humans by God for the purpose of procreation. For an individual to repress that desire is therefore no small effort. Writing to the widow Furia between 394 and 396, Jerome urges her to live the rest of her life in chastity. He recognizes, however, that whereas "all other sins are external" and may easily be avoided, only desire (libido) is internal. Implanted in humans by God in order to incite them to procreation, desire quickly exceeds its boundaries and becomes sinful. It is therefore a great feat of virtue to overcome this enemy within, to live in the flesh but not for the flesh.[51] Indeed, it is an act against nature to

49. For a helpful general treatment of Jerome's life and thought, see J. N. D. Kelly, *Jerome: His Life, Writings, and Controversies* (London: Duckworth, 1975). Kelly places Jerome's birth in the year 331, but others have argued for a later date, up to 347. See Brown, *The Body and Society*, 366, n.1. On Jerome's association with aristocratic Roman women see Clark, *Jerome, Chrysostom, and Friends*, 35–106 and Kelly, *Jerome*, 91–103. On Jerome's social network more broadly, and on the use of network analysis in historical reconstruction, see Elizabeth A. Clark, *The Origenist Controversy: The Cultural Construction of an Early Christian Debate* (Princeton: Princeton University Press, 1992), 11–42 (esp. 25–33); and L. Michael White, "Finding the Ties that Bind: Issues from Social Description," *Semeia* 56 (1992): 3–22.

50. Rosemary Radford Ruether, "Misogynism and Virginal Feminism in the Fathers of the Church," in *Religion and Sexism: Images of Women in the Jewish and Christian Traditions*, ed. Rosemary Radford Ruether (New York: Simon and Schuster, 1974), 177.

51. *Ep.* 54.9 (CSEL 54:475). Jerome held the view of many advocates for the virginal life that although God had encouraged procreation during the earlier period of the biblical patriarchs and under the "law," with the coming of Christ and the time of the "gospel," virginity and celibacy are the better choice (see for example *Adv. Jov.* 1.16–24 [*PL* 23.245C–255A]).

repudiate the natural function of the body—that is, sexual inter-course and procreation.[52] Here Jerome makes the same argument as Basil of Ancyra, that God actually added sexual desire to the "natural" fabric of the human body—and both make this point in the context of arguments in favor of virginity. Yet, like Basil, Jerome believes that there was no sex in paradise before the fall—it was the fall which made marriage necessary.[53]

Throughout his letters offering advice on ascetic living, Jerome warns of the ever-present dangers of sexual attraction and the ease with which his readers may slip into sin and lose their treasure of chastity. He often quotes I Corinthians 9:27 ("I mortify my body and bring it into subjection") and wonders how anyone can be confident of his or her chastity if even Paul is fearful of the power of the flesh.[54] So alarmed is he at the possibility of falling into sensuality that he refuses, in his letter to Eustochium (Paula's young daughter), to praise virginity—as others had done—but pro-poses rather to offer advice for its protection.[55] Jerome does not share Basil of Ancyra's optimistic view that the ascetic body can be controlled and transformed in this life into an angelic, incor-ruptible body in which lust no longer lives.[56] While Eustochium and other virgins may keep in mind their heavenly reward for their earthly struggles,[57] in this life they must remain fearful and vigilant. "As long as we are constrained in this fragile body, as long as we have our treasure in earthen vessels,[58] and the spirit lusts against the flesh and the flesh against the spirit,[59] there is no certain victory."[60]

---

52. *Ep.* 130.10 (CSEL 56:191).
53. On these ideas in Jerome see below, chap. 4.
54. *Epp.* 79.7 (CSEL 55:95); 22.5 (CSEL 54:149–150); 54.8 (CSEL 54:474).
55. *Ep.* 22.22–23 (CSEL 54:174–175): "virginitatem non efferimus, sed ser-vamus." Cf. *Ep.* 22.2 (CSEL 54:145): "non me nunc laudes virginitatis esse dicturum." This is a possible instance of borrowing from Basil of Ancyra's *De virginitate*. In his opening chapter Basil writes, Ἐγὼ δὲ σοι, . . . οὐχὶ παρθενίας ὕμνον (*PG* 30.672A); see Aubineau, *Grégoire de Nysse*, SC 119:519, n.3.
56. Basil of Ancyra, *De virg.* 51–53 (*PG* 30.772A–776A). Of course Basil also recognizes the possibility that, if lust should be allowed to creep back in due to contact with males, the virgin could well lose her achievement.
57. *Ep.* 22.41 (CSEL 54:209).
58. 2 Corinthians 4:7.
59. Galatians 5:17.
60. *Ep.* 22.3–4 (CSEL 54:146–148).

Jerome argues that the five senses are the "windows of the soul" through which vice has access and the individual is tempted to sinful pleasures. He uses the familiar metaphor of the chariot-eer controlling unruly horses to suggest that the soul must guide and control the natural operation of the senses. While a human can live without four of the senses—sight, hearing, smell, and touch—it is not possible to exist without tasting food. Therefore one must use discretion and moderation in diet in order to protect the soul from temptations to pleasure.[61]

Fasting takes on a key role in the ascetic life as a useful aid in the protection of bodily integrity. In fact, Jerome insists that it is *impossible* to preserve chastity without fasting.[62] He bases this argument on the physiological connection between eating and sexual desire. When the stomach is full and food goes undigested, the body is inflamed and the genitals are titillated.[63] Jerome is therefore concerned that ascetic men and women always eat in moderation and remain vigilant especially after a meal. When the body is full the mind becomes like watered ground in which the "thorns of lust" spring up. Thus he warns Eustochium to "seize the shield of faith" if sensuous thoughts distract her after she has eaten.[64]

An abundance of food leads to sexual desire by increasing the heat of the body. This is especially dangerous for young per-sons whose natural heat is strong enough that any additional heat from food or wine makes their bodies like fiery volcanoes.[65] The virgin or ascetic male will therefore follow a cooling regimen. Here Jerome refers specifically to Galen's dietary advice on the healthfulness of cooling foods for those in the prime of

61. *Adv. Jov.* 2.8–10 (*PL* 23.310B–313A).
62. *Ep.* 22.11 (CSEL 54:158).
63. *Ep.* 54.10 (CSEL 54:477).
64. *Ep.* 22.17 (CSEL 54:165).
65. *Ep.* 54.9 (CSEL 54:474–475). See also Dale Martin's discussion of Rufus of Ephesus's treatise on the "Regimen for Virgins" (*The Corinthian Body* [New Haven: Yale University Press, 1995], 224–226). Rufus argues that matur-ing girls should avoid foods such as meat and wine which heat the already-over-heated body and accelerate processes leading to sexual desire. The text Περὶ παρθένων διαίτης is found in Oribasius, *Libri Incerti* 18 (Ioannes Raeder, ed., *Oribasius: Collectionum medicarum reliquiae* [Amsterdam: Adolf M. Hakkert, 1964], 4:106–109).

life.[66] While meat and wine are useful for older persons who suffer from phlegm and coldness,[67] in general they are suitable only to those who indulge in sexual activity. By avoiding these foods the ascetic physically assists the soul in preserving chastity. In short, "without Ceres and Bacchus, Venus is cold."[68]

Jerome's arguments in favor of ascetic fasting are developed particularly in the second book of his treatise *Against Jovinian*, written in 393. A monk and celibate himself, Jovinian gained followers in Rome with his persuasive and scriptural critique of rigorous asceticism and monastic elitism. Although Jovinian's position must be pieced together from Jerome's summary, he apparently emphasized the power of baptism to remove sin and shield the Christian from the power of the devil. Baptized Christians are equal in perfection whether they are married or celibate, and whether they practice fasting or make thankful use of food. Further, there is only one heavenly reward for faithful Christians, not different rewards based on individual merit.[69] Jovinian opposed rigorous ascetic fasting and abstinence from particular foods—especially meat, based on the assertion that animals were created for use by humans. His case is strengthened by New Testament passages affirming that all food is clean[70] and that "nothing is to be rejected if it is received with thanksgiving."[71] After all, Paul himself had warned that "liars" would come forbidding marriage and the eating of certain foods, foods which were created by God for human consumption.[72]

Jovinian's criticism's landed too close to home for the rigorist Jerome, and Jerome's treatise reveals his strong defensive reaction.

---

66. *Ep.* 54.9 (CSEL 54:475–476). See also *Ep.* 125.7 (CSEL 56:124); *Adv. Jov.* 2.11 (PL 23.313B–C). On Jerome's use of Galen's work see Pierre Courcelle, *Late Latin Writers and Their Greek Sources*, trans. Harry E. Wedeck (Cambridge: Harvard University Press, 1969), 86–87. See also Arthur Stanley Pease, "Medical Allusions in the Works of St. Jerome," *Harvard Studies in Classical Philology* 25 (1914): 73–86.

67. *Ep.* 54.9 (CSEL 54:476).

68. Ibid.; *Adv. Jov.* 2.7 (PL 23.310A–B). Jerome is quoting from Terence's *Eunuchus*, 918.

69. *Adv. Jov.* 1.3 (PL 23.224). See Kelly, *Jerome*, 180–189.

70. Romans 14:20.

71. I Timothy 4:4.

72. I Timothy 4:1–3; *Adv. Jov.* 2.5 (PL 23.303A–304A).

In order to refute Jovinian's arguments Jerome asserts that animals were not originally created for human consumption and refers to the writings of Galen, Aristotle, Pliny, and others to show that there were numerous medical uses for them (as ingredients in various external remedies).[73] He borrows heavily from Porphyry's *De abstinentia* (without mentioning his source) in his descriptions of differing food preferences, food restrictions, and the value of abstinence in other religions and cultures.[74] This is followed by a string of biblical *exempla* of fasting. Here Jerome argues that even after Adam was cast out of paradise—because of his refusal to abstain from the fruit of one tree—humans were not allowed to eat animal flesh. It was only after the great flood, when God saw that humans were wicked and greedy, that they were given the freedom to eat meat.[75] Finally, Jerome defends himself against charges of heresy. Specifically, he attempts to distinguish his position from Marcion, Tatian, and those mentioned in 1 Timothy 4:3 who forbid marriage and command food abstinence. What these figures have in common, according to Jerome, is a disdain for the gifts of God in creation (that is, food and procreation). Jerome claims that his own advocacy of celibacy and fasting implies no such condemnation of creation.[76] In turn, he labels Jovinian as the Latin-speaking reincarnation of the heretic Basilides, the "master of luxury."[77]

Underlying Jerome's defense of fasting is his understanding of the connection between the pleasure of eating and sexual desire. Thus in response to Jovinian's arguments against ascetic refusal to eat meat, Jerome accuses his opponent of advocating both gluttony

---

73. *Adv. Jov.* 2.6 (*PL* 23.305A–306A).

74. Ibid., 4.7; 13–14 (*PL* 23.307D–310A; 315C–319B); Porphyry, *De abst.* 4.2–22 (Nauck, 228–269). This "flagrant instance of plagiarism" is discussed by Courcelle, *Late Latin Writers*, 73–74. See also Kelly, *Jerome*, 184.

75. *Adv. Jov.* 2.15–17 (*PL* 23.319B–326B); Genesis 6:5; 8:21; 9:1–3. J. N. D. Kelly points out that Jerome's chapters on biblical fasting are based largely on Tertullian's *De ieiunio* (*Jerome*, 184). Note that Jerome's argument that there was no meat-eating in paradise will be matched with the idea that there was no sexual activity before the fall (see the section on Jerome in chap. 5, below, and see *Adv. Jov.* 1.16; 29 [*PL* 23.246A; 263A]; *Ep.* 22.19 [CSEL 54:169]).

76. Ibid., 2.16 (*PL* 23.323B–324C).

77. Ibid., 2.37 (*PL* 23.350A–B).

and lust. He summarizes Jovinian's teachings as "fast rarely, marry frequently. For you cannot accomplish the work of marriage unless you consume mead, and meat, and solid food. Vigor is necessary for lust."[78] Jerome's teaching, in contrast, is "wherever there is chastity and sanctity, there is temperance."[79] Therefore the one who wishes to maintain bodily chastity will avoid heavy and heating foods. For a full stomach is the "seed plot of lust."[80]

Jerome levels particularly strong warnings against eating meat. Throughout his writings, meat takes on such dangerous qualities that it becomes a symbol for lustful indulgence. But according to Jerome meat-eating fuels not only the most gluttonous or sexually promiscuous behavior, but even marital procreation, which he has acknowledged as legitimate (if not particularly praiseworthy). He writes to the widow Salvina in 400 C.E.: "Let them eat flesh who serve the flesh, whose heat is worked off in sexual intercourse, who are bound to husbands and give attention to generation and offspring. Let the ones whose wombs carry fetuses fill their stomachs also with flesh."[81] Thus although Jerome knows that his views on sexual and dietary abstinence are vulnerable to the label of heresy, here he disdainfully links meat-eating and pregnancy as service to "the flesh."[82]

While warning against the dangers of heating foods Jerome recommends a cooling diet in general.[83] To the young widow Furia, for example, he suggests a cooling regimen that includes drinking only water, avoiding heating legumes (*legumina*—he does not identify which ones he classifies as heating), and avoiding whatever is flatulent and difficult to digest.[84] If her stomach is weak,

78. *Adv. Jov.* 2.37 (*PL* 23.351A).
79. *Ep.* 54.5 (CSEL 54:470).
80. *Adv. Jov.* 2.7 (*PL* 23.310A).
81. *Ep.* 79.7 (CSEL 55:96).
82. The connection between meat-eating and procreation will be central to our discussion of asceticism and paradise in chaps. 5 and 6.
83. On Jerome's cooling diet see also Aline Rousselle, "Abstinence et continence dans les monastères de Gaul méridionale à la fin de l'Antiquité et au début du Moyen Age: Étude d'un régime alimentaire et de sa fonction," in *Hommages à André Dupont: Études médiévales languedociennes* (Montpellier: Fédération historique de Languedoc méditerranéen et du Roussillon, 1974), 240; 249–250.
84. According to Galen all legumes are flatulent and difficult to digest, especially beans and chickpeas. Flatulence is sometimes removed, however,

Jerome does allow a little wine (1 Timothy 5:23). Vegetables or herbs (*holera*) are good for "young Christians" but, Jerome notes, they are harmless only if eaten in moderation—for undigested food and the consequent belches heat the body more than anything. Therefore it is best to keep a spare diet which leaves the belly always hungry.[85]

For the young monk Rusticus, Jerome recommends fasts to cool the heat of the body. Fasting is part of a lifestyle marked by sordid and simple dress; the avoidance of baths and women; scriptural study; and physical labor, including gardening and fishing.[86] Again Jerome cautions his reader against immoderate fasts, which cause indigestion, the "parent of lust."[87] He claims that some solitary monks have turned "melancholy" due to the "dampness of cells, immoderation of fasts, tediousness of solitude, and excessive

---

by proper preparation. For example when lentils are completely boiled the flatulence is avoided (*Pro puero epileptico consilium* 5 [Kühn 11:373–374]; cf. *Hippocratis de acutorum morborum victu liber et Galeni commentarius* 4.82 [Kühn 15:874–876]). Likewise roasting removes flatulence from chickpeas (*De alimentorum facultatibus* 1.22 [Kühn 6:534]; cf. Pliny, *Hist. nat.* 22.72,148 [Jones 6:398]). Galen classes beans and chickpeas among those foods that tend to generate semen (*De simplicium medicamentorum temperamentis ac facultatibus* 5.23 [Kühn 11:777]), but not legumes in general. In fact Galen recommends legumes, which are "not very nutritious," for the treatment of plethoric conditions in which the body has taken in more nourishment from food than it needs (*De sanitate tuenda* 6.6 [Kühn 6:409]). Finally, Galen classes lentils as heating and drying; however, as noted in chap. 2, he considers those foods that are both heating and drying (as opposed to heating and moistening) not to be generative of semen (*De san. tuenda* 5.8 [Kühn 6:351]; *De simp. med. temp. ac fac.* 5.23 [Kühn 11:776–777]; and *In Hippocratis vel Polybi opus de salubri victus ratione privatorum commentarius* 2 [Kühn 15:179]).

85. *Ep.* 54.10 (CSEL 54:476–477). The use of the words *legumina* and *holera* (or *olera*) in both ancient and modern sources is often confusing. Jacques André writes, "The word *legumina* designates primarily the edible plants in pods, of which one would eat the seeds, as opposed to vegetables properly called (*holera* or *olera*), of which one would eat the root or green parts, and to cereals (*frumenta*)" (*L'Alimentation et la cuisine à Rome* [Paris: Les Belles Lettres, 1981], 34). Thus *holera* could include roots, bulbs, shoots, herbs, gourds, and salad greens. See the appendix, "List of Alimenta" to Celsus's *De medicina* in W. G. Spencer, ed., *Celsus: De Medicina*, Loeb Classical Library (Cambridge: Harvard University Press, 1948 and 1953), 1:490–493.

86. *Ep.* 125.7–11 (CSEL 56:124–131).

87. Ibid., 7 (CSEL 56:124).

study."[88] To Paulinus of Nola Jerome writes, "Let your food be cheap and [taken] in the evening: vegetables and legumes, and once in a while as a great delicacy you might take some little fish."[89] He does not identify this as a cooling diet, but it is similar to those recommended to Furia and Rusticus.

In Jerome's letter to Eustochium, which may be read as a treatise on virginity, he instructs Eustochium to fast every day in moderation, never filling her stomach. He reminds her, "The one who mortifies her bodily members . . . is not afraid to say, 'I have become like a wineskin in the frost,[90] whatever moisture there was in me has been dried up.'"[91] Jerome is alluding to the notion that the moisture (humor) of the body, the abundance of which leads to sexual desire, is dried through fasting.[92] Although Jerome does not suggest a particular diet for Eustochium, he expresses contempt for virgins who eat meat and drink wine, and who brand those who do fast as "Manichean." These same women are in truth not virgins at all, Jerome says, as they are betrayed by the evidence of pregnancy.[93] Likewise, he condemns women who only pretend to fast:

> As soon as they see anyone, they groan, they lower the brow and with the face covered they free barely one eye for seeing. Their dress is dark, their girdle is made of sackcloth, their hands and feet are filthy; only the stomach—which cannot be seen—is inflamed by food.[94]

88. Ibid., 16 (CSEL 56:135). This letter, written in 411 C.E., demonstrates Jerome's apparent change in attitude toward solitary ascetic withdrawal as opposed to community life and ecclesiastical monasticism. Jerome also encourages Rusticus to aspire to be a cleric (17 [CSEL 56:136–137]). For a good overview of Jerome's early attraction to the desert and later disillusionment with solitary asceticism, see Philip Rousseau, Ascetics, Authority, and the Church in the Age of Jerome and Cassian (Oxford: Oxford University Press, 1978), 99–139.

89. Ep. 58.6 (CSEL 54:535).

90. Psalms 119:83.

91. Ep. 22.17 (CSEL 54:165–166).

92. Two manuscripts of Epistle 22 offer this reading of the above sentence, "whatever moisture of lust (umoris libidinis) there was in me has been dried up" (CSEL 54:166). Jerome usually writes of fasting as cooling as opposed to heating. The opposition of drying/moistening is found in other ascetic writers, including Basil of Ancyra and John Cassian. See also Rousselle, "Abstinence et continence," 248–250.

93. Ep. 22.13 (CSEL 54:160–161).

94. Ibid., 27 (CSEL 54:184).

Therefore the true virgin is known by the sincerity and intensity of her fasts. Not only does fasting help protect her from the sexual temptations threatening her prized integrity, true fasting does not lead to prideful displays of bodily neglect. The body of the virgin, cool and dry, pale and thin from fasting,[95] is a "temple" more precious to God than any gold or silver vessel.[96] She must therefore guard the temple of her body and give no man access. Only her bridegroom, Jesus, may come to her in her chamber, gaze upon her, play with her, and touch her.[97]

It is clear that Jerome associates meat-eating with the increase of heat in the body and therefore with sexual function. It is not surprising, therefore, that his recommended diet for a young child—who has not begun to mature sexually—is significantly different from that for an adult or adolescent ascetic. In his letter to Paula's daughter-in-law Laeta (403 C.E.), Jerome suggests that Laeta allow her own infant daughter (named after her grandmother) to eat meat, bathe, and drink wine for her stomach. These indulgences are made because severe abstinence is dangerous for children, and may cause such weakness that "her feet fail before they begin to run."[98] Her food should consist of "small vegetables, the best wheat flour (*simila*), and sometimes small fish."[99] Even so, Paula's eating habits should be such that she is always left hungry. Yet again Jerome warns against "long and immoderate fasts in which weeks are linked together and even oil in food and apples are avoided," especially for young people. Such fasts are dangerous because extreme abstinence is short-lived and often leads to gluttony, whereas moderation and regularity allows

95. Ibid., 17 (CSEL 54:164).

96. Ibid., 23 (CSEL 54:175).

97. Ibid., 25 (CSEL 54:178–180); Patricia Cox Miller, "The Blazing Body: Ascetic Desire in Jerome's Letter to Eustochium," *Journal of Early Christian Studies* 1 (1993): 21–45.

98. *Ep.* 107.8 (CSEL 55:299); cf. *Ep.* 54.9 (CSEL 54:475).

99. *Ep.* 107.10 (CSEL 55:301). Elsewhere Jerome classes *simila* among difficult to procure or extravagant foods which the one who fasts regularly should not eat (*Ep.* 52.12 [CSEL 54:435]; cf. *Ep.* 52.6 [CSEL 54:425]). On *simila* see also Celsus *De medicina* 2.18.4 (Spencer 1:192). Celsus classes *simila* as the second strongest wheat, next to *siligo*. See also Naum Jasny, *The Wheats of Classical Antiquity*, The Johns Hopkins University Studies in Historical and Political Science 62/3 (Baltimore: The Johns Hopkins Press, 1944), 67.

the ascetic to maintain perpetual abstinence.[100] While Jerome counsels moderation and even mild indulgence in young Paula's regimen, nevertheless her goal is the same as that of the adult recipients of Jerome's epistolary advice: "by means of vigils and fasts she mortifies her body and brings it into subjection,[101] . . . by means of the chill of continence she longs to extinguish the flame of lust and passions of burning youth."[102]

Jerome's disapproval of immoderate fasting in these letters must be balanced with the more rigorous tone in letters dating from earlier in his career. For example, in 384 C.E. Jerome wrote to Marcella praising her sister Asella, who had been dedicated to Christian virginity since the age of ten. From the age of twelve Asella practiced an extreme asceticism. Enclosed in a narrow cell, "she performed fasting for recreation, hunger was refreshment." Her food consisted of bread, salt, and cold water.[103] She ate only every two or three days, and continued in this regimen until she was fifty. Asella's abstinence can only be described as severe. Yet Jerome claims that her body remained healthy and her digestion good.[104] He does not question her rigorous self-denial, but rather holds her up as an example—to other young girls—of the "pattern of the perfect life."[105]

The disparity between Jerome's praise of one girl's meager diet and his recommendation, almost twenty years later in Letter 107, that another young girl follow a significantly more moderate and varied regimen may in part be due to the controversy surrounding the death of Paula's daughter Blesilla in 384. Widowed after only seven months of marriage,[106] Blesilla was converted to asceticism at the age of twenty. In dramatic contrast to her former frivolous and worldly life, she pursued a life of fasting, simple dress, prayer, study, and penitence.[107] Blesilla's fierce asceticism caused enough

---

100. *Ep.* 107.10 (CSEL 55:301–302).
101. 1 Corinthians 9:27.
102. *Ep.* 107.11 (CSEL 55:302).
103. *Ep.* 24.2–3 (CSEL 54:215).
104. Ibid., 4 (CSEL 54:216).
105. Ibid., 1 (CSEL 54:214).
106. *Ep.* 22.15 (CSEL 54:162–163).
107. *Ep.* 38.2–4 (CSEL 54:290–291).

scandal at Rome—and therefore enough criticism of Jerome—that Jerome felt compelled to defend himself and Blesilla in a letter to Marcella. He claimed that Blesilla's paltry food should not scandalize others, especially since John the Baptist ate locusts.[108] Indeed, Christian ascetics should not be criticized for imitating the apostles.[109]

Less than four months after her conversion, Blesilla was dead. The whispered accusations at her funeral were (according to Jerome) that the girl was "killed by fasting," and that the "detestable race of monks" should therefore be driven out of Rome for leading Paula and her beloved daughter astray.[110] Jerome's letter of condolence to the grieving Paula betrays his bitter resentment at these accusations. Downplaying the shocking nature of such an early death, he instead praises the self-mortification that marked Blesilla's last weeks of life. "Her steps tottered due to illness, and her thin neck barely held her pale, trembling face upright. And yet she always held either a prophet or a gospel in her hand."[111] He then reminds Paula that Christians should greet death with joy, since paradise is open to them. As Blesilla now "rules with Christ," Paula's tears are "detestable," "filled with sacrilege," and "completely filled with unbelief."[112] Although Jerome's harsh tone may have been due to his own grief and a sincere desire to comfort Paula, nevertheless it amounts to a flinching self-defense against the stings of anti-ascetic criticism.

Another factor influencing Jerome's tempered language on fasting and physical asceticism may have been the resounding negative reaction—even among his supporters—to the excesses of his treatise *Against Jovinian*. Jerome's friends "were shocked by the violence and crudity of his language, and by his eagerness to crush Jovinian rather than persuade him, but even more by the

---

108. Ibid., 3 (CSEL 54:291).
109. Ibid., 5 (CSEL 54:292).
110. *Ep.* 39.6 (CSEL 54:306). Kate Cooper discusses this episode in the context of her analysis of Roman aristocratic social responses to asceticism (*The Virgin and the Bride: Idealized Womanhood in Late Antiquity* [Cambridge: Harvard University Press, 1996], 68–72, 81–83).
111. Ibid., 1 (CSEL 54:294).
112. Ibid., 6 (CSEL 54:305–306).

derogatory view of marriage which his hysterical exaltation of virginity entailed."[113] As noted earlier, his advocacy of extreme ascetic denial brought accusations of heresy against him. The ensuing discussion focused on the issues of marriage and celibacy,[114] but the larger issue was the definition of the norm, the "pattern" of the Christian life.[115]

The tension in Jerome's writings between admiration of uncompromising ascetic regimen and sober calls for moderation is also seen in his three extant *Lives* of ascetic holy men.[116] The *Life of Paul the First Hermit*, for example, was written during or shortly after Jerome's experiment with solitary ascetic withdrawal at Chalcis in the Syrian desert (c.375 C.E.). In addition to its undisguised attempt to assert the primacy of Paul of Thebes over Antony as the first Christian to retreat into the Egyptian desert,[117] the work reveals Jerome's early attraction to and confidence in the solitary life.[118]

A different emphasis appears in his later (390) *Life of Hilarion*. Jerome notes in the opening sentences that some people had unfairly criticized Paul (as depicted in his *Life*) for his solitude and inaccessibility—he then adds with sarcasm that he fully expects them to criticize Hilarion for being too sociable.[119] Hilarion began his ascetic career as a disciple of the great Antony. After two months of observing his lifestyle and methods of abstinence, Hilarion found that the crowds of people who came to Antony for healing and exorcism were too much to bear, and—in imitation of Antony himself[120]—set off into the wilderness of Palestine at the age of fifteen to fight his ascetic battles alone.[121] After twenty-two

113. Kelly, *Jerome*, 187.

114. See Jerome's apology written to Pammachius in 393 or 394, *Ep.* 49 (CSEL 54:350–387); Kelly, *Jerome*, 179–194.

115. For further examples of Jerome's conflicting emphases on moderation and rigorism in fasting compare *Epp.* 52.11–12; 17 (CSEL 54:434–436; 440–441); 108.19–21 (CSEL 55:332–338); and 130.11 (CSEL 56:191).

116. For general discussions of Jerome's *Lives*, see Rousseau, *Ascetics, Authority, and the Church*, 133–139 and Kelly, *Jerome*, 170–174.

117. *Vita S. Pauli primi eremitae* 1 (*PL* 23.17A–19A).

118. *Vita Pauli* 6; 9; 10 (*PL* 23. 21B; 24B–26A).

119. *Vita S. Hilarionis* 1 (*PL* 23.30B).

120. Rousseau, *Ascetics, Authority, and the Church*, 137.

121. *Vita Hil.* 3–8 (*PL* 23.31A–33A).

years of solitude, Hilarion was approached by a brave woman seeking a cure for her sterility. Hilarion resisted at first, but soon prayed for her and she was healed. Hilarion then spent the rest of his life surrounded by disciples and people in need of healing and exorcism. Yet although Hilarion's life of service to others—so different from Paul's life of self-imposed exile—was equal to Paul's in holiness and virtue, nevertheless Jerome tells us that as an old man and head of a large monastery Hilarion wept, longing for his former lonely abode.[122]

Just as Jerome's *Lives* include significant differences in emphasis on the issue of solitary withdrawal, so also on the role of fasting a subtle tension is displayed. In the case of two of the holy men—Hilarion and Malchus—Jerome writes that they began their ascetic careers with a period of training and fasting to bring the flesh into submission. Malchus spent many years with a group of monks in the desert of Chalcis, "earning [his] provisions with manual labor and restraining the lasciviousness of the flesh with fasting."[123] The *Life of Hilarion* is much more explicit about this initial struggle against fleshly desires. The devil attacked the delicate young Hilarion by titillating his senses and igniting in his adolescent body the "flames of lust." Hilarion fought sexual desire as a true ascetic champion: he defiantly mortified his body with hunger, thirst, and hard labor.[124] Thus Jerome continues a central theme of his treatment of fasting in his letters of advice: fasting is a primary and effective weapon in the battle against sexual desire.

Jerome describes the particular foods that sustained Paul and Hilarion. He reports that soon after the hermit Paul fled into the Egyptian desert to avoid persecution, he found a cave in which to live, close to a palm tree and stream. Paul lived here for the rest of his life, as the palm tree provided him with food and the materials for clothing. Jerome anticipates the reader's disbelief in Paul's incredible diet, and asserts that he himself has seen one monk who lived for thirty years on barley bread and muddy water and

---

122. Ibid., 29 (*PL* 23.44A–B).
123. *Vita Malchi monachi captivi* 3 (*PL* 23.57A).
124. *Vita Hil.* 5 (*PL* 23.32A–B).

another who sustained himself on five dried figs per day.[125] Later in his life Paul tells Antony that for sixty years he has been regularly and miraculously provided with half-loaves of bread—just enough for one person.[126]

Jerome provides great detail on Hilarion's diet. The reader is immediately struck by the intentional variety in his nonetheless simple fare. From the age of twenty to the age of thirty-five, Hilarion changed his eating habits about once every three years. At first he ate only soaked lentils, then for three years only bread, salt, and water. For another three years he was sustained on wild herbs and roots, and then barley bread and vegetables cooked without oil. Jerome then writes,

> But seeing that his eyes were dimming and that his whole body was wrinkling with crusty spots and dry mange, he added oil to his previous diet and continuously until his sixty-third year he maintained this pace of abstinence, tasting nothing else—neither fruit nor legumes nor anything whatsoever.

When his health began to fail as on old man, Hilarion stopped eating bread and began to drink "a broth [made] from farina and crushed vegetables." Although his body was changing, Jerome reports, Hilarion's mind remained vital and he maintained his rule of life even on feast days or when he was ill.[127]

Whereas Jerome had felt compelled to acknowledge that the dietary abstinence of Paul the hermit was fantastic, even miraculous, he presents Hilarion's regimen as not miraculous, but in fact practical. His diet is simple and austere, certainly, but not unbelievable. More important, Hilarion reportedly modified his diet at times, in response to bodily need, adding oil to his food when

---

125. *Vita Pauli* 5–6 (*PL* 23.21A–22A). To Egyptian ascetics, the palm tree was "an extrememly important source of various raw materials and of food." The core of the trunk could be dried and ground into a kind of flour, as could the fruit. Juice and sap were made into wine, and the leaves could be used for thatching dwellings and weaving baskets (Maria Dembińska, "Diet: A Comparison of Food Consumption Between Some Eastern and Western Monasteries in the 4th–12th Centuries," *Byzantion* 55 (1985): 435–436). See also Darby, et al., *Food: The Gift of Osiris*, 2:722–733.

126. *Vita Pauli* 10 (*PL* 23.25C–26A).

127. *Vita Hil.* 11 (*PL* 23.33C–34A).

he developed a skin condition and altering his diet again in old age. Jerome's *Lives* of Paul and Hilarion, therefore, reveal the same tensions as were seen in his letters. While on the one hand Jerome uses the language of moderation, on the other he admires heroic fasting and believes that chastity cannot be protected without strict dietary abstinence.[128] For all of his assertive bravado in argumentation, one senses in Jerome's letters and treatises an underlying "insecurity" on the question, "How should one live?"[129] Even more so after the death of Blesilla, his star ascetic exhibit, and the controversies surrounding his treatise against Jovinian and his *Life of Paul the First Hermit*, this question remains.

To return, then, to Jerome's understanding of the physiological connection of eating and sexual desire: his representation of fasting, just as his representation of virginity, is notable for its relentless emphasis on the corporeal. Like Basil of Ancyra before him, Jerome argues that since desire itself is naturally implanted in humans in order to encourage procreation, it is all the more dangerous—an "enemy within."[130] Jerome also shares some of Basil's distinctive ideas about the operation of the bodily senses and the relation of diet and sexual function. Unlike Basil, however, Jerome displays no confidence in the possibility that the human body—even the virginal body—might be controlled or transformed in this life to the extent that lust or the passions are eliminated.[131] Yet he does consider fasting to be an effective tool in the ascetic life, not to attain perfection but to assist in the preservation of chastity. To this end Jerome enlists the physiological theories and dietetic advice of various pagan authors, especially Galen

128. *Ep.* 22.11 (CSEL 54:158).
129. Rousseau, *Ascetics, Authority, and the Church,* 118, citing *Ep.* 54.1.
130. *Ep.* 54.9 (CSEL 54:475).
131. On Jerome's strong opposition to the notion of passionlessness (ἀπάθεια) see, e.g., his *Ep.* 133.4 (CSEL 56:244–247); Brown, *The Body and Society,* 373–386. For Basil of Ancyra's emphasis on passionlessness, incorruptibility, and the removal of lust from the virgin's flesh see esp. *De virg.* 50–52; 58 (PG 30:768B–776A; 785B–788A); Ton H. C. Van Eijk, "Marriage and Virginity, Death and Immortality," in *Epektasis: Mélanges patristiques offerts au Cardinal Jean Daniélou,* ed. Jacques Fontaine and Charles Kannengiesser (Paris: Beauchesne, 1972), 225–227.

on the heat and moisture of the body. He seems to have actually read some of Galen's treatises, including *On the Preservation of Health* and *On the Mixing and Faculties of the Simple Medicines.*[132] In fact, the basic ascetic diet recommended by Jerome—non-heating legumes, vegetables, and fish—is quite similar to that prescribed by Galen for those suffering from "plethoric" conditions.[133] Jerome thus cites contemporary medical theory and authorities for validation of the practical, physical usefulness of fasting in guarding the fragile treasure of chastity.

John Cassian

The fourth ascetic theorist who makes explicit use of medical and physiological concepts to argue for the efficacy of fasting in maintaining sexual renunciation is John Cassian (c.365–c.433). His *Institutes* and *Conferences* were written between 420 and 426, after he had arrived in Marseilles and founded two monasteries there, and were intended to address the specific needs of Western monks in Gaul. Cassian was trained in asceticism, however, in Bethlehem and the Egyptian desert,[134] and had been a disciple of some of the true ascetic virtuosos of the Egyptian desert—including Evagrius of Pontus (who will be discussed in chapter 4). When Castor, the bishop of Apt, called on Cassian to write the *Institutes* as a guide for the monastery Castor was founding, he appealed in particular to Cassian's firsthand knowledge of the traditions of the Eastern, especially Egyptian, ascetic fathers.[135] Cassian

132. Courcelle, *Late Latin Writers*, 86–87.

133. Galen recommends legumes, vegetables, fish, and birds that would not contribute to the excess of humors and excrements in the body (*De san. tuenda* 6.6 [Kühn 6:407–410]).

134. The chronological details of Cassian's time in Bethlehem and Egypt cannot be determined with specificity. Owen Chadwick places Cassian's arrival in Bethlehem at "not later than 392, and perhaps some years earlier," and his departure for Egypt as probably before 386, when Jerome arrived in Bethlehem, as there is no evidence that Cassian met Jerome there (Owen Chadwick, *John Cassian*, 2nd ed. [Cambridge: Cambridge University Press, 1968], 10–11). See also Rousseau, *Ascetics, Authority, and the Church*, 169–176; and E. Pichery, ed., *Jean Cassien: Conférences*, SC 42, 54, 64 (Paris: Éditions du Cerf, 1955, 1958, 1959), 42:9–13.

135. *De institutis coenobiorum*, Preface, 3 (Jean-Claude Guy, ed., *Jean*

therefore proposes to describe what he learned about the institutions and rules of the most ancient monasteries, in order to provide instruction on the way to attain "the perfect life." But he
also notes that he will modify certain Egyptian customs with
those of Palestine and Mesopotamia, as the Egyptian practices
may be too rigorous and difficult for Western monks or not suitable to the climate of Gaul.[136] Cassian understands himself, then,
as the bearer of the tradition of the holy ascetic pioneers of the
East and, at the same time, the intentional translator and modifier
of that tradition for a new generation in different circumstances.

Cassian describes the *Institutes* as a guide for the precepts of
the "outer" or "exterior" person and the institutions of the
monastic community, while the *Conferences*—Cassian's written
account of conversations with Egyptian holy men—are intended
to address the issues of "inner discipline, the perfection of the
heart, and the life and doctrine of the anchorites."[137] Philip
Rousseau has argued, however, that while Cassian is usually
"regarded as a 'contemplative' writer, in the theological tradition
of Origen and Evagrius," and while he often seems to regard solitary asceticism as superior to community life, "distinctions in his
work—between contemplative and active; between community
and solitude—are by no means as clear as one may imagine."[138]
Rousseau identifies a subtle shift in emphasis in Cassian's *Conferences*—from a definite separation of cenobitic (communal) and
eremitic (solitary) monasticism, to the notion of these as stages in

---

Cassien: Institutions cénobitiques, SC 109 [Paris: Éditions du Cerf, 1965],
24].

136. Ibid., Preface 7–9 (SC 109:28–32). See Rousseau, *Ascetics, Authority,
and the Church,* 177–188. Rousseau points out that Cassian was concerned
about what he saw as the "instability" and lack of discipline among the
ascetic groups and individuals in Gaul. He argues that Cassian's promise to
tone down the harsh customs of Egyptian ascetics for Western practitioners
was a thinly disguised suggestion that few Western monks could equal the
purity of the Egyptian fathers, and that Cassian "thought there were few in
his audience likely to have achieved such perfection that they were ready for
the rigors of the solitary life" (184–186).

137. *Inst.* 2.9 (SC 109:74); see also *Conlationes,* Preface (SC 42:74–75).

138. Rousseau, *Ascetics, Authority, and the Church,* 177. I will point out
similar problems with applying these distinctions to Evagrius of Pontus's
ascetic theory below.

the individual monk's spiritual progress, and finally to an appreciation of the benefits of "social asceticism" despite "theoretical emphasis on the excellence of the eremitic life." Cassian came to regard community life as necessary and useful for the individual, not only for training in ascetic method, but for the protection of spiritual development against the dangers of pride.[139]

Cassian's audience is neither a particular male or female ascetic who needs advice on daily regimen, nor a reader who is meant to be inspired by the abstract philosophical praise of virginity, but a male ascetic community. What is most interesting for this study is Cassian's use of the Egyptian desert tradition, its models of ascetic behavior, and its methods of fasting, combined with Greco-Roman medical theory, in order to deal with a particular problem among male ascetics—the disturbing experience of wet dreams or nocturnal emissions.

For the monk intent on achieving the goal of perpetual and perfect chastity, the occurrence of nocturnal emissions—especially when accompanied by dreams or images—was an unexpected reminder of a spirit not yet perfect or completely purified. Further, such illusions and images served as signs of some negligence or lust, which may be hidden deep in the soul during the day but which emerges during sleep.[140] Thus Cassian emphasizes the power of thoughts, images, memories and fantasies in the individual's "battle" against the vice of fornication.[141]

---

139. Ibid., 177–183. See also Chadwick, *John Cassian*, 53–54.

140. *Inst.* 6.10–11 (SC 109:274); *Con.* 12.7–8 (SC 54:131–135); and see David Brakke, "The Problematization of Nocturnal Emissions in Early Christian Syria, Egypt, and Gaul," *Journal of Early Christian Studies* 3 (1995): 446–460.

141. E.g., *Inst.* 6.3 (SC 109:264–266); 6.11–13 (SC 109:274–278); *Con.* 7.15 (SC 42:258–260); 12.7 (SC 54:131–132); 15.10 (SC 54:219–220); 19.16 (SC 64:53–55); 22.2–3 (SC 64:116–119). This emphasis on thoughts and images in ascetic spirituality is inherited from Evagrius of Pontus (see below, chap. 4). Michel Foucault has pointed out that the role of the individual's thoughts, imaginations, and will is so central to Cassian's treatment of fornication that he nowhere deals with actual, physical sexual activity, or even the intention of engaging in a sexual act: "Cassian is interested in the movements of the body and the mind, images, feelings, memories, faces in dreams, the spontaneous movements of thoughts, the consenting (or refusing) will, waking and sleeping" ("The Battle for Chastity," in *Western Sexuality: Practice and*

Cassian also recognizes the role of diet in the occurrence of nocturnal emissions. He refers to the familiar notion that excess nutrition leads to a buildup of bodily humors, including semen. In the second conference of Abba Moses he writes:

> That which has once been collected inside [*in medullis*] because of an abundance of food is necessarily discharged, and it is expelled by a law of nature itself, which does not allow an abundance of any superfluous humor whatsoever to reside in it, as this is harmful and injurious. And for this reason our body must be chastised by an always rational and measured frugality, so that if, while remaining in the flesh, we are not able to be completely free of this natural necessity, at least it happens more rarely—and not more than three times in the course of the whole year—that we are sprinkled with these impurities. But still it is discharged without any pruritus during a quiet sleep, and not elicited by a false image—the sign of a hidden lust.[142]

To reduce the frequency of nocturnal emissions, then, the fathers recommend that monks limit their intake of food and water, thus reducing bodily humors.[143] But fasting alone cannot bring about such a state of tranquility. While Cassian affirms the physiological connection between eating and the buildup of semen in the body, and claims that gluttony and fornication exist naturally in human beings, nevertheless he returns again and again to the state of the monk's soul, his innermost thoughts, the purity of his heart. True chastity is not merely a physical state of sexual continence. Continence is usually maintained in spite of and in the struggle against the lusts of the flesh. But "perfect chastity is distinguished from the laborious beginnings of continence by a perpetual tranquility." For the one who is truly chaste the experience

---

Precept in Past and Present Times, ed. Philippe Ariès and André Béjin, trans. Anthony Forster [Oxford: Basil Blackwell, 1985], 20. But see also Elizabeth A. Clark, "Foucault, the Fathers, and Sex," *Journal of the American Academy of Religion* 56 [1988]: 627–630).

142. Cassian, *Con.* 2.23 (SC 42:134).

143. *Inst.* 6.22–23 (SC 109:286–288); *Con.* 12.11 (SC 54:139); *Con.* 22.3; 6 (SC 64:116–117; 123); on the problem of nocturnal emissions among the monks of Egypt see the passage, discussed in chap. 1, in *HM* 20.1–4 (André Jean Festugière, ed., *Historia Monachorum in Aegypto,* Subsidia hagiographica 53 [Brussels: Société des Bollandistes, 1971], 118–119).

of natural bodily movements during the night is not accompanied by any lustful desire and, further, the "members" are quieted by a "commandment of chastity."[144]

Thus the highest level of chastity is achieved when one is no longer bothered by illusions of feminine phantasms during the night.[145] Very few reach this level of perfection, but Cassian reports that Serenus was so advanced in chastity that he was not even subject to natural stirrings. He received this special grace from God after intense prayer, fasting, and vigils.[146] True chastity, then, is a mental condition as much as it is a physical state; nevertheless there are physical signs of its achievement—chiefly the cessation of nocturnal emissions. Similarly, while fornication cannot be completely repressed by physical means, fasting is promoted as a necessary and useful weapon in the struggle. Indeed, Cassian writes, "with any change in eating, the quality of our purity is necessarily changed as well."[147]

In the course of the *Institutes* and *Conferences,* Cassian gives very few direct dietary prescriptions regarding specific foods. While his descriptions of the diets and rules of fasting among Eastern ascetics amount to recommendations for Gallic monks, they nevertheless do not have the force of a *rule.*[148] Cassian tempers his descriptions of Eastern customs with repeated calls for moderation and consideration of individual ability and bodily condition. He reports that he himself was taught that, while all were under the same "rule of chastisement regarding the continence (*continentia*) of the mind and the virtue of the soul," the type of food as well as frequency of meals must vary according to age, sex, and physical condition: "The weak (*enervatus*) food of soaked legumes is not agreeable to everyone, nor is a frugal regimen of fresh vegetables suitable to all, nor is a strict repast of

144. *Con.* 12.11 (SC 54:137–140); cf. *Inst.* 6.4 (SC 109:266).
145. *Con.* 12.7 (SC 54:132).
146. *Con.* 7.1–2 (SC 42:244–245). Serenus received a vision at night in which an angel came to him and removed a "flaming tumor of flesh" from his viscera; the angel then announced to Serenus that the burning lusts of his flesh had been removed and he had received perpetual bodily purity.
147. *Inst.* 6.23 (SC 109:286).
148. Chadwick makes this observation regarding Cassian's description of Egyptian clothing (Chadwick, *John Cassian,* 57–58).

dried bread allowed to all."[149] Yet every monk, no matter what the state of his health and strength, attains to purity of heart and "perfect virtue" by restraining the lusts of the flesh, by taking care of the body but not its desires.[150] In determining the proper intensity of fasting, then, the monk should weigh in the scales of discretion the purity of his soul on one side and his bodily strength on the other.[151]

One should choose food that "tempers the heat of burning concupiscence," is easy to prepare, cheap enough that it may be purchased in large quantities, and suitable to the common use of the community. The fathers, according to Cassian, thought that diets deviating from what was customary and common were polluted by vanity. Specifically, Cassian finds no merit in excluding bread from the monastic diet. Thus none of the most esteemed and advanced fathers avoided eating bread, and likewise none of those who *did* abstain from bread (and instead ate legumes or vegetables or fruit) was counted among those who had received the gift of discretion.[152]

The usual daily fast described by Cassian consisted of two small loaves or biscuits of dried bread (*paxamatia*), which were eaten at the ninth hour[153] with a brine (*muria*) of salt and water,

149. *Inst.* 5.5 (SC 109:196–198); On moderation in fasting see also *Inst.* 5.9 (SC 109:202–204); 6.23 (SC 109:286); *Con.* 2.16–17 (SC 42:131–132); 2.22 (SC 42:133–134).
150. *Inst.* 5.7–8 (SC 109:200–202).
151. *Con.* 21.22 (SC 64:96).
152. *Inst.* 5.23 (SC 109:230–232); see also *Con.* 2.19 (SC 42:133), where Abba Moses reports that the "elders" had discouraged those who ate only legumes, vegetables, or fruit, and proposed instead the best daily food of two small dried breads. Aline Rousselle has suggested that Cassian's disapproval of abstinence from bread may be related to the avoidance of bread among the followers of Cybele (*Porneia: De la maîtrise du corps à la privation sensorielle IIe–IVe siècles de l'ère chrétienne*, Les chemins de l'Histoire [Paris: Presses Universitaires de France, 1983], 213). See also Rudolph Arbesmann, "Fasten, Fastenspeisen, Fasttage," in *Reallexikon für Antike und Christentum*, ed. Theodor Klauser (Stuttgart: Anton Hiersemann, 1969), 7:461; idem, *Das Fasten bei den Griechen und Römern*, Religionsgeschichtliche Versuche und Vorarbeiten, 21,1 (Giessen: Alfred Töpelmann, 1929; reprint, Berlin: Alfred Töpelmann, 1966), 84–85.
153. *Con.* 2.26 (SC 42:137); 12.15 (SC 54:144); 21.23 (SC 64:98).

to which one drop of oil was added.[154] On Saturdays and Sundays the monks throughout the East relaxed their daily fast. Cassian feels compelled to explain this to his Western audience, as many in Rome observed a Saturday fast. He explains that those in the East were not continuing any Jewish practice, but the weariness of the body after five days of rigorous fasting required two days of relaxation.[155] An extra meal was served on Saturdays and Sundays but was not obligatory.[156] Cassian also mentions soaked legumes and vegetables,[157] lentils,[158] and lentil porridge (*athera*),[159] which may have been eaten by the monks themselves or their guests. As the "greatest delights" among the Eastern ascetics Cassian lists cherlock (*labsanion*) soaked in salted water,[160] leaves of leeks, toasted or parched salt (*sal frictum*),[161] olives, and small salted fish or sardines (*maenomenia*).[162] He also describes the meal prepared by Serenus for his guests, which included *sal frictum*, three olives, five roasted chickpeas, two prunes, and one fig for each person. In addition, Serenus prepared a sauce[163] to which

154. *Con.* 8.1 (SC 54:9).
155. *Inst.* 3.9–10 (SC 109:112–114).
156. Ibid., 3.12 (SC 109:16).
157. Ibid., 5.5 (SC 109:198).
158. *Con.* 19.6 (SC 64:43).
159. Ibid., 15.10 (SC 54:219). Pliny refers to *athera* as a decoction of wheat which is useful as a medicine (*Hist. Nat.* 22.57,121 [Jones 6:380]).
160. *Inst.* 4.11 (SC 109:134); 4.22 (SC 109:152). Cassian cautions that *labsanion* is too harsh for the more fragile monks of the West. The word *labsanion* (or *lapsanion*) is apparently applied to various field weeds and mustards. Pliny classes *lapsana* among wild cabbages and claims that it relaxes the bowels (*Hist Nat.* 20.37,96 [Jones 6:56]). See also André, *L'alimentation*, 33, 47.
161. The meaning of *sal frictum* is not clear. It could refer either to drying or to rubbing. "Rubbed salt" would be table salt as opposed to block salt. Pliny discusses the "artifical" methods of obtaining salt by drying water from salt pools. He claims that in Egypt salt is made "from the sea itself, which flows into the soil, . . . soaked by the Nile." He also reports that the brine from salted foods (*muria salsamentorum*) could be reboiled and evaporated in order to make salt (*Hist. Nat.* 31.39,81–40,83 [Jones 8:426–428]). See also Darby, *Food: The Gift of Osiris* 1:449, and Rousselle, "Abstinence et continence," 249.
162. *Inst.*, 4.22 (SC 109:152).
163. *Liquamen* often refers to a sauce made from decomposing fish and

he added extra drops of oil; this he served in place of his usual brine.[164]

Cassian distinguishes between diets that include cooked food and those that consist primarily of raw or dried food. These regimens are also generally distinguished—but not strictly exclusive—in early monastic sources.[165] In the *Institutes* Cassian reports that in Palestine, Mesopotamia, Cappadocia, and all over the East—excluding Egypt—the task of cooking food for the brothers in the community was assigned weekly. He tells the story of certain monks assigned to cook who discovered that the wood supply was low. Rather than disappoint the others by serving them dried food (*xerofagia*), the monks wandered all over the desert towards the Dead Sea in search of wood.[166] In contrast, the monks of Egypt avoided the distraction from their regular rule of labor by permanently appointing one monk to tend the kitchen and by usually eating dried and uncooked food.[167] But Cassian does record an episode in which Paphnutius was burned by the fire while preparing lentil porridge.[168] This indicates some variation, perhaps on feast days.

Although Cassian does not himself classify individual foods as "drying" or "cooling," he writes that the monk's goal is in general to dry and cool the body.[169] Aline Rousselle has shown that the foods identified by Cassian as part of the Egyptian ascetic diet are among those considered drying by the Galenic medical tradition. She compares Cassian's regimen specifically to the foods

---

salt (also called *garum,* in Greek γάρος). On *garum* see André, *L'alimentation,* 195–198; Rousselle, "Abstinence et continence," 245; and now Robert I. Curtis, *Garum and Salsamenta: Production and Commerce in Materia Medica,* Studies in Ancient Medicine 3 (Leiden: E. J. Brill, 1991). Curtis discusses the production of and commerce in *garum* and fish products in the ancient Mediterranean world as well as their dietary and medicinal uses. On salt-fish products in ancient medicine, see 27–37.

164. *Con.* 8.1 (SC 54:9–10).

165. See chap. 1.

166. *Inst.* 4.19–21 (SC 109:146–150).

167. Ibid., 4.22 (SC 109:150–152).

168. *Con.* 15.10 (SC 54:219).

169. On cooling see *Inst.* 5.23 (SC 109:230); 6.17 (SC 109:282). On drying see *Con.* 12.11 (SC 54:139): the monk should mortify the excess even in

discussed by Oribasius (c.320–c.400), the physician to the emperor Julian.[170] Oribasius was heavily influenced by Galen and compiled many volumes of excerpts from various ancient medical writers. Rousselle points out that in Oribasius and others "the foods that relax the stomach, such as lentils, salted olives, figs, grapes, and prunes, were considered drying."[171] Indeed, all of the various foods in the diet recommended by Cassian are included in "the drying regimen of the physicians."[172]

Galen writes, for example, that lentils are heating and drying,[173] and can relax the stomach or have the opposite effect, depending on the method of preparation. Boiled in water and seasoned with salt or *garum* and oil, lentils are laxative.[174] Salt is drying,[175] as are figs and prunes,[176] and *garum* is drying and heating.[177] As noted above in the discussion of Jerome, Galen claims that flatulence is removed from chickpeas when they are roasted (as the ascetic Serenus served them to his guests).[178] Rousselle has pointed out that the leek (Latin: *porrum*, Greek: πράσον), which is "the only green vegetable recommended by Cassian"—as he

---

regard to the use of water, "so that the mass of daily humors might flow more slowly in the dried up members;" and 22.6 (SC 64:124): the monk, being under the grace of virginity rather than the law of marital procreation, has the impure humors dried up in him, and thus becomes like the good eunuchs of Isaiah 56:4-5 who keep the Lord's sabbaths and covenant, and are rewarded with "a name better than sons and daughters."

170. Rousselle, "Abstinence et continence," 242–249; see also idem, *Porneia*, 220–221.

171. Rousselle, *Porneia*, 220.

172. Idem, "Abstinence et continence," 249.

173. *De san. tuenda* 5.8 (Kühn 6:351); *In Hippocratis vel Polybi opus de salubri victus* 2 (Kühn 15:179). Again, foods that are heating and at the same time *drying* (as opposed to moistening) are *not* generative of semen, according to Galen (*De simp. med. temp. ac fac.* 5.23 (Kühn 11:776–777).

174. *De alim. fac.* 1.18 (Kühn 6:525).

175. Ibid., 3.41 (Kühn 6:745–747).

176. *De san. tuenda* 5.8–9 (Kühn 6:351–353). Rufus of Ephesus claimed that figs relax the stomach, speed digestion, and are drying (Fragment #471 from Arrhazi [Daremberg and Ruelle, 546]).

177. *De simp. med. temp. ac fac.* 11.13 (Kühn 12:377).

178. Yet, again, Galen does write that the chickpea "incites the impulses to sexual intercourse and at the same time therefore is believed to be generative of semen" (*De alim. fac.* 1.22 [Kühn 6:533–534]).

thought cherlock to be too harsh for Western monks—is also considered drying in Oribasius.[179] Galen describes the leek, along with other plants with edible bulbs such as garlic and onion, as bitter or acrid, with the power to cut thick and sticky humors, and of little nutritious value.[180] Wild leek is more bitter and dry than cultivated leek, and thus more powerful in cutting humors and clearing obstructions. It is used to provoke urine or menses when these are retained due to thick and sticky humors.[181] The leek is often eaten as a condiment or "dainty" rather than as a food in itself.[182]

Our understanding of the possible relation of Cassian's diet to ancient medical theory is complicated, however, by the fact that there is evidence that the leek was understood to be an aphrodisiac. Rufus of Ephesus, for example, in his treatise *On Satyriasis and Gonorrhea* includes the leek among foods which seem to incite towards sexual activity.[183] Pliny also asserts that the leek is an aphrodisiac.[184] Thus while Cassian himself may well have understood the leek to be a agent for drying the excess humors of the body, there is no consensus among late ancient writers as to its effects on the physiology of sexual desire. As is the case with salt[185] and lettuce[186] in the ascetic diet, varying cultural understandings of specific foods and the traditional lore attached to them as well as geographical and economic access to different foods must be taken into consideration.

The issues are complicated further in that Cassian's diet is imported or transplanted from Egypt to Gaul. Although his detailed recounting of the foods eaten or not eaten by the Egyptian heroes is a regulating device, nevertheless it is significant

179. "Abstinence et continence," 249; and *Porneia*, 220. There is literary evidence for the wide cultivation and eating of leeks in ancient Egypt (Darby, *Food: The Gift of Osiris*, 2:673–675).

180. *De alim. fac.* 2.71 (Kühn 6:658–659). The root or bulb is more bitter than the stalk and leaves (Ibid., 2.61 [Kühn 6:646]).

181. *De simp. med. temp. ac fac.* 6.1.31 (Kühn 11:825).

182. *De alim. fac.* 2.43 (Kühn 6:630). See also André, *L'Alimentation*, 32.

183. Περὶ σατυριάσμου καὶ γονορροίας 48 (Daremberg and Ruelle, 81).

184. *Hist. nat.* 20.21,47 (Jones, 6:29).

185. See p. 88, n.23.

186. See chap. 2, n.111.

that Cassian's account is descriptive rather than prescriptive. Moreover, he makes allowances for the weaker bodily constitutions and different climate of the West, and frequently reminds his audience that no one should be overburdened with severe fasting. He reports that the desert ascetics recommended the harsh fasting diet of two small loaves per day, yet he refers—albeit sometimes critically—to other ascetics who ate vegetables and legumes during their regular fast.[187] The modern reader is left to wonder exactly how austere Cassian expected the daily regimen of the Western monastic communities to be. On the topic of diet, as elsewhere, Cassian seems finally to be attempting a delicate balance between deep admiration for the awesome abstinence of the Egyptians and practical awareness of the limitations—and, indeed, possibilities—of the Western communal monks.[188]

Cassian's writings moreover reveal the importance of diet in the overall process of monastic self-definition—particularly in the period after the deaths of the ascetic pioneers and in the Western setting of corporate monasticism. While in his wistful descriptions of the harsh and humble regimen of the Egyptians one detects Cassian's sense that the glory days will not be recaptured in Gaul, nevertheless he holds up Eastern models as standards for imitation in the West. Jack Goody, in his sociological analysis of food in various cultures, has emphasized that food and the method of its preparation are factors in "'placing' oneself in rela-

---

187. *Inst.* 5.23 (SC 109:230–232); *Con.* 2.19 (SC 42:133).

188. Philip Rousseau has identified similar tensions in Cassian between regulating for the community life while arguing for the superiority of eremitic monasticism, and providing for the monks' greater involvement in "the world" and the church while still defending "the esoteric—the maintenance of an exclusive group, governed by arcane principle." He explains: "It is not that Cassian was not able to make up his mind on these issues. He felt it was impossible, or rather imprudent, to commit himself in public on one side or the other. For he had a deep sense of obligation to the past, to the 'traditio maiorum'; and this would have urged upon him the need for fidelity, a fidelity embracing many potentially conflicting traditions. It would have been immensely difficult for any man in his position, or in his period, to repudiate or ignore the practice of heroes so recently dead, so powerful a force in the memory and life of their disciples" (*Ascetics, Authority, and the Church*, 235).

tion to others."[189] That is, what an individual eats—and does not eat—helps to identify that individual as part of a larger group or culture with similar food behaviors. This identity may be ethnic (Irish-Americans often celebrate Saint Patrick's Day with a meal of corned beef and cabbage), economic (wealthy people eat caviar), geographical (North Carolinians pride themselves on their barbecue), or gendered ("real men don't eat quiche"). It is often, of course, religious. Thus in passing on the foods and fasting diet of the East, Cassian transmits a crucial element of tradition, discipline, and group identity to new communities struggling to define themselves.

Moreover, Cassian imports the tradition of the masters in order to address a specific male monastic issue: nocturnal emissions. But he often employs the language of Greco-Roman medical explanations as well in arguing for the efficacy of rigorous fasting for reducing the frequency of wet dreams. Cassian understands that the inextricable link between gluttony and fornication is due not only to the physiological "cause and effect" of eating and the buildup of bodily humors. It is also due to the psychological connection between the vices of gluttony and fornication in the depths of the soul.[190] Finally, however, these two arenas cannot be separated: diet affects the monk in body and in soul. Indeed, just as the pagan physician Galen argued that the physical κρᾶσις is directly related to the state of the soul,[191] Cassian assures the monks of Gaul that change in diet produces a change in the "quality of our purity."[192]

John Cassian presents an essentially practical and optimistic

189. Jack Goody, *Cooking, Cuisine and Class: A Study in Comparative Sociology*, Themes in Social Sciences (Cambridge: Cambridge University Press, 1982), 2. On the importance of bodily details such as eating for the "inscribing" of culture, see also Pierre Bourdieu, *The Logic of Practice*, trans, Richard Nice (Stanford, CA: Stanford University Press, 1990).

190. On the vices of the soul in Cassian and Evagrius of Pontus see below, chap. 4.

191. Galen, *De loc. aff.* 3.10 (Kühn 8:191); *De san. tuenda* 1.8 (Kühn 6:39–40).

192. *Inst.* 6.23 (SC 109:286).

program for the attainment of "the perfect life."[193] He seems confident that the ascetic struggle for purity and the highest levels of chastity will produce changes in this earthly life. Indeed, as the bodily humors are dried up and the episodes of involuntary nocturnal emissions become rare or even nonexistent, the monk's body becomes like the bush in the vision of Moses: surrounded by the flames of lust, it does not burn.[194] Thus, Cassian writes, "already in this body we begin to possess in some way that which is promised to the holy ones by the prophet: 'When you walk through fire you will not be consumed, and the flame will not burn in you.'"[195] He wants to assure his audience of anxious and sometimes despairing[196] monks that the achievement of such chastity is possible, if uncommon. A recorded conversation with Abba Chaeremon is revealing. Chaeremon is asked how long and what abstinence is necessary in order to acquire confidence in one's chastity. His response is remarkably straightforward and practical: If the monk withdraws from useless conversation, anger, and earthly concern, if he eats only two small loaves and sleeps only three or four hours per day, and recognizes that he requires God's mercy in addition to his own efforts, in six months he should be able to recognize "that perfection is not impossible for him."[197]

Food Deprivation and Sexual Function

John Cassian, Jerome, Gregory of Nyssa, and Basil of Ancyra all understood the benefits of ascetic fasting to include the slowing of the bodily processes that lead to sexual desire. Aline Rousselle has demonstrated that modern research on the effects of food

---

193. Ibid., Preface, 8 (SC 109:30).
194. *Con.* 12.11 (SC 54:139–140); Exodus 3:2.
195. *Con.* 12.11 (SC 54:139–140); Isaiah 43:2.
196. See, e.g., *Con.* 7.3 (SC 42:246–247); 12.9 (SC 54:136); 22.2 (SC 64:116).
197. *Con.* 12.14–15 (SC 54:143–144). Rousseau, in reference to Chaeremon's "formula" for success, writes, "With what ominous ease such a brief and clearcut distillation of experience could become a changeless and impersonal principle!" (*Ascetics, Authority, and the Church*, 226–227).

deprivation confirms the ancient theory to some extent.[198] One of the most exhaustive studies was conducted at the University of Minnesota from 1944 to 1945.[199] Rousselle has previously discussed in detail the results of this study in relation to ascetic diets, but it will be worth our while to review the experiment and Rousselle's conclusions. The subjects of the Minnesota controlled experiment in semi-starvation were thirty-two healthy young male volunteers who were conscientious objectors to World War II. The experiment involved first a twelve-week control period during which the subjects consumed an average of 3,492 calories per day. During the following twenty-four weeks of semi-starvation the men were limited to an average of 1,570 calories per day. The twelve-week period of restricted rehabilitation saw the average caloric intake increase gradually to around 3,500.[200]

The researchers found that many of their conclusions matched the observations of those who studied the effects of "natural" and wartime food shortages and famines. The most common physical changes due to experimental semi-starvation included weight loss and emaciation, "wasting of muscle," edema (retention of fluids in bodily tissue and cavities), hair loss, increased tolerance to heat, decreased tolerance to cold, lowered pulse rate, and lowered basal metabolism. The subjects also experienced a marked increase in depression, apathy, tiredness, weakness, and irritability. Food became the overwhelming preoccupation of the hungry men, and they began to exhibit peculiar food behaviors such as excessive use of salt and spices, salt craving, "souping" their food in an attempt to increase its bulk, saving bits of food for later consumption, prolonging meals for up to two hours, and reading cookbooks and collecting recipes. Many took up smoking, drank excessive amounts of coffee, and chewed gum constantly. Some vowed to become cooks after the end of the experiment. The men reported and discussed in sensuous detail their daydreams of

198. Rousselle discusses this connection in "Abstinence et continence," 252–253, and *Porneia,* 222–226.
199. Ancel Keys, Joseph Brožek, et al., *The Biology of Human Starvation,* 2 vols. (Minneapolis: University of Minnesota Press, 1950).
200. Ibid., 1:63–78.

favorite foods. For a few of the subjects, however, the group's pre-occupation with food was irritating and discouraging. One labeled it "nutritional masturbation."[201]

One of the most marked and common effects of prolonged food deprivation—in the Minnesota experiment as well as numerous studies of starving populations in war or famine—is a weakening or loss of sexual desire and activity.[202] The researchers at Minnesota found that by the end of the twenty-four weeks of semi-starvation "sexual feeling and expression . . . were virtually extinguished in all but a few of the subjects." They also report that "masturbation and nocturnal emissions ceased or were greatly reduced in frequency. Sex fantasies and sex dreams were reported to have decreased in number, and when present they were much attenuated." During the rehabilitation period, the sex drive returned only very slowly.[203] The researchers attributed the decrease in sexual desire in starvation or semi-starvation in part to the body's own "adaptive mechanisms protecting the individual organism from nonessential energy expenditure." Experiment results also showed a marked decrease in the production and excretion of male sex hormones (ketosteroids) as well as a reduction in semen volume and changes in its morphology.[204] Although the Minnesota experiment involved only male subjects, the authors note previous studies documenting widespread amenorrhea among women suffering from food deprivation.[205]

201. Ibid., 2:819–834.
202. Ibid., 2:906–913. One study found reduction in sexual interest and activity to occur in seventy to ninety percent of the population during prolonged famine (913).
203. Ibid., 2:839–840. It is an interesting parallel with our study of late antiquity that some of the men in the Minnesota experiment expressed relief at the cessation of their urge to masturbate. These men were described as having religious aversion to the practice.
204. Ibid., 1:755–757, 761–763; 2:840.
205. Ibid., 1:749–750. See also Emmanuel Le Roy Ladurie, "Famine Amenorrhoea (Seventeenth-Twentieth Centuries)," in Biology of Man in History, ed. Robert Forster and Orest Ranum, trans. Elborg Forster (Baltimore: The Johns Hopkins University Press, 1975), 163–178. This connection between food deprivation and amenorrhea will help to illuminate some texts dealing with ascetic women and to interpret the symbolic and physiological connec-

The Minnesota experiment thus documented both physiological and psychological aspects of the decline in sexual interest. This decline occurred at a daily caloric intake level of around 1500–1600. It is therefore a fair assumption that the monks of Gaul or Egypt would have experienced a loss of sexual appetite and a reduction in the frequency of nocturnal emissions and erections if in fact they followed the diet described by John Cassian for any significant length of time. Indeed, Rousselle estimates that the individual items in Cassian's daily fast—bread, brine, and oil—would provide around 930 calories. Even the special meal served by Serenus to his guests, which included a few olives, roasted chickpeas, prunes, and a fig, would provide only around 1,069 calories.[206] In light of the modern research just presented, Cassian's recommended weekday diet can only be described as one of semi-starvation.[207] On Saturdays and Sundays, however, the monks were permitted to relax their fast and add an extra meal on a voluntary basis. Cassian very sensibly notes that extra food was necessary at times due to the extreme weakness of the body after five fasting days.[208] These foods probably included legumes, vegetables, *athera*, and dried fish.

In sum, Cassian's practical and clear assertion (through the voice of Chaeremon) that six months of rigorous fasting, vigils, and reliance on God should be enough to bring one close to the goal of chastity—which is known in part by the cessation of sensuous dreams and nocturnal emissions—seems firmly based in his observations of the heroic fasters of the Egyptian desert and confirmed by modern research in semi-starvation.

It is clear that Greco-Roman physiological models inform ascetic advice on diet. Basil, Gregory, Jerome, and John Cassian share a basic understanding that the preservation of sexual chastity is affected by diet and the bodily processes of nutrition and digestion. In this sense fasting is part of an overall system for

---

tions between female fasting, virginity, and "becoming male," discussed below in chap. 6.

206. Rousselle, "Abstinence et continence," 250–252.

207. Ibid. Rousselle concludes that the desert monks must have eaten dried fish and legumes more frequently than Cassian suggests (252).

208. *Inst.* 3.9–10 (SC 109:112–114).

managing the body; like the physician, dietitian, or athlete, the ascetic woman or man must maintain a vigilance and knowledge of the powers and effects of various foods. Common medical wisdom thus appears as an integral and logical aspect of ascetic advice. It should also be clear from the previous discussion, however, that the physiological details are interwoven in an intricate web of argumentation. As we examine more closely other strands in this web, we will discover the extent to which the physical realities of bodily discipline are integrated into ascetic theology and spirituality.

CHAPTER FOUR

The Mother of All Vice: Gluttony and the Health of Body and Soul

WHEN, IN THE LATE FOURTH CENTURY, Evagrius of Pontus wrote his treatise on opposing virtues and vices, he began with this indictment of gluttony (γαστριμαργία):

> Gluttony is the mother of lust (πορνεία), the nourishment of evil thoughts, laziness in fasting, obstacle to asceticism, terror to moral purpose, the imagining of food, sketcher of seasonings, unrestrained colt, unbridled frenzy, receptacle of disease, envy of health, obstruction of the [bodily] passages, groaning of the bowels, the extreme of outrages, confederate[1] of lust, pollution of the intellect, weakness of the body, difficult sleep, gloomy death.

He praises the opposing virtue, abstinence (or *enkrateia*, ἐγκράτεια), as

> the bit of the belly, the whip of insatiability, the stable of moderation, the muzzle of voraciousness, renunciation of recreation, prescription of austerity, chastisement of idle thoughts, eye of vigils, the dissipation of burning desire, pedagogue of the body, defense tower of [ascetic] labor, fortification of character, restraint of lifestyle and repression of passions, mortification of the [bodily] members, renewal of the soul's life, imitation of the resurrection, the society for sanctification.[2]

---

1. The meaning of the word σύμμιστος is uncertain, and may be a corruption of σύμμεστος (full) or συμμύστης (fellow initiate, companion, etc.). See E. A. Sophocles, *Greek Lexicon of the Roman and Byzantine Periods (From B.C. 146 to A.D. 1100)* (New York: Frederick Ungar, 1957), 2:1028.
2. Evagrius, *De vitiis quae opposita sunt virtutibus*, 2 (PG 79.1141A–B).

Evagrius's recitation invokes many of the images central to the fourth-century discussion of gluttony, the passions, fasting, and the Christian body. Building on the discussion in the two previous chapters concerning first the connections between regimen and food behaviors to virtue and the "health" of the soul and, second, the physiological models of nutrition and arguments for ascetic fasting, in this chapter the focus shifts from fasting to its opposite vice, gluttony. Specifically, we will analyze the concept of glut-tony in the works of two Christian writers, Evagrius of Pontus and John Chrysostom, in order to highlight the discussion of diet and desire as it relates to the interaction of soul and body.

In early Christian ascetic literature, gluttony is a vice of the soul with physical causes and effects, a psychological enemy that can be battled in part by physical methods. The concept of glut-tony as a vice or passion of the soul, often as the first vice, is com-mon, and is rooted in a long-standing *topos* of the Hellenistic moralist tradition.[3] Among ancient Christian writers, Evagrius of Pontus develops the concept of the vices of the soul most system-atically. His treatment of the relationship between the soul's eight vices—particularly the vices of gluttony and sexual lust—is dynamic, influential for later writers in the East and West, and an integral element in his theory of ascetic spirituality. Evagrius per-haps demonstrates best the ascetic understanding that eating and

3. In addition to the texts of Evagrius and Cassian, which will be discussed here, see also, e.g., Galen, *De cognoscendis curandisque animi morbis* 6 (C. G. Kühn, ed. *Galeni Opera Omnia* [Leipzig: K. Knobloch, 1823; reprint, Hildesheim: Georg Olms, 1965], 5:27–28); Basil of Ancyra, *De vera virgini-tatis integritate* 46–47 (PG 30.760B–764A); Gregory of Nyssa, *De virginitate* 21.2 (Michel Aubineau, ed., *Grégoire de Nysse: Traité de la virginité*, SC 119 [Paris: Éditions du Cerf, 1966], 506); Basil of Caesarea, *De ieiunio homiliae* 1.9 (PG 31.181A); idem, *Sermo asceticus et exhortatio de renuntiatione sae-culi, et de perfectione spirituali* 6 (PG 31.640B); Pseudo-Athanasius, *Vita et gesta Sanctae beataeque magistrae Syncleticae* 49 (PG 28.1516C–1517A). For discussions in Christian sources of the effects of food and types of diet on the soul see Jerome, *Ep.* 54.10 (Isidorus Hilberg, ed., *Eusebii Hieronymi Epistulae*, CSEL 54–56 [Vienna: Tempsky, 1910–1918], 54:477); John Chrysostom, *Homilia X in Genesim* 2 (PG 53.83); idem, *Homilia LVII in Matthaeum* 4 (PG 58.563); Basil of Ancyra, *De virg.* 10 (PG 30.688C–689B); and Pseudo-Athanasius, *De virginitate* 7 (Eduard F. von der Goltz, ed., Λόγος σωτηρίας πρὸς τὴν παρθένον (De virginitate): Eine echte Schrift des Athanasius, TU 29,2a [Leipzig: J. C. Hinrichs, 1905], 41).

sexual desire are connected psychologically as well as physiologically.

Among early Christian writers, however, representations of gluttony vary significantly, often according to audience (lay or ascetic): gluttony is by some accounts the consumption of gross amounts of rich food and drink resulting in obesity, laziness, and immobility; by other accounts it is the desire for a small change in the normal dietary regimen.[4] Therefore, before I analyze Evagrius's writings addressed to practicing ascetics, I will discuss John Chrysostom's vivid descriptions, in homilies addressed to urban congregations in Antioch and Constantinople, of the physical effects of unrestrained eating, in order to illustrate these different approaches to gluttony and the gluttonous body. We will see that, according to both authors, fasting (whether occasional lay observation of ecclesiastical fasts or individual commitment to a daily regimen) results in specific changes in the body and the soul which help to identify the members of a spiritual elite.

Gluttony in John Chrysostom's Homilies

In Christian discussions of the value of fasting, medical arguments concerning the physical effects of overindulgence or dietary abstinence are common. Herbert Musurillo has identified and discussed this "hygienic motif" in early Christian authors, who argue that fasting and a light diet in general produce numerous health benefits, including better digestion, drier humors, clearer eyes, and easier sleep and breathing.[5] The argument from

4. John Cassian, for example, distinguishes three types of gluttony: the desire for a more delicate diet, the desire to gorge on huge amounts of food, and the desire to eat before the established hour (*Conlationes* 5.11 [E. Pichery, ed., *Jean Cassien: Conférences*, SC 42 (Paris: Éditions du Cerf, 1955), 199]).

5. Herbert Musurillo, "The Problem of Ascetical Fasting in the Greek Patristic Writers," *Traditio* 12 (1956): 17–19. Basil of Caesarea, e.g., notes in his homilies on fasting that medical opinion warns of the dangers of overeating and recognizes the usefulness of food abstinence (ἀσιτία) not only for the treatment of illness but for the maintenance of good health in general (*De ieiunio hom.* 1.4; 1.9; 2.7 [*PG* 31.168C; 177A; 193C–D]). Indeed, writes Basil, fasting is the "mother of health" (ibid., 1.7; 2.7 [*PG* 31.173C; 193C]). See also Asterius of Amasea's homily on the lenten fast, in which he reminds his congregation that fasting removes excess matter (ὕλη) from the body, and is good

health is particularly prominent in the works of John Chrysostom (c.349–407),[6] priest of Antioch, and later, bishop of Constantinople, known for his eloquence in preaching and his entanglement in conflicts with the Empress Eudoxia and with the anti-Origenist party. Chrysostom urges virgins and laypersons alike to avoid luxury and overeating which lead to "countless" afflictions including gout, headache, corrupted humors, stomach tension, dizziness, and dimming vision.[7] His sermons referring to ecclesiastical fasts or moderation in diet are peppered with graphic accounts of the physical consequences of gluttony. Just as a ship overloaded with cargo must get rid of excess, so also the human body burdened by quantities of food greater than that required for the normal processes of digestion must rid itself of excess through vomiting.[8] Like a swollen, bursting bottle or a

---

for the veins, stomach, digestion, eyes, breathing, and sleep (*Homiliae* 14.2 [C. Datema, ed., *Asterius of Amasea: Homilies I–XIV* (Leiden: E. J. Brill, 1970), 206–207]); Pseudo-Athanasius, *De virginitate* 7, in which fasting is said to heal disease and dry up bodily humors (von der Goltz, 41); and Jerome, *Adversus Jovinianum* 2.10–11 (*PL* 23.313B–314C) on illness caused by gluttonous eating and medical treatments by means of "thin" diet. On the medical use of fasting see Arbesmann, "Fasten, Fastenspeisen, Fasttage" in *Reallexikon für Antike und Christentum,* ed. Theodor Klauser (Stuttgart: Anton Hiersemann, 1969), 7:467–468 and idem, *Das Fasten bei den Griechen und Römern,* Religionsgeschichtliche Versuche und Vorarbeiten, 21/1 (Giessen: Alfred Töpelmann, 1929; reprint, Berlin: Alfred Töpelmann, 1966), 118–126.

    6. The date of Chrysostom's birth is not certain, but is placed between 344 and 354. Robert Wilken accepts the 349 date (*John Chrysostom and the Jews: Rhetoric and Reality in the Late Fourth Century,* The Transformation of the Classical Heritage 4 [Berkeley: University of California Press, 1983], 5). Herbert Musurillo points out that Chrysostom's arguments for moderation and health in fasting represent a later view. In earlier treatises such as *De compunctione* (*PG* 47.393–422) Chrysostom praises the harshness of the ascetic diet and suggests that concern for bodily health is not appropriate to the ascetic life (Musurillo, "The Problem of Ascetical Fasting," 7–8). Chrysostom's change of emphasis on the health effects of fasting may also be related to the fact, reported by Socrates and Sozomen, that Chrysostom's own early austerities left him with a permanently weak stomach and problems with digestion (Socrates, *Historia Ecclesiastica* 6.4 [*PG* 67.672B]; Sozomen, *Historia Ecclesiastica* 8.9 [*PG* 67.1541A]).

    7. *Hom. X in Gen.* 2 (*PG* 53.84); *De virginitate* 69 (*PG* 48.585).

    8. *Homilia XVI in Acta Apostolorum* 4 (*PG* 60.133–134). Plutarch also compares the gluttonous body to an overloaded cargo ship (*De tuenda sani-*

sewer clogged with filthy sludge, the stuffed body spews forth waste through every channel. Chrysostom is not at all subtle when he reminds the Christians of Antioch that the products of gluttony are "discharge, phlegm, mucus running from the nose, hiccups, vomiting, and violent belching."[9] But the most shameful result of gluttony—and, indeed, its most graphic symbol—is excrement. Chrysostom states bluntly, "The increase in luxury is nothing but the increase in excrement."[10] The physical reality of bodily waste is here the vivid sign of sinful immoderation.

In his zeal to encourage regular and sincere fasting among the laity, Chrysostom frequently returns to the idea that gluttonous behavior and the gluttonous body are shameful. Not only does the physical well-being of the individual's body suffer, but her or his status and respect in the household and community are threatened as well by dishonorable excess. Thus the drunken woman shames herself before others: "The free woman disgraces herself in the theater of her slaves, and the slave woman likewise in turn [disgraces herself] among [other] slaves."[11] Nothing is so shameful and ugly, Chrysostom remarks, as a woman who lives in gluttony and drunkenness, who belches out the disgusting smells of wine and spoiled meat and who is unable to lift herself up for all her weight. Her habits are not merely unhealthy; they are "rude," "slavish and thoroughly low-born."[12] Likewise the drunken man is "ridiculous in the eyes of his servants, ridiculous in the eyes of his enemies, pitiful in the eyes of his friends."[13] Here the emphasis is not so much on the physical ill effects of overindulgence in food and drink as on the possibility that one might make a fool of oneself in front of others—particularly those of equal or lesser social standing. Thus Chrysostom appeals to the individual's

---

tate praecepta 10,127c; 22,134c [Frank Cole Babbitt, ed., *Plutarch's Moralia*, Loeb Classical Library (Cambridge: Harvard University Press, 1971), 2:242; 2:276]).

9. *Homilia XIII in epistolam I ad Timotheum* 3–4 (*PG* 62.569–570).

10. Ibid., 4 (*PG* 62.569–570). On the disgrace of vomit, excrement, and the rest, see also *Homilia LXX in Matthaeum* 4 (*PG* 58.660)

11. *Hom. LVII in Matt.* 4 (*PG* 58.564).

12. *Homilia XXVII in Acta Apostolorum* 2 (*PG* 60.207).

13. Ibid.

sense of shame and the instinct to preserve and enhance social position through proper appearance and decorum. In so doing he invokes the very instincts of social snobbery that he often criticizes.[14]

Chrysostom also stresses that gluttony is a danger to health, the cause of diseases of both body and soul,[15] and the source of many evils,[16] but his homilies are striking for their consistent focus on the human body as an object of scrutiny by others and the locus of shame. Indeed, Chrysostom's homilies might well illustrate Robert Parker's assertion that in the ordered society of antiquity "the concrete vehicle of honour is the body."[17] His use of the rhetoric of shame in order to influence the behavior and lifestyle of his audience is further developed in frequent comparisons of dishonorable slaves of passion to their holy, abstinent counterparts.[18] While the woman stuffed with meat and drink is

14. See the discussion and references in Alain Natali, "Christianisme et cité à Antioche à la fin du IVe siècle d'après Jean Chrysostome," in *Jean Chysostome et Augustin*, ed. Charles Kannengiesser, Théologie historique 35 (Paris: Beauchesne, 1975), 57–58. Natali observes that between wealthy Christians and pagans in Antioch there existed "a true solidarity of class, a community of moral and cultural reflexes which associated Christians and pagans in the same activity, the service of the city" (57). See also the discussion and references in Wilken, *John Chrysostom and the Jews*, 21, 26–27. For a study of Antioch in the time of Chrysostom see especially André-Jean Festugière, *Antioche païenne et chrétienne: Libanius, Chrysostome et les moines de Syrie*, Bibliothèque des écoles françaises d'Athènes et de Rome, 194 (Paris: Éditions E. de Boccard, 1959). Peter Brown emphasizes the importance of the idea of shame in Chrysostom's thought in *The Body and Society: Men, Women, and Sexual Renunciation in Early Christianity*, Lectures on the History of Religions 13 (New York: Columbia University Press, 1988), 315–317.

15. *Hom. XXVII in Acta* 2 (*PG* 60.206–207). Foods sought not for nourishment but for indulgence become causes for spiritual and physical disease. Chrysostom elsewhere praises the monk's victory "over all the diseases," including the table, money, glory, and envy (*Hom. LXX in Matt.* 4 [*PG* 60.660]).

16. *Homilia I in Genesim* 2 (*PG* 53.23). Chrysostom labels gluttony (ἀδη-φαγία) the "source and patron of numerous evils for the human race" in a passage dealing with the good and bad *exempla* of fasting in scripture.

17. Robert Parker, *Miasma: Pollution and Purification in Early Greek Religion* (Oxford: Clarendon Press, 1983), 325–327.

18. On Chysostom's rhetorical style, see Wilken, *John Chrysostom and the Jews*, 104–127; and George A. Kennedy, *Greek Rhetoric under Christian*

ugly and shameful, the woman who resists gluttony is noble, self-controlled, and fair of form. What is more, "the beautiful state of her soul is conferred upon her body."[19] Similarly, those who live in luxury (τρυφή) allow themselves to be victims to all the passions and desires that arise from it like so many heads of the mythical Hydra. In contrast, Chrysostom describes and praises the nearby monks who have conquered passionate desires as if slaying the multi-headed monster.[20] Monks and other abstinent Christians are subject to neither the whims of the flesh nor the pressures of worldly society, but the lazy man who is always filling his stomach "lies exposed to all who wish to do him harm—if not to all people, then to all passions."[21] Thus those who are immoderate in lifestyle and eating show themselves to be weak victims and ignoble slaves to their own uncontrolled flesh.

One of the clearest examples of Chrysostom's attempts to shame his audience into proper behavior appears in his thirteenth homily on Ephesians. Here Chrysostom urges Christians to put off the ways of "the Gentiles," or those separated from God due to ignorance and greed,[22] and to put on the "garment" of righteousness and virtue. Virtue is not difficult to accomplish, he insists, and as evidence he points to the ascetics who live in the mountains near Antioch and practice severe renunciation.[23] Among these "noble athletes" are young girls who had been accustomed

---

Emperors (Princeton: Princeton University Press, 1983), 241–254. On the use of shame in persuasive argument see Aristotle, *Rhetorica*, 1383b–1385a (John Henry Freese, ed., *Aristotle: The "Art" of Rhetoric*, Loeb Classical Library [Cambridge: Harvard University Press, 1967], 210–220); and on the use of shame in early Christian rhetoric, see Elizabeth A. Clark, "Sex, Shame, and Rhetoric: En-Gendering Early Christian Ethics," *Journal of the American Academy of Religion* 49 (1991): 221–245.

19. *Hom. XXVII in Acta* 2 (*PG* 60.207).

20. *Hom. LXX in Matt.* 3–4 (*PG* 58.658–660). On Chrysostom's relationship to monasticism and ascetic withdrawal see Jean-Marie Leroux, "Saint Jean Chrysostome et le monachisme," in *Jean Chrysostome et Augustin*, ed. Charles Kannengiesser, Théologie historique 35 (Paris: Beauchesne, 1975), 125–144. For his own experience of the ascetic life, see Socrates, *HE* 6.3–4 (*PG* 67.665A–672C); Sozomen, *HE* 8.2; 9 (*PG* 67.1513B–1520A; 1537C–1541A).

21. *Homilia XXXV in Acta Apostolorum* 2–3 (*PG* 60.255–256).

22. Ephesians 4:17–19.

23. *Homilia XIII in epistolam ad Ephesios* 1–3 (*PG* 62.93–97).

to the most delicate, sedentary, pampered lifestyle before being caught by the "flame of Christ." Now, like "noble champions," they eagerly enter the contest. Chrysostom describes their rough clothing, long vigils, rigorous fasts, hard labor, and ministry to the sick. He notes that they work even harder than their household servants.[24] The tenor of the homily changes, however, when Chrysostom turns his attention from the ascetic triumphs of fragile young virgins to the behavior of his lay audience:

> But I demand nothing of this sort from you, as you *want* to be surpassed by women. Yet at least, so far as they are not burdensome, practice these things: control the hand and the licentious eyes. What is so difficult, tell me, what is so hard to manage? . . . Are you unable to dispose of your wealth? At least do not seize the wealth of others, or do wrong to them. Are you unable to fast? At least do not lead yourself into luxury [τρυφήν]. . . . I do not say, take care of the sick; but at least order your servant to do so. Do you see that this is not burdensome? For how could it be, when tender girls have from a great distance run past us? Let us be ashamed, I urge you, . . . women surpass us and obscure us. How ridiculous! What a dishonor! We [males] hold the place of the head, and are conquered by the body [females].[25]

Thus we see that in Chrysostom's homilies, gluttony, or "luxury" in general, is not only physically and spiritually unhealthy but also shameful and dishonorable to the public self. Chrysostom describes, as seen above, three aspects of this shamefulness: the physical repulsiveness of the glutton's body, the threat to social status by the weak or "slavish"[26] behavior of one controlled by desire, and the violation of gender hierarchies when lazy males allow themselves to be humiliated by the superior virtue of disciplined females.[27] Thus while Chrysostom tries on the one hand to separate Christians from their allegiance to the roles and standards of urban society, he appeals on the other hand to the impulses of social elitism and hierarchies in order to fill the ranks of the *Christian* elite. This elite consists both of the urban faith-

24. Ibid., 3 (*PG* 62.98).
25. Ibid., 3–4 (*PG* 62.98–99).
26. *Hom. XXVII in Acta* 2 (*PG* 60.207).
27. Cf. Aristotle, *Rhetorica* 1367a (Freese, 94): male virtues or actions are naturally more noble than female, as males are naturally superior.

ful, who are morally and spiritually distinguished from their pagan neighbors; and ascetic monks and virgins, who are distinguished from lay Christians by their total devotion to God, separation from the distractions of worldly pleasures, and pursuit of virtue.

In his book on rhetoric, Aristotle repeats the traditional saying that "shame dwells in the eyes." That is, shame is conferred or felt when others *see* shameful behavior or the evidence of it.[28] In the case of immoderate eating, then, the person should feel ashamed both by the act of eating gluttonously and the evidence of the act—the obese, ill, lumbering, malodorous body. But in Chrysostom's homilies, not only shame, but also honor, "dwells in the eyes."[29] Just as shameful excess is visible to all, so also honorable abstinence is reflected in the noble appearance of the body.[30]

This is true even of those whom Antiochene Christians cannot see with their own eyes—the monks and female ascetics in the mountains around the city. For Chrysostom manages to "show" them to his audience by means of extended ekphrases on their appearance and lifestyle. In the fourteenth homily on 1 Timothy, for example, he describes the monastery as a "calm harbor" where there is fasting, solitude, singing of hymns, and serenity. The monasteries are "like beacons shining from on high to those approaching at a distance; they remain at the harbor, drawing everyone into their own calm." Here there is no disturbance from worldly concerns, no arguments, bloodshed, or impurity. The monks awaken quickly, refreshed from pure sleep, their hearts and minds not made sluggish by excess food. Their "hands are always pure, for their sleep is regular" and free from fantasies.[31] In

---

28. Ibid., 1384a–b (Freese, 214–218).

29. For a related discussion see Blake Leyerle, "John Chrysostom on the Gaze," *Journal of Early Christian Studies* 1 (1993): 159–174.

30. Indeed, Chrysostom even argues that the body of the one who fasts gives off a sweet smell that is pleasant to others (*Homilia X de statuis* 1 [PG 49.111].

31. Chrysostom seems to be hinting that the monks, because of their dietary abstinence, have few problems with polluting nocturnal emissions or wet dreams; *Homilia XIV in epistolam I ad Timotheum* 3–5 (PG 62.575–578); see also *Hom. LXVIII in Matt.* 3–5 (PG 58.643–648), in which Chrysostom invites his congregation to "observe" the "pleasant spectacle" of the monks' way of life; and *Hom. LXX in Matt.* 3–4 (PG 58.658–661).

stark contrast to the shameful, frenzied excess of the gluttonous body, then, the bodies of monks and virgins display serenity and repose. Chrysostom's interpretation and representation of gluttony in this way weaves together Christian moral exhortation and guidance concerning specific acts of piety with standard rhetorical themes of honor and shame as well as the more general physiognomic approach that links appearance to character and body to soul.

The texts discussed thus far are directed to an audience of primarily lay Christians. These people continue to live "in the world," raise families, and maintain households. Although he urges his congregation to observe regular ecclesiastical fasts and points to local ascetics as examples of perfection, nevertheless Chrysostom does not expect the majority to follow an ascetic regimen.[32] The most he expects is that they not overindulge in either food or sexual activity. "Use the baths," he writes, "take care of your body, throw yourself into the marketplace, have your household, let your servants serve you, and make use of food and drink; but everywhere drive out excess. For this is what causes sin."[33] Thus John Chrysostom's homilies reflect an effort to balance a realistic assessment of his flock's needs and abilities with his challenge that they lead their lives, care for their bodies, and eat in such a manner as to distinguish themselves against the pagan crowd as Christians.[34] His gross caricatures of gluttons,

32. But see Peter Brown, *The Body and Society*. Brown points out that Chrysostom was also concerned that lay Christians not simply delegate responsibility for *enkrateia*, almsgiving, and scriptural study to the monks. On the contrary, Chrysostom preached the ideal of the Christian household as a "little monastery, ruled by the same precepts of the Gospel as those mediated by the monks on the distant mountainside" (311–312).

33. *Hom. XIII in Eph.* 3 (*PG* 62.97).

34. On this see especially *De inani gloria* 19, in which Chrysostom urges parents to raise their son as an "athlete for Christ." Chrysostom explicitly denies that he expects children to be prepared for the monastic life—although he would like it to be the case, nevertheless he accepts that this would be too great a burden for most families (Anne-Marie Malingrey, ed., *Jean Chrysostome: Sur la vaine gloire et l'éducation des enfants*, SC 188 [Paris: Éditions du Cerf, 1972], 102–104). Still, the boy should be brought up in discipline, abstinence, and reverence. The "gates" of his senses must be guarded against corrupting stimuli (23–63 [SC 188:108–162]), and the parents must teach him to fast, pray, keep vigils, and avoid the theater (79–80 [SC 188:182–186]).

painted in broad strokes, are in one sense the images of the human body unrestricted, undelineated, and unconstructed by Christian *enkrateia*. If we turn now to Evagrius of Pontus and his writings intended for audiences of practicing ascetics, the image of the glutton is more delicately drawn.

Gluttony and the Passions of the Soul in Evagrius of Pontus

Evagrius of Pontus's (c.345–399) career is remarkable for its synthesis of heroic spiritual achievement as an ascetic in the Egyptian desert and intricate philosophical speculation and systematization as a theorist and writer.[35] Born in the town of Ibora in Pontus, Evagrius was ordained lector by Basil of Caesarea, and studied with and was ordained deacon by Gregory of Nazianzus, whom he refers to as "our wise teacher" and "the righteous Gregory."[36] A personal crisis led him to Jerusalem, where he was counseled and converted to the monastic life by Melania the Elder. Melania sent him on his way to Nitria and the Cells, areas of the lower Egyptian desert famous for distinguished ascetic individuals.[37] In Egypt, Evagrius was a disciple of Macarius the Great and Macarius of Alexandria, and was associated with the "Tall Brothers" and other monks who would, after Evagrius's death in

35. Useful secondary sources on Evagrius include John Eudes Bamberger, *Evagrius Ponticus: The Praktikos and Chapters on Prayer*, Cistercian Studies Series 4 (Kalamazoo: Cistercian Publications, 1981), xxiii–xciv; Derwas J. Chitty, *The Desert a City: An Introduction to the Study of Egyptian and Palestinian Monasticism under the Christian Empire* (Crestwood, N.Y.: St. Vladimir's Seminary Press, 1966), 49–53; Antoine Guillaumont and Claire Guillaumont, "Évagre le Pontique," *Dictionnaire de spiritualité* 4 (1961): 1731–1744; idem, *Évagre le Pontique: Traité Pratique ou le moine*, SC 170 (Paris: Éditions du Cerf, 1971), 21–112; Antoine Guillaumont, "Un philosophe au désert: Evagre le Pontique," *Revue de l'histoire des religions* 181 (1972): 29–56; and Michael O'Laughlin, "Origenism in the Desert: Anthropology and Integration in Evagrius Ponticus" (Th.D. diss., Harvard Divinity School, 1987).

36. Evagrius, *Pr.* 89; epilogue (Antoine and Claire Guillaumont, eds., *Évagre le Pontique: Traité pratique ou le moine*, SC 171 [Paris: Éditions du Cerf, 1971], 680; 712).

37. Palladius, *HL* 38 (Cuthbert Butler, ed., *The Lausiac History of Palladius*, 2 vols., Texts and Studies 6/1–2 [Cambridge: Cambridge University Press, 1898 and 1904], 2:116–120).

399, be caught up in the controversy over "Origenist" thought with Bishop Theophilus of Alexandria.[38]

In contrast to John Chrysostom, Evagrius writes exclusively for an elite ascetic audience. He is concerned not with the daily interaction of lay Christians with the lures and dangers of urban society, but with the daily struggle against the thoughts and demons that threaten the attainment of passionlessness, knowledge, and pure prayer. Two important features of Evagrius's treatment will be examined here: the relationship between gluttony, renunciation, and health; and the role of gluttony and lust as vices of the soul. While Chrysostom and others stress the health *benefits* of fasting (in order to encourage congregations to observe weekly and Lenten fasts),[39] Evagrius is keenly aware of the possible dangers from a meager diet. This issue of fasting and health is especially prominent in the first book of the *Antirrheticus*, Evagrius's handbook of scriptural verses for "answering back" to evil, demon-inspired thoughts that tempt one to vices.[40] The first book

38. On Evagrius's companions in Egypt see *HL* 11; 24; 35 (Butler, 2:32–34; 77–78; 101–102); *HM* 27 (Latin version of Rufinus, *PL* 21.448–449); Socrates *HE* 4.23 (*PG* 67.516A–521B); Sozomen, *HE* 6.30 (*PG* 67.1384B–1388A). See Gabriel Bunge's recent study on Evagrius's relationship to the two Macarii, "Évagre le Pontique et les deux Macaire," *Irénikon* 56 (1983): 215–227, 323–360. On Evagrius and the Origenist controversy, see Chitty, *The Desert a City*, 49–61; Antoine Guillaumont, *Les 'Képhalaia Gnostica' d'Évagre le Pontique et l'histoire de l'Origénisme chez les Grecs et chez les Syriens*, Patristica Sorbonensia 5 (Paris: Éditions du Seuil, 1962); Francis X. Murphy, "Evagrius Ponticus and Origenism," in *Origeniana Tertia*, ed. Richard Hanson and Henri Crouzel (Rome: Ateneo, 1985), 253–269; Elizabeth A. Clark, "New Perspectives on the Origenist Controversy: Human Embodiment and Ascetic Strategies," *Church History* 59 (1990): 145–162; idem, *The Origenist Controversy: The Cultural Construction of an Early Christian Debate* (Princeton: Princeton University Press, 1992), esp. 43–84. See now Samuel Rubenson's study, in which he argues that Antony himself played a key role in the development of Origenist theology in Egypt and served as a link between Origen and Evagrius (*The Letters of St. Antony: Monasticism and the Making of a Saint*, Studies in Antiquity and Christianity [Minneapolis: Fortress Press, 1995]).

39. See n.5, p. 4.

40. The Syriac text with a translation back into the Greek is found in W. Frankenburg, ed., *Euagrius Ponticus: Syrischer Text, griechische Retroversion*, Abhandlungen der königlichen Gesellschaft der Wissenschaften zu Göttingen, Philologisch-historische Klasse, Neue Folge, 13,2 (Berlin: Weidmann, 1912), 472–545. I rely on the Greek translation here.

is devoted to the struggle "against the thoughts of gluttony." Despite (or perhaps due to) the formal structure of the text, it conveys a sense of immediacy and the very real hunger, loneliness, anxiety, and physical discomfort of rigorous renunciation. Half of the sixty-nine verses address fears of illness and physical weakness from fasting or fears of starvation or running out of food.[41] For example, Evagrius writes, "Against the thoughts that hinder us in our way of life by frightening us and saying that a miserable death comes from harsh fasting—[response:] 'I shall not die, but I shall live, and recount the deeds of the Lord' [Psalms 118:17]."[42] Elsewhere he recognizes the despair brought on by thoughts of pain in the stomach, liver, and kidneys,[43] or the thought that the physical torments of asceticism destroy the body yet are of no use to the soul.[44] Further, demons try to discourage the ascetic in his or her rule of life by conjuring up images and memories of family meals, feast days, and fellowship.[45] Or they suggest the smallest digressions in the daily regimen, such as eating before the established hour[46] or adding a few vegetables,[47] fruits,[48] or a little cooked food[49] to the diet. The demons of gluttony thus prey on human weaknesses and frailty of resolve by means of anxious thoughts about bodily health and comfort. But Evagrius intends to fortify ascetic resolve by warning others of the demons' methods and offering scriptural verses as weapons with which to do battle.[50] Fears of hunger or illness from fasting—based, no doubt, on the experience of those realities in the desert—are to be resisted and shut out of the mind.

41. See, e.g., sentences 1; 5; 8; 13; 14; 15; 16; 19; 21; 22; 26; 34; 35; 43; 44; 47; 48; 49; 50; 51; 52; 56; 57; 59; 65; 67; 69. Book 1 of the *Antirrheticus* is in Frankenberg, 475–485.

42. *Ant.* 1.19 (Frankenberg, 477).

43. Ibid., 1.56 (Frankenberg, 483).

44. Ibid., 1.65 (Frankenberg, 483). On gluttony and anxiety over bodily health see also *Pr.* 7 (SC 171:508–510).

45. *Ant.* 1.3; 25; 29; 32; 36; 38; 39; 40; 60 (Frankenberg, 475–483).

46. Ibid., 1.7 (Frankenberg, 475).

47. Ibid., 1.45; 53 (Frankenberg, 481; 483).

48. Ibid., 1.54 (Frankenberg, 483).

49. Ibid., 1.59 (Frankenberg, 483).

50. The ascetic should imitate Christ, who also answered the suggestions of the devil with words from scripture (*Ant.*, preface [Frankenberg, 473]).

Yet Evagrius's emphasis on the harsh treatment of the body found in the *Antirrheticus* must be balanced with his calls for moderation in other writings. In the *Praktikos*, for example, Evagrius quotes Macarius the Great on the need to keep the body in good health[51] and warns that crafty demons encourage those who are ill or weak to fast more severely or to exhaust themselves by physical exertion.[52] The one who is ill should eat the foods necessary for the improvement of health and should not feel sad about the temporary change in regimen.[53] Indeed, Palladius reports that Evagrius himself altered his diet when he became ill late in life:

> [Evagrius] said, "Since I arrived in the desert I have not eaten lettuce[54] or any other green vegetable, or fruit, or grapes, or meat, nor [have I taken] baths." Later, in his sixteenth year of living without cooked food, because of weakness in the stomach his flesh needed to partake of food cooked over a fire; he did not eat bread, but he partook of vegetables or barley gruel or legumes for two years. In this manner he finished his life, having communicated in the church at Epiphany.[55]

The writings of Evagrius therefore reflect what is a more general ambivalence among ascetic authors over issues of rigorism or moderation, and attitudes toward illness or bodily health.[56] As

---

51. *Pr.* 29 (SC 171:566–568).

52. Ibid., 40 (SC 171:592).

53. *Rerum monachalium rationes* 10 (*PG* 40.1264A).

54. This may be further evidence of an Egyptian tradition which understood lettuce to be an aphrodisiac (see chap. 2, n.111).

55. *HL* 38 (Butler 2:122). The Coptic version of this text notes that the elders forced Evagrius to alter his diet (E. Amelineau, ed., *Historia Lausiaca* [Paris: Ernest Leroux, 1887], 112). I am grateful to Blake Leyerle for her translation of the Coptic.

56. For general studies of Christian attitudes toward health, illness, and medicine in late antiquity, see Darrel W. Amundsen, "Medicine and Faith in Early Christianity," *Bulletin of the History of Medicine* 56 (1982): 326–350; Susan Ashbrook Harvey, "Physicians and Ascetics in John of Ephesus: An Expedient Alliance," *Dumbarton Oaks Papers* 38 (1984): 87–93; Peregrine Horden, "The Death of Ascetics: Sickness and Monasticism in the Early Byzantine Middle East," in *Monks, Hermits and the Ascetic Tradition*, ed. W. J. Sheils, Studies in Church History 22 (Oxford: Basil Blackwell for the Ecclesiastical History Society, 1985), 41–52; Vivian Nutton, "From Galen to Alexander, Aspects of Medicine and Medical Practice in Late Antiquity,"

Jerome, discussed earlier, seems to struggle to balance admiration for rigorous ascetic lifestyle with advice on moderation, so also Evagrius holds in tension the recognition of illness as a normal aspect of the disciplined life which must simply be endured[57] with the practical need to maintain the body in good health.[58]

Given this ambivalence in Evagrius, then, it is nonetheless clear that his writings reflect the physical hardship witnessed and experienced in the Egyptian desert. This is quite naturally in contrast to the emphases in Chrysostom's sermons, born out of an urban setting and addressed to a largely non-ascetic audience, and leads to further distinctions in the representation of fasting and gluttony. One significant distinction is in terms of the expected effects of fasting on the health of the body. Another involves the definition of gluttony and the portrayal of the gluttonous body. Chrysostom's gluttons are obese, lazy slaves to the belly whose bodies are like sewers clogged with rotting, corrupting sludge.[59] They are pathetic laughingstocks who can barely move and who

---

Dumbarton Oaks Papers 38 (1984): 1–14; and Owsei Temkin, *Hippocrates in a World of Pagans and Christians* (Baltimore: The Johns Hopkins University Press, 1991).

57. E.g., *Ant.* 1.3; 34; 43; 44; 48; 51; 57; 59 (Frankenberg, 475; 479–483).

58. *Pr.* 29 (SC 171:566–568). Often this tension seems to amount to contradiction. In his *Sententiae ad virginem*, Evagrius instructs the virgin, "Do not scorn your sister because she eats, and do not be elated at your abstinence; for you do not know what the Lord has determined nor who will stand in his presence" (*Sententiae ad virginem* 50 [Hugo Gressmann, ed., *Nonnenspiegel und Mönchsspiegel des Euagrios Pontikos*, TU 39, 4b [Leipzig: Hinrichs, 1913], 150]. Sentences 9 and 10 also stress moderation in fasting [Gressmann, 146]). Here Evagrius downplays the importance of physical asceticism in the spiritual life. This is not surprising. Yet in the next sentence he writes, "The one who pities her bloodshot eyes and her wasted flesh will not rejoice in the passionlessness of her soul." (Ibid., 51 [Gressmann, 150]). Now physical hardship seems expected, if not necessary. I do not want to overemphasize this tension in Evagrius—again, it seems to run throughout ascetic literature in the late fourth century. The overall position of Evagrius appears to be that while illness and hardship should not be feared and might even be expected as consequences of rigorous discipline, nevertheless they should not be sought out for their own sake or in order to confirm individual ascetic prowess. Here as elsewhere Evagrius is concerned with the danger of pride developing with ascetic accomplishments—a danger especially likely in monastic communities.

59. John Chrysostom, *Hom. XIII in I Tim.* 4 (PG 62.569–570).

behave shamefully in front of their servants.[60] In contrast, Evagrius's "gluttons" are the ascetics who would like a few vegetables with their rock-hard piece of bread. Gluttony for Evagrius is not so much the gorging on huge amounts of fancy food as it is the nagging desire for variety, for satiety, for security, for fellowship, for health. It thus represents much more than just the desire for food; it is the desire for the former lifestyle and community that have been renounced by those in the desert.

Evagrius most often treats the subject of gluttony in the context of discussions of the eight vices or evil thoughts or *logismoi* (λογισμοί).[61] This concept appears in many of Evagrius's works and provides the organizing structure for the *Antirrheticus* as well as a large section of the *Praktikos*,[62] and the treatises *On the Eight Spirits of Evil*[63] and *On the Vices Opposed to Virtues*.[64] The eight vices are gluttony (γαστριμαργία), lust (πορνεία), love of money (φιλαργυρία), sadness (λύπη), anger (ὀργή), listlessness (ἀκηδία), vainglory (κενοδοξία), and pride (ὑπερηφανία).[65] They are dynamically interrelated and dependent on each other,[66] and they are the favorite tools of demons who would interrupt progress in discipline. In his treatise *On the Various Evil Thoughts*, for example,

60. *Hom. XXVII in Acta* 2 (*PG* 60.207); *Hom. LVII in Matt.* 4 (*PG* 58.564); *Hom. XXXV in Acta* 3 (*PG* 60.256).

61. Evagrius most often uses the word λογισμοί to mean *evil* thoughts inspired by demons and freely interchanges the terms "thoughts of" and "demon of" or "spirit of" a certain vice (A. and C. Guillaumont, *Évagre le Pontique*, SC 170:56–57, 64–65). For general discussions of the theory of the *logismoi* see esp. ibid., SC 170:63–93; Irénée Hausherr, "L'origine de la théorie orientale des huit péchés capitaux," *Orientalia Christiana* 30 (1933): 164–175; and now Clark, *The Origenist Controversy*, 75–84.

62. *Pr.* 6–33 (SC 171:506–576).

63. *De octo spiritibus malitiae* (*PG* 79.1145A–1164D).

64. *De vitiis quae oppositiae sunt virtutibus* (*PG* 79.1140B–1144D). For a discussion of the Greek and Syriac texts see J. Muyldermans, ed., *Evagriana Syriaca: Texts inédits du British Museum et de la Vaticane*, Bibliothèque du Muséon 31 (Louvain: Publications universitaires/Institut orientaliste, 1952), 59–60.

65. *Pr.* 6 (SC 171:506–508). In the treatise *De octo spir. mal.* anger appears before sadness (*PG* 79.1153C). Each of the vices also appears in the older non-Christian moralist theories.

66. On the order of the vices see A. and C. Guillaumont, *Évagre le Pontique*, SC 170:90–93; and Hausherr, "L'origine," 171–173.

Evagrius explains that the first demons to oppose ascetic practice are those who excite gluttony and the appetites, followed by those who stir up greediness, and those who compel one to seek the respect or honor of others. These demons appear one after the other in turn. "For it is not possible to fall into the hands of the spirit of *porneia* without having fallen from gluttony."[67] Likewise, anger does not arise without quarrels or struggles over food, possessions, or glory. Indeed, the example of Jesus demonstrates that it is imperative to overcome these three types of demonic temptations, as he himself was tempted with suggestions of gluttony, greed, and vainglory.[68]

Evagrius's theory of the eight vices is further elaborated by John Cassian, in his *Institutes* and *Conferences*.[69] Cassian is more explicit than Evagrius about the direct causal connection between the vices. Thus gluttony leads to sexual lust (*fornicatio*), lust leads to avarice, and so on. Likewise, victory over gluttony is the first step in the repression of all vices.[70] The last two vices, vainglory and pride, arise not necessarily from an indulgence of the

67. *De diversis malignis cogitationibus* 1 (*PG* 79.1200D–1201A). The text of the treatise, which is included in the *PG* among the works of Nilus but is attributed to Evagrius in many of the Greek manuscripts, appears in *PG* 79.1200D–1233A, supplemented by *PG* 40.1240A–1244B and the chaps. in J. Muyldermans, *A travers la tradition manuscrite d'Évagre le Pontique*, Bibliothèque du *Muséon* 3 (Louvain: Bureaux du *Muséon*, 1932), 47–55.

68. *De div. mal. cog.* 1 (*PG* 79.1201A–B); Matthew 4:1-11.

69. *De institutis coenobiorum* 5 (Jean-Claude Guy, ed., *Jean Cassien: Institutions cénobitiques*, SC 109 [Paris: Éditions du Cerf, 1965], 186–258); *Con.* 5 (SC 42:187–217). Cassian follows Evagrius's order of the vices in *De octo spir. mal.* , with anger before sadness. See Michel Foucault's discussion of Cassian, "The Battle for Chastity," in *Western Sexuality: Practice and Precept in Past and Present Times*, ed. Philippe Ariès and André Béjin, trans. Anthony Forster (Oxford: Basil Blackwell, 1985), 14–25. It must be noted that while the influence of Evagrius on Cassian is undeniable, and that much of Cassian's ascetic method and theory is clearly Evagrian, Cassian does not mention Evagrius by name. This no doubt reflects the controversy over "Origenist" theology in the late fourth and early fifth century (see the sections on Evagrius and Jerome in chap. 5, below). Further, Cassian translates the Evagrian system to the West with many of its suspect features toned down—for example in place of Evagrius's emphasis on *apatheia* Cassian stresses "purity of heart" as the ascetic goal. On these issues see esp. Guillaumont, *Les 'Kephalaia Gnostica,'* 77–80.

70. *Inst.* 5.3 (SC 109:192); *Con.* 5.10 (SC 42:197–199).

preceding six, but in fact from their successful extirpation. After a certain amount of success in the battle against evil vices, the ascetic is at risk of becoming proud and boastful. The danger of falling into pride is also a prominent theme in Evagrius and the Evagrian tradition. Evagrius recognizes that the one distinguished in virtue might easily begin to think that she or he, not God, is alone responsible for ascetic achievements.[71]

Cassian notes that gluttony is unique among the eight evil thoughts because it can never be completely eradicated—the desire for food is essential for sustaining human life.[72] Gluttony and sexual lust are further distinguished because they exist naturally in human beings, they both require an external object of desire, and they are both consummated in a bodily act. As physical passions with corporeal effects, gluttony and lust require corporeal asceticism for their repression. Such ascetic practices include fasting, vigils, and acts of contrition. Cassian thus compares gluttony and lust to diseases which merit complicated remedies.[73] He elaborates Evagrius's theory of the struggle against these vices by offering, as discussed earlier, a detailed physiological explanation of both the causal relationship between gluttony and sexual desire as well as the effectiveness of fasting as a treatment against lustful desires.

Some of Evagrius's descriptions of the relationship between gluttony and lust are almost metaphorical; others are more physiological. For example, he compares food—as "the material of the belly" that feeds desire—to wood as the material that feeds the flame of fire. Just as a fire dies down when the wood gives out, so also lustful desire is extinguished by lack of food.[74] But on the other hand, Evagrius warns, as a fading fire is rekindled by additional wood, "fading lust is rekindled by satiety of food." Therefore the ascetic man or woman must not yield to the desires of the body:

71. E.g. *Pr.* 14 (SC 171:532–534).
72. *Con.* 5.19–20 (SC 43:211–212).
73. Ibid., 5.4 (SC 42:190–192).
74. *De octo spir. mal.* 1 (*PG* 79.1145A).

Do not pity the body bitterly complaining of weakness, nor fatten it up with extravagant food. For if it recovers, it will rise up against you and it will wage battle against you without truce until it captures your soul, and it will hand you over as a slave to the passion of *porneia*. A body deprived of food is an obedient horse, and it will never throw off its rider, for the one constricted by the bit submits and yields to the hand of the driver. Likewise the body tamed by hunger and vigils neither skips away from the rational control (λογισμός) that mounts it, nor will it whinny from being stirred by passionate impulse.[75]

Sexual desire is therefore checked in the first place by control of the appetite for food and discipline of the body. Evagrius describes the pleasures of taste as the source and cause of lust, and abstinence as the source of chastity. Indeed, "abstinence engenders chastity (σωφροσύνην), but gluttony is the mother of licentiousness."[76] In particular, Evagrius recommends limiting the intake of water as a means toward chastity (πρὸς σωφροσύνην).[77] He himself, according to the *Historia monachorum*, took very little water in his diet, teaching that "the demons frequently approach places full of water," and that excessive moisture in the body generates fantasies.[78] Evagrius explains that food provides the "material" for the increase in lust, but he does not go so far as Cassian or Basil of Ancyra, who actually describe the process of digestion and the buildup of sexual humors in the body. He seems, however, to assume that others understand this physiological relationship.

75. Ibid., 3 (*PG* 79.1148B–C).

76. Ibid., 4 (*PG* 79.1148C–D). See also *De vitiis* 2 (*PG* 79.1141A): "Gluttony is the mother of *porneia*"; and *De octo spir. mal.* 5 (*PG* 79.1149C): "A column rests on its base, and the passion of *porneia* rests on satiety (κόρῳ)."

77. *Pr.* 17 (SC 171:542). See also *Sententiae ad monachos* 102 (Gressmann, 162): "Weigh your bread in the balance and drink your water in moderation, and the spirit of *porneia* will flee from you;" Socrates, *HE* 4.23 (*PG* 67.517A–B).

78. *HM* 20.15 (André-Jean Festugière, ed., *Historia monachorum in Aegypto*, Subsidia hagiographica 53 [Brussels: Société des Bollandistes, 1971], 123); Latin version of Rufinus: ch. 27 (*PL* 21.449A–B). See also his *Epistula ad Melaniam* 7, where Evagrius notes, "I have the habit of eating once a day" (Martin Parmentier, trans., "Evagrius of Pontus' 'Letter to Melania,'" *Bijdragen, tijdschrift voor filosophie en theologie* 46 [1985]: 14 [English translation from Syriac]).

Much of Evagrius's treatment concentrates on the connection of vices (and virtues) in the thoughts.[79] This emphasis on thoughts is especially clear in the *Antirrheticus*, which has a separate book for each of the eight *logismoi* and their demons. Evagrius intends to expose the ways in which demons operate through thoughts that can turn the mind away from its goal of perfection. Sins of actions or deeds must be avoided, but the sins of thought are more subtle and more devastating. Indeed, while demons work against most people through their deeds, they attack monks though their thoughts.[80] Likewise, the monk strives "to stand before the tribunal of Christ" not as a "solitary man" but as a "solitary mind," that is, as one who has conquered not only sin that comes from action but also—and more importantly—sin that comes through thoughts in the mind.[81]

According to Evagrius, demons inspire evil thoughts by arousing memories and images of sensible objects.[82] These thoughts of sensations and sensible objects then bring desire, which in turn leads to pleasure.[83] Images clutter the mind and so distract the monk or virgin from prayer.[84] Demons also battle the ascetic at night by means of images in dreams.[85] Further, demons know by external signs whether one is susceptible to their evil manipulations. Thus "either some spoken word or movement of the body" becomes a sign for the passions of the soul—a sign by which

79. As discussed in chap. 3, it is his disciple John Cassian who will spell out the implications of Evagrius's teaching for the benefit of Western monks anxious to rid themselves of sexual desire.

80. *Pr.* 48 (SC 171:608).

81. *Ant.* , Preface (Frankenberg, 475).

82. E.g., *De oratione* 10; 44–46 (*PG* 79.1169B–C; 1176C–D); *De div. mal. cog.* 2; 16 (*PG* 79.1201B; 1217C–D) and [long recension] 24 (Muyldermans, 48–49); and *Ant.* passim. For a fuller discussion of Evagrius's understanding of the role of images and thoughts, see Clark, *The Origenist Controversy*, 43–84.

83. *Pr.* 4 (SC 171:502).

84. *De oratione* 50 (*PG* 79.1177B); *Sent. ad virg.* 38 (Gressmann, 149).

85. E.g., *Ant.* 2.15; 19; 34; 53; 60 (Frankenberg, 487; 489; 493); *De div. mal. cog.* [long recension] 26; 28 (Muyldermans, *A travers la tradition manuscrite d'Évagre le Pontique*, 50–51). On the role of dreams in the thought of Evagrius, see F. Refoulé, "Rêves et vie spirituelle d'après Évagre le Pontique," *La vie spirituelle: Supplément* 14 (1961): 470–516.

demons perceive whether their thoughts have taken root.[86] Demons require these outward signs because they are not able to know *directly* what is in the human heart.[87] John Cassian likewise stresses that demons are able to detect by outward signs what is hidden in a monk's soul. For example, writes Cassian, if the demons see a monk anxiously looking at the sun to determine how close it is to mealtime, they know that he has already admitted gluttony into his thoughts. Or if the monk submits to their lustful suggestions without resistance, or if they see that his flesh is aroused, it is a sure sign that "the dart of lust is already fixed in his innermost soul."[88] This emphasis on external signs of internal conditions is significant because it further highlights the importance of the external presentation of the ascetic body. We may assume that if demons are able to determine the extent of a monk's perfection by his outward demeanor and actions, then observant humans may be able to make similar physiognomic judgments of each other.

The individual must keep careful watch over his or her own thoughts, and must develop the skill of discerning which thoughts are dangerous. Here Evagrius sounds much like a professional diagnostician. He advises the ascetic to observe carefully and note the strength, frequency, duration, and source of different types of thoughts.[89] Not all thoughts are from demons, but those resulting in unnatural anger or desire certainly are demonic in origin.[90] It is also important to distinguish between different types of demons, which are identified according to the sense objects they cause to be present in the thoughts.[91] For example, the demon of *porneia* brings to the monk images or dreams of women,[92] while

---

86. *Pr.* 47 (SC 171:606).
87. *De div. mal. cog.* 27 (PG 79.1232B–1233A).
88. *Con.* 7.15 (SC 42:258–259).
89. *Pr.* 50 (SC 171:614–616).
90. *De div. mal. cog.* 2 (PG 79.1201C–D). See also *Pr.* 80 (SC 171:668): thoughts from angels bring a peaceful state, whereas thoughts from demons are disquieting.
91. *Pr.* 43 (SC 171:598–600).
92. E.g., *Ant.* 2.1; 6; 15; 32; 35; 36; 37 (Frankenberg, 485; 487; 489; 491).

the demon of greed inspires thoughts of former riches or possessions.[93]

Through such observation and discernment, the dedicated ascetic will learn the various strategies and weaknesses of demons, the particular times when each is most active, and the methods of resistance best suited to different passions. Specifically, Evagrius notes that young monks tend to battle against hunger and fornication while older monks must contend against passions such as anger. "Exhort the old [monks] to master their anger, but the young [to master] their belly. For the psychic demons (οἱ ψυχικοί . . . δαίμονες) battle against the former, but for the most part physical demons (οἱ σωματικοὶ) battle against the latter."[94] Further, physical demons seem to weaken sooner than do demons that affect the passions of the soul.[95] Thus the progression of evil thoughts is in some ways chronological and in relation to the progression of the individual through the ascetic life. During the earlier periods of renunciation the individual will most probably be bothered with thoughts of food and physical relationships, while later the temptation will be weariness or pride in ascetic achievement.

Therefore the struggle against the passions of the flesh and physical methods such as fasting, hard work, and sleeplessness are only the first stages in the effort to conquer all of the *logismoi* and their passions. Moreover, the resistance to all of the passions is not an end in itself but only the prerequisite for the next phase in the spiritual life—the cultivation of knowledge, contemplation, and pure prayer. Evagrius's system thus distinguishes—but does not separate—two phases in the ascetic journey, phases designated as the *praktike* or active (πρακτική) and the *gnostike* or contemplative (γνωστική).[96] The practical phase of monastic life is

93. Ibid., 3.50 (Frankenberg, 501).
94. *Gnostikos* 31 (Antoine Guillaumont and Claire Guillaumont, eds., *Évagre le Pontique: Le Gnostique*, SC 356 [Paris: Éditions du Cerf, 1989], 146; Frankenberg, *Euagrius Ponticus*, 551]).
95. *Pr.* 36 (SC 171:582).
96. Evagrius's system is influenced by the long tradition in antiquity of distinctions between practical or ethical and theoretical or mystical dimensions of the spiritual life (Susanna Elm, "Evagrius Ponticus' *Sententiae ad*

marked by ascetic training and the pursuit of virtue, with the goal
of "purifying the passionate part of the soul."[97] Passionlessness
(*apatheia*), which is at a lower level in spiritual progress than
higher forms of contemplation and knowledge, is thus the result
of closing the mind against thoughts and images that stir up
desire. "Love (ἀγάπη) is the descendant of *apatheia*, and *apatheia*
is the flower of *praktike*."[98]

At the level of *gnostike*, or contemplation, the goal is not
passionlessness, which is assumed, but spiritual knowledge or
theology.[99] Nevertheless the individual does not stop using
ascetic methods or cultivating virtues. In the *Gnostikos*, for
example, Evagrius warns the one who has already progressed to
the level of *gnostike*, "do not soften the dietary regimen in your
life and do not insult the *apatheia* by humiliating it with a fat
body."[100] Yet the focus of ascetic endeavor has shifted from physical techniques to spiritual contemplation. At the level of contemplation there is also a change in the types of demons one must
face: "Those of the demons who lay hold of the passionate part of
the soul are said to oppose the *praktike*. Those again who annoy
the rational part are called the enemies of every truth and the
opponents of contemplation."[101]

Here we recognize the Platonic concept of the tripartite soul,
that is, that the soul is made up of the concupiscible

Virginem," *Dumbarton Oaks Papers* 45 (1991): 107–109; Bernard McGinn,
"Asceticism and Mysticism in Late Antiquity and the Early Middle Ages," in
Asceticism, ed. Vincent L. Wimbush and Richard Valantasis (New York:
Oxford University Press, 1995), 58–74.

97. *Pr.* 78 (SC 171:666). For a good discussion of the *praktike* see A. and
C. Guillaumont, *Évagre le pontique*, SC 170:38–63. I have chosen to leave the
word *praktike* untranslated, but it suggests physical asceticism or ascetic
techniques and practices. On the passionate part of the soul, see below.

98. *Pr.* 81 (SC 171:670). There are degrees of passionlessness (*apatheia*).
Imperfect *apatheia* or "small" *apatheia* is reached when one has successfully
resisted the demons of the physical passions (gluttony, fornication, and
greed), while perfect *apatheia* is obtained by victory over all of the eight
thoughts, although one may still be subject to vainglory (*Pr.* 60 [SC 171:640];
De div. mal. cog. 16 [PG 79.1217B]; Guillaumont, "Un philosophe," 42–43; A.
and C. Guillaumont, *Évagre le Pontique*, SC 170:98–112).

99. *Pr.* 84; 87 (SC 171:674; 678).

100. *Gn.* 37 (SC 356:158; Frankenberg, *Euagrius Ponticus*, 551]).

101. *Pr.* 84 (SC 171:674).

(ἐπιθυμητικόν), the irascible (θυμικόν), and the rational (λογισ-τικόν) parts. The first two together make up the "passionate part of the soul."[102] Although Evagrius nowhere systematically divides the eight vices, demons, or the passions strictly according to this theory, throughout his writings certain vices and virtues are linked to certain parts of the soul. These instances, taken together, suggest a general—though never explicit—division of the vices according to the tripartite soul. Gluttony, *porneia*, and the love of money are associated with the concupiscible soul; sadness, anger, and *acedia* (weariness) seem to be linked to the irascible soul; and vainglory and pride to the rational soul.[103]

102. A. and C. Guillaumont, *Évagre le Pontique*, SC 170:104–105.
103. Ibid., 93–94. A. Guillaumont stresses the need for caution in linking Evagrius's theory of the vices too strictly to the theory of the tripartite soul, as Evagrius himself does not explicitly link the two. R. Draguet has suggested that the passions are divided between only the concupiscible and irascible parts of the soul, with gluttony, *porneia* (lust) and the love of money belonging to the former and the remaining five belonging to the latter. He acknowledges, however, that Evagrius does not make such an explicit division ("L'*Histoire Lausiaque*, une oeuvre écrite dans l'esprit d'Évagre," *Revue d'histoire ecclésiastique*, 41 [1946]: 331). F. Refoulé, on the other hand, associates the first three thoughts with the concupiscible part, anger with the irascible part, and vainglory and pride with the rational part of the soul, or *nous*. As for sadness and weariness, these do not fit simply into any one of the three parts, and so Refoulé labels them "intermediary" vices ("Rêves et vie spirituelle," 485–488). In Evagrius's writings themselves one finds that certain vices are clearly identified as belonging to a particular part of the soul, while other vices are not specifically placed. I will discuss briefly some of the suggestive passages on this issue. Gluttony and *porneia* (and probably the love of money) are associated with the concupiscible or desiring part of the soul (*Pr.* 54 [SC 171:624]). To battle the vices of the concupiscible soul Evagrius suggests fasting, hard work, vigils, solitude, and sleeping on the ground (*Pr.* 15; 22 [SC 171:536; 552]; *De div. mal. cog.* 2; 3 [PG 79.1201D; 1204B–C]). Likewise, in the *Praktikos*, he identifies the *virtues* of the concupiscible soul as chastity, love, and abstinence (*Pr.* 89 [SC 171:680–688]), and in his treatise on vices and virtues Evagrius opposes the vices of gluttony, *porneia*, and the love of money to the virtues (respectively) of abstinence, chastity, and poverty (*De vitiis* 2–3 [PG 79.1141A–D]). Anger obviously belongs to the irascible part of the soul, and sadness probably also (in *Pr.* 22 [SC 171:552] Evagrius mentions both anger and sadness in relation to the irascible soul). The demons affecting it use images that provoke fear and hostility (*Pr.* 54 [SC 171:624–626]; *Ant.* 4–5 [Frankenberg, 503–521]; *De octo spir. mal.* 9–12 [PG 79.1153C–1157C]). To battle against the demons of sadness and anger Evagrius recommends chanting Psalms; forbearance; and acts of mercy (*Pr.* 15 [SC 171:536–538]; *De div.*

In order to train the two passionate parts of the soul, different methods are required for each. Now the passions of the concupiscible soul are the "passions of the body" or "physical passions."[104] Evagrius argues that physical passions require physical methods

---

mal cog. 2; 3 [PG 79.1201D; 1204B–C]) and as the virtues of the irascible soul he names courage and endurance (Pr. 89 [SC 171:680–688]). Evagrius also opposes the virtues of gladness and forbearance to sadness and anger in De vitiis 3 [PG 79.1141D–1144B]). The vice of acedia or weariness defies easy categories. In the Praktikos (36 [SC 171:582]) Evagrius states that weariness (the "noontide" demon) affects the entire soul. Elsewhere Evagrius mentions sadness and weariness together (Sent. ad virg. 39 [Gressmann,149]). Further, in the treatise on vices and virtues (De vitiis 4 [PG 79.1144B–C]) the particular vice of weariness is opposed by the particular virtue of endurance (ὑπομονή), which Evagrius elsewhere identifies as a virtue of the irascible soul (Pr. 89 [SC 171:680–688; cf. 28 [SC 171:564]). In relation to the rational part of the soul Evagrius does not name particular vices explicitly. But there are demons that trouble the rational soul or nous as there are techniques, such as prayer and reading, for cleansing the nous (see e.g. Pr. 15; 84; 89 [SC 171:536; 674; 680–688]; De div. mal. cog. 3 [PG 79.1204B–C]; and Kephalaia gnostica 1.53 [Antoine Guillaumont, ed., Les six Centuries des Képhalaia gnostica d'Évagre le Pontique, Patrologia Orientalis 28,1 (Paris: Firmin-Didot, 1958), 43, from the French translation]). Some of these passages suggest a special link between the vices of vainglory and pride with the logistikon. E.g., Evagrius explains that some demons attack the human as a human, while others attack the human as an irrational being. The second group of demons provoke anger and desire, which are passions that humans share with animals. Thus to the extent that humans have some irrational element, they are subject to these passions and their vices. But the first group of demons operate against the rational element in humans and provoke "pride, vainglory, envy, and censoriousness—by which none of the irrational animals is affected" (De div. mal. cog. 21 [PG 79.1224B–C]). In the same treatise Evagrius again groups the attacks of demons according to anger, desire, and vainglory (long recension 28 [Muyldermans, A travers la tradition manuscrite d'Évagre le Pontique, 51]). These passages thus suggest that the rational element in the human is subject to the vices of pride and vainglory. Finally, it should be noted that John Cassian clearly groups vices according to the tripartite division of the soul, although these vices are not limited to the eight. As vices of the rational soul Cassian includes vainglory and pride; of the irascible soul he includes "furor," sadness, and weariness; and of the concupiscible soul he names gluttony, lust (fornicatio), and the love of money (Con. 24.15 [SC 64:187]).

104. Pr. 35–36 (SC 171:580–582); Gn. 31 (SC 356:146 [= Frankenberg (chap. 135a), 551]). The passions of the irascible part are to be identified with the "psychic" passions (A. and C. Guillaumont, Évagre le Pontique, SC 170:112; and SC 171:587).

for their suppression. Thus while reading, vigils, and prayer are effective against a wandering mind, "hunger, work, and withdrawal" put out the flames of bodily desire.[105] Fasting is, then, particularly suited for battling against physical passions, especially thoughts of gluttony and *porneia:* a frugal diet helps to drive away visions of shameful acts from the monk's imagination;[106] hunger and thirst help the virgin to reduce "evil desires."[107]

While "the passions of the body are cut off by means of abstinence (*enkrateia*)," writes Evagrius, "those of the soul [are cut off] by spiritual *agape*."[108] To heal the irascible soul Evagrius therefore recommends not bodily asceticism but patience and acts of mercy. Further, he advises the monk or virgin to *use* the passions of one part of the soul in order to counteract those of another. Anger is "useful medicine" against the demon of lust. The one who is struggling with sexual desire should therefore call upon the strength of his or her own incensed spirit.[109] Evagrius also opposes vainglory to *porneia,* arguing that "it is not possible for both to attack the soul at the same time. For the one offers honor, but the other is the patron of dishonor."[110] Therefore one is able to resist the temptations of the demon of vainglory by pretending to be affected by the opposing demon of sexual desire. The usefulness of applying opposites in order to fight off particular demons is prominent in Evagrius's practical advice. He warns the anchorite that when the demons see that the irascible soul is aroused, they will suggest that solitude is good, when in fact solitude is harmful to one suffering from anger. Likewise, demons stir up love of humanity and desire for company in one who is afflicted with desire, yet the presence of other bodies is dangerous for that person. Therefore the anchorite must carefully discern the suggestions of demons and do the opposite. In his prescrip-

---

105. *Pr.* 15 (SC 171:536); *De div. mal. cog.* 2 (*PG* 79.1201D).

106. *De div. mal. cog.* 16 (*PG* 79.1217C–D).

107. *Sent. ad virg.* 40 (Gressmann, 149).

108. *Pr.* 35 (SC 171:580). Elm points out, "thus ἀγάπη, love, is ἐγκράτεια of the soul" ("Evagrius Ponticus' *Sententiae ad Virginem,* " 110, n.91).

109. *De div. mal. cog.* 16 (*PG* 79.1217D–1220A); *Ant.* 2.22 (Frankenberg, 489). In these passages Evagrius quotes Psalms 4:4, "Be angry and do not sin."

110. *Pr.* 58 (SC 171:636).

tions for healing the soul beset by demonic threats, Evagrius thus applies the therapy of opposites, familiar both in Hippocratic and Galenic medicine as well as Stoic psychagogy.[111]

It is important to remember that the concupiscible and irascible parts of the soul are the seats not only of evil thoughts or vices, but of virtues as well.[112] Thus the former is the seat of desire—not only sexual desire, gluttony, or greed, but also the desire for virtue and knowledge of God. Likewise the latter is the seat not only of useless anger, but also courage and strength. The health of the soul requires not the suppression of the passionate part, but its orientation toward proper objects: "The reasonable soul works according to nature when its concupiscible part desires virtue, its irascible part fights for it, and its rational part undertakes the contemplation of existing things."[113]

111. Ibid., 22 (SC 171:552); see also *De div. mal. cog.* long recension 22 (Muyldermans, *A travers la tradition manuscrit d'Évagre le Pontique,* 47), where Evagrius warns that none of the anchorites who is angry, sad, or afflicted with vainglory should seek solitude. As discussed in chap. 2, the use of opposites is a method found in medicine, and in particular in the writings of Galen. But Galen recommends the application of opposites not only in order to maintain the health of the body. He also finds it useful for the health of the soul. In his treatise on the passions of the soul, Galen notes that the "power of irascibility" may help one to fight against "the other [power], which the ancient philosophers called the concupiscible, and which rushes irrationally toward the pleasures of the body" (*De cognoscendis curandisque animi morbis* 6 [Kühn 5:27]). On the opposition of anger and desire, see also Plato, *Respublica* 440a (Paul Shorey, ed., *Plato: The Republic,* 2 vols., Loeb Classical Library [Cambridge: Harvard University Press, 1963], 1:400) and *SVF,* ed. Hans von Arnim (Leipzig: B. G. Teubner, 1903–1924; reprint, 1964), 3:133 (no.489).

112. In chapter 89 of the *Praktikos,* Evagrius lists the virtues of the tripartite soul. The virtues of the rational part are prudence, comprehension, and wisdom; of the concupiscible part the virtues are chastity, *agape,* and abstinence; of the irascible part the virtues are courage and endurance. Justice is a virtue of the entire soul (SC 171:680–688). On the traditional sources of this passage see the editors' note (SC 171:681–683). John Chrysostom also discusses the virtues and vices of the tripartite soul in *De inani gloria* 65 (SC 188:162–164).

113. *Pr.* 86 (SC 171:676); *Keph. Gn.* 3.59 (PO 28.121–123), where Evagrius argues that all evil comes from the intellect, *thumos,* or *epithumia,* but it comes from using these parts, which were created by God, *contrary* to nature. On the contemplation of existing things see A. Guillaumont, "Un philosophe," 44–45. On the relationship between Evagrius, Clement of

In the ascetic theory of Evagrius, then, desire is not to be eradicated from the soul. On the contrary, desire, like irascibility, is necessary to the pursuit of virtue, *apatheia*, and spiritual knowledge.[114] The ascetic goal is to cleanse the concupiscible part of the soul of evil desires—including gluttony, *porneia*, and greed—and preserve useful desire. Basil of Ancyra illustrated this same idea by prescribing the ascetic's "sacrifice" not of the entire liver (which represents desire in general) but only the lobe of the liver (which represents evil desire).[115] Evagrius demonstrates that in Christian ascetic theory the goal of *apatheia* does not include the complete absence of passion and desire, but rather the absence of desire that is directed toward physical objects of pleasure and the reorientation of the desiring element in the soul toward spiritual objects.[116] Geoffrey Harpham has captured this paradoxical role of desire in asceticism:

> Desire is, of course, asceticism's abiding problem. But it is simply wrong to say, as so many have, that Christian asceticism excludes desire, for it manifestly exploits the desires to achieve spiritual perfection, to be united with God, to reach a condition of stability and permanence. While asceticism recognizes that desire stands between human life and perfection, it also understands that desire is the only means of achieving perfection, and that the movement towards ideality is necessarily a movement of desire.[117]

For Evagrius, the turning of the soul toward the cultivation of knowledge is such a "movement of desire"—desire, finally, to be with Christ in original unity.[118] It is a movement from practical

---

Alexandria, and the Stoic theory of *apatheia* see A. and C. Guillaumont, *Évagre le Pontique*, SC 170:98–112, and see the discussion of the soul's virtues in Musonius Rufus in chap. 2, above.

114. See, e.g., *De div. mal. cog.* 17 (*PG* 79.1220B). Further, for Evagrius the physical body is good and necessary for the fulfillment of the *praktike* (*Pr.* 53 [SC 171:620]; Guillaumont, *Les 'Kephalaia Gnostica,'* 110–113; A. and C. Guillaumont, *Évagre le Pontique*, SC 170:106–107).

115. See chap. 3.

116. This is nowhere represented more explicitly than in the *Sententiae ad virginem*, where the virgin's spiritual object of desire—the heavenly bridegroom—is very much the source of pleasure (see below, chap. 6).

117. Geoffrey Galt Harpham, *The Ascetic Imperative in Culture and Criticism* (Chicago: University of Chicago Press, 1987), 45.

118. The *Kephalaia Gnostica* is the best source for Evagrius's teaching on

ascetic exercises—beginning with fasting—to *apatheia, agape,* and *gnosis.*[119] Fasting, then, is one of the first steps in the process of healing the soul. Just as gluttony, as the first of the eight evil thoughts, produces the other *logismoi* if unchecked, so also fasting facilitates the cultivation of all virtues by beginning the process of detachment from[120] or destruction of[121] bodily desires. While satiety dulls the intellect[122] and inhibits prayer,[123] fasting "will cleanse you of transgressions and sins; it exalts the soul, sanctifies the mind, drives away demons, and prepares [you] to be near God."[124]

It is true that much of Evagrius's work focuses on the psychological struggles of asceticism. His analysis of demonology and the workings of thoughts in the soul is developed into a complex theory. Yet it would be inaccurate to minimize the place of physical asceticism in Evagrius's theory, to separate *praktike* from *gnostike.* First, while Evagrius distinguishes between and ranks these as phases in the spiritual life, they are both crucial to the entire process of salvation and reintegration into original unity. Indeed, Evagrius himself is known in early monastic sources not only for his vast learning and abilities in the discernment of thoughts, but also for his "incredible" abstinence.[125] Palladius even reports that at the end of his life Evagrius measured his own success in the desert by his endurance in fasting and by the fact that, before his death, he had been free of fleshly desires for three years.[126] Progress in the spiritual life is made through struggle,

---

original unity of all intellects, the fall or "movement" of all intellects save Christ away from contemplation of God in that unity, and the return of intellects to reintegration with Christ. See, e.g., *Keph. Gn.* 2.3; 3.2; 3; 28; 6.33–34 (PO 28.61; 99; 109; 231).

119. E.g., *Pr.* prologue, 8; 81; 91 (SC 171:492; 670; 692–694).
120. *De div. mal. cog.* 3 (*PG* 79.1204A).
121. Ibid., 2 (*PG* 79.1201D); *Sent. ad virg.* 40 (Gressmann, 149).
122. *De octo spir. mal.* 2 (*PG* 79.1145C).
123. *De oratione* 50 (*PG* 79.1177B).
124. *Rerum mon.* 10 (*PG* 40.1261D).
125. *HM* (Latin) 27 (*PL* 21.449A). For other sources which highlight both Evagrius's high level of learning as well as his ascetic guidance and achievements, see *HM* 20.18 (Festugière, 123); *AP* Evagrius, 6–7 (*PG* 65.176A); *HL* 38 (Butler, 2:120–121); Coptic *HL* (Amelineau, 112–115).
126. *HL* 38 (Butler 2:122).

through practical methods which help the individual resist temptation to evil desire. This effort of resistance, *askesis,* is the beginning of salvation: "Take away temptations and nobody will be saved."[127]

But further, we paint ourselves into a methodological corner if we as historians base our analysis of the ascetic life on Evagrius's distinction between the practical and the contemplative. We cannot reconstruct early Christian ascetic practice solely on the basis of the theoretical articulation of its practitioners, any more than one could reconstruct the playing of a game solely on the basis of the rules abstracted and articulated by its players.[128] Thus although Evagrius theorized his experience into a dazzling system (and his theory is itself deserving of scholarly analysis and may continue to inspire modern practitioners), simply to transfer the language and principles of Evagrius's model to scholarly descriptions of ascetic practice is problematic. A more useful approach is represented by Luke Dysinger's recent study, in which he argues that the interpretation of Evagrius's theory of prayer (which is often seen as apophatic) needs to take into account not only Evagrius's rhetorical stress on wordless and imageless prayer, but also what we know about the daily ritual of psalmody, in which recitations and prostrations alternated with periods of silent prayer. This ritualized practice, which was repeated over and over again each day, provides a "bridge" that allows us to integrate the two "sides" of Evagrius.[129]

---

127. *AP* Evagrius, 5 (*PG* 65.176A).

128. Pierre Bourdieu writes, "Just as the teaching of tennis, the violin, chess, dancing or boxing extracts a series of discrete positions, steps or moves, from practices that integrate all these articficially isolated elementary units of behaviour into the unity of an organized, oriented practice, so informants tend to present either general norms (always accompanied by exceptions), or remarkable 'moves', because they cannot appropriate theoretically the practical matrix from which these moves can be generated and which they possess only in practice" (*The Logic of Practice,* trans. Richard Nice [Stanford: Stanford University Press, 1990], 102).

129. Luke Dysinger, "The Significance of Psalmody in the Mystical Theology of Evagrius of Pontus," *Studia Patristica* 30 (1997): 175–181. I am grateful to Fr. Dysinger for sharing an early copy of his article with me.

Abstinence and the Control of Passion

Evagrius argues that through ascetic practices, such as fasting, acts of mercy, and prayer, the soul is healed and "the new human comes into existence, restored according to the image of the creator, in whom—because of the holy *apatheia*—there is neither male nor female, and—because of the one faith, and *agape*—neither Greek nor Jew, . . . slave nor free."[130] The monk is able to judge progress in this "holy *apatheia*" by means of certain signs, just as demons are able to determine the state of the individual's soul by means of external clues. Freedom from wicked and distracting thoughts, and in particular calm sleep which is undisturbed by images and fantasies is "proof of *apatheia*."[131]

The absence of polluting and disturbing dreams is also one of the factors in John Chrysostom's description of the high level of sanctity among monks. Both Chrysostom and Evagrius define a level of holiness and passionlessness that few have yet attained. Chrysostom, in the homilies discussed in this chapter, appeals to his congregation's sense of shame in order to inspire some to seek a higher level of spiritual honor and achievement, whether in the midst of the city or as new ascetic recruits. Evagrius writes for those who have already chosen the "perfect" life of ascetic struggle and contemplation.[132] His disciples are members of an ascetic elite. Yet both groups must struggle against attachment to

---

130. *De div. mal. cog.* 3 (*PG* 79.1204C); cf. Galatians 3:28.

131. *Pr.* 64 (SC 171:648); *De div. mal. cog.* 4 (*PG* 79.1204D); and see Refoulé, "Rêves et vie spirituelle," 488–493. Although Evagrius's discussion of dreams as an indicator of the state of the soul does not extend explicitly, as in Cassian, to the problem of nocturnal emissions, this issue is certainly implied.

132. In *De justis et perfectis* Evagrius draws a distinction between the "just," who fulfill the minimum requirements of the gospel, and the "perfect" who strive for complete imitation of Christ. While the "just" may avoid adultery, theft, and anger, the "perfect" have no desire, keep no possessions, and love those who torment them as much as any other person (1; 2; 8 [Muyldermans, *Evagriana Syriaca*, 105–106 (Syriac); 143–144 (French). I am using the French translation.]). In the prologue to the *Praktikos* Evagrius suggests that some teachings should be kept secret and restricted to an elite group, "so that we not cast pearls before swine" (SC 171:492–494).

the desires, pleasures, and temptations of this world. And both lay and ascetic Christians may evaluate progress in virtue and the soul's health in part by changes in the body's demeanor, shape, gestures, and movements. Gluttony, for both authors, represents the unrestrained body, the undisciplined soul; fasting represents the beginning of the process of reorienting the soul towards God, the kingdom, and original blessing. Fasting is a first step on the path that leads the individual into the very life of the angels.[133] We must now turn our attention to this eschatological concept, its role in fourth-century ascetic theory, and its relationship to ascetic fasting.

133. Chrysostom writes that monks who have slain the Hydra of passions receive some of the blessings of the resurrection in this life. Almost "bodiless," they live angelic lives (Hom. LXX in Matt. 3–4 [PG 58.658–660]). For Evagrius, through apatheia the human imitates the angels (see A. and C. Guillaumont, Évagre le Pontique, SC 170:107–108). In Evagrius's metaphysical and ontological system fallen intellects have three types of bodies (all created through Christ or the Logos in the "second creation" of bodies and the material world). The level of body as well as the corresponding level of contemplation is determined according to the extent of the intellect's fall from original unity. The three levels of bodies are those of the angels, humans, and demons (e.g. Keph. Gn. 1.68; 3.4; 5.11 [PO 28.49; 99; 181]). In the process of salvation, the fallen intellect can pass from one level of body to another. The goal is the passage of intellects to the angelic state and finally to bodiless unity (e.g., Keph. Gn. 2.77; 79; 3.20; 47–48; 66; 6.69 [PO 28.91–93; 105; 117; 125; 247]). For general discussions of Evagrius's theory of bodies and angels, see A. and C. Guillaumont, "Évagre le Pontique," 1739–1741; A. Guillaumont, Les 'Kephalaia Gnostica,' 249–252; Murphy, "Evagrius Ponticus," 256–258; and the section on Evagrius in chap. 5.

CHAPTER FIVE

Fasting and the Return to Paradise

THE COLLECTED SAYINGS of the desert fathers record a story about Abba John the Dwarf. One day John announced to his brother, "I want to be free from care, like the angels are free from care, not working, but constantly serving God." Stripping off his cloak, he left his brother and wandered off into the desert. But after a week had passed John returned and knocked on his brother's door. John's brother asked "Who are you?" John replied, "I am John, your brother." But his brother responded, "John has become an angel, and is no longer among human beings," and refused to let him in. The next morning, opening the door, he said to John, "You are a man and you must again work in order to eat." John fell down before his brother and begged forgiveness.[1] Another story concerns Macarius of Alexandria. When invited, for the second day in a row, to eat with a group of brothers, Macarius said, "You must eat, children, because you are still flesh; but I do not want to eat now."[2] These two incidents illustrate the tension, found throughout ascetic literature, between the ideal of "angelic" perfection and the persistent reality of physical needs. John the Dwarf was humbled to learn that he could not survive if he completely disregarded the needs of his body; but Macarius, like so many other heroes of the desert, nevertheless tried to live—to

---

1. *AP* John the Dwarf 2 (*PG* 65.204C–205A).
2. *AP* Macarius of Alexandria 1 (*PG* 65.304D).

whatever extent possible—as if he were no longer flesh.[3] The requirements for shelter, clothing, food, and the labor by which to meet these requirements signal the limitations of the human condition, which is marked finally by the inescapable facts of bodily existence: suffering, illness, and death. Yet the ideal of living without bodily cares or physical suffering—as the angels live, and as Adam and Eve lived before the fall—informs much of monastic hagiography and ascetic discourse.[4]

Bryan S. Turner has argued that the sociology of medicine and the sociology of religion overlap on these same issues of "human suffering and the indignity of death." Medicine and religion are in this sense "inevitably cultural responses to the problem of theodicy."[5] Both systems and their discourses are concerned with the questions of and responses to embodiment.[6] I have shown that, in early Christian asceticism, medical or physiological models and techniques blend with spiritual advice and theological speculation to form a coherent religious lifestyle. This lifestyle is based in part on the "management of desire by diet."[7] Thus, as we have

3. In the *Lausiac History*, Palladius relates that Macarius once irritated the monks of the Pachomian community at Tabennisi by eating nothing but a few cabbage leaves for the whole of Lent. The brothers complained to their leader, "From where did you bring this bodiless man (ἄσαρκον) for our condemnation? Either throw him out, or else know that we are all leaving you." (Palladius, *HL* 18 [Cuthbert Butler, ed., *The Lausiac History of Palladius*, 2 vols., Texts and Studies 6/1–2 (Cambridge: Cambridge University Press, 1898 and 1904), 2:52–53]).

4. On the themes of the angelic life and the return to paradise in early monastic writings, see P. Suso Frank, *Angelikos Bios: Begriffsanalytische und begriffsgeschichtliche Untersuchung zum 'engelgleichen Leben' im frühen Mönchtum*, Beiträge zur Geschichte des alten Mönchtums und des Benediktinerordens, 26 (Munich: Aschendorff, 1964).

5. Bryan S. Turner, *The Body and Society: Explorations in Social Theory* (Oxford: Basil Blackwell, 1984), 83–84.

6. Gregory of Nyssa keenly identifies this connection in his treatise *On the Soul and the Resurrection*. People are so afraid of death, he writes, that "all thought about living comes from the fear of death." Thus the importance of physicians and medical methods for controlling illness and prolonging life. Indeed, all worldly enterprises—including the building of homes, agriculture, fortifications, and warfare—aim finally at preserving human life for as long as possible in the face of inevitable and terrifying death (*De anima et resurrectione* [*PG* 46.13A–B]).

7. I borrow Turner's phrase (*The Body and Society*, 3).

seen, certain ascetic writers exhibit a medical "confidence" that physical techniques and regimens will enhance individual holiness by transforming the body itself—making it less and less of a stumbling block and more of a companion to human communion with the divine.

In the following pages I will discuss some of the ways in which ascetic practices in general—and fasting and virginity in particular—are related to early Christian visions of original humanity, the fall, and eschatological fulfillment. First, I will set the background for this discussion by briefly overviewing two myths, found in the poems of Hesiod, that were influential in the development of Greco-Roman ideas concerning the human condition and the problem of corporeality, and that continued to influence the Christian discussion. Both the myth of the golden age and the tales surrounding Prometheus are concerned with the state of the earliest mortals and the origins and development of "evils" such as labor, conflict, the differentiation of two sexes, illness, and death. Changes in human diet also figure in these myths of origin, and later philosophers such as Porphyry argue for modification of contemporary dietary practices based in part on their understanding of the first human food.

Turning to the Christian material, I will show that, in several ascetic writers of late antiquity, the ideal ascetic body is a visible sign or representation of both the original, pure human body of paradise and the incorruptible condition of the paradise to come. Ascetic discipline looks back to the garden and forward to the kingdom. By fasting, as by chastity and renunciation of "the world," the ascetic aligns herself or himself with ideal humanity—the perfect, trouble-free humanity created "in the image of God,"[8] and the future humanity restored to that image. By fasting, one not only imitates the obedient eating required of Adam and Eve, but also imitates the angels, who do not eat, but are completely rational beings devoted to the worship and service of God.

In the protological and eschatological arguments underlying ascetic theories, the imitation of the angels and the restoration of paradise are linked. The condition of the redeemed in the

---

8. Genesis 1:26-27.

kingdom of God will be like that of the angels;[9] but the resurrection is nothing less than the "restoration of the fallen ones back to the ancient state. . . . bringing back to paradise the one who was cast out of it."[10] I will highlight these themes as they relate to the ascetic practice of fasting and the ideal of virginity, in the writings of those treated earlier, as well as in Basil of Caesarea, Pseudo-Athanasius, and others. As I argued in chapter three, fasting and self-denial were expected by some authors to alter the form and functions of the ascetic body. Here I will discuss how these physical changes relate to the eschatological hope that one might overcome the suffering and limitations of the flesh and once again dwell in communion with God and the angels in paradise.

Humanity in the "Golden Age"

Reflection on the harsh realities of the human condition, including labor, violence, bodily suffering, decay, and death, has led often to reappraisals of the course of history and the value of human "progress." A negative view of the current state of humanity, a realization that things and people are not as they should be, may in turn result in a positive valuation of life in earlier times. Such "primitivism" is well represented in ancient Greco-Roman literature.[11] The earliest known explicit treatment of the theme of a better past is from the seventh century B.C.E., in Hesiod's *Works and Days*.[12] According to Hesiod, the first humans were a "golden

---

9. Here the sayings attributed to Jesus in the synoptic Gospels are key: "for in the resurrection they neither marry nor are given in marriage, but they are like angels in heaven" (Matthew 22:30); "for when they rise from the dead, they neither marry nor are given in marriage, but they are like angels in heaven" (Mark 12:25); "the children of this age marry and are given in marriage; but those who are deemed worthy to attain to that age and to the resurrection from the dead neither marry nor are given in marriage; for they cannot die any longer, because they are equal to angels and are children of God, being children of the resurrection" (Luke 20:34-36).

10. Gregory of Nyssa, *De hominis opificio* 17 (*PG* 44.188C–D).

11. See the very useful study and collection of texts by Arthur O. Lovejoy and George Boas, *Primitivism and Related Ideas in Antiquity*, A Documentary History of Primitivism and Related Ideas, vol. 1, Contributions to the History of Primitivism (Baltimore: The John Hopkins Press, 1935).

12. Hesiod, *Opera et dies*, 109–201 (M. L. West, ed., *Hesiod: Works and Days* [Oxford: Oxford University Press, 1978], 100–104).

race" of mortals made by immortal gods in the time of Cronus. These people of the "golden" age did not experience unhappiness, labor, grief, or any evil. Death was as gentle as falling asleep. The earth spontaneously bore food for their happy feasting, and they lived in peace with each other, with animals, and with the gods.[13]

After this golden race was "covered by earth," a new race of silver was created.[14] These humans were "much worse by far." Their lives were shorter; they were foolish, injurious toward each other, and impious toward the gods. For this they were "hidden away" by an angry Zeus. The people of the Bronze Age, created next by Zeus, were such lovers of violence that they destroyed themselves. Hesiod then reverses the deterioration of the races by describing the fourth race of semidivine heroes as more just and righteous. Although these heroes destroyed themselves in war, Zeus gave them life after death on the "islands of the blessed," where their existence was like the life of the golden age—happy and abundant with food given by the earth. Finally, Hesiod tells of the current race of iron. As the golden age was characterized by peace, comfort, piety, and bounty, the Iron Age is full of suffering, labor, war, impiety, dishonorable behavior, and all forms of evil. The end of the Iron Age is not foretold in Hesiod's account, but as he himself wishes that he had died *before* or been born *after* this wicked race, he suggests that he expects some better condition after its demise.

In Hesiod's account, diet is one of the indicators of the superiority of the golden race. Although the poet does not explain the origins of meat-eating within this tale, we can assume that the first diet was vegetarian, as we are told that the earth provided abundant food automatically. It is equally important for Hesiod that, whatever food the people of the golden age ate, they did not toil or resort to violence in order to procure it. In contrast, later races were subject to hard work and violence.[15] What is *suggested*

13. Lovejoy and Boas note that Hesiod's golden age is characterized not by frugal living, as is the case in other accounts, but by idleness and feasting (*Primitivism*, 28).

14. Hesiod gives no reason within this account for the disappearance of the golden race, but he notes that they exist now as *daimones* who protect humans (121–123 [West, 100–101]).

15. For a discussion of the question of food in Hesiod's myth of the ages

in Hesiod—that early vegetarianism and harmony with animals was superior to later killing and flesh-eating—is elaborated in the works of later authors.[16]

The Neoplatonic philosopher Porphyry (third century C.E.) is a valuable source on this topic, as he quotes from or summarizes the arguments of several thinkers, including Empedocles, Theophrastus, and Dicaearchus, in his *On Abstinence from Animal Food*. Empedocles (fifth century B.C.E.), for example, taught that history and the cosmos flow in cycles in which the forces of friendship (φιλία) and strife (νεῖκος) dominate in turns. Arguing against animal sacrifice, he asserted that in earliest times friendship dominated and was possessed by everyone, and that because humans believed that they were related to other living beings, they did not kill animals. It was only after the opposing forces of strife and war came into prominence that injustice and injury toward animals as well as toward other humans were practiced.[17] Aristotle's student Theophrastus (c.370–c.288 B.C.E.) also argued that the earliest, purest religious practices did not include animal sacrifice. His history of sacrificial offerings in *On Piety* is known to us primarily by Porphyry's summary.[18] According to Theophrastus, the first humans to live in Egypt sacrificed not animals or even first-fruits, but grass, which the earth produced long before trees and animals. As trees appeared, and then various grains, these were then offered in sacrifice to the gods.[19] As time

---

see Johannes Haussleiter, *Der Vegetarismus in der Antike*, Religionsgeschichtliche Versuche und Vorarbeiten, 24 (Berlin: Alfred Töpelmann, 1935), 54–56; and Daniel A. Dombrowski, *The Philosophy of Vegetarianism* (Amherst: University of Massachusetts Press, 1984), 19–21. While Dombrowski uses ancient sources to bolster the modern case for vegetarianism, his survey of the ancient material (pp.19–119) is accessible and useful.

16. Haussleiter traces this view and alternatives to it through several authors in his chapter "The Prehistory of Food in Light of Vegetarianism" (*Der Vegetarismus*, 54–78).

17. Porphyry, *De abstinentia* 2.21–22 (August Nauck, ed., *Porphyrii Philosophi Platonici: Opuscula Selecta* [Leipzig: Teubner, 1886; reprint, Hildesheim: Georg Olms, 1963], 150–152). See also the discussions and texts cited in Lovejoy and Boas, *Primitivism*, 32–34; and Haussleiter, *Der Vegetarismus*, 157–163.

18. *De abst.* 2.5–32 (Nauck, 135–162). See Haussleiter, *Der Vegetarismus*, 237–245; Dombrowski, *The Philosophy of Vegetarianism*, 71–74.

19. *De abst.* 2.5–6 (Nauck, 135–136).

progressed, dietary practices also changed. Theophrastus repeats the traditional saying, "enough of the oak (ἅλις δρυός)," to signify the shift from a diet of acorns to a new diet (including grains, breads, and then meat) and new methods of procuring and preparing food (including agriculture and hunting).[20] The habits of flesh-eating and blood sacrifices began, according to Theophrastus, not from some good cause, but due to famine or another ill fortune. Further, humans were punished for this defilement and "transgression" (παρανομία): some became atheists while others developed misconceptions of divinity.[21]

Porphyry uses Empedocles and Theophrastus to support his case against both the consumption of meat and the continuing use of animal sacrifices in Greco-Roman religious practice.[22] The thrust of his argument is that these habits are recent features in the steady decline of the human condition away from its harmonious beginnings. The original condition of humanity is further elaborated in Porphyry's selection from Dicaearchus's *Life in Greece* (fourth century B.C.E.).[23] Dicaearchus refers back to Hesiod's golden race of humans who were "akin to" the gods[24] and far superior to our own race. Killing no animals, needing no labor for food, the first humans did not know agriculture or any other art. Theirs was a life of leisure, but not luxury. For while the earth produced enough food to meet their needs, they ate frugally due to scarcity.[25] Yet their light, vegetarian diet led also to the superior health of the golden race. Dicaearchus emphasizes that they suffered no disease: "for none of [the physicians'] instructions will be found more favorable to health than that which

20. Ibid., 2.5–7 (Nauck, 136–138); Pierre Vidal-Naquet, "Plato's Myth of the Statesman, the Ambiguities of the Golden Age and of History," *Journal of Hellenic Studies* 98 (1978): 132. On the proverb "enough of the oak," see Lovejoy and Boas, *Primitivism*, 95, n.159.

21. *De abst.* 2.7–9 (Nauck, 137–140).

22. It should be noted that Porphyry says his treatise, and thus his arguments for vegetarianism, are directed to those who lead a philosophical life—not to those who practice mechanical arts, athletes, soldiers, sailors, or public speakers (ibid., 1.27 [Nauck, 104]).

23. Ibid., 4.2 (Nauck, 228–231).

24. Ibid. (Nauck, 229).

25. This is in contrast to Hesiod's description of the feasting of the golden race.

[says] not to make superfluous excrement, from which those ones always kept their bodies pure."[26] The purity and health of the first bodies were matched by the health of the first human relationships: there were no wars or disputes to divide people.[27]

But in later times, because of the multiplication of desires and love of possessions, humanity slipped away from its peaceful condition and simple diet and into first the pastoral life and then the agricultural life. Little by little, people became more cruel toward each other and animals, eventually degenerating into farmers, warriors and meat-eaters. Dicaearchus's account of human history thus adds several significant dimensions to the Hesiodic outline: the ancient Greeks were "akin to" the gods while later humans were made from an "adulterated and inferior material"; lack of knowledge of any art, including agriculture or war, accounted for their life of leisure; their bodies were healthier, free of disease, and without excess waste; the specific cause of their deterioration was desire for possessions and distinction; and finally, Porphyry notes, abstinence from animal food was no less important than any other factor in their happy life.[28]

These few examples of "primitivism" in ancient thought present the most important features of this tendency. Yet the opposing view—that the human condition has *improved* through time and with the developments of culture and technological arts—is also articulated in the ancient sources. In this view the first humans led a miserable, beastly existence. Subject to attacks from wild animals as well as the elements, unable to provide themselves with food or warm shelter, suffering from poor nutrition and diseases, their life was not to be envied. On the contrary, whether through invention from necessity or the gifts of beneficent gods (such as Prometheus or Demeter), the use of fire, farming techniques, cooking, animal husbandry, language, medicine, and political power were seen as civilizing progress.[29] Porphyry

26. Porphyry, *De abst.* 4.2 (Nauck, 229).
27. Ibid. (Nauck, 230).
28. Ibid. (Nauck, 230–231).
29. A prominent example of this view is found in Aeschylus's *Prometheus Bound*, 440–506. Here Prometheus is portrayed as the cultural hero by whose grace the first humans learned how to survive. In the play Prometheus reports that he took pity on the helpless and miserable mortals and so taught them

himself indicates that some critics of vegetarianism used this type of argument. They claimed, according to Porphyry, that the ancients avoided meat not out of piety (οὐ δι᾽ εὐσέβειαν), but because they did not yet know how to cook with fire.[30]

If we return to Hesiod and the story of Prometheus's deception of Zeus and gifts to mortals—as related in the *Theogony* and *Works and Days*—the ultimate value of cultural developments is ambiguous.[31] Prometheus is portrayed as one who steals the fire (hidden by Zeus as a punishment for Prometheus's earlier trickery)[32] because he wants to help mortals. Yet Prometheus's gift of stolen fire provokes Zeus to dispatch another "gift" to mortals: the first woman, Pandora, with her jar of evils which, once released, change the condition of humanity forever.[33] Mortals once lived like the gods and survived without unhappiness or hard work; now they are separated from the gods and their bodily lives are full of struggle, pain, disease, and death. The earth once provided enough ready-to-eat food; people must now work for every morsel to satisfy their daily hunger. The planting, cultivation, harvesting, preparation, and cooking of grain are now necessary to produce what was once freely available. Finally, the first race of mortals experienced themselves as integrated, unified "humans"

the use of fire as well as other cultural arts such as mathematics, language, the use of animals for work, navigation, medicine, the interpretation of dreams, sacrifice, and metal work: in short, "all arts [were given] to mortals from Prometheus" (Herbert Weir Smyth, ed. *Aeschylus*, 2 vols., Loeb Classical Library [Cambridge: Harvard University Press, 1963], 1:254–258). For other examples of "anti-primitivism" in antiquity see esp. Lovejoy and Boas, *Primitivism*, 192–221, 368–388; and Haussleiter, *Der Vegetarismus*, 64–78.

30. *De abst.* 1.13 (Nauck, 96).

31. See *Theogonia* 507–616 (M. L. West, ed., *Hesiod: Theogony* [Oxford: Oxford University Press, 1966], 130–134) and *Opera et dies* 42–105 (West, 97–100). In the latter work, the story of Prometheus's theft of fire and Zeus's retaliatory "gift" of Pandora and her jar of evils is placed directly before the myth of the ages, but the two tales are separate units which do not harmonize with each other (West, *Hesiod: Works and Days*, 172–173).

32. The *Theogony* is clear that Zeus hid the fire from humans after Prometheus tricked him in the distribution of the sacrificial ox (535–569 [West, 131–133]). But in *Works and Days* the poet explains only that Zeus was angry at being deceived earlier by Prometheus (42–52 [West, 97]).

33. *Opera et dies* 54–105 [West, 97–100]. In the *Theogony* the first woman does not have a name, neither does she carry a jar. She is identified as the source of the female race (*Theogonia* 570–593 [West, 133]).

(ἄνθρωποι); now they are males with separate female counterparts. What is more, men must struggle endlessly like worker
bees in order to fill the bellies of drone-like, lazy, voracious
women.[34] Thus, as Jean-Pierre Vernant observes, the "developments" in human civilization—in particular, sacrifice, agriculture, and marriage—signify the human condition after the golden
age.[35] While human survival has depended on the learning of various arts, their very existence and necessity signify the loss of
original harmony and effortlessness.

The Hesiodic myths of Prometheus and the golden age present
many of the themes and ambiguities that run throughout Greco-
Roman literature on the origins of human civilization and the
question of the source of evil and suffering. What is significant for
this study of ascetic behavior is the way in which views of the
earliest human condition informed behavior and lifestyle as well
as eschatological expectation. If the earliest state was better than
ours or even perfect, then it becomes a model for us to imitate if
we wish to perfect ourselves. Specifically, if the early humans ate
no meat, then we would do well to follow a vegetarian diet. This
is certainly the implication in Porphyry's use of Empedocles,[36]

34. *Theogonia* 594–602 (West, 134); see also Jean-Pierre Vernant, "At
Man's Table: Hesiod's Foundation Myth of Sacrifice," in *The Cuisine of Sacri-
fice among the Greeks*, ed. Marcel Detienne and Jean-Pierre Vernant, trans.
Paula Wissing (Chicago: University of Chicago Press, 1989), 60–78. Vernant
points out that in Hesiod "the idle and lewd aspect of the *gaster* is found par-
ticularly projected on women" (60). On *gaster* and the female see also Giulia
Sissa, *Greek Virginity*, trans. Arthur Goldhammer, Revealing Antiquity 3
(Cambridge: Harvard University Press, 1990), 59–70.

35. Vernant writes: "Sacrificial practice is presented as the first result and
most direct expression of the distance created between men and gods on the
day that Prometheus started his road to rebellion. The myth connects the ritual of sacrifice to primordial events that have made men what they are, mortal creatures living on earth in the midst of countless ills, eating grain from
the fields they have worked, and accompanied by female spouses. In other
words, men have become a race of beings completely separated from those to
whom at the outset they were very close, living together and sitting at the
same tables to share the same meals—the Blessed Immortals, residing in
heaven and fed on ambrosia, toward whom now rises the smoke of sacrificial
offerings" ("At Man's Table," 24).

36. According to Plutarch, Empedocles taught that the imprisonment of
human souls in mortal bodies is a punishment for flesh-eating (*De esu car-*

Theophrastus, and Dicaearchus; Porphyry himself is clear: "let us imitate the golden race, let us imitate those who were free."[37] For Porphyry, the eating of meat represents the attachment to irrational passions; a lighter, vegetable diet is one step in the process of returning to our former intellectual natures.[38]

Christian Asceticism and the Return to Paradise

The Genesis Account of Paradise and the Fall

In the Jewish and Christian account of creation (Genesis 1–3), the first human is created "in the image of God,"[39] given dominion over the animals, and supplied with food from every plant in

---

nium 1.7,996b–c [Harold Cherniss and William C. Helmbold, eds., *Plutarch's Moralia*, Loeb Classical Library (Cambridge: Harvard University Press, 1957), 12:558]).

37. Porphyry, *De abst.* 3.27 (Nauck, 227). The vegetarians of the golden age were free from slavery to the body and its passions.

38. Ibid., 1.30–31 (Nauck, 107–110). The Pythagorean and Orphic cults, while beyond the scope of the present study, are of course primary examples from antiquity of the avoidance of meat based on beliefs about the human condition and eschatology. In Pythagoreanism, the doctrine of metempsychosis and the pure vegetable food of the golden age are both stressed as justification for a strict vegetarian diet among at least some adherents (see Marcel Detienne, "La cuisine de Pythagore," *Archives de sociologie des religions* 29 [1970]: 141–162; Walter Burkert, *Lore and Science in Ancient Pythagoreanism*, trans. Edwin L. Minar, Jr. [Cambridge: Harvard University Press, 1972], 180–185; and Robert Parker, *Miasma: Pollution and Purification in Early Greek Religion* [Oxford: Clarendon Press, 1983], 291–299). Among the Orphics, the myth of the murderous sacrifice and consumption of Dionysus by the Titans—and the belief that humans were made out of the burnt ashes of the Titans punished for their crime—supported a vegetarian lifestyle. By refusing to participate in animal sacrifice (seen as the perpetuation of the Titan's cannibalism) and leading a vegetarian and ascetic life, the Orphic hoped to rise above the Titanic ashes of the present human condition and return to original purity. Thus Robert Parker writes, "the purifications of Empedocles and Orpheus had a specific eschatological meaning, because they released the soul from a burden of personal inherited guilt" (*Miasma*, 300). On Orphic anthropogony and eschatology see also Vernant, "At Man's Table," 43–51 (comparing Hesiod's account of original sacrifice with the Orphic version of the "sacrifice" of Dionysus); and Marcel Detienne, *Dionysus Slain*, trans. Mireille Muellner and Leonard Muellner (Baltimore: The Johns Hopkins University Press, 1979), 68–94. In general see Haussleiter, *Der Vegetarismus*, 79–163.

39. Genesis 1:26-27.

paradise.[40] God instructs Adam, however, that he may not eat of the tree of the knowledge of good and evil.[41] The original harmony and blessedness in the garden is lost when Adam and Eve disobediently eat the fruit of this very tree. They then discover their own nakedness and make garments out of leaves in order to cover their bodies. God punishes the offenders and the instigating serpent by diminishing the quality of their bodily lives. He puts enmity between the serpent and humans. Women will now experience pain in childbirth and be dominated by their husbands; men will now toil endlessly against cursed ground in order to produce food to eat—food which formerly was freely available. Finally, humans will now have their lives cut short by inevitable death, and their days will be counted off outside of the garden of Eden.[42] Thus in the Genesis myth of creation, as in Hesiod's poems, the "fallen" condition of humanity is characterized by suffering, conflict, gender hierarchy, agricultural labor, and death.[43] By the late fourth century, as we will see, Christian ascetic writers came to focus increasingly on another aspect of original human experience: the place of sexuality both inside the garden and after the fall.[44] The ascetic focus on the problem of

40. Ibid. 1:28–29.
41. Ibid. 2:16–17.
42. Ibid. 3:1–24.
43. In early Christian interpretations of Genesis, as in pagan philosophical interpretations of the "golden age," there are differing views of the ultimate value of human invention and technology. On this see Marguerite Harl, "La prise de conscience de la 'nudité' d'Adam: Une interprétation de Genèse 3,7 chez les Pères Grecs," *Studia Patristica* 7, TU 92 (Berlin: Akademie-Verlag, 1966): 486–495. Harl analyzes texts by Basil of Caesarea and Origen to illustrate two tendencies in interpretation on this issue. One tendency is to interpret the innocence of the garden (signaled by Adam's ignorance of his nudity) as freedom from worldly entanglements and freedom for the pursuit of contemplation. In this understanding, the inventions of human technology (beginning with the weaving of aprons from leaves) are seen as distractions from the contemplation of divinity. Another interpretation saw the developments of human culture as a positive exercise of God-given intellect and inventiveness.
44. Recent studies of this issue include Peter Brown, *The Body and Society: Men, Women, and Sexual Renunciation in Early Christianity*, Lectures on the History of Religions 13 (New York: Columbia University Press, 1988); Elizabeth A. Clark, "Heresy, Asceticism, Adam, and Eve: Interpretations of

sexuality and the praise of virginity as the means by which to return to paradise must be understood in the context of these broader anthropological and eschatological issues: What does it mean to be human and embodied? How are humans related to God? How will fallen humanity return to God and the purity of the garden?

In her remarkable interpretation of the Genesis story, Elaine Scarry notes of the fall of Adam and Eve:

> Part of the knowledge that comes with eating of the tree of good and evil is that they stand, without protest, as creatures with bodies in the presence of one who has no body. It is crucial that these two be said together: the problematic knowledge is not that man has a body; the problematic knowledge is not that God has no body; the problematic knowledge is that man has a body and God has no body—that is, that the unfathomable difference in power between them in part depends on this difference in embodiedness.[45]

Thus the reality of their own naked bodies is not "problematic" for the first humans until they gain knowledge of it through their rebellious eating. Having their eyes opened, Adam and Eve react to their new knowledge by performing "their first cultural act wholly independent of God, the weaving of leaves into aprons."[46] Scarry understands the aprons of leaves as the first "artifacts," the first products of human technology, the first effort by humans to

---

Genesis 1–3 in the Later Latin Fathers," in *Ascetic Piety and Women's Faith: Essays on Late Ancient Christianity,* Studies in Women and Religion 20 (Lewiston, N.Y.: Edwin Mellen Press, 1986), 353–385; Elaine Pagels, *Adam, Eve, and the Serpent* (New York, Random House, 1988); and Ton H. C. Van Eijk, "Marriage and Virginity, Death and Immortality," In *Epektasis: Mélanges patristiques offerts au Cardinal Jean Daniélou,* ed. Jacques Fontaine and Charles Kannengiesser (Paris: Beauchesne, 1972), 209–235.

45. Elaine Scarry, *The Body in Pain: The Making and Unmaking of the World* (New York: Oxford University Press, 1985), 209. See chap. 4 in general and pp. 191–198 on the realms of body (for humans) and voice (for God) in Hebrew Scripture. For a striking contrast in emphases see Jean-Pierre Vernant, "Dim Body, Dazzling Body," in *Fragments for a History of the Body,* ed. Michel Feher, trans. Anne M. Wilson (New York: Zone, 1989), 1:19–47. Vernant discusses the archaic Greek understanding of the body of the gods as a "super-body," a body of splendor, on which archaic culture modeled the ideal human body.

46. Scarry, *The Body in Pain,* 209.

project the body "out into the material world" and free the body of "the pressures and limitations of embodiment"[47] by the act of making.[48] God's response to the human attempt to "cover" the reality of body is to make their bodily experience more painfully obvious:

> The body is made a permanently preoccupying category in the pain of childbirth, the pain of work required to bring forth food, and the on-going unease in relation to any fixed shelter. God accepts their woven refusal to walk naked in His presence and, simultaneously, makes the physical acts of eating and generation, work and rest, themselves complex and cutting nets of difficulty.[49]

Scarry's analysis helps us to focus on the centrality of the problem of embodiment in human endeavor, religious vision, and self-understanding. Ascetic writers in the late fourth century return again and again to the Genesis story in order to argue for the fruitfulness of the ascetic project. In short, the ascetic life becomes a method and means by which one participates in the reversal of the sin of Adam and Eve. The paradise to come will be like the paradise of Eden—before enmity between the sexes, struggle against the elements, and terror of certain death. For some advocates, the ascetic life brings at least partial realization of the blessings of paradise here, in this life, in this body. Rather than participate in the continual making and remaking of this world (by worldly pursuits and desires, worldly eating, and procreation), the ascetic man or woman participates in the paradise still to come—yet already being made present and manifest in his or her "angelic" body. Thus a new self, a new body, and a new society are constructed.

Fasting and the Return to the Garden

The ascetic writers we have discussed previously show a keen awareness that the limitations and frustrations of the body are reminders of the fall, and that Adam and Eve had not been subject

---

47. Ibid., 251.
48. See also Harl, "La prise de conscience," passim.
49. Scarry, The Body in Pain, 209–210.

to such limitations before their sin. For example, John Chrysostom writes that the first humans, while being in the body, nevertheless were not "subject to" their bodies. They had no need for the protection of shelter or clothing, as their condition was "pain free" and "angelic."[50] Along with the blessings of paradise and its abundant food from trees and plants came God's command that Adam and Eve observe a simple rule of abstinence from the fruit of the tree of knowledge. For Chrysostom this prefigures fasting.[51] Asterius, the bishop of Amasea in the late fourth century, contrasts the abstinence required in paradise with the fasting required after the fall. "The law of fasting would not have been given to us," he writes, "if the law of the first abstinence (τῆς πρώτης ἐγκρατείας) had not been transgressed." Further, had the first humans not been disobedient in their eating, there would be no need for seeds, planting, cultivation, irrigation, or animal husbandry; all of the painful labors necessary in order to feed ourselves result from the fall.[52] Thus fasting, whether lay or ascetic, recalls not only the fall and sinfulness, but also the first, blessed abstinence in the midst of the freely available food of paradise. Normal eating, or worldly eating, in this context takes on all the symbolic weight of the fall and the pains of embodiment. Eating is one stage in the cycle of hunger, work, satiety, and emptying. Humans must continually "make" and "remake" themselves[53] until they are removed from this cycle by their deaths.

Other early Christian writers, like Chrysostom and Asterius, stress that the first sin of Adam and Eve was eating or gluttony and that our fasting is in some sense a response to or redress for

---

50. *Homilia XVI in Genesim* 1 (*PG* 53.126).

51. *Homilia I in Genesim* 2 (*PG* 53.23).

52. Asterius of Amasea, *Homiliae* 14.4 (C. Datema, ed., *Asterius Of Amasea: Homilies I–XIV. Text, Introduction and Notes* [Leiden: E. J. Brill, 1970], 207–208).

53. See Scarry, *The Body in Pain*: "At its most modest, man's recreation of himself occurs in his activity of providing himself with sustenance to renew his body each day. The activity of eating, regarded as an exclusively natural process when initiated and controlled by animal instinct, becomes in its entry into human consciousness the starting place of self-artifice, the first occasion of man's assumption of his responsibility for his own making and remaking" (251).

their sin.[54] Among authors of the period, Basil of Caesarea (c.330–c.379)[55] makes this point strongly. God's first commandment that the dwellers in paradise not eat from the tree of knowledge was "the legislation of fasting and abstinence. If Eve had fasted from the tree, we would not have the need to fast now."[56] Fasting is necessary as repentance: "Because when we did not fast we fell from paradise, let us fast now, in order that we may return to it."[57] Similarly, Chrysostom notes that "incontinence of the stomach" cast Adam out of paradise,[58] and Evagrius of Pontus remarks that "the desire for food sparked disobedience, the pleasure of taste threw [us] out of paradise."[59] The individual is thus put in the position of Adam and Eve, and is free to choose obedience (and life in paradise) through his or her fasting. Basil of Caesarea states this quite bluntly, "if you subdue your belly, you will live in paradise, but if you do not subdue [it], you will be a victim of death."[60]

54. See Herbert Musurillo, "The Problem of Ascetical Fasting in the Greek Patristic Writers," *Traditio* 12 (1956): 16–17, n.43; 23.

55. The date of Basil's death is the subject of recent debate, and could be as early as 377. See the discussion in Philip Rousseau, *Basil of Caesarea*, The Transformation of the Classical Heritage 20 (Berkeley: University of California Press, 1994), 360–363.

56. Basil of Caesarea, *De ieiunio homiliae* 1.3 (*PG* 31.168A); idem, *Regulae fusius tractatae* 16.2 (*PG* 31.957C). See also Theodorich Pichler, *Das Fasten bei Basileios dem Grossen und im antiken Heidentum*, Commentationes Aenipontanae 11 (Innsbruck: Universitätsverlag Wagner, 1955), 30–32, 39–41.

57. *De ieiunio hom.* 1.3–4 (*PG* 31.168A–B). Note that while Asterius claims that *enkrateia* was required in paradise but fasting is a consequence of the fall, Basil of Caesarea says that fasting was prescribed in the garden.

58. *Homilia XIII in Matthaeum* 1 (*PG* 57.209).

59. *De octo spiritibus malitiae* 1 (*PG* 79.1145B). On the theme of the gluttony of Adam and Eve as the first sin, see also, e.g., Pseudo-Athanasius, *De virginitate* 6 (Eduard F. von der Goltz, ed., *Λόγος σωτηρίας πρὸς τὴν παρθένον (De virginitate): Eine echte Schrift des Athanasius*, TU 29,2a [Leipzig: J. C. Hinrichs, 1905], 40); Basil of Caesarea, *Sermo asceticus et exhortatio de renuntiatione saeculi, et de perfectione spirituali* (hereafter *De renun.*) 6–7 (*PG* 31.640A–641A); idem, *Regulae fusius tractatae* 16.2 (*PG* 31.957C); Jerome, *Epistulae* 22.10; 130.10 (Isidorus Hilberg, ed., *Eusebii Hieronymi Epistulae*, CSEL 54–56 [Vienna: Tempsky, 1910–1918], 54:157–158; 56:189); and idem, *Adversus Jovinianum* 2.15 (*PL* 23.319B; 321A–B).

60. *De renun.* 7 (*PG* 31.641B).

Thus fasting is required in part because our first ancestors did not meet the more simple requirement of abstinence. But there is another, broader aspect to this connection between Christian fasting and the food of paradise. By fasting we imitate or "return to" the original state of humanity before the fall. This, indeed, is the goal of the ascetic life in general, as will become clear. But fasting imitates a particularly significant aspect of the life of the first humans and is a key element in the individual's renunciation of worldly concerns and orientation toward the kingdom. Basil of Caesarea writes that while fasting is a necessary form of repentance, it is also "the image of the way of life in paradise."[61] What characterizes that way of life? "Wine was not in paradise, [there was] not yet animal sacrifice, not yet meat-eating." Both wine and meat were introduced into the human diet, Basil points out, only after the flood.[62] Jerome likewise argues that the first foods of paradise did not include meat or wine, which were permitted for human consumption after the flood, and only because God saw the hardness of the human heart. Further, Jerome argues, as Christ is "Alpha and Omega, the beginning and the end,"[63] once

---

61. *De ieiunio hom.* 1.3 (*PG* 31.168A).

62. Ibid., 1.5 (*PG* 31.169B); Genesis 9:3, 20–21. See also *Homiliae de hominis structura* 2.6–7 (Alexis Smets and Michel van Esbroeck, eds., *Basile de Césarée: Sur l'origine de l'homme (Hom. X et XI de l'Hexaéméron)*, SC 160 [Paris: Éditions du Cerf, 1970], 238–246). These two homilies on the origin of humanity have been attributed to both Basil of Caesarea and Gregory of Nyssa, and the discussion of their authenticity continues. Smets and van Esbroeck argue that they are Basilean. See the editors' comments in SC 160:13–26, and Jean Gribomont, "Notes biographiques sur s. Basile le Grand," In *Basil of Caesarea: Christian, Humanist, Ascetic,* ed. Paul Jonathan Fedwick, 2 vols. (Toronto: Pontifical Institute of Mediaeval Studies, 1981), 1:33–34. Emmanuel Amand de Mendieta reviews previous opinions on the issue of authorship and argues that while Basil was not the author "in the full sense of the term," the homilies were written by a "compiler" who was probably a monk and used Basil's notes on the topic. Therefore the works are "Basilean" in ideas and teaching ("Les deux homélies sur la création de l'homme que les manuscrits attribuent à Basile de Césarée ou à Grégoire de Nysse," in *Zetesis: Album amicorum* [Antwerp: De Nederlandsche Boekhandel, 1973], 695–716). In his recent study of Basil, Philip Rousseau has also recognized the homilies as "essentially the work of Basil" (*Basil of Caesarea,* 318, n.1).

63. Revelation 1:8; 22:13.

Christ has come we should return to the ways of the beginning. That is, we should avoid divorce, circumcision, and meat-eating.[64] Jerome borrows material from Porphyry's *On Abstinence from Animal Foods* in order to establish the antiquity and ubiquity of food abstinence, and refers to Dicaearchus's views on the golden age in support of the belief that the earliest, meatless diet was the most noble.[65] While Jerome urges abstinence from meat and wine in particular, he and other ascetic authors nevertheless concede that they could both be included in the diet of persons who were either quite young, old, or ill.[66]

Fasting imitates the life in the Garden of Eden not only in terms of specific dietary rules. It also recalls the early state of innocence and detachment from concerns for acquiring food and maintaining a food supply. To fast is symbolically to remove oneself—if

64. *Adv. Jov.* 1.18 (*PL* 23.247B–248A). Basil of Caesarea, unlike Jerome, managed to avoid appearing to condemn the eating of meat. Jerome and others who argued for an essentially vegetarian regimen faced charges of heresy from their Christian opponents who could easily counter, as Jovinian did, with New Testament passages downplaying the importance of food avoidance. Such passages include Romans 14:20, 1 Timothy 4:1-5, and Matthew 11:19 (see *Adv. Jov.* 2.5–17 [*PL* 23.303A–326B]). Tertullian also argues in his treatise (written around 208–211 C.E.) in defense of Montanist fasts that the first foods were from plants and trees and that meat and fish were allowed into the diet only because people had shown themselves to be unable to observe a simple abstinence (*De ieiunio* 4 [A. Reifferscheid and G. Wissowa, eds., *Tertulliani Opera*, CSEL 20 (Vienna: Tempsky, 1890), 278]). Nevertheless, Tertullian insists that now *all* Christians should observe extended periods of fasting. This is a key distinction between Tertullian's pre-monastic view of the church and later ascetic writers such as Jerome who believe that rigorous fasting and other such renunciations are not expected of everyone, but only of "those who desire to be perfect," that is, the elite group of ascetic men and women (*Adv. Jov.* 2.6 [*PL* 23.307B]).

65. *Adv. Jov.* 2.13 (*PL* 23.315C–316A). Jerome's discussion of the actual diet of paradise reflects the same focus on the physical as we saw earlier in his discussion of fasting and sexual desire.

66. As discussed in chap. 3, Jerome recommends to Laeta that she include meat and wine in her young daughter's diet (*Ep.* 107.8 [CSEL 55:299]). For other examples of special dietary allowances of meat and/or wine, see Basil of Caesarea, *Sermones ascetici* 1.4 (*PG* 31.877A); Evagrius of Pontus, *Sententiae ad virginem* 10 (Hugo Gressmann, ed., *Nonnenspiegel und Mönchsspiegel des Euagrios Pontikos*, TU 39, 4b [Leipzig: Hinrichs, 1913], 146); Pseudo-Athanasius, *De virg.* 8; 12 (von der Goltz, 43; 45).

only temporarily—from the worldly obsession with food and the fear of hunger and death, and to align oneself instead with those who were free to contemplate and to commune with the divine. The simple food of the ascetic diet contrasts with the gluttonous desire for delicacies and satiety that characterizes worldly eating. This desire for food is part of the general turning away from God and toward the needs of the flesh. Basil of Caesarea sees this shift represented when Adam and Eve make coverings to hide their newly discovered nakedness. The invention of clothing is only the beginning of human entanglement in technology, invention, and labor. As humans became more and more preoccupied with the requirements of their vulnerable and mortal bodies, they lost the freedom and leisure for contemplation.[67]

To turn one's attention away from the needs of the body and back toward spiritual realities—through physical asceticism and contemplation—is thus to return to the original condition of humanity and original intimacy with God.[68] For John Chrysostom, monks and virgins already have to some extent recaptured this state. Describing their way of life to his congregation, Chrysostom compares monks to Adam before the fall. Their work is what Adam's was: like Adam, they have no worldly anxieties, and they speak freely (μετὰ παρρησίας) with God.[69] Yet these monks are not only like Adam; in their continual prayer, praise, and service to God, they are similar to the angels and imitate the work of the angels. They are unencumbered by worldly sorrows,

67. *Quod Deus non est auctor malorum* 6–9 (*PG* 31.344A–352B), discussed in Harl, "La prise de conscience," 488–490.

68. P. Suso Frank writes, "The renunciation of the world realized in monastic asceticism and the familiar association with God achieved in monastic contemplation brought the monk nearer to the state of Adam in paradise" (*Angelikos Bios*, 106–107).

69. *Homilia LXVIII in Matthaeum* 3 (*PG* 58.643–644). This intimate and free association with God is commonly understood as one of the blessings lost with the fall. Gregory of Nyssa writes that in the original state Adam the first-formed (ὁ πρωτόπλαστος) was not yet clothed by the tunics of skins but looked "freely (ἐν παρρησίᾳ) on the face of God, not yet judging the beautiful by means of taste and sight" (*De virginitate* 12.4 [Michel Aubineau, ed., *Grégoire de Nysse: Traité de la virginité*, SC 119 (Paris: Éditions du Cerf, 1966), 416–418]). On Gregory's spiritual interpretation of taste and sight, see below.

labor, or business—in contrast to those in Chrysostom's audience who are caught up in "commotion and the market."[70] Their superior food is not cooked meat, but the sayings of God, which are like a "wonderful honey."[71]

This characterization of the ascetic life as the life of the angels is common in early Christian literature.[72] Fasting in particular is often associated with the angelic state. By his or her meager diet the monk or virgin imitates the angels, who do not eat, and even achieves the "rank of angels."[73] In general the ascetic understanding of the "angelic life" can be summarized as living while in the body as if one were without a body (as the angels are without physical bodies).[74] Thus Chrysostom writes that the monks he praises "already pursue the ways of the angels. They do not marry, nor are they given in marriage, nor sleep too much, nor live in luxury, but except for a few certain things, they have become even

70. Chrysostom, *Hom. LXVIII in Matt.* 3 (*PG* 58.644).

71. Ibid., 5 (*PG* 58.646).

72. See Frank, *Angelikos Bios*, passim.

73. Pseudo-Athanasius, *De virg.* 7 (von der Goltz, 41): "Fasting is the life of the angels, and the one who practices it has the rank of the angels (ἀγγελικὴν τάξιν ἔχει)." On fasting and the angelic life in monastic literature, see the discussion and citations in Frank, *Angelikos Bios*, 23–27. Characterizations of fasting as angelic are not limited to works directed to ascetic audiences or about ascetic heroes. Basil of Caesarea, for example, in his homilies on fasting tells his audience that fasting is good for marriage, the household, the market, and the city (*De ieiunio hom.* 1.7; 9; 11; 2.7 [*PG* 31.173C–176B; 181A; 184B; 196A]). This is far from the monastic renunciation of the world and reflects Basil's concern to influence lay Christians in their daily activities. He also insists that fasting is "the likeness to the angels (and) the companion to the righteous" (ibid., 2.6 [*PG* 31.193A]). Yet it seems that in general it is among those who have "withdrawn" from "the world" and follow an ascetic way of life that the likeness to the angels is actually realized. Thus in another text directed to a monastic audience, Basil writes that while the Gospel of course relates to married people as well as celibates, nevertheless the celibate person strives actually to participate in the angelic way of life (*De renun.* 2 [*PG* 31.629D]). Gregory of Nyssa describes the angelic lifestyle of Macrina's community of virgins as such that their life was "between the human and the incorporeal nature" and Macrina herself as so detached from the flesh that it was "as if an angel providentially took on human form" (*De vita Macrinae* 11; 22 [Pierre Maraval, ed., *Grégoire de Nysse: Vie de Sainte Macrine*, SC 178 (Paris: Éditions du Cerf, 1971), 178–180; 214]).

74. In Evagrius's system angels *do* have *material* bodies (see p. 201).

bodiless."[75] These monks, as embodied mortals, must still eat and sleep, acquire food, and seek shelter. Yet they are nearly "bodiless" because they have removed themselves as much as possible from worldly society, which remains focused on the whims of the body, and instead become part of an "angelic" society, which is focused on the things of God.

As Chrysostom's comments and the two stories from the *Sayings of the Fathers* cited at the beginning of this chapter illustrate, the ascetic ideal is to exist as if without this suffering, mortal flesh even while in it. Yet it is indeed paradoxical that this realization of bodilessness is achieved to a great extent by means of rigorous, intentional, and careful application of physical methods of renunciation. Thus while the worldly focus on the pleasures of the body is rejected, the ascetic focus on the body's sanctification and response to the "technologies" of renunciation remains. The bodilessness of the angels is imitated and confirmed in the very bodies of human beings.

Fasting, Virginity, and Eschatology

The angelic life is an eschatological concept that informs and motivates Christian ascetic discourse and imagery. We imitate the angels now and perhaps some will realize angelic status even while in the human body, but in the resurrection we will surely live like them. Thus the angelic life and the return to paradise are linked in eschatological expectation.[76] The ascetic theorists of the late fourth century focus more and more on the role of virginity and the renunciation of sexual activity in the restoration of the original state of creation.[77] In the ideology and images surrounding

75. *Homilia LXX in Matthaeum* 4 (*PG* 58.660). For other examples of the angelic life as living as if out of the body see also Jerome, *Ep.* 130.10 (CSEL 56:190–191); Gregory of Nyssa, *De vita Macrinae* 11 (SC 178:178–180); and Basil of Ancyra, *De vera virginitatis integritate* 51 (*PG* 30.772A–B).

76. Frank, *Angelikos Bios*, 106–108, 120–121.

77. Peter Brown, "The Notion of Virginity in the Early Church," in *Christian Spirituality: Origins to the Twelfth Century*, ed. Bernard McGinn, John Meyendorff, and Jean Leclercq, World Spirituality 16 (New York: Crossroad, 1985), 429–433; P. Thomas Camelot, "Les traités 'de virginitate' au IVe siècle," in *Mystique et continence: Travaux scientifiques du VIIe Congrès*

virginity, food and the desire for food become intertwined with sexual desire and the activity of procreation. The preceding chapters have shown that early Christian sources connect pleasurable eating to sexual drive—as they connect fasting to the preservation of chastity—in discussions that show the interdependence of physiological processes and psychological condition. Eating and sexual activity are also connected in ascetic arguments concerning the fall and the coming kingdom. Both activities carry with them the burdens of mortality, labor, and pain. They are absolutely necessary for the preservation of individual lives and the survival of humanity, but have been affected by the fall and are tainted by the desire and passions that now attach to them. These appetites, while necessary and "natural," identify humans as embodied in the face of the bodiless condition of God and the angels and bind us to worldly endeavors. All of the struggles, labors, and passions that accompany our embodiment since the fall tend to separate us even further from our original intimacy with God and our trouble-free existence.[78] Thus eating and sexual activity are primary arenas for ascetic training, and their renunciation becomes the starting point of the reorientation toward paradise.[79]

---

international d'Avon, Études Carmélitaines (Brugge: Desclée de Brouwer, 1952), 281–286.

78. Aside from these associations with early Christian interpretations of the human condition, the social and economic connections between food and sex are recognized by modern sociologists and anthropologists such as Jack Goody, who writes, "Food and sex must both be related to the central human process of production and reproduction" (Cooking, Cuisine, and Class: A Study in Comparative Sociology, Themes in the Social Sciences [Cambridge: Cambridge University Press, 1982], 37, 191–193). The cultural and psychological linking of eating and sexual desire is explored by modern scholars of anorexia nervosa. See the fine overview of the scholarship and the development of the modern disease in Joan Jacobs Brumberg, Fasting Girls: The Emergence of Anorexia Nervosa as a Modern Disease (Cambridge: Harvard University Press, 1988), esp. 171–188; and for a more cultural and political approach, see Susan Bordo, Unbearable Weight: Feminism, Western Culture, and the Body (Berkeley: University of California Press, 1993), esp. 32–36 and 45–69.

79. Of course the association of eating and procreation with the fall and mortality is not new to the fourth-century material. The association between marriage and death—and celibacy and angelic immortality—is already

If fasting is distinctive of the angelic life, however, virginity is its "immortal crown."[80] Especially in fourth-century treatises on the subject, virginity becomes particularly associated with the return to the original perfection, immortality, and incorruptibility of humanity. The individual virgin removes herself or himself from procreation's cycle of birth and death. The virgin's pure and intact body recalls the incorruptibility of the garden—that is, the immunity to biological processes of decay, disease, and death—and anticipates the incorruptibility that will be restored in paradise. As Thomas Camelot writes, "the integrity of the flesh is thus situated in the center of the mystery of the economy of salvation." Virginity becomes "a sign and a hope."[81]

The interpretation of virginity's specific protological motivation and eschatological role—that is, its relation to the created state of original humanity and the consequences of the fall—is central to the patristic ideal of virginity. Further, the interpretation of the nature of sexuality and embodiment both in the garden and in the world after sin informs and underlies much of the theory of fasting—and, indeed, ascetic ideology in general. Fasting's eschatological motivations as well as the physiological expectations attached to it—especially the control of sexual desire—must

---

implied in Luke 20:34-36, and encratic and gnostic texts portray the cessation of marriage and procreation as the key to the resurrection or the liberation of the spirit. See Van Eijk, "Marriage and Virginity, Death and Immortality," 212–224; Brown, *The Body and Society,* 83–121; Gilles Quispel, "The Study of Encratism: A Historical Survey," in *La tradizione dell'Enkrateia: Motivazioni ontologiche e protologiche,* ed. Ugo Bianchi (Rome: Ateneo, 1985), 35–82; Giulia Sfameni Gasparro, "Asceticism and Anthropology: *Enkrateia* and 'Double Creation' in Early Christianity," in *Asceticism,* ed. Vincent L. Wimbush and Richard Valantasis, (New York: Oxford University Press, 1995), 127–146; idem, "Image of God and Sexual Differentiation in the Tradition of *Enkrateia*: Protological Motivations," in *Image of God and Gender Models in Judaeo-Christian Tradition,* ed. Kari Elisabeth Børresen (Oslo: Solum Forlag, 1991), 138–171; and Robert McL. Wilson, "Alimentary and Sexual Encratism in the Nag Hammadi Tractates," in *La tradizione dell'Enkrateia,* 317–339. On the fourth-century sources for encratism see Georges Blond, "L'hérésie' encratite vers la fin du quatrième siècle," *Recherches de science religieuse* 32 (1944): 157–210.

80. Pseudo-Athanasius, *De virg.* 24 (von der Goltz, 59).
81. Camelot, "Les traités 'de virginitate'," 283–284.

be understood in relation to the broader theological and practical issues of the body and sexuality. Because there are important distinctions among ascetic interpreters on these issues, it will be helpful to consider several writers individually and in some detail, and then to draw conclusions about the role of the physical effects of asceticism in confirming individual or group "angelic" status.

Basil of Ancyra. As discussed earlier, Basil explains that in the beginning the Creator divided the original "root of corporeal being" for each of the species, including human beings, into male and female. Further, each fragment of original androgynous unity was endowed with a powerful desire for union with the other in sexual intercourse. By this means, the Creator was able to ensure the population of the earth through procreation.[82] It is curious that in this passage (which appears early in the treatise) there is very little theological context to the account of the creation of the sexes, nor is there any explanation for the Creator's need to accomplish the multiplication of the species through sexual desire and sexual intercourse. If not for a mention of Adam and two quotations from Genesis and Mark,[83] the passage could easily have been taken from a non-Christian philosophical or medical text. (Indeed, we saw a similar description of creation and sexual desire in Galen.) Later in the treatise, however, Basil returns to the theme of creation with a decidedly more "theological" slant. Here Basil argues for virginity as an angelic condition which anticipates—and to some extent realizes—the kingdom and restores paradise through its incorruptibility. Virginity is a splendid thing, writes Basil, representing "some pure seed of the resurrection and the incorruptible life," because virgins already live according to the ways of the resurrection:

> For if in the resurrection they neither marry nor are given in marriage, but are as angels [Matthew 22:30], and will become the children of God

82. *De virg.* 3 (*PG* 30.673B–676C).
83. Basil cites Genesis 1:28, "Be fruitful and multiply, and fill the earth," and Mark 10:7-8, "For this reason a man shall leave his father and his mother and be joined to his wife, and the two shall become one flesh" (ibid. [*PG* 30.673C; 676C]).

[Luke 20:36], those who practice virginity are angels, going around through human life in incorruptible flesh—and not some obscure angels, but exceedingly distinguished.[84]

What is more, while angels have no bodies and remain protected and close to God, with nothing to do violence to their nature, chaste humans must preserve their equality to the angels in spite of all the temptations of the devil and of the flesh. They "have preserved their angelic incorruptibility by means of virtue, in a manner which is very surprising to the Creator."[85] By their rejection of marriage and the fleshly passion that it represents and fosters, then, virgins receive the status of incorruptible angels and anticipate the condition of the kingdom, which is the restoration of paradise. Basil contrasts the "present life" sown by Adam through marriage to the "coming age" sown by Christ through virginal incorruptibility. While humanity followed Adam out of paradise and into marriages, the virgin now follows Christ back into paradise. This is so because there was no sexual intercourse or death before the fall, as there will be no sexual intercourse or death in the kingdom. It was only after their transgression and punishment, after their expulsion from the garden, that Adam and "the woman" had sexual relations.[86]

One may well wonder, then, how Basil's earlier discussion of the implanting of sexual desire, which he presents as taking place in conjunction with the command of Genesis 1:28 (before the fall) to "be fruitful and multiply," harmonizes with the notion that there was no sex in paradise. Basil deals with this issue in the context of his argument that, because of the need to populate the earth, the "Master of our nature" did not command virginity. He writes:

> For he who, for the necessity of marriage (διὰ τὸ ἀναγκαῖον τοῦ γάμου), contrived such a habit in the male toward the female and conversely in the female toward the male (as the treatise indicates at the beginning), so restoring the succession of their race to those who became mortals

84. *De virg.* 51 (*PG* 30.772A–B).
85. Ibid.
86. Ibid., 54 (*PG* 30.777B–C). The idea that Adam and Eve had intercourse only after the fall is not new with Basil (see Van Eijk, "Marriage and Virginity, Death and Immortality," 224–225).

out of immortals, and devising, as has been said somewhere,[87] immortality, and saying on account of this: 'Be fruitful and multiply,' how could it be that he could at that time command virginity?[88]

For Basil, sexual desire, marriage, and the command to fill the earth by means of procreation are the Creator's devices meant to restore a type of immortality to those who had lost original immortality in the fall. The succession of children in this sense is a consolation (παραμυθήσηται) for mortality.[89] If this passage is taken with the earlier description of the separation of the original androgyne, Basil seems to suggest that the separation of male and female and the implanting of desire took place at the time of the creation described in Genesis 1:27-28, that is, before the actual event of the fall and casting out of paradise. He does not discuss the order of these events,[90] but he is clear that there was no sexual intercourse in paradise, that death is a consequence of the fall, and that marriage is necessary because of death. Outside of paradise, the pleasure of sexual activity and the powerful longing for it, which have been woven into the fiber of human flesh, signify the original disobedience and punishment at the same time that they mercifully lead to continuing generations.[91]

While sexual desire and pleasure are created by God and are part of male and female nature,[92] it is clear that for Basil they are "natural" to a condition that would not exist without the first

87. See Van Eijk, who connects the idea of "immortality-by-posterity" to Platonism and Clement of Alexandria. He speculates that Clement may be Basil's source here ("Marriage and Virginity, Death and Immortality," 225).

88. De virg. 55 (PG 30.780A).

89. Ibid., 54 (PG 30.777C).

90. In contrast, Gregory of Nyssa, who shares some of Basil's ideas on these matters, argues that God gave the desire for intercourse and the command to be fruitful and multiply because God knew beforehand that humans would fall from equality with the angels (see the discussion below, and De hom. opif. 22 [PG 44.205A–B]).

91. Thomas Laqueur discusses this idea in late ancient and Renaissance thought: "On the one hand concupiscence and the irresistible attractions of sexual rapture stood as marks in the flesh of mankind's fall from grace, of the essential weakness of the will. But on the other hand pleasure was construed as precisely what compelled men and women to reproduce themselves" ("Orgasm, Generation, and the Politics of Reproductive Biology," *Representations* 14 [1986]: 12).

92. De virg. 3 (PG 30.673C–676C).

sin. Marriage was created by God and is not evil; but with the coming of Christ and the fullness of the earth, virginity has been re-introduced. In this sense virginity is both "against nature," that is, the nature which was devised as a consequence of mortality, and "above the law," that is, the law of Moses and the Gospel—neither of which commands virginity.[93] By abstaining from marriage and its corruption and passions, aided in the preservation of chastity by fasting and the constraint of the body,[94] the virgin follows Christ back to paradise, where she "already lives luxuriously with him without corruption."[95] The virgin therefore "already" achieves to some extent the original state of humanity. When Basil writes that the virgin "is eager to show herself naked and unaware of the pleasure of the body in which she lives,"[96] we are reminded of the nakedness without shame that Adam and Eve enjoyed in the garden.

Gregory of Nyssa. The themes of original creation, the fall, and the restoration of paradise are well developed in several of Gregory's works, especially *On Virginity, On the Soul and the Resurrection,* and *On the Making of Humanity.* His full treatment raises many of the issues central to the ascetic debate on the place of embodiment in creation and salvation. In addition, Gregory's anthropological and eschatological views have been the subject of considerable scholarly discussion in recent years.[97] To

---

93. Ibid., 55 (*PG* 30.780B).

94. The virgin knows that she must constrain her own nature in order to gain the kingdom (ibid., 4 [*PG* 30.677B]).

95. Ibid., 54 (*PG* 30.777B–C).

96. Ibid., 4 (*PG* 30.677A).

97. See esp. Monique Alexandre, "Protologie et eschatologie chez Grégoire de Nysse," in *Arché e Telos: L'antropologia di Origene e di Gregorio di Nissa,* ed. Ugo Bianchi, Studia Patristica Mediolanensia 12 (Milan: Vita e Pensiero, 1981), 122–169; Jean Daniélou, *Platonism et théologie mystique: Essai sur la doctrine spirituelle de saint Grégoire de Nysse,* 2nd ed., Théologie 2 (Paris: Éditions Montaigne, 1954); idem, *L'être et le temps chez Grégoire de Nysse* (Leiden: E. J. Brill, 1970); Gerhart Ladner, "The Philosophical Anthropology of Gregory of Nyssa," *Dumbarton Oaks Papers* 12 (1958): 61–94; Van Eijk, "Marriage and Virginity, Death and Immortality," 230–234; Eugenio Corsini, "Plérôme humain et plérôme cosmique chez Grégoire de Nysse," in *Écriture et culture philosophique dans la pensée de Grégoire de Nysse,* ed. Marguerite Harl (Leiden: E. J. Brill, 1971), 111–126.

attempt a summary of Gregory's thought in a few pages is therefore risky at best, yet such a summary is necessary in order to situate a discussion of virginity and eschatology. Central to Gregory
of Nyssa's theology is his emphasis on the original creation of
humanity in the image and likeness of God (Genesis 1:26-27).
While the image has been obscured in humans because of sin and
passions, it has not been completely lost and will be restored to
its full glory.[98] The "image of God" indicates the divine characteristics in humanity—including rationality, intellect, rulership,
virtue, free will, and freedom from passions.[99] It is this image and
these traits that exist "by nature" in humanity.[100] In the creation
in "the image of God"—which was not yet Adam, the man "of the
earth"[101]—there was no sexual differentiation, passion, taste,
sight, or mortality.[102] The "corruption of the biological life" was
unknown.[103]

98. De virg. 12.1–4 (SC 119:398–420).

99. De hom. opif. 5; 16 (PG 44.137A–C; 184B–C); De an. et res. (PG
46.57B–C); De virg. 12.2; 4 (SC 119:398–410; 416–420).

100. Gregory's notion of nature as the original created norm must be distinguished from other views of nature as what we think of as the "natural"
world or "natural" bodily functions. We saw that Basil of Ancyra, for example, usually associates "nature" with the senses, sexuality, and mortality. For
Gregory "nature" is the image of God and the rest has been added (Daniélou,
Platonisme et théologie mystique, 47–59. See also David L. Blank, "The Etymology of Salvation in Gregory of Nyssa's De Virginitate, " Journal of Theological Studies 37 n.s. [1986]: 85–86). Gregory does, however, sometimes
adopt the usage of "nature" to indicate the natural world and the instincts or
gender characteristics that humans experience as "natural" after the fall. For
example, he writes that he hesitates to call Macrina a woman when she has
gone above nature (De vita Macrinae, prolog [SC 178:140]). Lovejoy and Boas
have assembled a useful appendix distinguishing some of the various meanings and uses of "nature" in ancient literature (Primitivism, 447–456).

101. De hom. opif. 22 (PG 44.204D).

102. Ibid., 16; 17 (PG 44.181A; 188A–C); De virg. 12.2; 4 (SC 119:398–400;
416–418). Gregory uses scripture to bolster his argument. Among the verses
cited the most important are Luke 20:35-36, Romans 14:17 ("The kingdom of
God is not food and drink"), and Galatians 3:28 ("[In Christ] there is neither
male nor female"). To the objection that without sexual activity humans
would not have been able to reproduce themselves, Gregory responds, using
Luke 20:35-36, that as humans were like the angels before the fall, they could
have multiplied like the angels—whatever that mysterious angelic mode of
increase might be (De hom. opif. 17 [PG 44.188A–189B]).

103. Daniélou, Platonism et théologie mystique, 51. Gregory's language

For Gregory, creation in the image of God is that which is referred to in Genesis 1:26 and the first part of verse 27. With the last words of verse 27, "male and female he created them," however, Gregory sees a creation "apart from the prototype (ἔξω . . . τοῦ πρωτοτύπου)."[104] Like Basil of Ancyra, Gregory argues that the division into male and female was accomplished apart from the creation of an angelic, genderless human. Gregory deals more directly and fully with the question of the order and purpose of this division and departure from "the prototype." Because God knew beforehand that humans would freely choose sin and would fall away from their angelic condition into mortality, God distinguished male and female as part of a device by which humans would be able to continue to multiply and accomplish the fullness of the earth. And so it is only after the division that God gives the command to "be fruitful and multiply, and fill the earth" (Genesis 1:28). But while the human body was sexually differentiated, and the potential for sexual procreation devised before the fall, Gregory is clear that there was neither marriage nor labor nor birth in the garden.[105] It seems therefore that "in Paradise, sexuality was not yet operative; the creation of the sexes according to Genesis 1:27 involved only the possibility, not the necessity of sexual propagation."[106]

With the creation of male and female, humanity was linked to the "animal and irrational" parts of creation. From the divine nature the human possesses a "rational and intelligent" element, which does not include the distinction between male and female, and from the irrational life the human possesses "the bodily condition and form which is divided into both male and female."[107]

---

here is perhaps deliberately vague. Although one could understand him to be arguing for a *bodiless* first creation, without taste or sight or biological corruption, he does not go that far. No doubt Gregory has in mind the earlier criticism, by Methodius of Olympus (d. 311) and others, of Origen's views on bodilessness in the creation and the resurrection. This is also a factor in Gregory's interpretation of the tunics of skin (see below).

104. *De hom. opif.* 16 (*PG* 44.181A).

105. Ibid., 17 (*PG* 44.188A–B); *De virg.* 12.4 (SC 119:418).

106. Ladner, "The Philosophical Anthropology of Gregory of Nyssa," 90–91; 93.

107. *De hom. opif.* 16 (*PG* 44.181B–C).

Therefore, "the making of our nature is in some sense double, one made like God, and the other separated according to that distinction [of male and female]."[108] Knowing that humans would lose their angelic condition, God substituted the "beastly and irrational" method of generation—that is, sexual intercourse—for the angelic.[109] With his notion of the "double creation," then, Gregory has drawn out the implications of an idea we saw earlier in Basil of Ancyra, who argued that sexual differentiation and sexual procreation were added because of mortality and the "necessity of marriage."

Now, these additions to the original creation according to the prototype—both sexual difference and the mixture of the animal impulses—were set in place before the fall, as *potential* aspects of human embodiment.[110] But when humans chose, through free will, to sin, and were cast out of paradise, what was potential became operative. This occurred at Genesis 3:21, when God clothed Adam and Eve in the "tunics of skins" before sending them out of the garden. At this point humans actually "assumed that passible and passionate, corporeal-sexual condition"[111] that continues to mark their fall. The tunics of skin are the "form of the animal nature with which we were clothed because of our familiarity with the passionate life."[112] With them we were clothed with "sexual intercourse, conception, childbirth, uncleanness, nursing, feeding, excretion, the gradual growth to adulthood, the prime of life, old age, illness, death."[113] All the passions and sufferings of the biological, corruptible, mortal body were

---

108. Ibid.

109. Ibid., 17 (*PG* 44.189C–D). On Gregory's doctrine of double creation and the influence of Philo see Ladner, "The Philosophical Anthropology of Gregory of Nyssa," 80–86, and Daniélou, *L'être et le temps*, 89–93. See also Corsini, "Plérôme humain," 115–122; Aubineau, *Grégoire de Nysse*, SC 119:400–401, n.4; and Sfameni Gasparro, "Image of God," esp. 151–156.

110. Further, the animal impulses of anger and desire, while not part of the soul by nature, are nevertheless required for the survival of the body and not necessarily evil. They may be used toward either virtue or vice (*De an. et res.* [*PG* 46.64B–68A]).

111. Ladner, "The Philosophical Anthropology of Gregory of Nyssa," 88.

112. *De an. et res.* (*PG* 46.148C–149A).

113. Ibid.; *De virg.* 12.4; 13.1 (SC 119:416–418; 422).

received after the fall. Humanity fell from its proper angelic condition into the degraded condition of the beasts.[114]

In his interpretation of the tunics of skin, Gregory stops short
of identifying them with the body as such or with corporeality
itself. Earlier critics had accused Origen of Alexandria of teaching
that the true nature of humanity was bodiless and that the body
was a consequence of the fall. Although his own thought was
shaped by Origen, Gregory was familiar with and influenced by
the reaction against Origen's teachings, and his tempered language here reflects the theological debate.[115] Thus in Gregory's
treatment the tunics of skin are understood as the animal and
mortal state of the body, or "thick" corporeality. Gregory suggests
that the body before the fall, like the resurrection body, was not
thick and heavy (as are the tunics of skins), but "light" and
"airy."[116] Nevertheless, whatever corporeality there was in paradise is something quite other than the body as we know it—
which is subject to irrational passions,[117] pain, disease, and death.

It is, of course, the ultimate terror and indignity of death that
especially signifies our loss of original blessing. Gregory's writings
reveal his distinct awareness of the magnitude of the loss of

114. Monique Alexandre observes that this opposition between the
angelic and bestial states "plays a fundamental role in Gregory's thought." As
by the fall humanity fell into a bestial, sinful, mortal state, so by *askesis* one
returns to the angelic. "Gregory's anthropology at all points, protology,
history of salvation, eschatology, plays on this opposition angel/beast" ("Protologie et eschatologie," 135, n.64). See also Blank, "The Etymology of Salvation," 86.

115. Modern scholars have been eager to separate Gregory from the taint
of Origenism on the issues of the creation and resurrection body. See, e.g., the
discussion in Daniélou, *L'être et le temps*, 154–164 and 206–221. Daniélou
points out the influence of Methodius of Olympus's critique of Origen on the
thought of Gregory of Nyssa. For other discussions of the tunics of skin see
Daniélou, *Platonisme et théologie mystique*, 27–31, 55–60; Ladner, "The
Philosophical Anthropology of Gregory of Nyssa," 88–93; Aubineau, *Grégoire
de Nysse*, SC 119:159; 418–419 n.1; cf. Jean Gribomont, "Le panégyrique de la
virginité, oeuvre de jeunesse de Grégoire de Nysse," *Revue d'ascétique et
mystique* 43 (1967): 257–258.

116. *De an. et res.* (*PG* 46.108A).

117. The irrational passions such as anger, pleasure, and cowardice arise
in the individual because of our likeness to irrational animals (*De hom. opif.*
18 [*PG* 44.192A–193B]).

immortality and the fear of death that plagues every person. He emphasizes that God did not abandon humans because of their sin. The differentiation of male and female, sexual relations, and the tunics of skin have all been given to humanity as the means by which the fullness of the earth and of time will be accomplished in spite of the fall. Through irrational sexual intercourse, an activity humans now have in common with animals, the predetermined number of souls will be completed and all things will be restored in the necessary time.[118] Thus marriage was invented as a "consolation for death (παραμυθία τοῦ ἀποθνῄσκειν)."[119]

But while marriage is not evil and in fact is a merciful, corrective device serving the goal of salvation in the period after the fall, it is nevertheless primarily that which gives nourishment to death, supplying death with new bodies, keeping the cycle of sexual intercourse, corruption, and decay in motion.[120] Bodily procreation "is no more the origin of life than of death for human beings."[121] Thus, in Gregory's theology, sexual procreation, nutrition, physiological processes, and mortality are linked together as the bestial condition into which humanity degenerated through sin. Further, this condition, symbolized by the tunics of skin, makes the individual all the more susceptible to the irrational passions, which are fueled by exercise of the senses. As Ugo Bianchi observes in regard to Cappadocian theology, "the ontological connection" between "thick corporeality, sexuality, passion,

---

118. *De hom. opif.* 22 (*PG* 44. 205B–C). For the importance of time in Gregory of Nyssa see Brown, *The Body and Society*, 296–304.

119. *De virg.* 12.4 (SC 119:420). Van Eijk points out that Gregory does not explicitly claim that marriage is a way of achieving a kind of immortality through procreation, an idea, found in Basil of Ancyra, which traces back through the platonic tradition. Gregory is not as interested in marriage as "inferior" immortality as in marriage as nourishment to death ("Marriage and Virginity, Death and Immortality," 234).

120. The more "positive" view of marriage is present in the *De hom. opif.* In *De virg.* Gregory emphasizes only the link between marriage and death (12–14 [SC 119:398–444]). Van Eijk's analysis is especially useful ("Marriage and Virginity, Death and Immortality," 230–234); see also Aubineau, *Grégoire de Nysse,* SC 119:160–161.

121. *De virg.* 4.1 (SC 119:432).

sin" underlies Gregory's understanding of creation, the fall, and—as we shall see—salvation.[122]

Central to Gregory's discussion of salvation is the idea that the end-time or the kingdom of God will be like the beginning of creation; the resurrection will be a restoration (ἀποκατάστασις) of the paradise lost in the fall. Salvation involves the recovery of the image of God which is natural and proper in humanity, and the "restoration of our nature in its primitive form."[123] It follows that in the resurrection we will "cast away" the tunics of skin and all the animal, passionate, mortal, degrading processes that are associated with them.[124] Indeed, the resurrection is such an exact mirror of the original state that humanity must proceed back to paradise by retracing the steps by which Adam exited. Thus our first step toward paradise is to abstain from marriage, which was the last point in the departure from it.[125]

By living the life of virginity one imitates the angelic condition and turns away from the bestial state of fallenness.[126] Further, the virgin already receives some of the benefits of the resurrection now, in this life. What are those benefits? One is very practical—the virgin is freed from the miseries of marriage and child rearing. In addition, the angelic incorruptibility and purity of lifestyle anticipate the blessings promised in the resurrection.[127] But most importantly, virginity halts the power of death. While life "according to the flesh" always leads to death (through the

122. Ugo Bianchi, "L'intention du Colloque: Analyse historico-religieuse," in *Arché e Telos: L'antropologia di Origene e di Gregorio di Nissa,* ed. Ugo Bianchi, Studia Patristica Mediolanensia 12 (Milan: Vita e Pensiero, 1981), 16–17.

123. *De an. et res.* (*PG* 46.148A). See also *De hom. opif.* 17; 21 (*PG* 44.188C–D; 201A–204A); *De virg.* 12.4 (SC 119:416–418). For discussions see Alexandre, "Protologie et eschatologie," passim; Daniélou, *Platonisme et théologie mystique,* 84–115; idem, *L'être et le temps,* 205–226; Aubineau, *Grégoire de Nysse,* SC 119:204–207.

124. *De an. et res.* (*PG* 46.148C).

125. *De virg.* 12.4–13.1 (SC 119:416–424).

126. *De virg.* 14.4; 23.7 (SC 119:442; 558–560); *De hom. op.* 17 (*PG* 44.188C–189A).

127. *De virg.* 14.3–4 (SC 119:438–442).

continual begetting of new victims), virginity does not produce death, but life and incorruptibility. The virginal body itself, because it does not participate in the cycle of birth and death, becomes a "boundary (μεθόριος)"[128] between death and life. Death can exercise its power no longer through the bodies of virgins.[129] Although individual virginity does not bring the kingdom any sooner (as the extent of time is already predetermined), nevertheless the individual who removes herself or himself from "life according to the flesh" removes as well the temporal interval (διάστημα) of generations between the self and God.[130]

Returning to Gregory's image of retracing the steps back into paradise, then, release from marriage is the first. Next, those returning "to Christ" must "withdraw from the earthly hardship"[131] which humanity has endured after the fall, and put off the "'tunics of skins,' that is, 'the thoughts of the flesh.'" Next they must reject the coverings of leaves by which they have attempted to hide their shame and stand openly before the eyes of the Creator. "They must reject the deceits of both taste and sight," ignoring the advice of the serpent by gazing only upon beauty and repelling the taste for evil.[132] Thus the return to paradise, angelic

---

128. On μεθόριος in Gregory's thought see Daniélou, L'être et le temps, 116–132.

129. De virg. , 13.2–14.1 (SC 119:428–436).

130. Ibid., 14.4 (SC 119:440); Corsini, "Plérôme humain," 120–121. For this understanding I rely on Van Eijk, "Marriage and Virginity, Death and Immortality," 233–235. He writes: "For the individual who gives up marriage, time is virtually nonexistent. On this point he [Gregory] is joined by all those theologians who, starting from Lk. 20, 34-36, argue that the virgins already partake in the ἀφθαρσία: virginity is always realized eschatology; in virginity time, that is, the process of γένεσις καὶ φθορά, seems to come to an end" (235).

131. Ταλαιπωρία indicates hardship and distress, and Gregory would seem to be referring to reversing the punishment of suffering in agricultural labor and childbirth pronounced in Genesis 3:16-19, as his model is the events of the fall and expulsion from paradise. But to what extent Gregory is here advocating the rejection of physical labor is not clear. Cf. 23.3 (SC 119:532) where Gregory condemns idleness, and see Aubineau's comments (SC 119:423, n.4).

132. De virg. 12.4; 13.1 (SC 119:416–418; 422–426). On this see also De hom. opif. 19–20 (PG 44.197B–201A). Here Gregory explains that the tree of the knowledge of good and evil, from which the protoplast was commanded not to eat (Genesis 2:17), was used as a deceptive lure by the serpent, who

condition of original creation, and intimacy with God are the same stages, in reverse, by which Adam and Eve fell.[133]

In this passage the lifestyle and goals of virginity are highly spiritualized. The ascetic practices of sexual continence, withdrawal from the world, renunciation of the "thoughts of the flesh," control of the senses such as taste and sight, and contemplation are here expressed in terms of mystical ascent.[134] The sense of taste, for example, seems less a physiological reality than a metaphor for "appetite"—either the appetite for evil or the appetite for God. Gregory even interprets the food of paradise as spiritual food.[135] Yet it is interesting that he offers this spiritual reading of the Genesis myth in response to the very practical issue of the shame that some may feel because, like the "irrational animals," humans must eat to stay alive. Therefore one senses behind the allegory the daily bodily behaviors and struggles of individual persons. It seems likely as well that when Gregory writes of the need to "reject the deceits of both taste and sight" he has in mind not just a spiritual rejection of evil, but also ascetic dietary abstinence and control of the bodily senses[136]—by which one is identified with the blessed condition of paradise. Physical eating is for Gregory part of the beastly condition to which we have been subjected in this world. Just as the first human was free from this function and all of the degrading physical processes that go with it, so also we will be freed from it in the kingdom.[137]

---

gave its fruit a good appearance, that it might be "pleasing to the eyes and stimulate the appetite to taste" (197B). Thus it is by activating the powers of taste and sight that the serpent was able to deceive Eve into eating, "and that eating became the mother of death to humanity" (200D). Gregory also seems to play on the connection between the eyes or sight and sensual pleasures. Basil of Ancyra makes this connection as well when he notes that for Adam the "eyes of desire" for evil were opened after he experienced "the taste of pleasure" (De virg. 44 [PG 30.756D–757A]).

133. De virg. 13.1 (SC 119:422–424).

134. Daniélou, Platonisme et théologie mystique, 86–87.

135. De hom. opif. 19 (PG 44.196C–197B): When God gave permission to the one made in God's likeness to eat freely of "every tree in the garden" (Genesis 2:16), we should understand this as a reference to the tree of life.

136. Gregory discusses the usefulness of such a dietary regimen in De virg. (see chap. 3).

137. De hom. opif. 18–19 (PG 44.196A–D).

Thus Gregory of Nyssa's ascetic focus on the role and nature of virginity must be understood in the context of the broader issues of sin and the resulting corporeal sufferings of decay, corruption, and death. As Peter Brown has suggested, for Gregory sexual desire in itself was not the issue; "sexuality, for him, meant reproduction: and the continuity of the human race through reproduction was accepted by him as a sad, but faithful echo of the abiding purposes of God."[138] Through procreation God will bring the human race to completeness; yet in the midst of time each individual must face the terror and certainty of physical death. Gregory understands the human drive to produce future generations as an attempt "to block out the sight of the grave."[139] Through the life of virginity, however, one is able not only to face the enemy, death, but to block its power forever.

Basil of Caesarea. Gregory's anthropology, as it is articulated in these sources, touches on all the key elements of the fourth-century discussion of virginity and salvation. Protological and eschatological motivations for the ascetic life are significant in the writings of four other figures as well. Basil of Caesarea, Evagrius, Chrysostom, and Jerome all rely on arguments from creation, the fall, and paradise in their ascetic formulations. I will highlight the most important such arguments, especially as they relate to ideas found in Gregory and Basil of Ancyra.

In his *Ascetic Discourses,* Basil (brother of Gregory of Nyssa and bishop of Caesarea from 370)[140] notes that while humanity was created in the image and likeness of God, sinful action damaged the beauty of that image "by dragging down the soul toward passionate desires."[141] In order to return to primordial grace and to restore the image of God to its full beauty, then, one must turn away from passionate desires and cultivate *apatheia,* which is in the likeness of the creator. By imitating the divine freedom from passions, one achieves a likeness to God. Virginity, Basil writes, is

138. Brown, *The Body and Society,* 296.
139. Ibid., 297.
140. The most recent study is Philip Rousseau's *Basil of Caesarea.*
141. *Sermones ascetici* 1.1 (*PG* 31.869C–D).

a helpful ally to those who strive for this goal. But virginity is not simply abstaining from procreation; it is demonstrating incorruption in every aspect of life and character, including speech, sight, hearing, eating, and drinking.[142] Therefore the virgin must carefully avoid defilement of any worldly passion such as anger, envy, or vainglory, and orient herself or himself instead toward the incorporeal, angelic life.[143]

Basil writes that the "angelic nature" is "to be free from the yoke of marriage, not to be excited by any other beauty, but to gaze intently on the divine face."[144] The angelic condition as here defined is thus like that of the first human creation in paradise. And the first human was created in the likeness of God. For the bishop of Caesarea as for Gregory, then, the ascetic project revolves around the restoration of the image and likeness of God through imitation in this life of the original, angelic state of paradise. Virginity imitates the freedom from marriage and procreation that was enjoyed before the fall and will be enjoyed in the resurrection.[145] It is "the spiritual life in the flesh, the heavenly life on earth."[146]

As shown earlier, Basil of Caesarea asserts that fasting imitates another aspect of the freedom of paradise, the freedom from a complicated, meat-based diet. While Gregory of Nyssa interprets the diet of paradise spiritually, Basil is more literal in his description of the vegetarian regimen of humans and animals before the fall. He does not go so far as to insist on vegetarianism, as God has permitted the use of animal food after the fall; nevertheless he suggests that those who now desire "to lead their lives in imitation of the life of paradise" make use of fruits and grains, and reject as useless whatever is superfluous or excessive.[147] It is clear that for Basil the diet that includes meat and a wide variety of foods and delicacies is one more result of the fall out of simplicity and undistracted contemplation and into worldly complications

142. Ibid. (*PG* 31.869D–872A).
143. Ibid., 1.2 (*PG* 31.873A–B).
144. Ibid.
145. *De hom. structura* 2.11 (SC 160:256–258).
146. *Epistula* 46.2 (*PG* 32.372B–C).
147. *De hom. structura* 2.6–7 (SC 160:238–246).

and entanglements.[148] He does not condemn the eating of any one type of food,[149] but he contrasts the simple diet of paradise to the desire for variety that attaches to worldly eating: "Since we no longer gaze upon the tree of life, nor glory in that Beauty, henceforth butchers and bakers and a variety of pastries and fragrant foods have been given to us for enjoyment, and some such things console us (παραμυθούμενα) for our fall from that place."[150]

Both Basil of Ancyra and Gregory of Nyssa wrote of marriage as a consolation for death or the loss of mortality. Here Basil of Caesarea uses the same language of consolation in regard to diet. Thus eating and sexual activity are linked again as aspects of the lifestyle that is granted to humans by a merciful God in light of the loss of original blessing. Neither marriage nor meat-eating is condemned as evil, but both are distinctive activities of the corporeal condition after sin and the technologies of culture outside of the garden. Moreover, those who live now in imitation of the angelic life or in anticipation of the return to paradise should avoid both sexual activity and complicated, heavy diets—as they avoid worldly passions and enterprise.

Evagrius of Pontus. Michael O'Laughlin has observed that "the central problem in interpreting Evagrius" is that he "was both a theologian and a teacher of monasticism; as such, he produced a varied corpus of literature, ranging from simple ascetic observations to esoteric theological speculation."[151] When taken together, Evagrius's esoteric reflections on the origin of bodies and the human body and his more "practical" advice on lifestyle (discussed earlier) constitute an ascetic vision dazzling in its scope. The known body of his work manifests the direct influence of Origen's theological speculations as well as the mature ascetic insight of one tested by the rigors of the Egyptian desert. Origen's

---

148. *Quod Deus* 6–9 (*PG* 31.344A–352B).
149. *Ep.* 199.28 (*PG* 32.725A); see Blond, "L''hérésie' encratite," 184–185.
150. *De hom. structura* 2.7 (SC 160:244).
151. Michael O'Laughlin, "New Questions Concerning the Origenism of Evagrius," in *Origeniana Quinta,* ed. Robert J. Daly (Leuven: University Press, 1992), 528–529.

influence is especially evident in the cosmological and eschatological speculations of Evagrius's "great doctrinal work,"[152] the
Kephalaia Gnostica,[153] and the *Letter to Melania*.[154] The *Kephalaia Gnostica* consists of six "centuries" or chapters of ninety sayings each. The sayings are obscure and secretive, as they are
directed to an elite ascetic audience prepared for the reception of
high spiritual instruction. The letter reportedly sent to Melania is
written in less cryptic language and provides a sort of summary of
Evagrius's doctrine.

It is significant that neither of these texts integrates specific
ascetic practices, such as fasting or celibacy, into the discussion.
Indeed, if one's understanding of Evagrius were based entirely on
the lofty philosophical and spiritual formulations of these writings, one would not necessarily recognize the Evagrius distinguished by his rigorous ascetic discipline. It is important,
therefore, to consider Evagrius's vision as a whole. In part because
of the very different types of texts that have been attributed to
Evagrius, scholars have not been entirely successful in forming a
complete picture of the philosopher-monk. What is more, scholarly discourse on a particular topic, in this case Evagrius, often

152. Antoine Guillaumont and Claire Guillaumont, "Évagre le Pontique,"
Dictionnaire de spiritualité 4 (1961): 1734.

153. Antoine Guillaumont, ed., *Les six Centuries des Kephalaia gnostica*
d'Évagre le Pontique, PO 28,1 (Paris: Firmin-Didot, 1958).

154. The Syriac text of the *Epistula ad Melaniam* published by Frankenberg is not complete (W. Frankenberg, ed., *Euagrius Ponticus: Syrischer Text,*
griechische Retroversion, Abhandlungen der königlichen Gesellschaft der
Wissenschaften zu Göttingen, Philologisch-historische Klasse, Neue Folge,
13,2 [Berlin: Weidmann, 1912], 612–619). Martin Parmentier has translated
the complete Syriac text into English ("Evagrius of Pontus' 'Letter to Melania,'" *Bijdragen, tijdschrift voor filosofie en theologie* 46 (1985): 8–21. On
Evagrius's relation to Origen and Origenism see esp. Antoine Guillaumont,
Les 'Képhalaia Gnostica' d'Évagre le Pontique et l'histoire de l'Origénisme
chez les Grecs et chez les Syriens, Patristica Sorbonensia 5 (Paris: Éditions du
Seuil, 1962); Elizabeth A. Clark, "New Perspectives on the Origenist Controversy: Human Embodiment and Ascetic Strategies," *Church History* 59
(1990): 145–162; idem, *The Origenist Controversy: The Cultural Construction of an Early Christian Debate* (Princeton: Princeton University Press,
1992), 43–84; Francis X. Murphy, "Evagrius Ponticus and Origenism," in *Origeniana Tertia,* ed. Richard Hanson and Henri Crouzel (Rome: Ateneo, 1985),
253–269.

takes on a uniformity of interpretation, including categories and terminology. Thus often the tendency is to ascribe Evagrius's "practical" teachings to the influence of the desert fathers and his metaphysical and eschatological speculations to philosophical influences outside of the desert. But this division runs the risk of oversimplifying not only Evagrius, a complex ascetic personality, and his teachers, but also the nature of desert asceticism.[155] The scholarly problem of integrating Evagrius the theologian and Evagrius the monk is, of course, part of the larger problem of relating theory and practice, discussed in chapters one and four.

The Evagrian system begins and ends with the unity of rational minds and God. The first creations were minds or intellects (νόες), not the material world, bodies, or souls. Just as when rivers flow into the sea they are absorbed into it and the sea changes them completely into "its own nature, color, and taste (γεῦμα)," and there is no differentiation, so also before sin minds were "at one" in God, without distinction.[156] Created for the purpose of knowing God,[157] the minds were "naked," incorporeal, rational, and pure.[158] But by some "movement (κίνησις)" caused by free will, and their own negligence, the minds fell from the unity with and knowledge of God and lost the equality and unity between themselves.[159] As

155. See, e.g., Antoine Guillaumont, "Un philosophe au désert: Evagre le Pontique," *Revue de l'histoire des religions* 181 (1972): 32–33, 43–44; Antoine Guillaumont and Claire Guillaumont, "Évagre le Pontique," 1737–1738; Michael O'Laughlin, "Origenism in the Desert: Anthropology and Integration in Evagrius Ponticus," Th.D. diss., Harvard Divinity School, 1987. Samuel Rubenson's approach to Evagrius and the Origenist tradition seems to me to be more integrating (*The Letters of St. Antony: Monasticism and the Making of a Saint*, Studies in Antiquity and Christianity [Minneapolis: Fortress Press, 1995]).

156. *Ep. ad Mel.* 6 (Parmentier, 13 [English translation]; Frankenberg, 619 [Greek retranslation from the Syriac]).

157. *Keph. Gn.* 1.50 (PO 28.41). All quotations from the *Kephalaia Gnostica* are my translations from the French.

158. E.g., *Keph.Gn.* 1.65; 3.24; 30; 31; 6.20; 85 (PO 28.47; 107; 111; 225; 253).

159. *Ep. ad Mel.* 6 (Parmentier, 12 [English translation], Frankenberg, 619 [Greek]); *Keph. Gn.* 1.77; 2.37; 3.3 (PO 28.53; 77; 99). One intellect only, Christ, remained united to God in essential knowledge. After the fall and before the reunifying of the intellects, Christ alone is "naked mind." On

the minds fell they became "souls" and were attached to "thick" bodies.[160]

For Evagrius, the Genesis account recalls not the first creation of intellects but the second creation of the material world and bodies.[161] His notion of the double creation is thus more explicit in its temporal order than Gregory of Nyssa's interpretation of the creation of humanity in Genesis 1:26-27 as being "in some sense double." In the *Kephalaia Gnostica* he writes:

> Before the movement, God was good, powerful, wise, creator of incorporeal beings, father of the rational beings [*logikoi*], and all-powerful; after the movement, He became creator of bodies, judge, governor, physician, shepherd, doctor, merciful and long suffering.[162]

It is clear that for Evagrius, the "first" beings were bodiless, and the "second" beings—bodies—were created only in response to the fall or "movement" of the first.[163] As the intellects fell and became souls,[164] they were attached to three different levels of bodies, according to the degree of their fall away from unity.[165] The highest level of body is that of the angels, followed by the body of humans and the body of demons. The bodies of angels are lighter, and the bodies of lower beings are heavier.[166] All three types of bodies are composed from the same four material elements mixed in different proportions. Evagrius writes, "In angels there is a predominance of *nous* and fire, in humans [there is a predominance] of *epithumia* and earth, in demons [there is a

---

Evagrian Christology see A. Guillaumont, *Les 'Kephalaia Gnostica,'* 117–119, 151–156.

160. *Keph. Gn.* 1.49; 58; 3.22; 28; 68; 6.20 (PO 28.41; 45; 107; 109; 125; 225); *Ep. ad Mel.* 6 (Parmentier, 12 [English translation]; Frankenberg, 619 [Greek]).

161. Guillaumont, *Les 'Kephalaia Gnostica,'* 103–113.

162. *Keph. Gn.* 6.20 (PO 28.225).

163. See also ibid., 1.50; 2.64 (PO 28.41; 87); Guillaumont, *Les 'Kephalaia Gnostica,'* 109.

164. *Keph. Gn.* 3.28 (PO 28.109): "The soul is the intellect which, by negligence, fell from unity and which, by lack of vigilance, descended to the level of *praktike*."

165. Ibid., 3.38 (PO 28.113).

166. Ibid., 2.68 (PO 28.87).

predominance] of *thumos* and air."[167] Thus angels and demons, like human beings, do have material bodies; it is the composition and mixture of the elements that determines the quality of those bodies.[168] While the original unity of minds and God is like the vast, inseparable waters of the sea, the fall of minds and their differentiation into various bodies is like the separation of rivers out of the sea. Each river changes according to the land through which it flows; so also, each fallen mind has "acquired the taste of the body to which it was bound."[169]

After the fall and embodiment, human beings are composed of both a rational element and an irrational, animal element. Our bodies are subject to the same movements, senses, and material elements as the bodies of animals.[170] With the beasts we also have desiring and incensive impulses in common.[171] But Evagrius is very clear that these impulses are concerned with "corporeal nature" and that therefore "the *thumos* and the *epithumia* do not appear to have been created with the rational nature before the movement."[172] The mind in its created state was free from the body and the passions associated with it. But with the fall "the soul ceased to be in the image of God and voluntarily became the image of animals, [and] it was subjected to all the movements of the body, which it got in common with beasts and animals, which are its relatives."[173] The full image of God will be restored only

167. Ibid., 1.68 (PO 28.49). On the composition of the human body see also *Ep. ad Mel.* 8 (Parmentier, 14–15).

168. Guillaumont, *Les 'Kephalaia Gnostica,'* 114–117.

169. *Ep. ad Mel.* 6 (Parmentier, 13 [English translation]; Frankenberg, 619 [Greek]).

170. *Ep. ad Mel.* 9 (Parmentier, 15–16 [English translation]).

171. *De diversis malignis cogitationibus* 21 (*PG* 79.1224B–C).

172. *Keph. Gn.* 6.85 (PO 28.253). For a discussion of the relation between mind, soul, and body as well as the parts of the soul, see O'Laughlin, "Origenism in the Desert," 153–164. O'Laughlin points out that the rational part of the soul might be considered a "direct extension of the *nous*" (153).

173. *Ep. ad Mel.* 9 (Parmentier, 16 [English translation]). Evagrius seems to suggest that the mind is in the image of God and enjoyed that image when it was in a "naked" or pure state, but after the fall or "movement," when the mind was no longer inclined to God and capable of unity, it was therefore no longer fully in the image of God (*Keph. Gn.* 3.32; 6.73 [PO 28.111; 247–249]; *Ep. ad Mel.* 3 [Parmentier, 10 (English translation); Frankenberg, 615 (Greek)]). See Guillaumont, *Les 'Kephalaia Gnostica,'* 109, n.131; and Clark, "New Per-

when the corporeal nature is cast off and the intellects once again become "naked" and united in perfect contemplation of the God-head.

The beginning of this process of salvation takes place in the body itself and through the corporeal senses, by means of contemplation and *praktike.* This is why in Evagrius's system the body is not evil; although embodiment is a consequence of sin, it is not a punishment. Rather, the body and the material world were created by a merciful God in order to make possible an elementary contemplation of the sensible world; from this contemplation the intellect can move to higher levels.[174] Contemplation of creation is the beginning of the knowledge of God.[175]

In the upward progress of salvation, through virtue and contemplation, the mind can pass from the level of the human body to that of the angelic body. But through further sin, lack of virtue, and ignorance, it can also descend to the level of the demonic body. What does this fluidity of movement between levels of bodies and contemplation mean in terms of the ascetic project? For Evagrius the goal of the *praktike,* or practical phase, of the ascetic life is the achievement of *apatheia.* While not the highest goal of the spiritual life, passionlessness is nevertheless the sign of success in practical ascetic discipline, and the point of transition into a higher level of contemplation.[176] Further, as angels have material bodies but are not subject to passions, human beings imitate the angels through *apatheia.*[177] But the Evagrian ascetic ideal

---

spectives on the Origenist Controversy," 151–152). Contrast Gregory of Nyssa's argument that the image of God has only been "obscured" by sin. In short, it is the mind and not the body which is in the image of God; when the mind is clothed with the body, it takes on the animal image.

174. Guillaumont, *Les 'Kephalaia Gnostica,'* 110–113.

175. *Ep. ad Mel.* 2 (Parmentier, 8–9 [English translation]; Frankenberg, 613 [Greek]); on the levels of contemplation or knowledge see e.g. *Keph. Gn.* 1.74; 75; 2.4; 5; 11; 20; 21; 61; 62; 63; 3.4; 10; 36; 42; 61; 4.11; 90; 6.2; 82 (PO 28.53; 61–63; 65; 69; 85; 99; 101; 113; 115; 123; 141; 175; 217; 251).

176. See the discussion in chap. 4, above. The impassibility of the soul is a lower achievement than the contemplation of worlds, incorporeal beings, and intelligibles, and the knowledge of the trinity (*Keph. Gn.* 1.70; 2.4 [PO 28.51; 61–63]).

177. Antoine Guillaumont and Claire Guillaumont, *Évagre le Pontique: Traité Pratique ou le moine,* SC 170 (Paris: Éditions du Cerf, 1971), 107–108.

does not stop at the *imitation* of angels or even equality with angels. In the world to come, the human actually *becomes* an angel and the human body becomes the angelic body.[178] If we imitate the angels now, we will become angels then; if our *apatheia* is imperfect now, then we will enjoy the perfect impassibility of the angelic body. Moreover, there are those among humans who advance so far in *praktike* and contemplation or prayer that they can be said to "eat the bread of angels" even now.[179] This suggests that Evagrius allows the possibility that some, while in human bodies, might attain perfect *apatheia*.[180] The human body, in general terms, is placed at the level between the angelic and the demonic bodies. But we have seen that these levels of bodies in Evagrius are not completely fixed. At the same time, the body of the monk or virgin, while human, is distinguished from other human bodies by its progress in perfection and *apatheia* and its movement toward the angelic condition.

Of course passing into the angelic body is not the end of salvation. Final unity will be achieved only after all bodies have been cast off and the minds are once again "naked" and united to God in perfect contemplation of the trinity. As the fall away from unity was marked by the creation of corporeal beings, so the return to unity will be marked by the dissolution of bodies and the minds' regaining of their original condition.[181] Considered

---

A. Guillaumont notes that for Evagrius passionlessness is a quality that applies not to incorporeal beings, but to embodied beings. When the minds are freed from bodies again, they will return to the state of "nudity" or purity, which is a much higher state than impassibility. Therefore *apatheia* belongs properly to the angels, "that is to say to those beings which have a body, but which are without any passion" (ibid.).

178. *Keph. Gn.* 3.65; 5.11; 6.24 (PO 28.125; 181; 227); On the succession of worlds in Evagrius see Guillaumont, *Les 'Kephalaia Gnostica,'* 115, 250–252.

179. *Keph. Gn* 1.23 (PO 28.27); see also *De oratione* 113 (*PG* 79.1192D); *De justis et perfectis* 13; 17 (J. Muyldermans, ed., *Evagriana Syriaca: Texts inédits du British Museum et de la Vaticane,* Bibliothèque du *Muséon* 31 [Louvain: Publications universitaires/Institut orientaliste, 1952], 107–108 [Syriac]; 144–145 [French]).

180. Antoine Guillaumont, "Un philosophe au désert," 49.

181. *Ep. ad Mel.* 5–6 (Parmentier, 11–13 [English translation], Frankenberg, 617–619 [Greek]); *Keph. Gn.* 1.26; 58; 2.17; 77; 3.66; 68; 4.34; 86; 5.19 (PO 28.29; 45; 67; 91; 125; 151; 173; 185). See also Guillaumont, *Les 'Kepha-*

together, then, Evagrius's cosmological and eschatological doctrine and his practical techniques of resistance against evil thoughts, images, and passions form an integrated ascetic system. As his notions of creation, the fall, and embodiment inform his ideals for the ascetic life, so the material body of the monk or virgin becomes the arena in which the drama of salvation history is played out and, to some extent, made manifest through bodily struggle and perfection. If in his more speculative writings, such as the *Kephalaia Gnostica* and the *Letter to Melania*, Evagrius seems to set aside physical efforts in the ascetic life, in his other writings, most notably the *Antirrheticus*, Evagrius reveals his sharp personal awareness of the predicament of embodiedness, and the day-to-day endurance of pain, hunger, illness, and loneliness required of the ascetic athlete.

John Chrysostom. Chrysostom's textual treatment of the themes of creation, the fall, and the human body in his homilies and in his treatise *On Virginity*[182] is more literal and less spiritualized than what we have seen in Gregory of Nyssa and Evagrius. He agrees with Basil of Ancyra, Gregory, Basil of Caesarea, and Evagrius that there was no sexual intercourse in the garden before the fall, and the virginity of the first humans is central to his arguments for the superiority of virginity in his own day. Yet he begins not with a spiritual, genderless body or an incorporeal mind, but with the male and female bodies of Adam and Eve.[183] Nevertheless,

---

laia Gnostica,' 115–117. Evagrius returns to the metaphor of the sea to express the unity of minds with God. As the rivers that flow into the sea become themselves part of its immensity and possess its qualities, "thus also he who observes the making perfect of all intellects, is amazed greatly and marvels because he sees all these various distinct knowledges as they merge into one essential and unique knowledge, and that all those become this one, forever" (*Ep. ad Mel.* 12 [Parmentier, 20 (English translation)]).

182. *PG* 48.533–596. See the introductions to the treatise by Elizabeth A. Clark in *John Chrysostom: On Virginity; Against Remarriage,* trans. Sally Rieger Shore, Studies in Women and Religion 9 (Lewiston, N.Y.: Edwin Mellen Press, 1983), vii–xlii; and Bernard Grillet in *Jean Chrysostome: La virginité,* ed. Herbert Musurillo and Bernard Grillet, SC 125 (Paris: Éditions du Cerf, 1966), 7–72. Grillet dates the treatise to 382, but notes that Musurillo argues for a date of 392 (25).

183. Chrysostom's interpretation of the "image of God" deserves

Chrysostom sees a great distinction between the bodily condition of the first pair before the fall and their state after their disobedience: the first humans were not subject to bodily needs. Their bodies were not troublesome sources of labor, pain, or anxiety.[184] They were naked and unashamed, yet their bodies did not require clothing or houses to protect them from the elements, nor did they labor for food. Another feature of this blessed and angelic life was the virginity of Adam and Eve. Chrysostom points out that before the fall and expulsion from the garden, there is, in Genesis, no mention of sexual intercourse: "For how [could there be intercourse], when they were not subject to the needs of the body?"[185] Thus the virginity of the first humans is for Chrysostom a key aspect of their general freedom from concern for their own bodily preservation—as individuals and as a species. Indeed, God himself could have multiplied the human race by means other than sexual intercourse, as he had created Adam and Eve.[186]

Chrysostom describes the "princely robe" and "radiant and bright garment" which clothed humans and provided for them against physical needs prior to the fall.[187] With the disobedience

---

comment here. Gregory of Nyssa and Evagrius represent the view that the image of God is above categories of human gender and is associated especially with the rational element in humanity. John Chrysostom departs from this view on two significant points. First, he associates the image not with rationality or intellect, but with control and governing authority. The image of God in humanity is thus expressed in their control over the earth and other living creatures. As God is sovereign over all, so humanity is sovereign on earth (*Homilia VIII in Genesim* 3–4 [*PG* 53.72–73]; *Homilia VII de statuis* 2 [*PG* 49.93]). Second, Chrysostom argues further that males in particular are in the image of God, and that this legitimates male domination and female subordination (e.g., *Hom. VIII in Gen.* 4 [*PG* 53.72–73]). On the other hand, Chrysostom elsewhere characterizes the first male and female as being equal in authority and control over the earth. This equality, however, was lost with the fall and Eve became subject to the male (*Homilia XVII in Genesim* 8 [*PG* 53.144–145]). For a fuller discussion of these issues see Elizabeth A. Clark, *Jerome, Chrysostom, and Friends: Essays and Translations*, Studies in Women and Religion 2 (Lewiston, N.Y.: Edwin Mellen Press, 1979), 3–6.

184. *De virginitate* 14 (*PG* 48.543–544); *Homilia XVIII in Genesim* 1; 2; 4 (*PG* 53.149; 150; 153); *Hom. XVI in Gen.* 1 (*PG* 53.126).

185. *Hom. XVIII in Gen.* 4 (*PG* 53.153); Genesis 4:1.

186. *De virg.* 14 (*PG* 48.544).

187. Ibid.; *Hom XVIII in Gen.* 1 (*PG* 53.149).

and fall from the garden, however, this carefree bodily condition was lost. Instead humans found their bodies to be subject to decay, death, pain, and hard work.[188] In place of their former garments humans were clothed in the "tunics of skin" (Genesis 3:21). Chrysostom does not interpret "the tunics of skin" as the degraded embodied state itself, but as the coverings provided by a merciful God for humans who were ashamed of their nakedness and vulnerability. Nevertheless they were intended as reminders of their sin, as our need for the protection of clothing should continue to remind us of the first sin and its consequences.[189]

Marriage and sexual procreation were introduced into practice, then, only after the entrance of mortality and after Adam and Eve proved themselves unworthy of the blessings of virginity.[190] Marriage is a concession to the weakness of humanity, granted in the beginning in our inferior, childlike state after the fall.[191] And procreation provides a great consolation in the face of mortality. It is an "image of the resurrection" for humanity caught in the grip of death.[192] But in contrast to Basil of Ancyra and Gregory of Nyssa, Chrysostom does not argue that marriage was *necessary* in order to fill the earth by means of sexual activity and child bearing. Indeed, he reminds his readers that the word and will of God, not marriage, increase the human population.[193] Further, Chrysostom explicitly downplays procreation as a justification for the practice of marriage. If in the beginning marriage was granted for the purpose of procreation, he writes, even more so it was allowed in order "to quench the burning desire of nature," that is, to provide a legitimate outlet for sexual desire and to avoid *porneia*. But now that the earth has been fully populated, only one justification remains: "the removal of intemperance and licentiousness."[194]

---

188. *De virg.* 14 (*PG* 48.544); *Hom. XVIII in Gen.* 3 (*PG* 53.151).
189. *Hom. XVIII in Gen.* 1–2 (*PG* 53.149–150).
190. Ibid., 4 (*PG* 53.153).
191. *De virg.* 16–17 (*PG* 48.545–546).
192. *Hom. XVIII in Gen.* 4 (*PG* 53.154).
193. *De virg.* 15 (*PG* 48.544). See also Van Eijk, "Marriage and Virginity, Death and Immortality," 227–230.
194. *De virg.* 19 (*PG* 48.547). Chrysostom elsewhere expresses the notion, seen in Basil of Ancyra and Jerome, that sexual desire is "natural" and

For Chrysostom, then, "virginity means abstinence not so much from procreation as from sexual intercourse."[195] Again this distinguishes his interpretation of virginity from Gregory of Nyssa's. Gregory emphasizes that in choosing virginity one opts out of the perpetuation of the cycle of birth and death, and that virginity breaks the power of death. But Chrysostom simply asserts that as marriage and death will not be operative in the resurrection, which is at hand, we should make ourselves worthy by rejecting marriage along with all other worldly entanglements.

> [In the kingdom there will be] no more marriage, no more labor pains, or pleasure and intercourse, or plenty of money, or management of possessions, food or clothing, or agriculture and sailing, or arts and architecture, or cities and houses, but some other condition and way of life. All these things will pass away a little later. . . . Why do we prefer a miserable life, when Christ calls us to a trouble-free [state]?[196]

Thus virginity represents the freedom from bodily and worldly necessities that characterizes the human experience of embodiment both before the fall and in the kingdom to come. And just as the first humans lived like the angels, so also the one who pursues virginity in this life *imitates* angelic existence. Angels neither marry nor are given in marriage, and they remain close to God and serve God continually. This is true also of virgins, asserts Chrysostom, who have detached themselves from the whirlwind of earthly activities and the anxieties of marriage. Virginity makes those on earth live like the beings who reside in heaven. "It does not let those invested with bodies be inferior to the incorporeal powers, and it leads those who are human to the zealous imitation of the angels."[197] In effect, those who choose virginity are "angels upon the earth," who, while still in the flesh and "subject to the necessity of nature," nevertheless live "as if" they were incorporeal and immortal dwellers in heaven.

---

implanted by God for the purpose of procreation. He is careful to distinguish between this natural desire and illicit lust or adultery. See, e.g., *Homilia II in epistolam ad Ephesios* 3 (*PG* 62.20); *Homilia V in epistola ad Ephesios* 4 (*PG* 62.42); *Commentarius in Epistolam ad Galatas* 5.3 (*PG* 61.669).

195. Van Eijk, "Marriage and Virginity, Death and Immortality," 228.
196. *De virg.* 73 (*PG* 48.587).
197. Ibid., 11; 68 (*PG* 48.540; 584–585).

For Chrysostom, the beauty of virginity is that it allows one to realize in one's own person the promise of the resurrection, the promise of salvation.[198] But if virginity looks forward to the resurrection, it also looks back to the garden. To at least some extent the virgin or monk recaptures the freedom from the needs and limitations of embodiment even while in the flesh. If he does not go as far as Evagrius, who understands physical embodiment to have taken place after the fall, nevertheless Chrysostom argues that our experience of the body is qualitatively different because of sin.

Jerome. We saw earlier that Jerome's ascetic viewpoint is notable for its emphasis on physical realities and the dangers of fleshly desires. This is certainly evident in his discussions of fasting and virginity. It also characterizes his understanding of the protological and eschatological motivations for the ascetic life. Jerome's treatment begins and ends with the physical bodies of male and female. His is thus an important alternative voice in this discussion of creation, embodiment, and salvation, and serves to highlight some of the practical ascetic issues at stake in theological debate. For Jerome these issues center around the limitations and possibilities of the human body—past, present, and future. Much of what Jerome has to say on these topics comes out of his writings in which he debates "Origenist" (Evagrian) views of cosmology, salvation, and the resurrection body, or explains away his own early admiration for the Alexandrian's speculations. Elizabeth Clark has shown that Jerome's position shifted over the years, from early (if not complete) acceptance of Origen's image of a bodiless and genderless resurrection (represented in Jerome's *Commentary* on Ephesians, which he wrote in the late 380s), to a later view, articulated in response to those who claimed that

---

198. Ibid., 79 (*PG* 48.592). See also *Homilia LXX in Matthaeum* 2–4 (*PG* 58.657–660), where Chrysostom describes the lifestyle of the monks who already receive some of the blessings of the resurrection. On the idea of asceticism and the realization of salvation in the embodied state see Jean-Marie Leroux, "Saint Jean Chrysostome et le monachisme," in *Jean Chrysostome et Augustin,* ed. Charles Kannengiesser, Théologie historique 35 (Paris: Beauchesne, 1975), 130–136.

Jerome himself held Origenist opinions. This later period, represented by most of the texts examined here, is marked by the influence of Evagrius on the Origenist tradition as well as intense and widespread debate. Now Jerome rejects the key Origenist notions of bodilessness, the restoration into oneness, and angelic perfection or passionlessness.[199] As Peter Brown has noted, Jerome finally embraced an understanding of the origins and nature of the human body that could not be reconciled with the "limitless fluidity of the human person" found in Origen's or Evagrius's spiritualizing anthropology.[200]

Jerome agrees with other late fourth-century ascetic writers that there was no sexual intercourse before the fall.[201] Adam and Eve were virgins in paradise; it was only after sin and the expulsion from the garden that they were married and began sexual relations.[202] Thus Jerome associates marriage with guilt and death,[203] and interprets the tunics of skin as the "tunic of marriage with which Adam was clothed when he was cast out of the paradise of virginity."[204] Further, the command to "be fruitful and multiply" was given only in order to "fill the earth," as if planting

199. Elizabeth A. Clark, "The Place of Jerome's Commentary on Ephesians in the Origenist Controversy: The Apokatastasis and Ascetic Ideals," *Vigiliae Christianae* 41 (1987): 154–171; idem, *The Origenist Controversy*, esp. 121–151 and 221–227. Clark argues that Jerome only really became aware of the importance of Evagrian thought in the early fifth century. See also Pierre Lardet, ed., *Saint Jérôme: Apologie Contre Rufin*, SC 303 (Paris: Éditions du Cerf, 1983), 1*–75*; J. N. D. Kelly, *Jerome: His Life, Writings, and Controversies* (London: Duckworth, 1975), passim.

200. Brown, *The Body and Society*, 380.

201. Elizabeth Clark notes that while Jerome's interpretation of the sexuality and marriage of Adam and Eve is similar to that of John Chrysostom, "Jerome's scheme . . . met with a far more negative reception in the West than Chrysostom's had in the East." This negative reaction in the West to the denegation of marriage in Jerome's treatise against Jovinian is one explanation for the more "generous" treatment of marriage that would come in Augustine's writings ("Theory and Practice in Late Ancient Asceticism: Jerome, Chrysostom, and Augustine," *Journal of Feminist Studies in Religion* 5 [Fall 1989]: 30–31; see also idem, "Heresy, Asceticism, Adam, and Eve," 353–385).

202. *Adv. Jov.* 1.16; 29 (*PL* 23.246A; 263A); *Ep.* 22.19 (CSEL 54:169).

203. *Ep.* 22.18–19 (CSEL 54:167–169).

204. *Ep.* 128.3 (CSEL 56:158).

and cultivating the "wood" of population. Now that the population has increased, and with the coming of Christ, however, the wood is ready to be "cut down" by virginity.[205]

Jerome thus echoes the now familiar theme that to practice the virginal life is to imitate the blessed condition of humanity in paradise before the fall. For Jerome the original virginity was not, however, the characteristic of bodiless minds, spiritual bodies, or even bodies not subject to physical needs, but the pure and undefiled state of real bodies not subject to lust. It follows that Jerome's arguments for and advice concerning the virginal life emphasize resistance to the pleasures and desires of the flesh. This acute awareness of the ever-present threat of falling into sinful desire is also apparent in his discussion of the present and future rewards of virginity. He does at times associate virginity with the "angelic life,"[206] but this is not a common image in his work. In fact Jerome seems to avoid language suggesting that the virgin might attain a state of angelic perfection in this life. In his letter to Eustochium, for example, he pointedly refuses to flatter the virgin's achievement with rhetorical displays placing her "already among the angels." He would by his words of advice inspire not pride in ascetic victories already won, but fear of the possibility that she may, through the negligence of self-confidence, lose her crown.[207]

While Gregory of Nyssa, Basil of Caesarea, and others write of virginity as the imitation of the incorporeal powers, Jerome

205. *Adv. Jov.* 1.16 (*PL* 23.246B–C); *De perpetua virginitate B. Mariae adversus Helvidium* 21 (*PL* 23.215B). For Jerome's full argument for the superiority of virginity over marriage see esp. the treatise against Jovinian (*PL* 23.221A–352C) and the letter to Eustochium (*Ep.* 22 [CSEL 54:143–211]).

206. E.g., *Adv. Helv.* 21 (*PL* 23.215A); *Ep.* 130.10 (CSEL 56:190–191); *Adv. Jov.* 1.12; 1.41 (*PL* 23.237C–238A; 282B).

207. *Ep.* 22.2–5 (CSEL 54:146–150). Jerome's ambivalence about the notion of angelic perfection among humans must be understood in the context of his efforts, after about 390 C.E., to separate himself from Origenist teachings and to condemn the teachings of Pelagius. He especially rejects the notion of *apatheia,* or passionlessness, and singles out Evagrius as its theorist (*Ep.* 133.3 [CSEL 56:246]). In his treatise against the Pelagians (415 C.E.), he associates Pelagian perfectionism with *apatheia* taught by Origen, Evagrius, and other "heretics" (*Dialogus adversus Pelagianos,* prologue [*PL* 23.518A]).

stresses that the virgin imitates Christ and Mary.[208] This further exemplifies his more physical, less metaphorical or spiritualized ascetic argumentation. Jerome's rhetorical emphasis is less on virginity as the overcoming of the evils of duality, extremes, time, or even the cycle of birth and death, and more on virginity as the resistance to the evil desires of the flesh. In the same way, Jerome rejects a spiritualized interpretation of the rewards of the ascetic life and the future resurrection. Against the Origenist notion of the restoration of all beings to a bodiless, genderless state—a notion Jerome himself had at one time found appealing—he insists on the resurrection of physical bodies that will retain their male or female sex.[209] In the resurrection our bodies will be perfected and will no longer experience lust; nor will the male and female sexual apparatus function as in this world. But our bodies will remain *human* bodies, male and female bodies.[210] Further, although we have been promised that we will be *like* angels in the resurrection,[211] Jerome writes, we will not actually *become* angels, for "the likeness to angels is not the changing of humans into angels, but the progress in immortality and glory."[212]

Our separate identities will not be erased in genderless angelic "bodies" or swallowed up into the undifferentiated sea of unity between God and minds (to borrow Evagrius's image), but will continue in the glory of paradise. Jerome scoffs at his opponents who would believe otherwise, imagining that their "little women" would grasp their breasts and strike at their wombs, saying, "What good is it if this fragile body is to rise again? If we will be like the angels in the future, we will have the bodily nature of angels as well."[213] But for Jerome the bodily resurrection of humans as males and females is a positive affirmation not only

---

208. *Ep.* 22.18; 38 (CSEL 54:168; 203).

209. Clark, "The Place of Jerome's Commentary," 156–157; Brown, *The Body and Society*, 379–384.

210. *Ep.* 75.2 (CSEL 55:31–32); *Adv. Jov.* 1.36 (PL 23.273).

211. Matthew 22:30; Mark 12:25; Luke 20:34-36.

212. *Contra Johannem Hierosolymitanum ad Pammachium* 31 (PL 23.400B); *Epp.* 75.2; 84.5–6; 108.23 (CSEL 55:31–32; 126–127; 340–341); *Adv. Jov.* 1.36 (PL 23.273).

213. *Ep.* 84.6 (CSEL 55:127); Brown, *The Body and Society*, 381–383.

of the bodily incarnation and resurrection of Christ,[214] but also of the individual struggles and rewards of ascetic men and women.[215]

In the writings of Jerome, sexual abstinence in general and virginity in particular recall and represent the ideal of human flesh without lust and sexual activity. To choose to struggle against the desires of the flesh in this life is to imitate the bodily condition of paradise before the fall and to anticipate the resurrection.[216] If Jerome hesitates to use the language of "realized eschatology," which we saw frequently in the writings of Basil of Ancyra, Gregory of Nyssa, Basil of Caesarea, and Chrysostom, this does not mean that he held no high expectations for ascetic achievement in this life. Indeed, we have seen that Jerome expects ascetic observances, especially fasting, to help preserve chastity in the struggle against the lusts of the flesh. Further, the mortification of the body takes on a special urgency and significance if one believes that *that* very body will rise and be glorified. Jerome writes,

> I do not condemn the flesh, in which Christ was born and resurrected; I do not despise the clay that, fired into a pure vessel, reigns in heaven. . . . I love the flesh that is chaste, virginal, fasting; I love not the works of the flesh, but its substance; I love the flesh that knows it is to be judged, that in martyrdom for Christ is killed, torn to pieces, and consumed by flames.[217]

Fasting and virginity are techniques that, like the potter's oven, fire the flesh and make it ready for the kingdom of heaven. It is clear that while Jerome's is one of the loudest and most severe voices in the late ancient Christian chorus chanting the hazards of embodiment, nevertheless the body itself, and the rigorous

214. Ibid.; *Adv. Jov.* 1.36 (*PL* 23.272C–273A); *Contra Joh. Hieros.* 23 (*PL* 23.390B–391B).

215. Clark, "The Place of Jerome's Commentary," 161–167; idem, "New Perspectives on the Origenist Controversy," 159–162; idem, *The Origenist Controversy*, 99–101, 122, and 129–132 on Jerome's arguments for the hierarchy of heavenly rewards and his opposition to Origen's concept of the final restoration of all beings to unity.

216. Frank, *Angelikos Bios*, 107–108.

217. *Ep.* 84.9 (CSEL 55:132).

methods for its control and transformation, remain central to his whole theory. What is especially important for this study is that all of the authors surveyed here, even those (such as Evagrius) with the most "spiritualized" or "disembodied" interpretations of the first creation and the future resurrection, regard the condition of the present body which has been manipulated by ascetic techniques as in some sense related to—or realizing—the past and future blessed condition of humanity.

The Body of Paradise

The ancient anthropological theories surveyed here reveal the extent to which concepts of the origins of embodiment, sexuality, and death inform ascetic programs and expectations; arguments for the connection between diet and sexuality contribute further to the ascetic hope that the present human body might be transformed.[218] The early Christian ascetic woman or man represents both symbolically and physically the promise of sanctification. Han Drijvers has written that in the body of the early Christian saint "the specific problems of human existence, food and sex, disease and death, are overcome in a symbolic and exemplary way."[219] Of course the physical limitations of embodiment cannot

218. For a general discussion of early Christian views of the resurrection body, and specifically the question of material continuity between the flesh-and-bones body and the resurrection, see now Caroline Walker Bynum, *The Resurrection of the Body in Western Christianity, 200–1336*, Lectures on the History of Religions, n.s. 15 (New York: Columbia University Press, 1995), 21–114. Bynum argues that early Christianity theories of resurrection were motivated not so much by concern with procreation, sexuality, gender, and the preservation of hierarchies (issues central to the analyses of Elaine Pagels, Elizabeth Clark, and John Gager) as by fear of bodily decay, absorption, and death (90–91, 109–113). I hope that my discussion has suggested that—in ascetic theories of returning to paradise and well as in practical ascetic advice—the issues of bodily change, corruption, and decay (emphasized by Bynum) are interwoven with and inseparable from concerns of gender, sexuality, and hierarchy. The corruptible and unruly body, death, hierarchy, and (in some views) even gender itself all result from the fall.

219. Han Drijvers, "The Saint as Symbol: Conceptions of the Person in Late Antiquity and Early Christianity," in *Concepts of Person in Religion and Thought*, ed. Hans G. Kippenberg, Yme B. Kuiper, and Andy F. Sanders, Religion and Reason 37 (Berlin: Mouton de Gruyter, 1990), 151–152.

be completely overcome, as Abba John the Dwarf was quick to learn. But if humans are unable to do without food or sleep, these may be restricted; and humans *are* able to survive without sexual activity.[220] Thus sexual abstinence takes on a particularly powerful role in ascetic ideology.

In the Genesis story of creation, the fall and punishment of the first humans were made perpetually real in the experience of the human body—as Elaine Scarry expresses it, the body was made "a permanently preoccupying category."[221] In the same way, progress back toward intimacy with God is also played out in the body. Scarry's analysis of Hebrew scripture is again helpful in our understanding of the ascetic body. She observes that throughout the Hebrew Bible, "it is in the body that God's presence is recorded." Thus in our very creation, in procreation, childbirth, eating, circumcision, and wounding, the bodiless God is substantiated and confirmed in the bodies of human beings. Likewise, "the failure of belief is, in its many forms, a failure to remake one's own interior in the image of God, to allow God to enter and to alter one's self. . . . Disobedience or disbelief or doubt in the scriptures is habitually described as a withholding of the body."[222] Opening the body to the presence of the divine, a willingness to allow one's own physical presence to record and announce the presence of God, these scriptural notions are continued and given new vitality in the ascetic life.

The body closed to the world and its enticements is a common image in Christian writings of late antiquity. Thus the five senses are like "windows" or "gates" which must be shut up to protect the soul and guard the body against the pollution of sensual pleasures. The author of the *Life of Syncletica*, for example, notes that Syncletica closed all of her senses like windows, and associated

220. Foucault makes this observation in relation to Cassian's writings on fornication (Michel Foucault, "The Battle for Chastity," in *Western Sexuality: Practice and Precept in Past and Present Times*, ed. Philippe Ariès and André Béjin, trans. Anthony Forster (Oxford: Basil Blackwell, 1985), 16.

221. *The Body in Pain*, 210.

222. Ibid., 191–204. Scarry cites several examples in which the resistance to belief is expressed in images of the withholding of the body—a turned shoulder, hardened heart, stopped up ears, stiffened neck, or stony face (203).

only with her "bridegroom," Christ. Syncletica herself taught that it was necessary to keep all of the senses chaste.[223]

Basil of Ancyra argues that the senses are like entrances into the house of the soul which must be guarded against intruding pleasures. He compares the single sensual pleasure to a soldier who comes to the house seeking lodging. If not turned away immediately, but allowed to come inside, that one soldier can affect the entire house. He leaves one of his weapons in the house even if he goes out, thus laying claim to the house and "making the home his own both for himself and for his comrades," whom he will no doubt invite back with him. In the same way the house of the soul must turn away pleasure. If even one small sensual pleasure is allowed to enter, it will lay claim to the entire soul and open the way for its "comrades," other pleasures, to enter.[224] The wise virgin will therefore not open her eyes indiscriminantly, she will stop up her ears to wicked talk, and restrain her sense of taste with the bit of rationality. If she must open the eyes of her body in order to admit the light "of the present life" she will keep the "eyes of the soul" closed. But on the other hand she will *open* the eye of her soul in order to receive the "true light and the Beauty which it illuminates."[225] The ascetic body is in this way closed to the corruption of the world, but it is open to the transforming and perfecting presence of the divine.[226]

Indeed, through ascetic renunciation and discipline, not only is the soul protected and made ready to receive divine light, but the body itself is changed. Thus Gregory of Nyssa reports that his sister Macrina's stomach was "just as we suppose [it will be] in the

---

223. Pseudo-Athanasius, *Vita et gesta Sanctae beataeque magistrae Syncleticae* 9; 24; 25 (*PG* 28.1492B; 1501B–C). The text was probably written in Egypt in the fifth century.

224. *De virg.* 15 (*PG* 30.700C–704A).

225. Ibid., 5 (*PG* 30.680A–B).

226. For other examples of the images of closing the senses like windows or gates see also Evagrius, *De ieiunio* 13 (Muyldermans, *Evagriana Syriaca*, 116 [Syriac]; 152 [French]); Jerome, *Adv. Jov.* 2.8 (*PL* 23.310B); Chrysostom, *De inani gloria et de educandis liberis* 23–63 (Anne-Marie Malingrey, ed., *Jean Chrysostome: Sur la vaine gloire et l'éducation des enfants*, SC 188 [Paris: Éditions du Cerf, 1972], 108–162).

resurrection, free from its own desires."[227] Likewise, she had attained such a state of holiness in her angelic life that when she died her body glowed.[228] By physical as well as contemplative efforts, the old, worldly self and body are "remade" into the new. Scarry has analyzed extreme forms of bodily asceticism and concluded that by "the annihilating power of pain" one's world is destroyed and new worlds are constructed:

> The self-flagellation of the religious ascetic, for example, is not (as is often asserted) an act of denying the body, eliminating its claims from attention, but a way of so emphasizing the body that the contents of the world are cancelled and the path is clear for the entry of an unworldly, contentless force. It is in part this world-ridding, path-clearing logic that explains the obsessive presence of pain in the rituals of large, widely shared religions as well as the imagery of intensely private visions, that partly explains why the crucifixion of Christ is at the center of Christianity.[229]

Other modern scholars have recognized, along with Drijvers and Scarry, this intimate connection between the body and belief. Bryan Turner has noted the "paradox" that the human body is "a natural environment, while also being socially constituted"; it is "a material organism, but also a metaphor."[230] Thus cultural and religious meanings and ideals are created and interpreted through the physical organism of the body and its behaviors or postures. Turner understands the problematic realities of embodiment to be at the center of sociological, medical, and religious theory: "the human body is subject to processes of birth, decay, and death which result from its placement in the natural world, but these processes are also 'meaningful' events located in a world of

227. *Epistula* 19 (*PG* 46.1076A).
228. *De vita Macrinae* 32 (SC 178:246).
229. Scarry, *The Body in Pain*, 33–34. Many of the texts we have dealt with stress moderation in asceticism, but Scarry's connection of physical hardship with the creation of new realities is still quite valid. Her discussion of real physical pain in relation to asceticism would certainly not be extreme if applied to texts such as Evagrius's *Antirrheticus*, the *Life of Syncletica*, Palladius's *Lausiac History*, the *Sayings of the Fathers*, and others. Thus for example the saying of Alonius, "If I had not destroyed everything, I would not have been able to build myself up" (*AP* Alonius 2 [*PG* 65.133A]).
230. Turner, *The Body and Society*, 7–8.

cultural beliefs, symbols and practices."[231] Our bodily attentions, labors, and stances are therefore laden with "symbolic potential."[232]

The early Christian ascetic ideal of overcoming the body's fallen condition of mortality and suffering is both realized and symbolized in the chaste, thin, mortified flesh of its adherents. Further, the disciplined flesh of the ascetic identifies her or him—both in *contrast* to the norms and practices of the larger society and perhaps at the same time in continuity with its *ideals*—with the smaller, elite society of those who "would be perfect."[233] As Margaret Miles has also argued, in the early Christian life it is "the physical practices—fasting, sexual abstinence, vigils, prayers, and exorcisms—that effectively deconstruct the person's physical and social habits and make possible the reconstruction of a new orientation."[234] Pierre Bourdieu's analysis pushes us even further to consider the ways in which "symbolic power works partly through the control of other people's bodies" and bodily details "can instill a whole cosmology."[235] Thus the "practical" aspects of ascetic culture should not be bracketed off from the theological. Moreover, Bourdieu insists that the centrality of the body should not be considered simply as a matter of "representation" or "body image," but rather of "incorporation" and "identification." He writes that the body "does not represent what it performs, it does not memorize the past, it *enacts* the past, bringing it back to life. What is 'learned by body' is not something that one has, like knowledge that can be brandished, but something that one is."[236]

---

231. Ibid., 58.

232. Ibid., 190.

233. Steven D. Fraade has argued, in reference to the Essenes, that elitist *askesis* can serve "as a way of bridging the gap between the movement's ideal and its ability to fulfill it" ("Ascetical Aspects of Ancient Judaism," in *Jewish Spirituality: From the Bible Through the Middle Ages,* ed. Arthur Green, World Spirituality 13 [New York: Crossroad, 1986], 269.

234. Margaret Miles, *Carnal Knowing: Female Nakedness and Religious Meaning in the Christian West* [Boston: Beacon Press, 1989], 40.

235. *The Logic of Practice,* trans. Richard Nice [Stanford: Stanford University Press, 1990], 69.

236. Ibid., 72–73.

In the ancient texts examined here, we thus see the dynamic interplay of body and belief, of physical configuration and theological speculation, of ascetic practices and eschatological expectations, of instilled bodily dispositions[237] and articulated, privileged theory.

The idealized bodily condition of the distant past and/or future informs both our present experience of the sufferings of embodiment and the rules and techniques by which we feed, care for, and model our bodies. Food and diet, gender differentiation and sexual procreation, embodiment and physical effort—all are woven together in the ancient discussion of human origins, nature, and destiny. This is evident in both Hesiod's myth of the golden age and the Genesis myth of creation, as well as in the later interpretations of the two accounts. In fourth-century ascetic theory, fasting and virginity are intimately linked both in the theological and anthropological understandings of creation and embodiment, and in the expectations that the future restoration to primitive wholeness will somehow be realized even now, in this place and in this body. When Jerome urges the widow Salvina to leave meat-eating to those who serve the flesh through sexual intercourse and procreation,[238] he is not only making a physiological argument; he is connecting the eating of meat and sexual activity as enterprises of fallen humanity.[239] The Christian ascetic no longer lends her or his body to the furtherance of earthly miseries; the body as well as the soul has been converted. Fasting and chastity symbolize and actualize the remaking of the present self and body according to an ancient and yet future ideal. How that ideal is related to the gendered body is the subject of the next chapter.

237. Ibid., 66–73.
238. *Ep.* 79.7 (CSEL 55:96).
239. See also Jerome, *Ep.* 22.19 (CSEL 54:168), where he connects marriage to agricultural labor as enterprises of life outside of paradise, and *Adv. Jov.* , 1.18 (*PL* 23.247B–248A), where Jerome notes that meat-eating and divorce were both concessions given to "hard-hearted" people only after the flood.

CHAPTER SIX

Fasting and the Female Body

IN THE PREVIOUS CHAPTERS I have examined various medical, philosophical, and eschatological approaches to diet and sexuality in late antiquity. These approaches and theories help to illuminate the logic of asceticism in general, and the intimate linkage of body and soul in relation to fasting and chastity in particular. In this chapter I will focus specifically on female asceticism and the representation of the female body in ascetic discourse. I will explore the ways in which medical or physiological theories contribute to the ascetic understanding of both the effects of food restriction on the female bodily experience and the eschatological goals of "becoming male" and the disappearance of gender differentiation. Diet is, as I have shown, an important factor in maintaining the overall health of the body and the proper balance of humors. This is no less true in the case of female reproductive fitness and the balance of the fluids associated with fertility— menstrual blood, milk, and female semen. Here we will turn to Christian ascetic texts and explore the discourse on diet, sexuality, and gender specifically in relation to female ascetics. Finally, we will be able to draw some conclusions about the relationship between the physical effects of food deprivation, the theological understanding of embodiment and gender, and the ideal of virginity.

Ascetic Women and Fasting in Early Christian Sources

The investigation of women's fasting behavior in early Christian asceticism, like the general study of women in Christian history, is affected by the almost total lack of sources by women. Our sources therefore present arguments *about* women, or instructions *to* women, but *by* male authors, priests, and spiritual authorities. While some of the recorded lives and sayings of holy women claim to transmit their actual words and teachings, and may reflect some of the realities of their disciplined life, these types of sources present all of the historical problems associated with hagiography. On the other hand, hagiographical sources can tell us much about the author's and audience's worldviews and expectations for holiness as well as gender roles.[1] Further, the genres of our sources are not absolutely distinct and separable. To cite just one example, Jerome's letter written to Eustochium after her mother Paula's death in the early fifth century contains many of the standard *topoi* of ascetic hagiographies, including extraordinary fasting, illness from harsh ascetic disciplines, accusations of madness against her, defense against "heretics," and foreknowledge of her own death.[2]

In any event, the male perspective of the sources limits the kinds of claims one can make about women's own experience and interpretation of asceticism. One can piece together the theological, ideological, and physiological arguments used by male theorists, biographers, and advisors in order to justify, represent, and

---

1. See the discussions of hagiography and historicity in Frank E. Reynolds and Donald Capps, eds., *The Biographical Process: Studies in the History and Psychology of Religion*, Religion and Reason 11 (The Hague: Mouton, 1976), 1–33; Charles F. Keyes, "Charisma: From Social Life to Sacred Biography," in *Charisma and Sacred Biography*, ed. Michael A. Williams, JAAR Thematic Studies 48/3–4 (Chambersburg, Pa.: American Academy of Religion, 1982), 1–22; Patricia Cox, *Biography in Late Antiquity: A Quest for the Holy Man*, The Transformation of the Classical Heritage 5 (Berkeley: University of California Press, 1983), xi–xvi. See also Evelyne Patlagean, "Ancient Byzantine Hagiography and Social History," in *Saints and Their Cults: Studies in Religious Sociology, Folklore and History*, ed. Stephen Wilson, trans. Jane Hodgkin (Cambridge: Cambridge University Press, 1983), 101–121.

2. Jerome, *Epistula* 108 (Isidorus Hilberg, ed., *Eusebii Hieronymi Epistulae*, CSEL 54–56 [Vienna: Tempsky, 1910–1918], 55:306–351).

control female ascetic behavior. Within those arguments one is able to detect what women might actually have been doing—in the case, for example, of instructions on women's dress, movements, associations with male ascetics, or activities in the church—but our sources do not permit us to see through the dark glass of male representation to women's own self-presentation or self-understanding. With these considerations in mind, then, we can approach our sources for evidence and argumentation concerning women's fasting practices as well as the physical results expected from fasting and the interpretation of those results. A broad range of sources are useful to this search, including some of the treatises, homilies, and letters discussed previously as well as instructions and *canons* dealing with topics in female asceticism and a number of *Lives* of holy women—some of which date from the fifth to the seventh centuries and are preserved in Greek, Coptic, and Syriac.

Survey of the Textual Evidence

It must first be noted that dietary abstinence is *in general* no less prominent a theme in early Christian accounts of or advice to male ascetics than it is in texts dealing with female ascetics. In the fourth- and fifth-century monastic sources, lives of holy men and women, and other ascetic texts, fasting is a regular and important exercise in both male and female asceticism.[3] (In contrast, Caroline Walker Bynum has found that by the Middle Ages, food asceticism becomes particularly associated with female piety in

---

3. The *Apophthegmata Patrum, Historia monachorum,* and *Historia Lausiaca* of Palladius record numerous accounts of fasting among male as well as female desert ascetics. All three deal with issues of moderation and extreme renunciation. For example, Palladius reports one story of a certain virgin who was said to have eaten only on Saturdays and Sundays for thirty years, and another concerning the monk Elpidius who also ate only on Saturdays and Sundays and who was so wasted from fasting that it was as if "the sun shone through his bones" (*HL* 20; 48 [Cuthbert Butler, ed., *The Lausiac History of Palladius*, 2 vols., Texts and Studies 6/1–2 (Cambridge: Cambridge University Press, 1898 and 1904), 2:63; 142–143]). For further examples and on fasting in these texts in general, see chap. 1. Note also the material on male fasting in John Cassian, Jerome, and Evagrius, above.

hagiographical material.[4]) Nevertheless, distinct emphases and concerns emerge in a variety of early Christian sources concerning female fasting. These include: encouraging women to fast frequently, reporting that female ascetics fast more rigorously than male ascetics, concern over immoderate or unregulated fasting in female ascetic communities, issues of authority and the control of lifestyle, and the association of fasting with the destruction of the female nature, characteristics, and functions of the female body.

Several texts encourage women in particular to fast or imply that women are more suited to fasting than men. In the *Canons* attributed to Hippolytus, virgins and widows are exhorted to "fast frequently and pray for the church."[5] The author of the Pseudo-Athanasian *Sermo exhortatorius* urges his readers to keep the regular Wednesday and Friday fasts of the church, adding that additional fasting is up to the individual: "if you desire, fast; if you desire, do not fast. But it is fitting for women to fast always."[6] Unfortunately, the author does not explain why this is so. In a passage similarly frustrating to the modern researcher, Basil of Caesarea notes that fasting is as proper and natural to women as breathing.[7] Elsewhere Basil argues that, being created in the image of God, women are equal to men in virtue and good works. He then asks, what man can imitate "the vigor of women in fasting,

---

4. This is shown by quantitative evidence as well as the emphasis on food as a cultural and religious symbol (*Holy Feast and Holy Fast: The Religious Significance of Food to Medieval Women*, The New Historicism: Studies in Cultural Poetics [Berkeley: University of California Press, 1987], 76–112).

5. *Canones Hippolyti* 32 (René-Georges Coquin, ed. *Les Canons d'Hippolyte*, PO 31,2 [Paris: Firmin-Didot, 1966], 402 [Arabic], 403 [French translation]). The date, author, and place of origin of the canons are debated, but Coquin dates them to the middle of the fourth century and argues for an Alexandrian origin (323–331). See the discussion and bibliography in Susanna Elm, '*Virgins of God': The Making of Asceticism in Late Antiquity*, Oxford Classical Monographs (Oxford: Clarendon Press, 1994), 228–230.

6. *Sermo exhortatorius* 2 (*PG* 28.1112A).

7. Basil of Caesarea, *De ieiunio homiliae* 2.2 (*PG* 31.188A–B): Γυναιξὶ δὲ, ὥσπερ τὸ ἀναπνεῖν, οὕτω καὶ τὸ νηστεύειν οἰκεῖόν ἐστι καὶ κατὰ φύσιν. This homily is not directed to an ascetic audience. On the contrary, Basil urges all Christians, young and old, wealthy and poor, to fast. He states, for example, that fasting is good for children as water is good for plants (188B).

their labor in prayer, the abundance of their tears, their readiness for good works?"[8]

The passage above from the *Canons of Hippolytus* suggests a particular ecclesiastical responsibility for widows and virgins to fast. The other passages testify—at least at a rhetorical level—to an affinity of women for dietary abstinence, although no theological or physiological explanations for such affinity are given. Peter Brown has argued that one of the factors for women's distinction in ascetic fasting may have been their increased confinement to home or controlled community:

> Deprived of the clear boundary of the desert, their energies less drained by hard physical labor and unable to expose themselves far from their place of residence for fear of sexual violence, virgins frequently defined themselves as separate from the world through an exceptionally rigid control of their diet. Woman ascetics were famous for their ability to endure preternaturally long fasts.[9]

In other words, if women's religious activity, service, and piety were less public and constrained by factors of gender and ecclesiastical or familial control, they might have been more likely to excel in the discipline of fasting. I will argue that, in addition to constraints on their activity, another critical factor in the association of women with food asceticism is the developing ideology of virginity and the theoretical framework, described in the previous chapters, that links eating to sexual desire, sexual desire to the fall, and the fall to embodiment (or at least bodily suffering), gender differentiation (or at least gender hierarchy), and death.

First, it will be helpful to review some of the key texts prescribing and regulating fasting for individual virgins or female ascetic communities. Some of this evidence has been examined in previous chapters, and we need not review it in detail here. In the discussion of Basil of Ancyra's treatise on virginity, the centrality of

---

8. Basil of Caesarea, *Homiliae de hominis structura* 1.18 (Alexis Smets and Michel van Esbroeck, eds., *Basile de Césarée: Sur l'origine de l'homme (Hom. X et XI de l'Hexaéméron)*, SC 160 [Paris: Éditions du Cerf, 1970], 214).

9. Peter Brown, *The Body and Society: Men, Women and Sexual Renunciation in Early Christianity*, Lectures on the History of Religions 13 (New York: Columbia University Press, 1988), 269.

regular dietary abstinence to the virginal life was clear. It is important to emphasize again that Basil argues both for the usefulness of fasting in the preservation of chastity and the need for moderation. He advises the virgin to choose those foods that have drying and cooling faculties in order to check the buildup of sexual humors. Similarly, Jerome's correspondence with or concerning the ascetic women Paula, Eustochium, Blesilla, Asella, and the others is peppered with advice concerning diet and the preservation of chastity. Like Basil of Ancyra, he expects ascetic women (and men) to fast regularly.

The Greek treatise on virginity attributed to Athanasius has a strong emphasis on fasting as central to the virginal life. Along with prayer and almsgiving, fasting is a great safeguard (φυλακτήριον).[10] It brings numerous spiritual and physical benefits: "it heals diseases, dries up the bodily humors, casts out demons, chases away wicked thoughts, makes the mind clearer and the heart pure, sanctifies the body and places the person before the throne of God."[11] The author encourages the virgin to remain steadfast in fasting—even if others tell her not to fast so often lest she become weak.[12] On the other hand, she must not scorn those who eat, nor allow the enemy to provoke her to a greater asceticism that will make her body "weak and useless."[13] She should

10. Pseudo-Athanasius, *De virginitate* 6 (Eduard F. von der Goltz, ed., *Λόγος σωτηρίας πρὸς τὴν παρθένον (De virginitate): Eine echte Schrift des Athanasius*, TU 29,2a [Leipzig: J. C. Hinrichs, 1905], 39–40. Von der Goltz argues for Athanasian authorship (see esp. 114–122), but others have rejected such an attribution. For an overview of scholarly opinion, see Michel Aubineau, "Les écrits de saint Athanase sur la virginité," *Revue d'Ascétique et de Mystique* 31 (1955): 144–151; Aubineau rejects Athanasian authorship, as does David Brakke in a more recent assessment ("The Authenticity of the Ascetic Athanasiana," *Orientalia* 63 (1994): 44–47.

11. Pseudo-Athanasius, *De virg.* 7 (von der Goltz, 41). On fasting to cast out demons, see Matthew 17:18-20. Some ancient manuscripts add verse 21, "but this kind [of demon] never comes out except by prayer and fasting." See also Herbert Musurillo, "The Problem of Ascetical Fasting in the Greek Patristic Writers," *Traditio* 12 (1956): 19–23. Musurillo notes that the demonic "motif" in fasting is "extremely rare among patristic writers" (20).

12. *De virg.* 6 (von der Goltz, 40).

13. On the influence of Evagrius of Pontus on this text, see von der Goltz, 72–74.

keep a measured regimen, fasting all year long and eating bread with vegetables prepared with oil in the evening. Her diet should be vegetarian: "all that is nonanimal is pure (πάντα ἁγνὰ ὅσα ἄψυχα)."[14] Wine is to be taken only for illness or in order to be hospitable.[15]

The pseudo-Athanasian treatise is distinguished by its emphasis on fasting and its specificity regarding regimen. Other texts oriented to virgins living either with their families, in small groups in homes, or in communities also portray fasting as an expected discipline. Parents are instructed to supervise the fasts of their virgin daughters in an anonymous fourth-century Greek treatise on virginity,[16] Eusebius of Emesa's homilies on virginity,[17] and the *Canons* attributed to Athanasius. In the latter

---

14. *De virg.* 8 (von der Goltz, 42–43). Some scholars have seen this vegetarian rule and the recommendation to "fast all year long" as evidence linking the treatise to the followers of Eustathius who were anathematized at the Council of Gangra, sometime in the middle of the fourth century, for allegedly fasting on Sundays and condemning meat-eating (see below). Von der Goltz, however, notes correctly that the practice of vegetarianism was widespread in Egyptian asceticism, and that the advice to fast all year long does not necessarily indicate that one is to fast on Sundays, which were traditionally excluded from fasting rules (119–120). See also Aubineau, "Les écrits de saint Athanase," 148. The line between advocacy of meat avoidance for ascetics and condemnation of all meat-eating (with the danger of seeming to condemn the gift of God to humans) is sometimes fuzzy or awkwardly drawn, as we saw in the positions of Jerome and Basil of Caesarea (above, chap. 5).

15. *De virg.* 12; 22 (von der Goltz, 45; 57).

16. *Homilia de virginitate* 18 (David Amand and Matthieu-Charles Moons, "Une curieuse homélie grecque inédite sur la virginité adressée aux pères de famille," *Revue bénédictine* 63 [1953]: 39). Although the homily focuses primarily on the virgin daughter and the authority of the father, parents are also encouraged to limit the food intake of their young son (63 [Amand and Moons, 53]). Amand and Moons date the homily to the early fourth century and argue against the attribution of the homily to Basil of Caesarea (19, 234–235, 238). Amand has argued for a Syrian origin of the homily ("La virginité chez Eusèbe d'Emèse et l'ascétisme familial dans la première moitié du IVe siècle," *Revue d'histoire ecclésiastique* 50 [1955]: 818; see also Arthur Vööbus, "Syrische Herkunft der Pseudo-Basilianischen Homilie über die Jungfräulichkeit," *Oriens Christianus* 40 [1956]: 69–77; and Concetta Aloe Spada, "Un'omelia greca anonima 'sulla verginità' [Rev. Bén. 63(1953)]," in *La tradizione dell'Enkrateia: Motivazioni ontologiche e protologiche*, ed. Ugo Bianchi [Rome: Ateneo, 1985], 603–623).

17. *Homiliae* 6.9; 7.9; 12; 13 (É. M. Buytaert, ed. *Eusèbe d'Émèse:*

collection, a number of canons discuss male virgins as well as female virgins who live in monasteries while others deal specifically with virgins who live at home.[18] For example, *Canon 92* instructs monks and female virgins alike to keep a perpetual fast, avoiding meat, fish, and wine.[19] *Canon 98*, however, concerns the virgin daughter who remains at home under the strict guidance of her parents. The author notes that there should be a virgin in every Christian household: "For the salvation of the whole house is this one virgin. And when wrath cometh upon the whole city, it shall not come upon a house wherein a virgin is." The parents must carefully observe their daughters to learn which one demonstrates the steadfastness, modesty, and obedience required for holiness. The virgin is not to eat meat or drink wine, and is to maintain her fast each day until evening. She is further instructed to prepare her own food, "cakes of bread and fried cakes and fine flour mixed with fat and honey."[20]

Several other sources testify to the importance of fasting in individual and community female asceticism during the fourth and fifth centuries.[21] But two in particular call for discussion:

Discours conservés en Latin, Spicilegium Sacrum Lovaniense, 26 [Louvain: Spicilegium Sacrum, 1953], 1:156–157; 181; 183–184). On homilies 6 and 7, home monasticism in the East, and parallels with the anonymous homily, see Amand, "La virginité chez Eusèbe d'Émèse," passim. Eusebius was born around 300 and died before 359.

18. Pseudo-Athanasius, *Canones* (Wilhelm Riedel and Walter E. Crum, eds. and trans., *The Canons of Athanasius, Patriarch of Alexandria, ca 293–373*, Texts and Translation Society 9 [London: William and Norgate, 1904; reprint, Amsterdam: Philo Press, 1973]). Riedel and Crum place the text in Egypt between 350 and 500 C.E. and argue that, although the case for Athanasian authorship is not conclusive, "the regulations of our canons are not in contradiction to the conditions of the age of Athanasius" (xiv, xxv). For a discussion of the Athanasian canons in the context of the development of female monasticism in Egypt, see Elm, *Virgins of God*, 231–233, 358.

19. Pseudo-Athanasius, *Can.* 92 (Riedel and Crum, 59 [English translation from the Arabic]). On women's communities see also *Can.* 48; 99 (Riedel and Crum, 35–36; 64–65).

20. Ibid., 98 (Riedel and Crum, 62–63 [English translation]). See also canons 103 and 104, in which the author forbids wealthy women to keep virgins as servants, and suggests that a wealthy woman without a virgin daughter may keep one of her maids as a virgin (Riedel and Crum, 66–67).

21. E.g., Basil of Caesarea, *Sermones ascetici* 2.2 (*PG* 31.888A–C); John

Evagrius of Pontus's *Sentences to a Virgin*[22] and the *Life of Syncletica* (yet another text transmitted under the name of Athanasius).[23] Syncletica's story is fascinating for its graphic depiction of the holy woman's endurance of suffering from various illnesses and bodily decay.[24] If she rejects medical attention for the disease that eats away at her lungs and gums,[25] Syncletica regards fasting as a "saving remedy" and "safeguard" which

---

Chrysostom, *Homilia XIII in epistolam ad Ephesios* 3 (*PG* 62.98); *Vita Melaniae Junioris* 22; 24; 25; 43; 56; 62 (Denys Gorce, ed., *Vie de Sainte Mélanie*, SC 90 [Paris: Éditions du Cerf, 1962], 172–178; 208–210; 238; 250); Gregory of Nyssa, *De vita Macrinae* 11 (Pierre Maraval, ed., *Grégoire de Nysse: Vie de Sainte Macrinae*, SC 178 [Paris: Éditions du Cerf, 1971], 176); Jerome, *Ep.* 108.20 [on Paula's monastery] (CSEL 55:334–336); J. Lebon, ed. and trans., "Athanasiana Syriaca I: 'Un Λόγος περὶ παρθενίας attribué à saint Athanase d'Alexandrie,'" *Le Muséon* 40 (1927): 212–213; and "Lettre aux vierges" in *S. Athanase: Lettres festales et pastorales en copte*, ed. and trans. L.-Th. Lefort, CSCO 150–151 (Louvain: L. Durbecq, 1955), 150:79 [Coptic], 151:60–61 [French]. On these last two works, preserved in Syriac and Coptic and attributed to Athanasius (with arguments in favor of Athanasian authorship) see also Aubineau, "Les écrits de Saint Athanase," 153–156, 160–169; and Brakke, "The Authenticity of the Ascetic Athanasiana," 19–25, 27–30. Both texts are now translated into English in Brakke's *Athanasius and the Politics of Asceticism*, Oxford Early Christian Studies (Oxford: Clarendon Press, 1995) 274–291, 303–309.

22. *Sententiae ad virginem* (Hugo Gressmann, ed., *Nonnenspiegel und Mönchsspiegel des Euagrios Pontikos*, TU 39,4b [Leipzig: Hinrichs, 1913], 143–151). For a full discussion of the sentences in the context of female monasticism see Susanna Elm, "Evagrius Ponticus' *Sententiae ad Virginem*," *Dumbarton Oaks Papers* 45 (1991): 97–120. Elm argues that Evagrius may have written the sentences for his friend and ascetic colleague, Melania the Elder, and for her community in Jerusalem (114–116).

23. Pseudo-Athanasius, *Vita et gesta Sanctae beataeque magistrae Syncleticae* (*PG* 28.1488A–1557B). On the date and origin of the Greek text (probably from fifth-century Egypt), see the introduction to the French translation by Sr. Odile Bénédicte Bernard, *Vie de Sainte Synclétique*, Spiritualité Orientale 9 (Begrolles-en-Mauges: Abbaye Notre Dame de Bellefontaine, 1972), iii–iv. The influence of Evagrius of Pontus is shown in this text by the emphasis on the power of thoughts (e.g. 8; 17; 26; 45; 88), the danger of pride (e.g., 10; 49–54), the chain of evils beginning with gluttony and *porneia* (26; 49), the active and contemplative life (86); and the particular emphasis on the dietary avoidance of water (17–18).

24. *Vita Sync.* 10; 98–99; 104–107; 110–112 (*PG* 28.1492C; 1548A–1549A; 1552B–1553A; 1553D–1557A). See also the sayings of Syncletica in *AP* Syncletica (*PG* 65.421A–428A), which share these same themes.

25. *Vita Sync.* 105; 111 (*PG* 28.1552B–C; 1556A–C).

brings weakness to the body but health to the soul.[26] She herself uses fasting and prayer to battle against thoughts inspired by the enemy,[27] and teaches that by controlling the belly (γαστρός) one is able also to control sexual pleasures (τῶν ὑπογαστρίων ἡδονῶν).[28] Thus fasting is here very closely associated with the physical methods necessary for spiritual development (an emphasis we see especially in Evagrius of Pontus), and eating is connected to sexual desire. Despite the rigors of Syncletica's own *askesis* and her advice to fast, however, she also warns against the dangers of pride in heroic fasts, and recommends that her disciples keep a regular, moderate regimen. In fact, the female anchorite who becomes proud because of her extreme asceticism should be placed in a community and compelled to eat twice a day.[29] A lack of moderation in fasting shows the influence of the enemy; therefore she urges others to "fast with logic and discipline."[30]

In his *Sentences to a Virgin,* Evagrius also balances the necessity for fasting with the requirement for regularity and humility. On the one hand, "hunger and thirst quench evil desires"[31] and the virgin should not pity her wasted flesh or bloodshot eyes.[32] Further, Evagrius recommends complete avoidance of meat and wine except for weak sisters.[33] On the other hand, he warns against irregularities and extremes in fasting: "Do not say, 'today I will eat and tomorrow I will not eat,' because you do this without prudence. For it will be harmful to your body and painful for your stomach."[34] Later he stresses that the virgin should not be scornful of those who eat, or puffed up in her own feats of abstinence, lest she not stand before the throne of God.[35] Evagrius hints here at some level of competition in fasting within the community, and seems eager to discourage immoderate abstinence.

26. Ibid., 10 (*PG* 28.1492B–C).
27. Ibid., 17–18 (*PG* 28.1496A–B).
28. Ibid., 29 (*PG* 28.1505A).
29. Ibid., 50 (*PG* 28.1517B–C).
30. Ibid., 53; 100 (*PG* 28.1520A–C; 1549A–B).
31. *Sent. ad virg.* 40 (Gressmann, 149).
32. Ibid., 51 (Gressmann, 150).
33. Ibid., 10 (Gressmann, 146).
34. Ibid., 9 (Gressmann, 146).
35. Ibid., 50 (Gressmann, 150).

Evagrius and Syncletica's biographer are witnesses (along with the writer of the treatise on virginity attributed to Athanasius) to the common tension in ascetic writers between clear admiration and praise for those who endure extreme regimens, and cautionary, sober calls for moderation and regularity in fasting.[36] Basil of Caesarea emphasizes moderation throughout his ascetic writings. In the *sermones ascetici*, directed to both male and female ascetics, Basil insists that discipline, community, and guidance are necessary for anyone undertaking the life of renunciation, and that immoderation in the mortification of the flesh is just as harmful as immoderation in the pleasures of the flesh.[37] Basil does not question the goodness of ascetic training, but encourages guidance: "Abstinence and all bodily mortification have some value, but if one follows one's own impulses, and does what is pleasing, and is not persuaded by the superior who gives counsel, then the harm done will be greater than the virtuous action."[38]

Discipline and obedience are especially required in communities of women, according to Basil:

> The life among women demands greater and more extraordinary decorum in the virtues of poverty, silence, obedience, and sisterly love, and strictness in regard to going out in public, caution in associations, [good] disposition towards others, and not having split groups. In all these things the life of virgins should achieve a greater zeal.[39]

Basil declares that virgins must obey their superior in all matters of community life and discipline, even if she should prevent their fasting or order them to take food for physical restoration.[40] Basil's

36. The theme of moderation in diet is common in texts dealing with both female and male asceticism. See Musurillo, "The Problem of Ascetical Fasting," 24–35; Rudolph Arbesmann, "Fasting and Prophecy in Pagan and Christian Antiquity," *Traditio* 7 (1949–1951): 32–40; P. Suso Frank, *Angelikos Bios: Begriffsanalytische und begriffsgeschichtliche Untersuchung zum 'engelgleichen Leben' im frühen Mönchtum*, Beiträge zur Geschichte des alten Mönchtums und des Benediktinerordens, 26 (Munich: Aschendorff, 1964), 26. See also the discussions of moderation in Basil of Ancyra, Gregory of Nyssa, Jerome, John Cassian, and Evagrius, above.

37. *Serm. asc.* 1.3; 2.1–2 (*PG* 31.873C–876D; 881B–888D).

38. Ibid., 2.2 (*PG* 31.884C).

39. Ibid. (*PG* 31.888A–B).

40. Ibid. (*PG* 31.888C).

advice on greater strictness among virgins and his warnings against individual impulse in fasting suggest that he is aware of cases of zealousness in fasting and physical renunciation among female ascetics. His words may reflect in part the controversies of the later fourth century over the place of renunciation in the Christian life and the definition of legitimate and "heretical" ascetic beliefs and practices. Often the debate centered on questions of fasting and the behavior of women, with wider issues of individual authority and ecclesiastical control.

Basil's own admiration for and association with Eustathius of Sebaste, whose followers were condemned at the council of Gangra, is no doubt a factor in his calls for obedience and moderation.[41] The bishops assembled in the mid-fourth century at Gangra[42] criticized the more rigorous interpreters of Eustathius's ascetic teaching for their beliefs and practices regarding marriage, diet and fasting, clothing, and the traditions of the established church.[43] The *Canons* accuse these ascetics of arrogance and irregularities in fasting. Anathematized are those who condemn marriage and encourage women and men to leave their spouses and neglect their children, and women who wear men's clothing and cut their hair as a declaration that they are no longer subject to men.

---

41. On Eustathius (c.300–c.377) and his ascetic leadership in Cappadocia, Pontus, and Armenia, see Socrates, *Historia ecclesiastica* 2.43 (*PG* 67.332B–333B); Sozomen, *Historia ecclesiastica* 3.14 (*PG* 67.1077C–1081A); Elm, *Virgins of God*, 106–112, 124–136; Jean Gribomont, "Le monachisme au IVe s. en Asie Mineure: de Gangres au Messalianisme," *Studia Patristica* 2, TU 64,9 (Berlin: Akademie-Verlag, 1957), 400–415; idem, "Eustathe de Sébaste," *Dictionnaire d'histoire et de géographie ecclésiastiques* 16 (1967): 26–33; idem, "Eustathe de Sébaste,"*Dictionnaire de spiritualité* 4 (1961): 1708–1712; and now Philip Rousseau, *Basil of Caesarea*, The Transformation of the Classical Heritage 20 (Berkeley: University of California Press, 1994), especially 23–24, 73–76, 239–245.

42. The date of the council is debated, with proposed dates ranging from 340 to 380. For a brief overview of the scholarly positions and an argument for a date of around 355, see T. D. Barnes, "The Date of the Council of Gangra," *Journal of Theological Studies* n.s. 40 (1989): 121–124.

43. See the canons of the council in Charles Joseph von Hefele, *Histoire des Conciles d'après les documents originaux*, 2nd ed. (Paris: Letouzey et Ané, 1907), 1.2:1032–1043.

The second *Canon* of the council addresses the issue of ascetic vegetarianism: "If anyone condemns those who with piety and faith eat meat (without blood, not sacrificed to idols, and not strangled), as if because of their partaking they have no hope, let that one be anathema."[44] Thus by their total vegetarianism and condemnation of all meat eating, the accused go beyond the church's usual recommendations against certain types of meat and challenge the established ecclesiastical order. What is more, the followers of Eustathius are also accused of both fasting on Sunday and ignoring traditional church fasts.[45] The "heretics" are thus both too rigorous and too lax. Either way, the validity of ecclesiastical authority and tradition is threatened.

The bishops conclude with a statement affirming the practice of asceticism in general but criticizing those who arrogantly exalt themselves over ordinary, non-ascetic Christians and "introduce innovations that are against scripture and the ecclesiastical canons."[46] Virginity, abstinence, withdrawal from worldly involvements, poverty, and simple dress are good when practiced with humility, in accordance with the teaching and traditions of the church, and without disdain for those who marry, eat meat, and are active in the world.[47]

Several important issues are raised by the *Canons* of Gangra. First, there is clear tension, if not conflict, between ordinary lay piety and lifestyle and ascetic discipline. The bishops are compelled to affirm both. Second, the followers of Eustathius seemed to break down traditional gender roles and even encourage some kind of equality between men and women. Thus the council anathematizes "any woman who, because of supposed asceticism, cuts her hair which God gave as a reminder of her subordination, as if undoing the command of subordination."[48]

---

44. Hefele, 1033. Recall that Basil of Caesarea is careful to separate himself from those who condemn the eating of meat in *Epistula* 199.28 (*PG* 32.725A).
45. *Canons* 18–19 (Hefele, 1.2:1040–1041).
46. Epilogue (Hefele, 1.2:1042–1043).
47. Ibid.
48. *Canon* 17 (Hefele, 1.2:1040). On heresy, asceticism, and issues of gender hierarchy see also Evelyne Patlagean, *Pauvreté économique et pauvreté*

Most important, the canons make clear that meat avoidance *in itself* is not the problem. Indeed, the regular avoidance of meat and wine, except for those who are weak or ill, seems to be the most common feature of renunciation in the ascetic texts discussed in this study.[49] The problem with vegetarianism for the bishops at Gangra, as for Jovinian and Basil of Caesarea, is the implied or actual criticism—even condemnation—of those who normally eat meat. Vegetarianism becomes a focal point for concern over ascetic elitism, divisions among Christians, and questions of individual and ecclesiastical authority.

Yet in another way, meat avoidance is *precisely* the problem. For it is precisely in behaviors and practices such as eating or not eating (as well as gender relations, marriage, and sexuality—all arenas for the construction of "heretical" *askesis*) that group identity and social conformity are rooted and maintained.[50] The same

---

sociale à Byzance: 4e–7e siècles, Civilisations et sociétés 48 (Paris: Mouton, 1977), 137–140; Elm, *"Virgins of God, "* 199 and passim, and Virginia Burrus, "The Heretical Woman as Symbol in Alexander, Athanasius, Epiphanius, and Jerome," *Harvard Theological Review* 84 (1991): 229–248.

49. This is not to say that meat was never eaten. See, e.g., *AP* Theophilus the archbishop 3; Poemen 170 (*PG* 65.200A; 364A–B); Maria Dembińska, "Diet: A Comparison of Food Consumption Between Some Eastern and Western Monasteries in the 4th–12th Centuries," *Byzantion* 55 (1985): 442; Evelyne Patlagean, *Pauvreté,* 41, 48–49, 136–137; idem, "Ancient Byzantine Hagiography," 106.

50. Jack Goody, *Cooking, Cuisine and Class: A Study in Comparative Sociology,* Themes in the Social Sciences (Cambridge: Cambridge University Press, 1982), 2. Robert Parker notes in relation to Pythagoreanism that, whatever the particular food avoided, food abstinence differentiates a group or individual from ordinary life: "The content of the restriction, though unlikely to be wholly arbitrary, is in a sense less important than its context. The rules are found where the individual is required to shed his profane self (actual fasting is found in the same contexts): as a preparation for initiation or incubation, and as part of the permanent abnormality of the Pythagorean life" (*Miasma: Pollution and Purification in Early Greek Religion* [Oxford: Clarendon Press, 1983], 365). Goody's analysis and Parker's assessment help us to understand the powerful role of food behavior in self-definition, whether in pagan and Christian antiquity or in modern societies. The work of Pierre Bourdieu on the role of bodily practices and the development of *habitus* has profound implications for understanding the role of food and dietary habits in "the purely social and quasi magical process of socialization, which is inaugurated by the act of marking" (*The Logic of Practice,* trans. Richard Nice [Stanford: Stanford University Press, 1990], 58. In general see 52–79).

bodily practices that establish and express ascetic culture can threaten the broader structure and institution of the church. Bourdieu observes that bodily "hexis" (that is, the body's demeanor and movements) is "political mythology realized, *embodied*, turned into a permanent disposition, a durable way of standing, speaking, walking, and thereby of feeling and thinking."[51] In other words, appearance and behavior "em-body" belief, and so easily become the focal points of debate and schism.

Further, the early Christian discussion of fasting, meat avoidance, and moderation takes on the same contours as the argumentation over virginity and marriage. We recall that Jovinian, one of the strongest anti-ascetic voices in the West, for example, criticizes the elitism of those who insist on the higher goodness of virginity or chastity and the importance of fasting. He also accuses Jerome and other ascetics of denying the goodness of creation and the gifts of God by despising marriage and meat-eating.[52] Jerome, in turn, takes great pains to insist that he does not condemn marriage by praising virginity, nor claim that every Christian must reject meat and wine. Both sexual and dietary renunciation are free choices, not commanded by God.[53] The argument that virginity and renunciation must be free choices, aspects of the "counsels of perfection" rather than commandments, and the insistence on the goodness of marriage in spite of the praise of chastity are standard in texts on virginity. They serve to distinguish the author's position from that of the "heretical" Manichaean, gnostic, or encratic groups,[54] while still allowing the

51. Bourdieu, *The Logic of Practice*, 69–70.
52. Jerome, *Adversus Jovinianum* (PL 23.221A–352D).
53. E.g., ibid., 1.3; 8; 12; 2.6; 16; 17 (PL 23.222A–224A; 231B–232C; 237A–240A; 307B–C; 323B–324B; 325B); *Epp.* 22.20; 79.7 (CSEL 54:170; 55:95–96). Of course, both Jerome's associates and his critics, like many a modern reader, seem unconvinced by these pronouncements.
54. For other sources on the themes of the goodness of marriage and the necessity that virginity be a free choice see, e.g., John Chrysostom, *De virginitate* 1–11 (PG 48.533–541); Basil of Ancyra, *De vera virginitate integritate* 55–58 (PG 30.777D–788A); Basil of Caesarea, *Sermo asceticus et exhortatio de renuntiatione saeculi, et de perfectione spirituali* 2 (PG 31.629A); Gregory of Nyssa, *De virginitate* 7.1 (Michel Aubineau, ed., *Grégoire de Nysse: Traité de la virginité*, SC 119 [Paris: Éditions du Cerf, 1966], 348–352); Eusebius of

author to advocate rigorous ascetic disciplines that, quite often, are practically indistinguishable from the behaviors condemned in "heretical" asceticism.

Arguments for fasting and virginity are therefore also concerned with issues of the goodness of creation, the definition of "heretical" behavior, and the formation of elitist groups of Christians distinguished by their discipline and renunciation. As the renunciation of marriage and the avoidance of ordinary food both signal one's orientation to the life of paradise or the life of the angels, so both behaviors identify the individual as a member of a select community of those who "would be perfect."[55]

The Eschatological Body: Female Nature, Becoming Male, and Pleasing the Bridegroom

But early Christian fasting is more than a technique for group identification. It is also an expression of theological concepts and a method for managing the body and its processes, as we have seen. This returns us to the issue of the evidence for and interpretation of women's fasting. How do Christian theorists and biographers in late antiquity represent the effects of fasting on the female body? What does the female ascetic "look like" in these textual portraits? How is this related to the ancient medical representation of femaleness?

Descriptions of the physical changes brought on by food deprivation emphasize reduction in sexual humors through drying and cooling, drying or shriveling of the breasts, and general destruction of the female characteristics or "nature" of the body. Basil of Ancyra, we have seen, places great emphasis on the avoidance of those foods that fill the body and the sexual organs with humors which must be expelled through sexual activity.[56] Through control of her diet, the virgin should be able to dry and cool the body, thus counteracting the heat and moisture that generate humors

---

Emesa, *Hom.* 6.6 (Buytaert, 155); anonymous *Hom. de virg.* 3–4 (Amand and Moons, 35–37); Lebon, "Athanasiana Syriaca I," 213–214; Pseudo-Athanasius, *Vita Sync.* 23; 77–78 (*PG* 28.1500C–1501A; 1532C–1533B).

55. Matthew 19:21.

56. *De virg.* 6; 7 (*PG* 30.681C–684B).

and desire for intercourse.[57] Given Basil's reported medical background and his use of Galenic theories on production of humors and the physiology of sexual desire and orgasm, we can assume that he expects the virgin to keep in check the buildup of female semen through dietary regimen. And John Cassian will argue later in the West that male celibates can similarly reduce the level of semen in their bodies by regular fasting.

But there is more. The virgin's physical regimen not only alters the internal processes of nutrition and sexuality; it is part of an overall effort to alter the external presentation of her body and thereby to diminish the sexually attractive power of her femaleness. Basil argues that at creation, in order that the female not be completely helpless in her subordination, the Creator placed in her body the power to attract the male. Thus her body was made more beautiful in form and pleasant to the touch, her appearance drawing the male to her.[58] The virgin, therefore, is intent on "destroying the pleasure of the female in herself, and cutting off the habit of the male towards [the female]."[59] Not only will she avoid beautifying herself, she will intentionally obscure her natural beauty. She must "make her look masculine and her voice hard, and in her walk and generally in every movement of her body constrain the enticements of pleasure."[60] The "form" of the female body, which was made alluring at creation, is made "pure" through virginity and asceticism.[61]

Further, Basil describes the virgin's body as "dead"; she has so purified her soul and body that lust no longer lives in her.[62] In an image that pushes the Stoic ideal to the extreme, Basil says that the virgin becomes like a sculpted image, unmoved by the assaults of the senses and unstimulated by thoughts and fantasies of pleasure.[63] By a kind of mystical castration she has cut off her female nature and its pleasure, and will receive all of the honor

57. Ibid., 8 (*PG* 30.685B–C).
58. Ibid., 3 (*PG* 30.676B–C).
59. Ibid., 19 (*PG* 30.708B).
60. Ibid., 16–18 (*PG* 30.704B–708B).
61. Ibid., 47 (*PG* 30.761A).
62. Ibid., 51–52 (*PG* 30.772A–773A).
63. Ibid., 58 (*PG* 30.785B–788A).

promised (in Isaiah 56:4-5) to the eunuchs who keep the Lord's sabbath.[64] Indeed, virgins should be admired more than continent males, Basil says, as they have conquered their own female nature:

> Although clothed in the female body, they have by means of asceticism beaten off the shape engendered from it for the sake of the soul, and have made themselves appear like men through excellence, just as their souls have been created equal. And just as men, through asceticism, pass from men to the rank of angels, so also these women, through asceticism, pass from women to the same rank as theirs.[65]

Yet although these virgins have struggled more valiantly than their chaste brothers, Basil is quick to note, in *this* life they are equal to men only in terms of the soul, "being lame (χωλευούσας) in that equality because of the garment of the female [body]." Only in the life to come will they be equal in all ways.[66] Therefore despite all of the necessary efforts to destroy the female pleasure in herself and to make herself appear masculine, despite the purity of body and soul achieved through great physical and spiritual effort, the virgin continues to be crippled by her physical body. Her virtue is equal to that of her male counterparts, but their equality extends only as far as the contours or touch of her

---

64. Ibid., 57–60 (*PG* 30.781A–793A). Basil of course warns the virgins against those who have undergone voluntary physical castration. In perhaps the most graphic passage of the treatise, Basil argues that the eunuch who has had his testicles removed is nevertheless quite able to rape an unsuspecting female (ibid., 61 [*PG* 30.793A–796D]). Aline Rousselle has argued that the religious castration of groups such as the Cybelene Galli had as its goals a kind of mystical preservation of childhood, infertility, and the preservation of vital breath—not sexual continence or the cessation of sexual activity (*Porneia: De la maîtrise du corps à la privation sensorielle IIe–IVe siècles de l'ère chrétienne*, Les chemins de l'Histoire [Paris: Presses Universitaires de France, 1983], 157–164).

65. *De virg.* 51 (*PG* 30.772B–C). Basil seems to suggest that female ascetics must first take on the rank of males. On ranks of men and angels see also Pseudo-Athanasius, *De virg.* 10 (von der Goltz, 44): "Put aside female mentality and take on courage and virility. For in the kingdom of heaven 'there is neither male nor female,' but all well-pleasing women take on the rank of men (πᾶσαι αἱ εὐαρεστήσασαι γυναῖκες ἀνδρῶν τάξιν λαμβάνουσιν);" and ibid., 7 (von der Goltz, 41): "Fasting is the life of the angels, and the one who makes use of it has angelic rank (ἀγγελικὴν τάξιν ἔχει)."

66. Basil of Ancyra, *De virg.* 51 (*PG* 30.772C).

feminine form. After all, even the virginal flesh that is called "dead" to lust is able to ignite the flames of passion—in herself as well as in others—by the slightest, most innocent touch.[67]

Thus the virginal body in Basil's treatise is represented as the dry, cool, insensitive statue of stone, a model of harmony and repose, a house closed up to protect the purity of the soul. But at the same time the body is the potential cause of her own or her brother's downfall because of its created power of sexual attraction—which, however, she is able to control and repress to a great extent through ascetic regimen and proper decorum.[68] If Basil is confident that through diet she can reduce the heat and moisture necessary to generate sexual humors; and that by obscuring her beauty, affecting masculinity in her appearance, and restricting her public exposure she can limit the occasions for sin, nevertheless her female body will remain a dangerous erotic zone for the rest of her female life.

Like Basil of Ancyra, Jerome employs the Galenic model of the four qualities of heat, cold, moisture, and dryness, and understands the faculties of foods to add to these qualities in the human body. He recommends cooling and drying regimens at some length to male and female ascetic friends, with the clear rationale that through fasting one controls the buildup of the heat and moisture necessary for the production of sexual humors and sexual desire. The "temple" of the virgin's body will be dry and cool, and she should associate only with companions who are likewise pale and thin from fasting.[69] Jerome's descriptions of the ideal ascetic female body emphasize the physical effects of abstinence from food and bodily pampering. Paula, who prescribed double fasts for those women in her monastery who struggled with lust, neglected her own health and despised eating to such an extent that her eyes were weakened from crying and she appeared "squalid with filth."[70] Poor Blesilla's teetering steps and thin neck

---

67. Ibid., 45; 53; 66 (*PG* 30.757B–760B; 776A–C; 804B–805A).

68. The virgin battles against *porneia* in herself, but she is also the source of temptation and sexual sin for those around her (e.g., ibid., 16; 35; 44–45 [*PG* 30.704B–705A; 740B–C; 756D–757A]).

69. *Ep.* 22.17; 23 (CSEL 54:164; 175).

70. *Epp.* 45.3; 108.19–21 (CSEL 54:325; 55:332–338).

are glowingly described by Jerome even as he defends himself
against criticism for encouraging the excessive abstinence that
probably caused her death.[71] And Jerome notes of Asella that her
"holy knees" became so hard from kneeling for prayer that they
looked like those of a camel.[72]

It is interesting that Jerome does not follow Basil of Ancyra and
suggest that virgins affect a masculine appearance, nor does he
tend to praise women for being "manly," though the attribution
of manliness to female ascetics is typical in the ascetic discourse
of the fourth and fifth centuries.[73] That Jerome does not adopt this
image is, I think, connected to his arguments against the notions
that *apatheia* is attainable in this life and that there will be no
more gender distinctions in paradise.[74] The chaste female body
Jerome describes is no insensitive statue. If in Basil of Ancyra's
treatise the virgin's body is "dead" because lust no longer lives in
it, if she should remove her mind and soul from her body to such a
degree of perfection that she is not even aware if she is in the body
or out of the body,[75] Jerome's virgin never forgets for a minute that
she is burdened by female flesh. For Jerome, female asceticism is
not so much a matter of blotting out or denying female nature as
it is the renunciation of the "natural" female functions of sexuality and procreation.[76] To this end, fasting is a necessary tool.

71. See chap. 3.
72. *Ep.* 24.5 (CSEL 54:216–217).
73. E.g., *AP* Sarah, 4 ("By nature I am a woman, but not by my thoughts.");
9 (*PG* 65.420D–421A); Palladius, *HL* 9 (Butler, 2:29); *Vita Mel.* Prologue (SC
90:126); Pseudo-Athanasius, *De virg.* 10 (von der Goltz, 44); Pseudo-Athanasius, *Vita Sync.* 15; 111 (*PG* 28.1493C–D; 1556B–C); Gregory of Nyssa, *Vita
Mac.* 10 (SC 178:172).
74. Jerome does use language about women going against their female
nature, but avoids the image of becoming male. For example, in his treatise
against Helvidius, Jerome contrasts the virgin to the wife, and suggests that
the virgin should not be called a woman. Since Jerome understands "woman"
to mean a married, sexually active female, the virgin is no longer identified by
this category. But he does not carry the image further to suggest that the virgin becomes male (*De perpetua virginitate B. Mariae adversus Helvidium* 20
[*PL* 23.214A]). Further, when Jerome praises the strength and virtue of women
and claims that they should be imitated by men, he does not refer to these
women as "manly" (e.g. *Epp.* 54.2; 66.13 [CSEL 54:467; 663–664]).
75. Basil of Ancyra, *De virg.* 66 (*PG* 30.804C).
76. *Ep.* 130.10 (CSEL 56:190–191).

Basil and Jerome have argued for the usefulness of fasting most explicitly based on the medical understanding of diet and sexual physiology. Both authors seem to interpret the medical model as suggesting that the virgin or chaste woman can through diet literally dry up the excess of female semen. Given the earlier discussion of the medical understanding of the effects of diet on the quality and quantity of blood, semen, menses, and milk in the female body, what other implications are there for the category of dryness? Can we argue that ancient ascetics expected the other fluid signs of femaleness—menstruation and full breasts—to be diminished by dietary restrictions?

Modern research on the physical effects of food deprivation suggests that severe or rigorous fasting could result in amenorrhea as well as atrophy of the mammary glands.[77] And Caroline Walker Bynum's research on medieval fasting has confirmed that the cessation of menstruation was commonly reported of female ascetics distinguished for their fasting.[78] But what can be said about late antiquity? For evidence on this issue, the treatises of ascetic theorists like Jerome, Basil, Evagrius, and the others provide nothing explicit. Intriguing clues are found, however, in the dozen or more hagiographical narratives, dating from the fifth to the seventh centuries, concerning female transvestites.[79] The basic plot of

77. Ancel Keys, Joseph Brožek, et al., *The Biology of Human Starvation*, 2 vols. (Minneapolis: University of Minnesota Press, 1950), 1:749–750; 759–753; Emmanuel Le Roy Ladurie, "Famine Amenorrhoea (Seventeenth–Twentieth Centuries)," in *Biology of Man in History*, ed. Robert Forster and Orest Ranum, trans. Elborg Forster (Baltimore: The Johns Hopkins University Press, 1975), 163–178. Keys and Le Roy Ladurie both acknowledge other factors, such as stress, contributing to amenorrhea.

78. Bynum, *Holy Feast and Holy Fast*, 122–123, 138, 148, 211, 214, 274, 394. Bynum also discusses the themes of miraculous lactation in virgins or healing oil exuding from the breasts of women who otherwise do not excrete "normal" fluids; she connects these themes to the medieval image of the lactating Christ (80, 122–123, 126, 211, 270–275).

79. For general studies of this literature and its earlier influences see John Anson, "The Female Transvestite in Early Monasticism: The Origin and Development of a Motif," *Viator* 5 (1974): 1–32; Khalifa Bennasser, *Gender and Sanctity in Early Byzantine Monasticism: A Study of the Phenomenon of Female Ascetics in Male Monastic Habit with a Translation of the Life of St. Matrona* (Ph.D. diss., Rutgers University, 1984); Marie Delcourt, "Female Saints in Masculine Clothing," in *Hermaphrodite: Myths and Rites of the*

these accounts involves a woman's desire to renounce the world, her use of male clothing as a disguise for flight and concealment of identity, and the eventual discovery of her true identity or gender.[80] The woman involved may be married, a virgin, or a repentant prostitute. Often she is assisted in her deception by an understanding priest or monk who supplies her with monastic garments or some other type of male clothing. Some of the women live alone as hermits, while others live disguised as monks within monastic communities. Some are found to be women only after their deaths, as their bodies are prepared for burial; others reveal themselves to family members grieving for their lost loved one.

The primary tool for disguising femaleness in these narratives is male clothing. For example, Hilaria, the daughter of a king, puts on the protective belt of a soldier in order to board a ship for Alexandria, and changes later into the monk's habit given to her by the desert father Pambo.[81] Euphrosyne, fleeing her father's home in Alexandria in order to avoid marriage, has her head shaved and is given a robe by an old ascetic man before entering a monastery as a eunuch.[82] And Pelagia, the beautiful dancer and actress of Antioch, is converted and baptized by bishop Nonnus who gives her his own hair shirt and mantle before she leaves for Jerusalem.[83] While clothing enables the female renouncer to

Bisexual Figure in Classical Antiquity, trans. Jennifer Nicholson (London: Studio Books, 1961), 84–102; Evelyne Patlagean, "L'histoire de la femme déguisée en moine et l'évolution de la sainteté féminine à Byzance," *Studi Medievali* Ser. 3, 17 (1976): 597–623. Anson has studied about twenty legends of female monks (13); Patlagean lists twelve (599–602). The narratives are preserved in Greek, Coptic, and Syriac.

80. Anson, "The Female Transvestite," 13.

81. *Vita Sanctae Hilariae* (James Drescher, ed., *Three Coptic Legends: Hilaria, Archellites, The Seven Sleepers,* Supplément aux annales de service des antiquités de l'Égypte 4 [Cairo: Institut Français d'archéologie orientale, 1947], 3; 6 [Coptic]; 72; 75 [English translation]).

82. *Vita Sanctae Euphrosynae* (Agnes Lewis Smith, trans., *Select Narratives of Holy Women from the Syro-Antiochene or Sinai Palimpsest,* Studia Sinaitica 10 [London: C. J. Clay and Sons, 1900], 51–52 [English translation from the Syriac]).

83. *Vita Pelagiae Antiochae* 41 (Sebastian P. Brock and Susan Ashbrook Harvey, eds. and trans., *Holy Women of the Syrian Orient,* The Transformation of the Classical Heritage 13. [Berkeley, University of California Press,

assume "maleness" in order to make her flight and continue to live in a monastic setting undetected, another key factor in the disguise is often the destruction of female appearance through harsh ascetic regimen.

One of the most explicit accounts of the effects of renunciation on appearance occurs in the story of Pelagia. Pelagia's biographer, reportedly a deacon of Antioch, first describes her appearance before her conversion, as she rode through the streets accompanied by her servants and admirers: "On her hands and feet she wore armbands, silks, and anklets decorated with all sorts of pearls, while around her neck were necklaces and strings with pendants and pearls. Her beauty stunned those who beheld her, captivating them in their desire for her." Her perfume and makeup, her shamelessness, her perfect white skin—everything about her appearance "incited everyone who set eyes on her to fall in love with her."[84] After years of harsh ascetic training and passing as the eunuch Pelagios, however, her appearance changed drastically. The deacon describes what he saw when he visited her on the Mount of Olives:

> I failed to recognize her because she had lost those good looks I used to know; her astounding beauty had all faded away, her laughing and bright face that I had known had become ugly, her pretty eyes had become hollow and cavernous as the result of much fasting and the keeping of vigils. The joints of her holy bones, all fleshless, were visible beneath her skin through emaciation brought on by ascetic practices. Indeed the whole complexion of her body was coarse and dark like sackcloth, as the result of her strenuous practice.[85]

The deacon did not even recognize her as a woman, much less as the most desirable woman in Antioch, for he did not "notice anything about her that resembled the manner of a woman."[86] Thus

---

1987], 58 [English translation from the Syriac]). The Greek texts are collected in Séminaire d'Histoire des Texts de l'École normale, *Pélagie la Pénitente: Métamorphoses d'une légende,* vol. 1, *Les textes et leur histoire* (Paris: Études Augustiniennes, 1981), 39–131.

84. *Vita Pel.* 4–6 (Brock and Harvey [English translation], 42–43).
85. Ibid., 45 (Brock and Harvey [English translation], 60).
86. Ibid.

the wearing away of Pelagia's feminine appearance is one element of her male disguise as well as the mark and symbol of her conversion and holiness.

Other similar hagiographies likewise emphasize the ravaging of female features through asceticism. Euphrosyne, for example, was so beautiful when she began her ascetic career that even though taken for a eunuch she proved tempting to other monks and was sent to live in an isolated cell. Later, however, she was not recognized by her own father because her beauty had been "withered" through constant fasting, vigils, and sleeping on the ground.[87] Apollinaria, after travelling to Alexandria desiring the ascetic life, escaped from her royal entourage and lived in a swamp for many years before becoming a disciple of Macarius. After years in the swamp, her hagiographer writes, "her body became like the shell of a tortoise. For it had been devoured by the mosquitoes." When she came out of the swamp, then, not even the blessed Macarius could guess that the "eunuch" was in fact a woman.[88] One modern commentator has called this type of brutal obliteration of the signs of femaleness "a motif of 'self-castration.'"[89] If the disguise of male clothing helps in the initial escape into the monastic life, then rigorous fasting, vigils, and other types of renunciation

---

87. *Vita Euphr.* (Lewis, 53; 56). The Lives of Pelagia and Euphrosyne are strong examples of the use of female beauty as a symbol of the temptation of males. The destruction of their beauty also removes the danger from their appearance. Emphasis on female responsibility for male lust runs throughout early Christian ascetic literature and has been discussed by modern scholars. On the transvestite narratives see Anson, who suggests that for male monastic writers "the fantasy of a holy woman disguised among their number represented . . . a psychological opportunity to neutralize the threat of female temptation" ("The Female Transvestite," 5). In general see Geoffrey Galt Harpham, *The Ascetic Imperative in Culture and Criticism* (Chicago: University of Chicago Press, 1987), 45–88; Margaret R. Miles, *Carnal Knowing: Female Nakedness and Religious Meaning in the Christian West* (Boston: Beacon Press, 1989), 70–77. Buiding on the analysis of Harpham, Miles writes, "As temptation, women's bodies played an indispensable role in the fantasy lives of male ascetics, a concentrated and localized form of the world-as-temptation, grist for the mill of the monk's resistance" (75).

88. *Vita Sanctae Apolinariae* (Greek text in Drescher, *Three Coptic Legends*, 156–157). The story of Apollinaria is similar to the Life of Hilaria, with a few differences in plot (see Anson, "The Female Transvestite," 19–21).

89. Anson, "The Female Transvestite," 20.

insure that the holy woman's body will no longer function or be recognized as female. Here the act of "becoming male" symbolized by the taking on of male garments is completed by the loss of the physical features of femaleness.

Further, at least two of the transvestite narratives specifically describe the near disappearance of the woman's breasts. Anastasia, who lived for twenty-eight years as a eunuch monk, was visited by Daniel of Scetis and his disciple just before her death. Preparing the body he thought was male for burial, Daniel's disciple discovered "women's breasts, looking like two shriveled up leaves."[90] And Hilaria's biographer notes that the monks with whom she lived accepted her as a eunuch, in part because of her monk's habit, but also because her breasts "were not as those of all women." Further, "she was shrunken with ascetic practices nor was she subject to the curse of women, since God Almighty ordained for her the thing appointed."[91] The Coptic word translated here by Drescher as "curse" is derived from the Greek πάθος, and so can have a range of meanings, including "condition," "emotion," and "suffering" or "illness." It would seem, however, that given the context (a physical description of a body that no longer appears female), we might understand this to be a reference to menstruation.

Of course the obliteration of the female characteristics of the body is here a hagiographical *topos*, and we cannot argue that each woman's body (or, indeed, any woman's body) changed in exactly the way described. But this is not really the important historical evidence provided by this literature. Rather, the transvestite narratives tell us something about the expectations for female holiness held by hagiographers and their audience, if not the holy women themselves. The taking on of male clothing and the general wearing away of female appearance through fasting

90. *Vita Anastasiae* (Brock and Harvey [English translation from the Syriac], 147). The story of Anastasia is included in a narrative cycle concerning Daniel of Scetis. Three Greek versions of the life have been edited by M. Léon Clugnet, "Vie d'Anastasie la Patrice," *Revue de l'orient chrétien* 5 (1900): 51–59. The three texts describe her breasts as "dry" (ξηρῶν [52]), "withered" (μεμαραμμένα [56]), and "dried up" (κατεξηραμένα [59]).

91. *Vita Hil.* (Drescher, 6 [Coptic]; 75 [English translation]).

and mortification symbolize more than the repression of female temptation by assuming "manliness." Anastasia's and Hilaria's dried-up breasts, Hilaria's release from the "curse of women"— these images suggest a repression of the *procreative* body. As we have seen, the fluids of the "healthy" female in ancient medical discourse are signs of fertility. Dried breasts and the absence of menstrual fluids, on the other hand, characterize women who are either too old or too young to bear children, or women who, because of illness, diet, or lifestyle, are not able to assume their social role as childbearers.

As noted above, when Apollinaria emerges from years of living in a mosquito-filled swamp, her body is "like the shell of a tortoise."[92] This metaphor suggests that Apollinaria's skin had become hard and rough like the texture of the shell; but it also presents the image of a hollow, dry shell empty of its fleshy innards. Apollinaria's body is no longer fit for procreation. It has become thin, dry, hard—in short, it is no longer "female." For the gender category of "female," in both medicine and theology, is defined in large part by sexuality, fertility, and procreation.[93]

Further, the quality of dryness in general has symbolic as well as physiological meaning. G. E. R. Lloyd has shown that in Greek science and philosophy, heat and moisture are generally associated with life and vitality, while cold and dryness are negatively valued as associated with the process of aging and death.[94] So too

92. *Vita Apolinariae* (Drescher, 157).

93. Kirsten Hastrup makes some helpful comments in her anthropological study of cultural sexual roles. She writes, "It seems, then, that the course of life of a woman is basically divided into three stages. The first stage is that of the unspecified, yet creative virgin; the next stage is that of the sexually specified, child-bearing woman, and the course is completed by a final return to unspecificity, this time of widowhood and of old women's impotence. . . . This course of life is peculiar to women. Only women's bodies can be used to define social status in this way" ("The Semantics of Biology: Virginity," in *Defining Females: The Nature of Women in Society*, ed. Shirley Ardner [New York: John Wiley and Sons, Halsted Press, 1978], 59–60).

94. G. E. R. Lloyd, "The Hot and the Cold, the Dry and the Wet in Greek Philosophy," *Journal of Hellenic Studies* 84 (1964): 100–101. Galen taught that aging was a process of drying and cooling (*De sanitate tuenda* 1.2; 5.3 [C. G. Kühn, ed., *Galeni Opera Omnia* (Leipzig: K. Knobloch, 1823–1833; reprint, Hildesheim: Georg Olms, 1965), 6:5; 319]).

in the ideology of asceticism, the dryness of the body signifies that the individual has removed herself or himself from service to the cycle of birth and death and is no longer enslaved by physical desire. The heat and moisture of sexual desire and procreative sexuality are diminished by fasting. Thus Jerome encourages Eustochium to fast regularly, so that she can say "I have become like a wineskin in the frost; whatever moisture there was in me has been dried up."[95] It is the same interpretation of the mortified, dry, and cool body of the virgin that underlies Basil of Ancyra's notion that her body is "dead" because lust no longer lives in it,[96] and Eusebius of Emesa's claim that for the virgin who lives in ascetic renunciation, concupiscence is dead and her body itself is a stranger to her.[97] The physical results of fasting and other ascetic disciplines—the mortified body, the sterile body—represent and confirm individual conversion, renunciation, and holiness. If we consider the protological association of sexuality, death, and the fall with the female, or with gender differentiation and hierarchy, then for a female ascetic to mortify her body to the point of unrecognized femaleness, even to the point of sterility, is truly to return to paradise.[98]

It is important to remember as well that medical writers of late antiquity clearly recognized the possibility of long-term amenorrhea as a result of lifestyle and dietary behaviors. Soranus and Aetios of Amida argue that, in itself, menstruation is not necessary for health, noting that "masculine" and active women often cease to menstruate.[99] Aetios goes so far as to suggest that, unless

95. Jerome, *Ep.* 22.17 (CSEL 54:165–166); Psalms 119:83.

96. Basil of Ancyra, *De virg.* 51–52 (*PG* 30.772D–773A).

97. Eusebius of Emesa, *Hom.* 7.13 (Buytaert, 184).

98. The image of the virgin as being dead or sterile toward the world but spiritually fertile is common in the ascetic literature used in this study, e.g., Gregory of Nyssa, *De virg.* 13.3 (SC 119:428–430); Pseudo-Athanasius, *De virg.* 14 (Von der Goltz, 48–49); Athanasius, "Lettre aux vierges" (Lefort, *S. Athanase: Lettres festales et pastorales en copte*, CSCO 150:95 [Coptic]; 151:77 [French]); Jerome, *Adv. Jov.* 1.16 (*PL* 23.246C). In medieval sources on female asceticism, the symbolism of the chaste body as fertile and life-giving becomes much more pronounced (see Bynum, *Holy Feast and Holy Fast*, 300 and passim).

99. See above, chap. 2 .

a woman wants to conceive, it would be better to prescribe a regimen "by which [means] the body of a woman may become so dry that it is not necessary [for her] to have menstrual periods."[100]

While references to withered breasts and (possibly) amenorrhea in the transvestite narratives do not constitute enough evidence in themselves to point to a trend in late ancient ascetic physiology, nevertheless, given all of the medical and theological arguments surveyed thus far, I would argue that amenorrhea must have been a recognized phenomenon among the most austere female ascetics, and that it would have been interpreted in much the same way as the cessation of nocturnal emissions among male ascetics such as those addressed by John Cassian—that is, as a sign of success in the battle with sexual desire. But even more, the drying of the female reproductive fluids symbolizes freedom from the culturally and socially defined status of "woman" as childbearer and the theological status of the female as the one in whose body the cycle of life and death is perpetuated.

The ascetic ideal of overcoming female nature or even of becoming male is thus closely linked to physical appearance and the effects of physical disciplines, especially virginity and fasting. Whether among the more radical interpreters of the eschatological vision of Galatians 3:28—such as the followers of Eustathius or the transvestite holy women who dressed in male clothing and cut their hair—or among the virgins counseled by Basil of Ancyra to affect masculinity through demeanor and decorum, the external presentation and appearance of the body seems in large part to determine gender identification. In this way early Christian ascetic texts confirm Laqueur's observation that in antiquity "to be a man or a woman was to hold a social rank, a place in society, to assume a cultural role."[101]

Yet the notion of "becoming male" can only be taken so far. In the transvestite narratives, there is almost always a revelation of

---

100. *Tetrabiblion* 16.53 (James V. Ricci, trans., *Aetios of Amida: The Gynaecology and Obstetrics of the VIth Century, A.D.* [Philadelphia: Blakiston, 1950], 56 [English translation]).

101. Thomas Laqueur, *Making Sex: Body and Gender from the Greeks to Freud* (Cambridge: Harvard University Press, 1990), 8.

the true female identity of the disguised monk, and often the woman is reconciled—although not permanently reunited—with the family she was forced to flee. (And of course the reader or hearer of the story is aware of the heroine's identity from the beginning.) Further, although Basil of Ancyra encourages virgins to try to look masculine, and praises the equality of female and male souls, in this life their female bodies continue to hinder them. Here is a fundamental tension within the patristic discourse on virginity. For while the virgin is virile in ascetic prowess and virtue, while she has lived against her own female nature, while she has renounced the suffering of marriage and childbirth for the freedom of virginity, in two ways she remains fundamentally female: her body, though mortified, is still the potential source of sexual temptation and sin; and though she has no earthly husband to control her, she is the "bride of Christ."

The metaphor of the bride of Christ is not applied exclusively to female virgins in early Christian literature; the soul or the church as bride, and Christ or God as bridegroom, are also common images, playing on erotic themes in the Song of Songs.[102] But in fourth-century ascetic writings "bride of Christ" language becomes more and more distinctive of discourse on female virginity. In choosing a life of perpetual chastity, the virgin becomes the spouse of Christ and belongs to him just as an earthly wife belongs to her husband; and a virgin who breaks her vow is guilty of adultery.[103] Thus the metaphor of marriage to Christ becomes a

102. Brown, *The Body and Society*, 274–276; and see the texts cited in G. W. H. Lampe, ed., *A Patristic Greek Lexicon* (Oxford: Oxford University Press, Clarendon Press, 1961), 928–930.

103. For examples of bride of Christ imagery in our sources see Basil of Ancyra, *De virg.* 23–29; 36; 37; 39–43; 50 (*PG* 30.716C–729B; 740C–745C; 748B–756C; 768B–772A); Evagrius, *Sent. ad virg.* 52; 55; 56 (Gressmann, 150–151); Gregory of Nyssa, *Vita Mac.* 22 (SC 178:214–216); Pseudo-Athanasius, *De virg.* 6; 24 (Von der Goltz, 40; 59); John Chrysostom, *De virg.* 1; 59 (*PG* 48.533; 580); Jerome, *Epp.* 22.1; 17; 25; 41; 107.7; 108.28 (CSEL 54:144–145; 166; 178–180; 209–210; 55:298; 347); Pseudo-Athanasius, *Vita Sync.* 7; 9; 92 (*PG* 28.1489B–C; 1492A–B; 1544C–1545A); anonymous *Hom. de virg.* 18; 44; 56–57; 108 (Amand and Moons, 39; 45; 49; 63); Eusebius of Emesa, *Hom.* 6.16; 18; 7.23; 26; 28 (Buytaert, 161; 162–163; 191; 193; 194); Athanasius, "Lettre aux vierges" (Lefort, *S. Athanase: Lettres festales et pastorales en copte*, CSCO 150:87–88 [Coptic]; 151:69–70 [French]); Lebon,

rhetorical tool in the effort of male writers to control and confine female religious behavior.

For example, Basil of Ancyra warns several times that the heavenly bridegroom sees everything that the virgin does, even when she is alone, and knows all of her secret thoughts. Basil reminds his reader that just as one who enters an earthly marriage leaves her father's house and pledges that her husband is the master and guardian of her life, the virgin pledges herself to the Lord, who is her guardian. For this virgin to then marry a mortal man is nothing short of adultery. In a vivid image, Basil describes the heavenly bridegroom watching as a mortal man dares to climb into the Lord's bed—a scenario Basil likens to the bride of a nobleman having sex with a slave in his master's bed.[104] The virgin, then, is under the control of the heavenly bridegroom as much as any earthly husband, and he monitors and knows all of her movements and thoughts. The image of the watchful and jealous eyes of the Lord strengthens Basil's case for increased seclusion and modesty among virgins.[105]

It is particularly important to note the ways in which the mortified female body is eroticized in relation to Christ. It is not simply that female desire is projected onto the heavenly bridegroom, but that her physical renunciations are, according to some authors, that which make her more desirable to her beloved. Pseudo-Athanasius, for example, exhorts the virgin addressed in his treatise,

---

"Athanasiana Syriaca I," 219; 225 [French translation from Syriac]; *Vita Mel.* 1; 42 (SC 90:130; 206–208); Basil of Caesarea, *Ep.* 46 (*PG* 32.369A–381B); Gregory of Nyssa uses bride of Christ imagery widely in *De virg.* Although he is explicit at one point that both men and woman desire union of the soul with the "incorruptible bridegroom" (20.4 [SC 119:498–502]), elsewhere in the treatise his words on marriage to Christ seem directed to females in particular (3.8 [SC 119:294]; and see the editor's comments, SC 119:145–146; 193–197).

104. *De virg.* 39 (*PG* 30.748B–749A); see also 27–29 (*PG* 30.725B–729B).

105. Jerome's letter to Eustochium is another important example of the use of Christ's authority and fidelity to regulate female behavior. He tells Eustochium not to wander around the city where she may be seduced, exposed, or attacked. "Jesus is jealous (*zelotypus*)," he writes, "he does not want your face to be seen by others" (*Ep.* 22.25 [CSEL 54:180]).

Adorn your body with this virtue [fasting], O virgin, and you will please the heavenly bridegroom. For those who are tied to the world and who beautify their bodies with sweet oils, fragrances, and perfumes, and with lavish garments and gold, in order to please men cannot please God. Christ does not require any of these things from you, but only a pure heart and an undefiled body which is mortified by fasting.[106]

Fasting adorns the body to please the bridegroom, Christ. It is a cosmetic technique placed in opposition to worldly cosmetics and ornamentation. In the *Life of Syncletica*, likewise, the holy woman teaches that while worldly women make themselves more attractive with baths, fragrant oils, and perfumes, those who desire to be more attractive to Christ adorn themselves, by means of rigorous asceticism, with virtues.[107] And Basil of Ancyra writes that the virgin must neglect everything, including her own beauty, to follow Christ, who is pleased by the appearance and decorum proper to his betrothed.[108] Her body itself is the nuptial chamber prepared for her heavenly bridegroom, who will therein lie with (συνευνάζειν) her soul as with a pure bride.[109]

Thus Christ is attracted to the virgin's mortified body just as earthly males would be attracted to the female body created for sexual pleasure. Though she should make herself appear masculine and stamp out the attraction of the female in her self-presentation toward earthly men, in relation to Christ her body is represented in quite feminine terms. Brought to perfection by fasting—dry and cool, thin and undefiled—her body is presented to Christ as if to an earthly husband. She will chastise her body and bring it into subjection, in order to deliver it pure to the bridegroom.[110]

What is more, writes Evagrius, if the female ascetic denies her-

106. *De virg.* 6 (von der Goltz, 40).
107. Pseudo-Athanasius, *Vita Sync.* 92 (*PG* 28.1544C–1545A).
108. *De virg.* 25–27; 36 (*PG* 30.721A–728A; 740C–744A).
109. Ibid., 27 (*PG* 30.725B). For similar eroticized images of Christ and the virgin, see Jerome, *Ep.* 22, esp. chap. 25 (CSEL 54:178–180).
110. Athanasius, "Lettre aux vierges" (Lefort, *S. Athanase: Lettres festales et pastorales en copte*, CSCO 150:90 [Coptic]; 151:71 [French]); 1 Corinthians 9:27.

self the pleasures of the flesh, in the kingdom all of her senses will be gratified and her union with Christ consummated:

> The virginal eyes will see the Lord. The virgins' ears will listen to his words. The virgins' mouth will kiss their bridegroom, and the virgins' nose will rush towards the scent of his perfume. Virginal hands will stroke the Lord, and the chastity of their flesh will be pleasing to him. The virginal soul will be crowned, and she will live forever with her bridegroom. A spiritual garment will be given to her, and she will celebrate a feast with the angels in heaven. She will light an inextinguishable lamp, and she will not lack oil in her vessels. She will receive everlasting wealth, and inherit the kingdom of God.[111]

All that the virgin has renounced—sensual pleasures, physical companionship, clothing, food, wealth, inheritance—she will receive in heaven and for eternity.

Such physical and erotic images of the heavenly reward for earthly self-denial are understandable only in the context of female asceticism,[112] and only in the context of a discourse that urged both the negation of female sexual desire and desirability as well as the directing of that desire toward Christ and the perfecting of desirability through ascetic mortification. Thus the male theorists, biographers, and homilists who argued for the value of the virginal life could hold in tension the images of the virgin as one who renounces femaleness and gains the "rank" of maleness, and one who gives herself to Christ in a spiritual marriage that

---

111. Evagrius of Pontus, *Sent. ad virg.* 55 (Gressmann, 151).

112. Susanna Elm has made the important observation that while Evagrius describes the spiritual goal for female ascetics as union with the divine through marriage to Christ the celestial bridegroom, in his parallel text addressed to a male audience, the *Sententiae ad monachos*, the goal of the ascetic life is union with the divine through gnosis. Thus while both male and female ascetics may achieve mystical union, Evagrius represents the female goal in the sexual imagery and metaphors of marriage, while he describes the male goal in terms of knowledge of God ("Evagrius Ponticus' *Sententiae ad Virginem*," 110–114). On the different goals of male and female continence in ascetic discourse see also the observations of Han Drijvers, "The Saint as Symbol: Conceptions of the Person in Late Antiquity and Early Christianity," in *Concepts of Person in Religion and Thought*, ed. Hans G. Kippenberg, Yme B. Kuiper, and Andy F. Sanders, Religion and Reason 37 (Berlin: Mouton de Gruyter, 1990), 150.

nevertheless "leaves the traditional pattern of the sexes intact."[113]

Female Flesh and Future Body

It is really no surprise that we end with paradox. On the one hand,
within the framework of the ascetic theory that we have explored
in these chapters, the virginal body comes to exemplify Christian
hope for return to the pure and trouble-free immortality of original humanity. The physical appearance or rhetorical image of the
virgin, who testifies by the evidence of her bodily mortifications
that she is no longer procreative and therefore no longer female,
represents the transformation of all humanity—from differentiated, corruptible, and mortal fallenness to wholeness and unity.[114]
On the other hand, the male delineation of the contours of female
piety seems driven by *fear* of the power and sexual danger
ascribed to the female body and to female "nature," within the
same discourse that praised virginity. Gender, or really the problem of femaleness, intrudes at every level, in every aspect of this
study, including physiological models, eschatological visions,
constructions of heresy, practical ascetic advice, and images of
creation, the fall, death, and desire.

Even within the lofty visions of genderless and bodiless unity,
femaleness defines and constricts the goals of ascetic piety.
Femaleness is that which must be overcome to achieve male

---

113. Drijvers, "The Saint as Symbol," 150. Averil Cameron has also com-
mented on the rhetorical space which allowed for the "coexistence" of the
denial of female desire and the erotic language surrounding the relationship of
virgin and Christ. She asks, "Should we be looking for a psychoanalytic explanation for this language, as one might be tempted to do? . . . Or is it rather
that the rhetoric has taken on a polarity which in asserting the negative also
licenses the positive?" ("Virginity as Metaphor: Women and the Rhetoric of
Early Christianity," in *History as Text: the Writing of Ancient History*, ed.
Averil Cameron [Chapel Hill: University of North Carolina Press, 1989],
200–201).

114. On Macrina as an "*exemplum* for a complete human being" see Elm,
Virgins of God, 102. And see Carolyn Walker Bynum's discussion of late
medieval piety, in which she argues that "femaleness" and the female body
symbolized humanity in relation to God (*Holy Feast and Holy Flesh*,
277–296).

rank, it provides the symbolic language for the fall and the power of death as well as for the ascetic's subordinate relationship to Christ, and it is the physical factor that causes the virgin to limp along in her earthly life, in spite of her achievements, behind her male ascetic counterparts. Basil of Ancyra's words capture the paradox of hope and fear that characterizes male ascetic discourse on virginity:

> while in the present life they are equal to men only in their soul, being lame in that equality because of the garment of the female body, in the coming age even they will be found equal in all ways, through virtue, to those [men] who have become angels. For if because they are made equal to the angels they neither marry nor are given in marriage, those [females] who accomplish this in the present life by means of asceticism show themselves to be like the angels in all ways; castrating the property of female and male bodies for sexual intercourse, I say, through virtue, and living—with naked souls—on earth with men.[115]

While Basil's vision of naked, fleshless souls projects the equality of male and female into the coming age, his treatise itself—like the Canons of the Council at Gangra, or Jerome's epistolary recollections of debates with Origenists, or so many other texts that offer glimpses of ancient piety—reminds us that *some* embodied women and men were intent on training, creating, and displaying the future body in the present flesh.

---

115. Basil of Ancyra, *De virg.* 51 (*PG* 30.772C); and see the discussion of this passage in Elm, *Virgins of God,* 120–121 and Ton H. C. Van Eijk, "Marriage and Virginity, Death and Immortality," in *Epektasis: Mélanges patristiques offerts au Cardinal Jean Daniélou,* ed. Jacques Fontaine and Charles Kannengiesser (Paris: Beauchesne, 1972), 226.

Bibliography

I. Primary Sources

Aeschylus. *Prometheus vinctus.* Herbert Weir Smyth, ed. *Aeschylus,* vol. 1. Loeb Classical Library. Cambridge, Mass.: Harvard University Press, 1963.

Aetios of Amida. *Tetrabiblion.* James V. Ricci, trans. *Aetios of Amida: The Gynaecology and Obstetrics of the VIth Century, A.D.* Philadelphia: Blackiston, 1950.

Apophthegmata Patrum. PG 65.71–440.

Aristotle. *De generatione animalium.* A. L. Peck, ed. *Aristotle: Generation of Animals.* Loeb Classical Library. Cambridge: Harvard University Press, 1979.

———. *Rhetorica.* John Henry Freese, ed., *Aristotle: The 'Art' of Rhetoric.* Loeb Classical Library. Cambridge, Mass.: Harvard University Press, 1967.

Arnim, Hans von. *Stoicorum Veterum Fragmenta.* 4 vols. Leipzig: B. G. Teubner, 1903–1924; reprint, 1964.

Asterius Amasenus. *Homilia* 14. C. Datema, ed. *Asterius of Amasea: Homilies I–XIV. Text, Introduction, and Notes.* Leiden: E. J. Brill, 1970.

Athanasius. "Athanasiana Syriaca I: 'Un Λόγος περὶ παρθενίας attribué à saint Athanase d'Alexandrie.'" Edited and translated by J. Lebon. *Le Muséon* 40 (1927): 205–248.

———. *S. Athanase. Lettres festales et pastorales en copte.* Edited and translated by L.-Th. Lefort. CSCO 150–151. Louvain: L. Durbecq, 1955.

———. *Vita Antonii. PG* 26.837–976.

Pseudo-Athanasius. *Canones.* Wilhelm Riedel and Walter E. Crum, eds. and trans. *The Canons of Athanasius, Patriarch of Alexandria, ca 293–373.* Texts and Translation Society 9. London: William and Norgate, 1904; reprint, Amsterdam: Philo Press, 1973.

———. *De virginitate.* Eduard F. von der Goltz, ed. Λόγος σωτηρίας πρὸς τὴν παρθένον *(De virginitate): Eine echte Schrift des Athanasius.* TU 29,2a. Leipzig: J. C. Hinrichs, 1905.

———. *Sermo exhortatorius. PG* 28.1107D–1114A.

———. *Vita et gesta Sanctae beataeque magistrae Syncleticae. PG* 28.1488–1557.

———. Odile Bénédicte Bernard, trans. *Vie de Sainte Synclétique.* Spiritualité orientale 9. Begrolles-en-Mauge: Abbaye Notre Dame de Bellefontaine, 1972.

Basil of Ancyra. *De vera virginitatis integritate. PG* 30.669–809.

———. A. Vaillant, ed. and trans. *De Virginitate de Saint Basile: Text vieux-Slave et traduction française.* Textes publiés par l'Institute d'Études slaves 3. Paris: Institut d'Études Slaves, 1943.

Basil of Caesarea. *De ieiunio homiliae 1–2. PG* 31.164–197.

———. *Epistulae. PG* 32.220–1112.

———. *Homiliae de hominis structura.* Alexis Smets and Michel van Esbroeck, eds., *Basile de Césarée: Sur l'origine de l'homme.* SC 160. Paris: Éditions du Cerf, 1970.

———. *Quod Deus non est auctor malorum. PG* 31.329–352.

———. *Sermo asceticus et exhortatio de renuntiatione saeculi, et de perfectione spirituali. PG* 31. 625–648.

———. *Sermones ascetici. PG* 31.869–888.

———. *Regulae [Regulae brevius tractatae* and *Regulae fusius tractatae]. PG* 31.889–1305.

Caelius Aurelianus. *De morbis acutis et chronicis.* I. E. Drabkin, ed. *Caelius Aurelianus on Acute Diseases and On Chronic Diseases.* Chicago: University of Chicago Press, 1950.

Cebetis tabula. John T. Fitzgerald and L. Michael White, eds., *The*

Tabula of Cebes. Texts and Translations 24, Greco-Roman Religions Series 7. Chico: Scholars Press, 1983.

Celsus. *De medicina.* W. G. Spencer, ed. *Celsus: De medicina.* 3 vols. Loeb Classical Library. Cambridge: Harvard University Press, 1948, 1953.

Clement of Alexandria. *Paedagogus.* Henri-Irénée Marrou, Marguerite Harl, Claude Mondésert, and Chantal Matray, eds., introduction by Henri-Irénée Marrou. *Clément d'Alexandrie: Le Pédagogue.* SC 70, 108, 158. Paris: Éditions du Cerf, 1960–1970.

———. *Stromata.* Claude Mondésert, ed., introduction by P. Thomas Camelot. *Clément d'Alexandrie: Les Stromates. Stromate II.* SC 38. Paris: Éditions du Cerf, 1954.

Epictetus. *Dissertationes.* W. A. Oldfather, ed. *Epictetus: The Discourses as Reported by Arrian, The Manual, and Fragments.* 2 vols. Loeb Classical Library. Cambridge: Harvard University Press, 1966–1967.

Eusebius of Caesarea. *Historia ecclesiastica.* Kirsopp Lake, J. E. L. Oulton, and H. J. Lawlor, eds. and trans. *Eusebius: The Ecclesiastical History.* 2 vols. Loeb Classical Library. Cambridge: Harvard University Press, 1980.

Eusebius of Emesa. *Homiliae 6–7.* É. M. Buytaert, ed. *Eusébe d'Émèse: Discours Conservés en Latin.* Spicilegium Sacrum Lovaniense 26. Louvain: Spicilegium Sacrum, 1953.

Evagrius of Pontus. *Antirrheticus.* In *Euagrius Ponticus: Syrischer Text, griechische Retroversion,* ed. W. Frankenburg, 472–545. Abhandlungen der königlichen Gesellschaft der Wissenschaften zu Göttingen, Philologisch-historische Klasse, n.F., 13,2. Berlin: Weidmann, 1912.

———. *De diversis malignis cogitationibus. PG* 79.1200–1233; supplemented by *PG* 40.1240–1244 and J. Muyldermans, ed. *A travers la tradition manuscrite d'Évagre le Pontique,* 47–55. Bibliothèque du *Muséon* 3. Louvain: Bureaux de *Muséon,* 1932.

———. *De ieiunio.* In *Evagriana Syriaca: Texts inédits du British Muséum et de la Vaticane,* ed. J. Muyldermans, 115–117;

150–153. Bibliothèque du *Muséon* 31. Louvain: Publications universitaires/ Institut orientaliste, 1952.

———. *De justis et perfectis.* In *Evagriana Syriaca: Texts inédits du British Muséum et de la Vaticane,* ed. J. Muyldermans, 105–109; 143–146. Bibliothèque du *Muséon* 31. Louvain: Publications universitaires/ Institut orientaliste, 1952.

———. *De octo spiritibus malitiae. PG* 79.1145–1164.

———. *De oratione. PG* 79.1165–1200.

———. *De vitiis quae oppositae sunt virtutibus. PG* 79.1140–1144.

———. *Epistula ad Melaniam.* In *Euagrius Ponticus: Syrischer Text, griechische Retroversion,* ed. W. Frankenburg, 612–619. Abhandlungen der königlichen Gesellschaft der Wissenschaften zu Göttingen, Philologisch-historische Klasse, n.F., 13,2. Berlin: Weidmann, 1912.

———. Martin Parmentier, trans. "Evagrius of Pontus' 'Letter to Melania.'" *Bijdragen, tijdschrift voor filosofie en theologie* 46 (1985): 2–38.

———. *Gnostikos.* Antoine Guillaumont and Claire Guillaumont, eds. *Évagre le Pontique: Le Gnostique.* SC 356. Paris: Éditions du Cerf, 1989.

———. *Kephalaia Gnostica.* Antoine Guillaumont, ed. and trans. *Les six Centuries des Kephalaia gnostica d'Évagre le Pontique.* PO 28,1. Paris: Firmin-Didot, 1958.

———. *Praktikos.* Antoine Guillaumont and Claire Guillaumont, eds. *Évagre le Pontique: Traité pratique ou le moine.* SC 170–171. Paris: Éditions du Cerf, 1971.

———. John Eudes Bamberger, ed. and trans., *Evagrius Ponticus: The Praktikos and Chapters on Prayer.* Cistercian Studies Series 4. Kalamazoo: Cistercian Publications, 1981.

———. *Rerum monachalium rationes. PG* 40.1252–1264.

———. *Sententiae ad monachos.* In *Nonnenspiegel und Mönchsspiegel des Euagrios Pontikos,* ed. Hugo Gressmann, 153–165. TU 39,4b. Leipzig: Hinrichs, 1913.

———. *Sententiae ad virginem.* In *Nonnenspiegel und Mönchsspiegel des Euagrios Pontikos,* ed. Hugo Gressmann, 146–151. TU 39,4b. Leipzig: Hinrichs, 1913.

Galen. C. G. Kühn, ed. *Galeni Opera Omnia,* 20 vols. Leipzig: K. Knobloch, 1821–1833; reprint, Hildesheim: Georg Olms, 1964–1965.

———. *De alimentorum facultatibus.* Kühn 6:453–748.

———. *De cognoscendis curandisque animi morbis.* Kühn 5:1–57.

———. *De curandi ratione per venae sectionem.* Kühn 11:250–316.

———. *De locis affectis.* Kühn 8:1–452.

———. *De naturalibus facultatibus.* Kühn 2:1–214.

———. *De sanitate tuenda.* Kühn 6:1–452.

———. *De semine.* Kühn 4:512–651.

———. *De simplicium medicamentorum temperamentis ac facultatibus.* Kühn 11:379–892; 12:1–377.

———. *De usu partium corporis humani.* Kühn 3:1–939; 4:1–366.

———. Margaret Tallmadge May, trans. *Galen: On the Usefulness of the Parts of the Body.* 2 vols. Ithaca: Cornell University Press, 1968.

———. *De venae sectione adversus Erasistratum.* Kühn 11:147–186.

———. *Hippocratis de acutorum morborum victu liber et Galeni commentarius.* Kühn 15:418–919.

———. *In Hippocratis vel Polybi opus de salubri victus ratione privatorum commentarius.* Kühn 15:174–223.

———. *Pro puero epileptica consilium.* Kühn 11:357–378.

———. *Quod animi mores corporis temperamenta sequantur.* Kühn 4:767–822.

———. *Quod optimus medicus sit quoque philosophus.* Kühn 1:53–63.

Gregory of Nyssa. *De anima et resurrectione.* PG 46.12–160.

———. *De hominis opificio.* PG 44.124–256.

———. *Epistula 19.* PG 46.1072–1080.

———. *De virginitate.* Michel Aubineau, ed. *Grégoire de Nysse: Traité de la virginité.* SC 119. Paris: Éditions du Cerf, 1966.

———. *De vita Macrinae.* Pierre Maraval, ed. *Grégoire de Nysse: Vie de Sainte Macrine.* SC 178. Paris: Éditions du Cerf, 1971.

Hesiod. *Opera et dies.* M. L. West, ed. *Hesiod: Works and Days.* Oxford: Clarendon Press, 1978.

———. *Theogonia.* M. L. West, ed. *Hesiod: Theogony.* Oxford: Clarendon Press, 1966.

Pseudo-Hippolytus. *Canones Hippolyti.* René-Georges Coquin, ed. and trans. *Les Canons d'Hippolyte.* PO 31,2. Paris: Firmin-Didot, 1966.

Historia monachorum in Aegypto. André-Jean Festugière, ed. *Historia Monachorum in Aegypto.* Subsidia hagiographica 53. Brussels: Société des Bollandistes, 1971.

———. [Latin translation of Rufinus] *PL* 21.391–462.

———. Norman Russell, trans. *The Lives of the Desert Fathers: The Historia Monachorum in Aegypto.* Introduction by Benedicta Ward. London: Mowbray; Kalamazoo: Cistercian Publications, 1980.

Homilia de virginitate [anonymous]. David Amand and Matthieu-Charles Moons. "Une curieuse homélie grecque inédite sur la virginité adressée aux pères de famille." *Revue bénédictine* 63 (1953): 18–69, 211–238.

Jerome. *Adversus Jovinianum. PL* 23.221–352.

———. *Contra Johannem Hierosolymitanum ad Pammachium. PL* 23.371–412.

———. *Contra Rufinum.* Pierre Lardet, ed. *Saint Jérôme: Apologie Contre Rufin.* SC 303. Paris: Éditions du Cerf, 1983.

———. *De perpetua virginitate B. Mariae adversus Helvidium. PL* 23.193–216.

———. *De viris illustribus. PL* 23.631–760.

———. *Dialogus adversus Pelagianos. PL* 23.517–618.

———. *Epistulae.* Isidorus Hilberg, ed. *Eusebii Hieronymi Epistulae.* CSEL 54–56. Vienna: Tempsky, 1910–1918.

———. *Vita Malchi Monachi Captivi. PL* 23.55–62.

———. *Vita S. Hilarionis. PL* 23.29–54.

———. *Vita S. Pauli Primi Eremitae. PL* 23.17–30.

John Cassian. *Conlationes.* E. Pichery, ed. *Jean Cassien: Conférences.* SC 42, 54, 64. Paris: Éditions du Cerf, 1955, 1958, 1959.

———. *De Institutis coenobiorum.* Jean-Claude Guy, ed. *Jean*

Cassien: Institutions cénobitiques. SC 109. Paris: Éditions du Cerf, 1965.

John Chrysostom. *Commentarius in Epistolam ad Galatas.* PG 61.611–682.

———. *De compunctione.* PG 47.393–422.

———. *De inani gloria.* Anne-Marie Malingrey, ed. *Jean Chrysostome: Sur la vaine gloire et l'éducation des enfants.* SC 188. Paris: Éditions du Cerf, 1972.

———. *De virginitate.* PG 48.533–596.

———. Herbert Musurillo and Bernard Grillet, eds. *Jean Chrysostome: La virginité.* SC 125. Paris: Éditions du Cerf, 1966.

———. *Homiliae 21 de statuis ad populum Antiochenum.* PG 49.15–222.

———. *Homiliae in Acta Apostolorum.* PG 60.13–384.

———. *Homiliae in Epistula ad Ephesios.* PG 62.9–176.

———. *Homiliae in Epistolam Primam ad Timotheum.* PG 62.501–600.

———. *Homiliae in Genesim.* PG 53.21–386.

———. *Homiliae in Matthaeum.* PG 57.13–472.

Liber Graduum. Ed. Michael Kmosko. *Patrologia Syriaca* 1,3. Paris: Firmin-Didot, 1926.

Musonius Rufus. Cora B. Lutz, ed. "Musonius Rufus. The Roman Socrates." *Yale Classical Studies* 10 (1947): 3–147.

Oribasius, *Libri Incerti.* Ioannes Raeder, ed. *Oribasius: Collectionum medicarum reliquiae* 4. Amsterdam: Adolf M. Hakkert, 1964.

Palladius. *Historia Lausiaca.* Cuthbert Butler, ed. *The Lausiac History of Palladius,* 2 vols. Texts and Studies 6/1–2. Cambridge: Cambridge University Press, 1898, 1904.

———. E. Amelineau, ed. *Historia Lausiaca.* Paris: Ernest Leroux, 1887.

Plato. *Phaedrus.* Harold North Fowler, ed. *Plato: Euthyphro, Apology, Crito, Phaedo, Phaedrus.* Loeb Classical Library. Cambridge: Harvard University Press, 1966.

———. *Respublica.* Paul Shorey, ed. *Plato: The Republic.* 2 vols. Loeb Classical Library. Cambridge: Harvard University Press, 1963.

————. *Symposium*. W. R. M. Lamb, ed. *Plato: Lysis, Symposium, Gorgias*. Loeb Classical Library. Cambridge: Harvard University Press, 1967.

————. *Timaeus*. R. G. Bury, ed. *Plato: Timaeus, Critias, Cleitophon, Menexenus, Epistles*. Loeb Classical Library. Cambridge: Harvard University Press, 1966.

Pliny. *Historia naturalis*. H. Rackman, W. H. S. Jones, and D. E. Eichkolz, eds. *Pliny: Natural History*. 10 vols. Loeb Classical Library. Cambridge: Harvard University Press, 1938–1963.

Plutarch. *De esu carnium*. Harold Cherniss and William C. Helmbold, eds. *Plutarch's Moralia* 12. Loeb Classical Library. Cambridge: Harvard University Press, 1957.

————. *De Iside et Osiride*. Frank Cole Babbitt, ed. *Plutarch's Moralia* 5. Loeb Classical Libray. Cambridge: Harvard University Press, 1962.

————. *De tuenda sanitate praecepta*. Frank Cole Babbitt, ed. *Plutarch's Moralia* 2. Loeb Classical Library. Cambridge: Harvard University Press, 1971.

————. *Quaestiones convivales*. Paul A. Clement and Herbert B. Hoffleit, eds. *Plutarch's Moralia* 8. Loeb Classical Library. Cambridge: Harvard University Press, 1969.

Porphyry. *De abstinentia*. August Nauck, ed. *Porphyrii Philosophi Platonici opuscula selecta*. Bibliotheca Scriptorum Graecorum et Romanorum Teubneriana. Leipzig: Teubner, 1886; reprint, Hildesheim: Georg Olms, 1963.

————. Thomas Taylor, trans. *On Abstinence from Animal Food*. London: Centaur Press, 1965.

Rufus of Ephesus. *Opera*. C. Daremberg and C. E. Ruelle, eds. *Oeuvres de Rufus de Éphèse*. Paris: 1897; reprint, Amsterdam: Adolf M. Hakkert, 1963.

Socrates. *Historia ecclesiastica*. PG 67.29–842.

Soranus. *Gynaikeia*. Owsei Temkin, trans. *Soranus' Gynecology*. Baltimore: The Johns Hopkins Press, 1956.

Sozomen. *Historia ecclesiastica*. PG 67.844–1630.

Tertullian. *De anima*. A. Reifferscheid and G. Wissowa, eds. *Tertulliani Opera*, 298–396. CSEL 20. Vienna: Tempsky, 1890.

————. *De ieiunio adversus psychicos.* A. Reifferscheid and G. Wissowa, eds. *Tertulliani Opera,* 274–297. CSEL 20. Vienna: Tempsky, 1890.

Veilleux, Armand, trans. *Pachomian Koinonia: The Lives, Rules, and Other Writings of Pachomius and his Disciples,* 3 vols. Vol. 1, *The Life of Saint Pachomius and his Disciples.* Vol. 2, *Pachomian Chronicles and Rules.* Cistercian Studies Series 45–46. Kalamazoo: Cistercian Publications, 1980–1981.

Vita Anastasiae. In *Holy Women of the Syrian Orient,* ed. and trans. Sebastian P. Brock and Susan Ashbrook Harvey, 143–149. The Transformation of the Classical Heritage 13. Berkeley: University of California Press, 1987.

Vita Melaniae Junioris. Denys Gorce, ed. *Vie de Sainte Mélanie.* SC 90. Paris: Éditions du Cerf, 1962.

Vita Pelagiae Antiochae. In *Holy Women of the Syrian Orient,* ed. and trans. Sebastian P. Brock and Susan Ashbrook Harvey, 41–62. The Transformation of the Classical Heritage 13. Berkeley: University of California Press, 1987.

————. Séminaire d'Histoire des Texts de l'École normale. *Pélagie la Pénitente: Métamorphoses d'une légende.* Vol. 1, *Les textes et leur histoire.* Paris: Études Augustiniennes, 1981.

————. M. Léon Clugnet, ed. "Vie d'Anastasie la Patrice." *Revue de l'orient chrétien* 5 (1900): 51–59.

Vita Sanctae Apolinariae. In *Three Coptic Legends: Hilaria, Archellites, The Seven Sleepers,* ed. James Drescher, 152–161. Supplément aux annales du service des antiquités de l'Égypte 4. Cairo: Institut Français d'archéologie orientale, 1947.

Vita Sanctae Euphrosynae. In *Select Narratives of Holy Women from the Syro-Antiochene or Sinai Palimpsest,* ed. and trans. Agnes Smith Lewis, 46–59. Studia Sinaitica 10. London: C. J. Clay and Sons, 1900.

Vita Sanctae Hilariae. In *Three Coptic Legends: Hilaria, Archellites, The Seven Sleepers,* ed. and trans. James Drescher, 1–13; 69–82. Supplément aux annales du service des antiquités de l'Égypte 4. Cairo: Institut Français d'archéologie orientale, 1947.

II. Secondary Sources

Achelis, H. *Virgines Subintroductae: Ein Beitrag zum VII Kapitel des I Korintherbriefs.* Leipzig: J. C. Hinrichs, 1902.

Alexandre, Monique. "Protologie et eschatologie chez Grégoire de Nysse." In *Arché e Telos: L'antropologia di Origene e di Gregorio de Nysse,* ed. Ugo Bianchi, 122–169. Studia Patristica Mediolanensia, 12. Milan: Vita e Pensiero, 1981.

Aloe Spada, Concetta. "Un'omelia greca anonima 'sulla verginità' (Rev. Bén. 63[1953])." In *La tradizione dell'Enkrateia: Motivazioni ontologiche e protologiche,* ed. Ugo Bianchi, 603–623. Rome: Ateneo, 1985.

Amand de Mendieta, David. "La virginité chez Eusèbe d'Émèse et l'ascétisme familial dans la première moité du IVe siècle." *Revue d'histoire ecclésiastique* 50 (1955): 777–820.

Amand de Mendieta, Emmanuel (David). "Les deux homélies sur la création de l'homme que les manuscrits attribuent à Basile de Césarée ou à Grégoire de Nysse." In *Zetesis: Album amicorum,* 695–716. Antwerp: De Nederlandsche Boekhandel, 1973.

Amundsen, Darrel W. "Medicine and Faith in Early Christianity." *Bulletin of the History of Medicine* 56 (1982): 326–350.

André, Jacques. *L'Alimentation et la cuisine à Rome.* Paris: Les Belles Lettres, 1981.

Andrews, Alfred C. "The Use of Rue as a Spice by the Greeks and Romans." *Classical Journal* 43 (1948): 371–373.

Anson, John. "The Female Transvestite in Early Monasticism: The Origin and Development of a Motif." *Viator* 5 (1974):1–32.

Arbesmann, P. Rudolph. *Das Fasten bei den Griechen und Römern.* Religionsgeschichtliche Versuche und Vorarbeiten 21/1. Giessen: Alfred Töpelmann, 1929; reprint, Berlin: Alfred Töpelmann, 1966.

———. "Fasten, Fastenspeisen, Fasttage." In *Reallexikon für Antike und Christentum,* ed. Theodor Klauser, 7:447–524. Stuttgart: Anton Hiersemann, 1969.

———. "Fasting and Prophecy in Pagan and Christian Antiquity." *Traditio* 7 (1949–1951): 1–71.

Armstrong, Arthur Hilary. "Gnosis and Greek Philosophy." In *Gnosis: Festschrift für Hans Jonas*, ed. B. Aland, 87–124. Göttingen: Vandenhoeck & Ruprecht, 1978.

Aubineau, Michel. "Les écrits de saint Athanase sur la virginité." *Revue d'Ascétique et de Mystique* 31 (1955): 140–173.

Aubert, Jean Jacques. "Threatened Wombs: Aspects of Ancient Uterine Magic." *Greek, Roman, and Byzantine Studies* 30 (1989): 421–449.

Barnes, T. D. "The Date of the Council of Gangra." *Journal of Theological Studies* n.s. 40 (1989): 121–124.

Barton, Tamsyn S. *Power and Knowledge: Astrology, Physiognomics, and Medicine under the Roman Empire*. The Body, in Theory: Histories of Cultural Materialism. Ann Arbor: The University of Michigan Press, 1994.

Behm, Johannes. "νῆστις, νηστεύω, νηστεία" In *Theological Dictionary of the New Testament*, ed. Gerhard Kittel, 4:924–935. Translated and edited by Geoffrey W. Bromiley. Grand Rapids: Eerdmans, 1967; reprint, 1973.

Bell, Catherine. *Ritual Theory, Ritual Practice*. New York: Oxford University Press, 1992.

Bell, Rudolph M. *Holy Anorexia*. Epilogue by William N. Davis. Chicago: University of Chicago Press, 1985.

Bennasser, Khalifa. *Gender and Sanctity in Early Byzantine Monasticism: A Study of the Phenomenon of Female Ascetics in Male Monastic Habit with a Translation of the Life of Matrona*. Ph.D. diss., Rutgers University, 1984.

Bianchi, Ugo. "L'intention du Colloque: Analyse historico-religieuse." In *Arché e Telos: L'antropologia di Origene e di Gregorio di Nissa*, ed. Ugo Bianchi, 9–35. Studia Patristica Mediolanensia, 12. Milan: Vita e Pensiero, 1981.

Blank, David. "The Etymology of Salvation in Gregory of Nyssa's *De virginitate*." *Journal of Theological Studies* n.s. 37 (1986): 77–90.

Blayney, Jan. "Theories of Conception in the Ancient Roman World." In *The Family in Ancient Rome: New Perspectives*, ed. Beryl Rawson, 230–236. Ithaca: Cornell University Press, 1986.

Blond, Georges. "L'hérésie' encratite vers la fin du quatrième siècle." *Recherches de science religieuse* 32 (1944): 157–210.

Bordo, Susan. *Unbearable Weight: Feminism, Western Culture, and the Body.* Berkeley: University of California Press, 1993.

Bourdieu, Pierre. *The Logic of Practice.* Translated by Richard Nice. Stanford, Calif.: Stanford University Press, 1990.

Boylan, Michael. "The Galenic and Hippocratic Challenges to Aristotle's Conception Theory." *Journal of the History of Biology* 17 (1984): 83–112.

Brakke, David. *Athanasius and the Politics of Asceticism.* Oxford Early Christian Studies. Oxford: Clarendon Press, 1995.

———. "The Authenticity of the Ascetic Athanasiana." *Orientalia* 63 (1994): 17–56.

———. "The Problematization of Nocturnal Emissions in Early Christian Syria, Egypt, and Gaul." *Journal of Early Christian Studies* 3 (1995): 419–460.

Brock, Sebastian P. and Susan Ashbrook Harvey, eds. *Holy Women of the Syrian Orient.* The Transformation of the Classical Heritage 13. Berkeley: University of California Press, 1987.

Brown, Peter. *The Body and Society: Men, Women and Sexual Renunciation in Early Christianity.* Lectures on the History of Religions 13. New York: Columbia University Press, 1988.

———. "The Notion of Virginity in the Early Church." In *Christian Spirituality: Origins to the Twelfth Century,* ed. Bernard McGinn, John Meyendorff, and Jean Leclercq, 427–443. World Spirituality 16. New York: Crossroad, 1985.

Brumberg, Joan Jacobs. *Fasting Girls: The Emergence of Anorexia Nervosa as a Modern Disease.* Cambridge: Harvard University Press, 1988.

Bunge, Gabriel. Évagre le Pontique et les deux Macaire." *Irénikon* 56 (1983): 215–227, 323–360.

Burkert, Walter. *Lore and Science in Ancient Pythagoreanism.* Translated by Edwin L. Minar, Jr. Cambridge: Harvard University Press, 1972.

Burrus, Virginia. "The Heretical Woman as Symbol in Alexander,

Athanasius, Epiphanius, and Jerome." *Harvard Theological Review* 84 (1991): 229–248.

Bynum, Caroline Walker. *Holy Feast and Holy Fast: The Religious Significance of Food to Medieval Women.* The New Historicism: Studies in Cultural Poetics. Berkeley: University of California Press, 1987.

———. *The Resurrection of the Body in Western Christianity, 200–1336.* Lectures on the History of Religions, n.s., 15. New York: Columbia University Press, 1995.

Cabrol, Fernand. "Jeûnes." *Dictionaire d'archéologie chrétienne et de liturgie* 7 (1927): 2481–2501.

Camelot, P. Thomas. "Les traités 'de virginitate' au IVe siècle." In *Mystique et Continence: Travaux scientifiques du VIIe Congrès international d'Avon,* 273–292. Études Carmélitaines. Brugge: Desclée de Brouwer, 1952.

Cameron, Averil. "Virginity as Metaphor: Women and the Rhetoric of Early Christianity." In *History as Text: The Writing of Ancient History,* ed. Averil Cameron, 184–205. Chapel Hill: University of North Carolina Press, 1989.

Cavallera, Ferdinand. "Basile d'Ancyre." *Dictionnaire de spiritualité* 1.2 (1932): 1283.

———. "Le 'De Virginitate' de Basile d'Ancyre." *Revue d'histoire ecclésiatique* 6 (1905): 5–14.

Chadwick, Henry. "Origen, Celsus, and the Stoa." *Journal of Theological Studies* 48 (1947): 34–49.

Chadwick, Owen. *John Cassian.* 2nd ed. Cambridge: Cambridge University Press, 1968.

Chitty, Derwas J. *The Desert a City: An Introduction to the Study of Egyptian and Palestinian Monasticism under the Christian Empire.* Crestwood, N.Y.: St. Vladimir's Seminary Press, 1966.

Clark, Elizabeth A. "Ascetic Renunciation and Feminine Advancement: A Paradox of Late Ancient Christianity." *Anglican Theological Review* 63 (1981): 240–257.

———. "Foucault, the Fathers, and Sex." *Journal of the American Academy of Religion* 56 (1988): 619–641.

———. "Heresy, Asceticism, Adam, and Eve: Interpretation of

Genesis 1–3 in the Later Latin Fathers." In *Ascetic Piety and Women's Faith: Essays on Late Ancient Christianity,* 353–385. Studies in Women and Religion 20. Lewiston, N.Y.: Edwin Mellen Press, 1986.

———. "Introduction" to *John Chrysostom: On Virginity; Against Remarriage.* Translated by Sally Rieger Shore. Studies in Women and Religion 9. Lewiston, N.Y.: Edwin Mellen Press, 1983.

———. *Jerome, Chrysostom, and Friends: Essays and Translations.* Studies in Women and Religion 2. Lewiston, N.Y.: Edwin Mellen Press, 1979.

———. "John Chrysostom and the *Subintroductae.*" *Church History* 46 (1977): 171–185.

———. "New Perspectives on the Origenist Controversy: Human Embodiment and Ascetic Strategies." *Church History* 59 (1990): 145–162.

———. *The Origenist Controversy: The Cultural Construction of an Early Christian Debate.* Princeton: Princeton University Press, 1992.

———. "The Place of Jerome's Commentary on Ephesians in the Origenist Controversy: The Apokatastasis and Ascetic Ideals." *Vigiliae Christianae* 41 (1987): 154–171.

———. "Sex, Shame, and Rhetoric: En-Gendering Early Christian Ethics." *Journal of the American Academy of Religion* 49 (1991): 221–245.

———. "Theory and Practice in Late Ancient Asceticism: Jerome, Chrysostom, and Augustine." *Journal of Feminist Studies in Religion* 5 (Fall 1989): 25–46.

Cooper, Kate. *The Virgin and the Bride: Idealized Womanhood in Late Antiquity.* Cambridge: Harvard University Press, 1996.

Corsini, Eugenio. "Plérôme humain et plérôme cosmique chez Grégoire de Nysse." In *Écriture et culture philosophique dans la pensée de Grégoire de Nysse,* ed. Marguerite Harl, 111–126. Leiden: E. J. Brill, 1971.

Courcelle, Pierre. *Late Latin Writers and Their Greek Sources.* Translated by Harry E. Wedeck. Cambridge, Mass.: Harvard University Press, 1969.

Cox, Patricia. *Biography in Late Antiquity: A Quest for the Holy Man.* The Transformation of the Classical Heritage 5. Berkeley: University of California Press, 1983.

Curtis, Robert I. *Garum and Salsamenta: Production and Commerce in Materia Medica.* Studies in Ancient Medicine 3. Leiden: E. J. Brill, 1991.

Daniélou, Jean. *L'être et le temps chez Grégoire de Nysse.* Leiden: E. J. Brill, 1970.

———. "Grégoire de Nysse et le Messalianisme." *Recherches de science religieuse* 48 (1960): 119–134.

———. *Platonisme et théologie mystique: Essai sur la doctrine spirituelle de saint Grégoire de Nysse.* 2nd ed. Théologie 2. Paris: Éditions Montaigne, 1954.

Darby, William J., Paul Ghalioungui, and Louis Grivetti. *Food: The Gift of Osiris.* 2 vols. London: Harcourt Brace Jovanovich, Academic Press, 1977.

Dean-Jones, Lesley. "The Cultural Construct of the Female Body in Classical Greek Science." In *Women's History and Ancient History,* ed. Sarah B. Pomeroy, 111–137. Chapel Hill: University of North Carolina Press, 1991.

Delcourt, Marie. "Female Saints in Masculine Clothing." In *Hermaphrodite: Myths and Rites of the Bisexual Figure in Classical Antiquity,* 84–102. Translated by Jennifer Nicholson. London: Studio Books, 1961.

Dembińska, Maria. "Diet: A Comparison of Food Consumption Between Some Eastern and Western Monasteries in the 4th–12th Centuries." *Byzantion* 55 (1985): 431–462.

Deseille, Placide. "Jeûne." *Dictionnaire de spiritualité* 8 (1974): 1164–1175.

Detienne, Marcel. "La cuisine de Pythagore." *Archives de sociologie de religions* 29 (1970): 141–162.

———. *Dionysos Slain.* Translated by Mireille Muellner and Leonard Muellner. Baltimore: The Johns Hopkins University Press, 1979.

Dodds, E. R. *Pagan and Christian in an Age of Anxiety.* Cambridge: Cambridge University Press, 1965; reprint, New York: W. W. Norton, 1970.

Dombrowski, Daniel A. *The Philosophy of Vegetarianism.* Amherst: University of Massachusetts Press, 1984.

Draguet, R. "L' *Histoire Lausiac,* une oeuvre écrite dans l'esprit d'Évagre." *Revue d'histoire ecclésiastique* 41 (1946): 321–364 and 42 (1947): 5–49.

Drijvers, Han J. W. "The Saint as Symbol: Conceptions of the Person in Late Antiquity and Early Christianity." In *Concepts of Person in Religion and Thought,* ed. Hans G. Kippenberg, Yme B. Kuiper, and Andy F. Sanders, 137–157. Religion and Reason 37. Berlin: Mouton de Gruyter, 1990.

Dysinger, Luke. "The Significance of Psalmody in the Mystical Theology of Evagrius of Pontus." *Studia Patristica* 30 (1997): 175–181.

Elliott, Alison Goddard. *Roads to Paradise: Reading the Lives of the Early Saints.* Hanover, N.H.: University Press of New England for Brown University Press, 1987.

Elm, Susanna "Evagrius Ponticus' *Sententiae ad Virginem.*" *Dumbarton Oaks Papers* 45 (1991): 97–120.

———. *'Virgins of God': The Making of Asceticism in Late Antiquity.* Oxford Classical Monographs. Oxford: Clarendon Press, 1994.

Evans, Elizabeth C. *Physiognomics in the Ancient World.* Transactions of the American Philosophical Society, 59,5. Philadelphia: The American Philosophical Society, 1969

Festugière, André-Jean. *Les moines d'orient: Culture ou sainteté.* 4 vols. Paris: Éditions du Cerf, 1961–1964.

———. *Antioche païenne et chrétienne: Libanius, Chrysostome et les moines de Syrie.* Bibliothèque des écoles françaises d'Athènes et de Rome. Paris: Éditions E. de Boccard, 1959.

Fitzgerald, John T. *Cracks in an Earthen Vessel: An Examination of the Catalogues of Hardships in the Corinthian Correspondence.* SBL Dissertation Series 99. Atlanta: Scholars Press, 1988.

Forbes, Robert J. *Studies in Ancient Technology* 3. 2nd ed. Leiden: E. J. Brill, 1965.

Foucault, Michel. "The Battle for Chastity." In *Western Sexuality: Practice and Precept in Past and Present Times,* ed.

Philippe Ariès and André Béjin, 14–25. Translated by Anthony Forster. Oxford: Basil Blackwell, 1985.

———. *The History of Sexuality*, 3 vols. Vol. 2, *The Use of Pleasures*. Vol. 3, *The Care of the Self.* Translated by Robert Hurley. New York: Random House, 1985–1986.

Fraade, Steven D. "Ascetical Aspects of Ancient Judaism." In *Jewish Spirituality: From the Bible Through the Middle Ages*, ed. Arthur Green, 253–288. World Spirituality 13. New York: Crossroad, 1986.

Francis, James A. *Subversive Virtue: Asceticism and Authority in the Second-Century Pagan World.* University Park: Pennsylvania State University Press, 1995.

Frank, P. Suso. *Angelikos Bios: Begriffsanalytische und begriffsgeschichtliche Untersuchung zum 'engelgleichen Leben' im frühen Mönchtum.* Beiträge zur Geschichte des alten Mönchtums und des Benediktinerordens 26. Munich: Aschendorff, 1964.

Gager, John G. "Body-Symbols and Social Reality: Resurrection, Incarnation and Asceticism in Early Christianity." *Religion* 12 (1982): 345–363.

Glad, Clarence Edvin. "Adaptability in Epicurean and Early Christian Psychagogy: Paul and Philodemus." Ph.D. diss., Brown University, 1992.

Gleason, Maud W. *Making Men: Sophists and Self-Presentation in Ancient Rome.* Princeton: Princeton University Press, 1995

Goody, Jack. *Cooking, Cuisine, and Class: A Study in Comparative Sociology.* Themes in the Social Sciences. Cambridge: Cambridge University Press, 1982.

Goulet-Cazé, Marie-Odile. "Le Cynisme à l'époque impériale." *Aufstieg und Niedergang der Römischen Welt* 2.36.4: 2720–2833.

Gourevitch, Danielle. *Le mal d'être femme: La femme et la médecine dans la Rome antique.* Realia. Paris: "Les Belles Lettres," 1984.

Gribomont, Jean. "Le dossier des origines du Messalianisme." In *Epektasis: Mélanges Patristiques offerts au Cardinal Jean*

Daniélou, ed. Jacques Fontaine and Charles Kannengiesser, 611–625. Paris: Beauchesne, 1972.

———. "Eustathe de Sébaste." *Dictionnaire d'histoire et de géographie ecclésiastiques* 16 (1967): 26–33.

———. "Eustathe de Sébaste." *Dictionnaire de spiritualité* 4 (1961): 1708–1712.

———. "Le monachisme au IVe s. en Asie Mineure: de Gangres au Messalianisme." *Studia Patristica* 2, 400–415. TU 64,9. Berlin: Akademie-Verlag, 1957.

———. "Monasticism and Asceticism: I. Eastern Christianity." In *Christian Spirituality: Origins to the Twelfth Century*, ed. Bernard McGinn, John Meyendorff, and Jean Leclercq, 89–112. Translated by Marie Miklashevsky. World Spirituality 16. New York: Crossroad, 1985.

———. "Notes biographiques sur s. Basile le Grand." In *Basil of Caesarea: Christian, Humanist, Ascetic*, ed. Paul Jonathan Fedwick, 2 vols., 1:21–148. Toronto: Pontifical Institute of Mediaeval Studies, 1981.

———. "Le panégyrique de la virginité, oeuvre de jeunesse de Grégoire de Nysse." *Revue d'ascétique et mystique* 43 (1967): 249–266.

Guillaume, Alexandre. *Jeûne et charité dans l'église latine, des origines au XIIe siècle en particulier chez Léon le Grand*. Paris: n.p., 1954.

Guillaumont, Antoine, and Claire Guillaumont. "Évagre le Pontique." *Dictionnaire de spiritualité* 4 (1961): 1731–1744.

———. *Les 'Képhalaia Gnostica' d'Évagre le Pontique et l'histoire de l'Origénisme chez les Grecs et chez les Syriens*. Patristica Sorbonensia 5. Paris: Éditions du Seuil, 1962.

———. "Un philosophe au désert: Evagre le Pontique." *Revue de l'histoire des religions* 181 (1972): 29–56.

Hankinson, James. "Actions and Passions: Affection, Emotion, and Moral Self-Management in Galen's Philosophical Psychology." In *Passions and Perceptions: Studies in Hellenistic Philosophy of Mind*, ed. Jacques Brunschwig and Martha C. Nussbaum, 184–222. Cambridge: Cambridge University Press, 1993.

———. "Galen's Anatomy of the Soul." *Phronesis* 36 (1991): 197–233.

Hanson, Ann Ellis. "Continuity and Change: Three Case Studies in Hippocratic Gynecological Therapy and Theory." In *Women's History and Ancient History*, ed. Sarah B. Pomeroy, 73–110. Chapel Hill: University of North Carolina Press, 1991.

———. "The Medical Writers' Woman." In *Before Sexuality: The Construction of Erotic Experience in the Ancient Greek World*, ed. David M. Halperin, John J. Winkler, and Froma A. Zeitlin, 309–337. Princeton: Princeton University Press, 1990.

Harl, Marguerite. "La prise de conscience de la 'nudité' d'Adam: Une interprétation de *Genèse* 3,7 chez les Pères Grecs." *Studia Patristica* 7, 486–495. TU 92. Berlin: Akademie-Verlag, 1966.

Harpham, Geoffrey Galt. *The Ascetic Imperative in Culture and Criticism*. Chicago: University of Chicago Press, 1987.

Harvey, Susan Ashbrook. "Physicians and Ascetics in John of Ephesus: An Expedient Alliance." *Dumbarton Oaks Papers* 38 (1984): 87–93.

Hastrup, Kirsten. "The Semantics of Biology: Virginity." In *Defining Females: The Nature of Women in Society*, ed. Shirley Ardener, 49–65. New York: John Wiley and Sons, Halsted Press, 1978.

Hausherr, Irénée. "L'origine de la théorie orientale des huit péchés capitaux." *Orientalia Christiana* 30 (1933): 164–175.

Haussleiter, Johannes. *Der Vegetarismus in der Antike*. Religionsgeschichtliche Versuche und Vorarbeiten 24. Berlin: Alfred Töpelmann, 1935.

Hefele, Charles Joseph von. *Histoire des conciles d'après les documents originaux*. 2nd ed. 9 vols. Paris: Letouzey et Ané, 1907–1918.

Héritier-Augé, Françoise. "Older Women, Stout-Hearted Women, Women of Substance." In *Fragments for a History of the Human Body*, ed. Michel Feher, 3: 281–299. Translated by Leigh Hafrey. New York: Zone, 1989.

————. "Semen and Blood: Some Ancient Theories Concerning Their Genesis and Relationship." In *Fragments for a History of the Human Body*, ed. Michel Feher, 3: 159–175. Translated by Tina Jolas. New York: Zone, 1989.

Hijmans, B.L. *Askesis: Notes on Epictetus' Educational System.* Wijsgerige Teksten en Studies 2. Assen: Van Gorcum, 1959.

Hock, Ronald F. "'By the Gods, It's My One Desire to See an Actual Stoic': Epictetus' Relations with Students and Visitors in his Personal Network." *Semeia* 56 (1993): 121–142.

Horden, Peregrine. "The Death of Ascetics: Sickness and Monasticism in the Early Byzantine Middle East." In *Monks, Hermits and the Ascetic Tradition*, ed. W. J. Sheils, 41–52. Studies in Church History 22. Oxford: Basil Blackwell for the Ecclesiastical History Society, 1985.

Janini Cuesta, José. "Dieta y virginidad: Basilio de Ancira y San Gregorio de Nisa." *Miscelánea Comillas* 14 (1950): 187–197.

Janin, R. "Basile d'Ancyre." *Dictionnaire d'histoire et géographie ecclésiastiques* 6 (1932): 1104–1107.

Jasny, Naum. *The Wheats of Classical Antiquity.* The Johns Hopkins University Studies in Historical and Political Science 62/3. Baltimore: The Johns Hopkins Press, 1944.

Kee, Howard Clark. *Medicine, Miracle and Magic in New Testament Times.* Society for New Testament Studies Monograph Series 55. Cambridge: Cambridge University Press, 1986.

Keenan, Mary Emily. "St. Gregory of Nyssa and the Medical Profession." *Bulletin of the History of Medicine* 15 (1944): 150–161.

Kelly, John Norman Davidson. *Jerome: His Life, Writings, and Controversies.* London: Duckworth, 1975.

Kennedy, George A. *Greek Rhetoric Under Christian Emperors.* Princeton, N.J.: Princeton University Press, 1983.

Keyes, Charles F. "Charisma: From Social Life to Sacred Biography." In *Charisma and Sacred Biography*, ed. Michael A. Williams, 1–22. JAAR Thematic Studies 48/3–4. Chambersburg, Pa.: American Academy of Religion, 1982.

Keys, Ancel, Josef Brožek, et al. *The Biology of Human Starvation*. 2 vols. Minneapolis: University of Minnesota Press, 1950.

King, Helen. "The Daughter of Leonides: Reading the Hippocratic Corpus." In *History as Text: The Writing of Ancient History*, ed. Averil Cameron, 13–32. Chapel Hill: University of North Carolina Press, 1989.

Kraemer, Ross. "The Conversion of Women to Ascetic Forms of Christianity." *Signs* 6 (1980–1981): 298–307.

Ladner, G. B. "The Philosophical Anthropology of Gregory of Nyssa." *Dumbarton Oaks Papers* 12 (1958): 61–94.

Lampe, G. W. H., ed. *A Patristic Greek Lexicon*. Oxford: Oxford University Press, Clarendon Press, 1961.

Laqueur, Thomas. *Making Sex: Body and Gender from the Greeks to Freud*. Cambridge: Harvard University Press, 1990.

———. "Orgasm, Generation, and the Politics of Reproductive Biology." *Representations* 14 (1986): 1–41.

Le Bachelet, X. "Basile d'Ancyre." *Dictionnaire de théologie catholique* 2 (1903): 461–463.

Le Roy Ladurie, Emmanuel. "Famine Amenorrhoea (Seventeenth-Twentieth Centuries)." In *Biology of Man in History*, ed. Robert Forster and Orest Ranum, 163–178. Translated by Elborg Forster. Baltimore: The Johns Hopkins University Press, 1975.

Leroux, Jean-Marie. "Saint Jean Chrysostome et le monachisme." In *Jean Chrysostome et Augustin*, ed. Charles Kannengiesser, 125–144. Théologie historique 35. Paris: Beauchesne, 1975.

Leroy, F. J. "La tradition manuscrite du 'de virginitate' de Basile d'Ancyre." *Orientalia Christiania Periodica* 38 (1972): 195–208.

Lesky, Erna. *Die Zeugungs- und Vererbungslehren der Antike und ihr Nachwirken*. Wiesbaden: Akademie der Wissenschaften und der Literatur, 1950.

Leyerle, Blake. "Clement of Alexandria on the Importance of Table Etiquette." *Journal of Early Christian Studies* 3 (1995): 123–141.

―――. "John Chrysostom on the Gaze." *Journal of Early Christian Studies* 1 (1993): 159–174.

Lilla, Salvatore R.C. *Clement of Alexandria: A Study in Christian Platonism and Gnosticism.* Oxford Theological Monographs. Oxford: Oxford University Press, 1971.

Lloyd, G. E. R. "The Hot and the Cold, the Dry and the Wet in Greek Philosophy." *Journal of Hellenic Studies* 84 (1964): 92–106.

―――. "Scholarship, Authority and Argument in Galen's *Quod animi mores*." In *Le opera psicologiche di Galeno*, ed. Paola Manuli and Mario Vegetti, 9–42. Naples: Bibliopolis, 1988.

―――. *Science, Folklore and Ideology: Studies in the Life Sciences in Ancient Greece.* Cambridge: Cambridge University Press, 1983.

Long, A. A. *Hellenistic Philosophy: Stoics, Epicureans, Sceptics.* New York: Charles Scribner's Sons, 1974.

―――. "Soul and Body in Stoicism." *The Center for Hermeneutical Studies in Hellenistic and Modern Culture: Colloquy 36.* Berkeley: Center for Hermeneutical Studies, 1980.

Lovejoy, Arthur O. and George Boas. *Primitivism and Related Ideas in Antiquity.* A Documentary History of Primitivism and Related Ideas, vol. 1. Contributions to the History of Primitivism. Baltimore: The Johns Hopkins Press, 1935.

MacCulloch, J. A. "Fasting (Introductory and non-Christian)." In *Encyclopaedia of Religion and Ethics*, ed. James Hastings, 5:759–765. Edinburgh: T. & T. Clark, 1937.

MacDermot, Violet. *The Cult of the Seer in the Ancient Middle East.* Berkeley: University of California Press, 1971.

Maclean, A. J. "Fasting (Christian)." In *Encyclopaedia of Religion and Ethics*, ed. James Hastings, 5:765–771. Edinburgh: T. & T. Clark, 1937.

Malherbe, Abraham J., ed. *The Cynic Epistles: A Study Edition.* Society of Biblical Literature Sources for Biblical Study 12. Missoula: Scholars Press, 1977.

―――. "Self-Definition Among Epicureans and Cynics." In *Jewish and Christian Self-Definition 3, Self-Definition in the*

Greco-Roman World, ed. Ben F. Meyers and E. P. Sanders, 46–59. Philadelphia: Fortress Press, 1982.

Markus, R. A. *Christianity in the Roman World*. Currents in the History of Culture and Ideas. London: Thames and Hudson, 1974.

Martin, Dale B. *The Corinthian Body*. New Haven: Yale University Press, 1995.

McGinn, Bernard. "Asceticism and Mysticism in Late Antiquity and the Early Middle Ages." In *Asceticism*, ed. Vincent L. Wimbush and Richard Valantasis, 58–74. New York: Oxford University Press, 1995.

Meeks, Wayne A. *The Moral World of the First Christians*. Library of Early Christianity. Philadelphia: The Westminster Press, 1986.

Miles, Margaret R. *Carnal Knowing: Female Nakedness and Religious Meaning in the Christian West*. Boston: Beacon Press, 1989.

Miller, Patricia Cox. "The Blazing Body: Ascetic Desire in Jerome's Letter to Eustochium." *Journal of Early Christian Studies* 1 (1993): 21–45.

———. "Desert Asceticism and 'The Body from Nowhere.'" *Journal of Early Christian Studies* 2 (1994): 137–153.

Murphy, Francis X. "Evagrius Ponticus and Origenism." In *Origeniana Tertia*, ed. Richard Hanson and Henri Crouzel, 253–269. Rome: Ateneo, 1985.

Musurillo, Herbert. "The Problem of Ascetical Fasting in the Greek Patristic Writers." *Traditio* 12 (1956): 1–64.

Natali, Alain. "Christianisme et Cité à Antioche à la fin du IVe siècle d'après Jean Chrysostome." In *Jean Chrysostome et Augustin*, ed. Charles Kannengiesser, 41–59. Théologie historique 35. Paris: Beauchesne, 1975.

Noonan, John T., Jr. *Contraception: A History of Its Treatment by the Catholic Theologians and Canonists*. Enlarged ed. Cambridge: Harvard University Press, Belknap Press, 1986.

North, Helen. *Sophrosyne: Self-Knowledge and Self-Restraint in Greek Literature*. Cornell Studies in Classical Philology 35. Ithaca: Cornell University Press, 1966.

Nussbaum, Martha C. *The Therapy of Desire: Theory and Practice in Hellenistic Ethics.* Martin Classical Lectures, n.s., 2. Princeton: Princeton University Press, 1994.

Nutton, Vivian. "From Galen to Alexander, Aspects of Medicine and Medical Practice in Late Antiquity." *Dumbarton Oaks Papers* 38 (1984): 1–14.

O'Laughlin, Michael. "New Questions Concerning the Origenism of Evagrius." In *Origeniana Quinta,* ed. Robert J. Daly, 528–534. Leuven: University Press, 1992.

———. "Origenism in the Desert: Anthropology and Integration in Evagrius Ponticus." Th.D. diss., Harvard Divinity School, 1987.

Onians, Richard Broxton. *The Origins of European Thought About the Body, the Mind, the Soul, the World, Time, and Fate.* Philosophy of Plato and Aristotle. Cambridge: Cambridge University Press, 1951; reprint ed., New York: Arno Press, 1973.

Pagels, Elaine. *Adam, Eve, and the Serpent.* New York: Random House, 1988.

Parker, Robert. *Miasma: Pollution and Purification in Early Greek Religion.* Oxford: Clarendon Press, 1983.

Patlagean, Evelyne. "Ancient Byzantine Hagiography and Social History." In *Saints and Their Cults: Studies in Religious Sociology, Folklore and History,* ed. Stephen Wilson, 101–121. Translated by Jane Hodgkin. Cambridge: Cambridge University Press, 1983.

———. "L'histoire de la femme déguisée en moine et l'évolution de la sainteté féminine à Byzance." *Studi Medievali* Ser. 3, 17 (1976): 597–623.

———. *Pauvreté économique et pauvreté sociale à Byzance: 4e–7e siècles.* Civilisations et sociétés 48. Paris: Mouton, 1977.

Pease, Arthur Stanley. "Medical Allusions in the Works of St. Jerome." *Harvard Studies in Classical Philology* 25 (1914): 73–86.

Perkins, Judith. "The 'Self' as Sufferer." *Harvard Theological Review* 85 (1992): 245–272.

————. *The Suffering Self: Pain and Narrative Representation in the Early Christian Era.* London: Routledge, 1995.

Pichler, Theodorich. *Das Fasten bei Basileios dem Grossen und im Antiken Heidentum.* Commentationes Aenipontanae 11. Innsbruck: Universitätsverlag Wagner, 1955.

Pigeaud, Jackie. *La maladie de l'ame: Étude sur la relation de l'ame et du corps dans la tradition médico-philosophique antique.* Paris: Les Belles Lettres, 1981.

Porter, Roy. "History of the Body." In *New Perspectives on Historical Writing,* ed. Peter Burke, 206–232. University Park: Pennsylvania State University Press, 1991.

Preus, Anthony. "Galen's Criticism of Aristotle's Conception Theory." *Journal of the History of Biology* 10 (1977): 65–85.

Quispel, Gilles. "The Study of Encratism: A Historical Survey." In *La tradizione dell'Enkrateia: Motivationi ontologiche e protologiche,* ed. Ugo Bianchi, 35–82. Rome: Ateneo, 1985.

Rabel, Robert J. "Diseases of the Soul in Stoic Psychology." *Greek, Roman, and Byzantine Studies* 22 (1981): 385–393.

Rader, Rosemary. "Fasting." In *Encyclopedia of Religion,* ed. Mircea Eliade, et al., 5:286–290. New York: Macmillan, 1987.

Refoulé, F. "Rêves et vie spirituelle d'après Évagre le Pontique." *La vie spirituelle: Supplément* 14 (1961): 470–516.

Renehan, R. "On the Greek Origins of the Concepts Incorporeality and Immateriality." *Greek, Roman, and Byzantine Studies* 21 (1980): 105–138.

Reynolds, Frank E. and Donald Capps, eds. *The Biographical Process: Studies in the History and Psychology of Religion.* Religion and Reason 11. The Hague: Mouton, 1976.

Riddle, John M. *Contraception and Abortion from the Ancient World to the Renaissance.* Cambridge: Harvard University Press, 1992.

Rist, John M. "Are You a Stoic? The Case of Marcus Aurelius." In *Jewish and Christian Self-Definition* 3, *Self-Definition in the Greco-Roman World,* ed. Ben F. Meyers and E. P. Sanders, 23–45. Philadelphia: Fortress Press, 1982.

————. *Stoic Philosophy.* Cambridge: Cambridge University Press, 1969.

Rousseau, Philip. *Ascetics, Authority, and the Church in the Age of Jerome and Cassian.* Oxford: Oxford University Press, 1978.

————. *Basil of Caesarea.* The Transformation of the Classical Heritage 20. Berkeley: University of California Press, 1994.

————. *Pachomius: The Making of a Community in Fourth-Century Egypt.* The Transformation of the Classical Heritage 6. Berkeley: University of California Press, 1985.

Rousselle, Aline. "Abstinence et continence dans les monastères de Gaul méridionale à la fin de l'Antiquité et au début du Moyen Age: Étude d'un régime alimentaire et de sa fonction." In *Hommages à André Dupont, Études médiévales langue-dociennes,* 239–254. Montpellier: Fédération historique de Languedoc mediterranéen et du Roussillon, 1974.

————. "Observation féminine et idéologie masculine: Le corps de la femme d'après les médecins grecs." *Annales: Économies, Sociétés, Civilisations* 35 (1980): 1089–1115.

————. *Porneia: De la maîtrise du corps à la privation sensorielle IIe–IVe siècles de l'ère chrétienne.* Les chemins de l'Histoire. Paris: Presses Universitaires de France, 1983.

Rubenson, Samuel. *The Letters of St. Antony: Monasticism and the Making of a Saint.* Studies in Antiquity and Christianity. Minneapolis: Fortress Press, 1995.

Ruether, Rosemary Radford. "Misogynism and Virginal Feminism in the Fathers of the Church." In *Religion and Sexism: Images of Women in the Jewish and Christian Traditions,* ed. Rosemary Radford Ruether, 150–183. New York: Simon and Schuster, 1974.

Scarborough, John. *Roman Medicine.* Ithaca: Cornell University Press, 1969.

Scarry, Elaine. *The Body in Pain: The Making and Unmaking of the World.* New York: Oxford University Press, 1985.

Schümmer, Johannes. *Die altchristliche Fastenpraxis mit beson-derer Berücksichtigung der Schriften Tertullians.* Liturgie-geschichtliche Quellen und Forschungen, 27. Munich: Aschendorff, 1933.

Sfameni Gasparro, Giulia. "Asceticism and Anthropology:

Enkrateia and 'Double Creation' in Early Christianity." In *Asceticism*, ed. Vincent L. Wimbush and Richard Valantasis, 127–146. New York: Oxford University Press, 1995.

———. "Image of God and Sexual Differentiation in the Tradition of *Enkrateia*: Protological Motivations." In *Image of God and Gender Models in Judaeo-Christian Tradition*, ed. Kari Elisabeth Børresen, 138–171. Oslo: Solum Forlag, 1991.

Shaw, Teresa M. "Creation, Virginity and Diet in Fourth-Century Christianity: Basil of Ancyra's *On the True Purity of Virginity.*" *Gender & History* 9 (1997): 579–596.

Sissa, Giulia. *Greek Virginity.* Translated by Arthur Goldhammer. Revealing Antiquity 3. Cambridge: Harvard University Press, 1990.

———. "Subtle Bodies." In *Fragments for a History of the Human Body*, ed. Michel Feher, 3: 133–156. Translated by Janet Lloyd. New York: Zone, 1989.

Smith, Wesley D. "The Development of Classical Dietetic Theory." In *Hippocratica: actes du Colloque hippocratique de Paris, 4–9 septembre 1978*, ed. M. D. Grmek, 439–448. Colloques internationaux du Centre national de la recherche scientifique 583. Paris: Éditions de centre national de la recherche scientifique, 1980.

Sophocles, E.A. *Greek Lexicon of the Roman and Byzantine Periods (from B.C. 146 to A.D. 1100).* 2 vols. New York: Frederick Ungar, 1957.

Spanneut, Michel. *Le Stoïcisme des pères de l'église de Clément de Rome à Clément d'Alexandrie.* New ed. Patristica Sorbonensia. Paris: Éditions du Seuil, 1957.

Staats, Reinhart. "Basilius als lebende Mönchsregel in Gregors von Nyssa *De virginitate.*" *Vigiliae christianae* 39 (1985): 228–155.

———. "Messalianism and Anti-Messalianism in Gregory of Nyssa's *De Virginitate.*" *Patristic and Byzantine Review* 2 (1983): 27–44.

Stewart, Columba. '*Working the Earth of the Heart': The Messalian Controversy in History, Texts, and Language to AD*

431. Oxford Theological Monographs. Oxford: Clarendon Press, 1991.

Temkin, Owsei. *Galenism: Rise and Decline of a Medical Philosophy*. Ithaca: Cornell University Press, 1973.

———. *Hippocrates in a World of Pagans and Christians*. Baltimore: The Johns Hopkins University Press, 1991.

Turner, Bryan S. *The Body and Society: Explorations in Social Theory*. Oxford: Basil Blackwell, 1984.

———. "The Body Question: Recent Developments in Social Theory." In *Regulating Bodies: Essays in Medical Sociology*, 33–66. London and New York: Routledge, 1992.

Van Eijk, Ton H. C. "Marriage and Virginity, Death and Immortality." In *Epektasis: Mélanges patristiques offerts au Cardinal Jean Daniélou*, ed. Jacques Fontaine and Charles Kannengiesser, 209–235. Paris: Beauchesne, 1972.

Veilleux, Armand. "The Origins of Egyptian Monasticism." In *The Continuing Quest for God: Monastic Spirituality in Tradition and Transition*, ed. William Skudlarek, 44–50. Collegeville, Minn.: Liturgical Press, 1982.

Veith, Ilza. *Hysteria: The History of a Disease*. Chicago: University of Chicago Press, Phoenix Books, 1970.

Vernant, Jean-Pierre. "At Man's Table: Hesiod's Foundation Myth of Sacrifice." In *The Cuisine of Sacrifice among the Greeks*, ed. Marcel Detienne and Jean-Pierre Vernant, 21–86. Translated by Paula Wissing. Chicago: University of Chicago Press, 1989.

———. "Dim Body, Dazzling Body." In *Fragments for a History of the Human Body*, ed. Michel Feher, 1: 19–47. Translated by Anne M. Wilson. New York: Zone, 1989.

Vidal-Naquet, Pierre. "Plato's Myth of the Statesman, the Ambiguities of the Golden Age and of History." *Journal of Hellenic Studies* 98 (1978): 132–141.

Von Staden, Heinrich. "Hairesis and Heresy: The Case of the *haireseis iatrikai*." In *Jewish and Christian Self-Definition*. Vol. 3, *Self-Definition in the Greco-Roman World*, ed. Ben F.

Meyer and E. P. Sanders, 76–100. Philadelphia: Fortress Press, 1982.

————. "Spiderwoman and the Chaste Tree: The Semantics of Matter." *Configurations* 1 (1992): 23–56.

Vööbus, Arthur. *History of Asceticism in the Syrian Orient.* 2 vols. CSCO 184 (Subsidia 14) and 197 (Subsidia 17). Louvain: Secrétariat du CorpusSCO, 1958–1960.

————. "Syrische Herkunft der Pseudo-Basilianischen Homilie über die Jungfräulichkeit." *Oriens Christianus* 40 (1956): 69–77.

Walzer, Richard. "New Light on Galen's Moral Philosophy." *Classical Quarterly* 43 (1949): 82–96.

Ward, Benedicta. "Introduction" to *The Lives of the Desert Fathers: The Historia Monachorum in Aegypto.* Translated by Norman Russell. London: Mowbray; Kalamazoo: Cistercian Publications, 1981.

White, L. Michael. "Finding the Ties That Bind: Issues from Social Description." *Semeia* 56 (1993): 3–22.

————. "Scholars and Patrons: Christianity and High Society in Alexandria." In *Christian Teaching: Studies in Honor of LeMoine G. Lewis,* ed. Everett Ferguson, 328–342. Abilene: ACU Press, 1981.

Wilken, Robert L. *John Chrysostom and the Jews: Rhetoric and Reality in the Late Fourth Century.* The Transformation of the Classical Heritage 4. Berkeley: University of California Press, 1983.

Wilson, Robert McL. "Alimentary and Sexual Encratism in the Nag Hammadi Tractates." In *La tradizione dell'Enkrateia: Motivazioni ontologiche e protologiche,* ed. Ugo Bianchi, 317–332. Rome: Ateneo, 1985.

Wimbush, Vincent L., ed. *Ascetic Behavior in Greco-Roman Antiquity: A Sourcebook.* Studies in Antiquity and Christianity. Minneapolis: Fortress Press, 1990.

————. and Richard Valantasis, eds. *Asceticism.* New York: Oxford University Press, 1995.

Winkler, Gabriele. "The Origins and Idiosyncrasies of the Earliest Form of Asceticism." In *The Continuing Quest for God:*

Monastic Spirituality in Tradition and Transition, ed. William Skudlarek, 9–43. Collegeville, Minn.: Liturgical Press, 1982.

Yarbrough, Anne. "Christianization in the Fourth Century: The Example of Roman Women." *Church History* 45 (1976): 149–165.

Ziehen, Ludwig. "Νηστεία." In *Realencyclopaedie der classischen Altertumswissenschaft*, ed. A. Pauly and G. Wissowa, 17/1:88–107. Revised ed. Stuttgart: J. B. Metzler, 1936.

Index

In cases where a topic appears in the main text and in a note or notes on the same page, only the page number is listed here, unless the note is not directly related to the discussion preceding the note number. Titles of ancient sources refer only to instances where the actual title appears in the main text or in discussions within notes, not to every discussion of that source.